Inventory and Production Management in Supply Chains

Inventory and Production Management in Supply Chains

Edited by
Bertie Graham

WILLFORD PRESS

www.willfordpress.com

Published by Willford Press,
118-35 Queens Blvd., Suite 400,
Forest Hills, NY 11375, USA

ISBN: 978-1-64728-522-7

Cataloging-in-Publication Data

Inventory and production management in supply chains / edited by Bertie Graham.
     p. cm.
Includes bibliographical references and index.
ISBN 978-1-64728-522-7
1. Business logistics. 2. Inventory control. 3. Production management.
4. Production planning. I. Graham, Bertie.
HD38.5 .I58 2023
658.7--dc23

For information on all Willford Press publications
visit our website at www.willfordpress.com

Contents

             Permissions

             List of Contributors

             Index

Preface

This book has been an outcome of determined endeavour from a group of educationists in the field. The primary objective was to involve a broad spectrum of professionals from diverse cultural background involved in the field for developing new researches. The book not only targets students but also scholars pursuing higher research for further enhancement of the theoretical and practical applications of the subject.

Supply chain management (SCM) deals with the management of materials and information across the entire supply chain. SCM majorly focuses on three areas, namely, information flow, inventory management and production management. Businesses must develop and optimize techniques for managing inventory and production throughout their supply chains. Inventory management is an area of management that deals with the control of the entire stock of a company. Inventory control and warehouse management are parts of the overall inventory management process. The movement of items within a warehouse comes under the purview of inventory control whereas managing the stock at a specific location falls under warehouse management. Production management or operations management is a management area that involves planning, organizing, directing and controlling all the activities of production. This book provides comprehensive insights on inventory and production management in supply chains. A number of latest researches have been included to keep the readers up-to-date with the global concepts in this area of study. The book aims to serve as a resource guide for students and experts alike.

It was an honour to edit such a profound book and also a challenging task to compile and examine all the relevant data for accuracy and originality. I wish to acknowledge the efforts of the contributors for submitting such brilliant and diverse chapters in the field and for endlessly working for the completion of the book. Last, but not the least; I thank my family for being a constant source of support in all my research endeavours.

Editor

Learning from Incidents: A Supply Chain Management Perspective in Military Environments

Raffaele Cantelmi [1,2], **Giulio Di Gravio** [1]🆔 **and Riccardo Patriarca** [1,*]🆔

[1]   Department of Mechanical and Aerospace Engineering, Sapienza University of Rome, Via Eudossiana,
       18-00184 Rome, Italy; raffaele.cantelmi@uniroma1.it (R.C.); giulio.digravio@uniroma1.it (G.D.G.)
[2]   Land Armaments Directorate, Ministry of Defence, Via di Centocelle, 301-00187 Rome, Italy
*   Correspondence: riccardo.patriarca@uniroma1.it

Abstract: Supply chain management (SCM) represents a crucial role in the military sector to ensure operation sustainability. Starting from the NATO handbook for military organizational learning, this paper aims at investigating the link between technical inconveniences and sustainable supply chain operations. Taking advantage of the learning from incidents (LFI) models traditionally used in the risk and safety management area, this paper proposes an information management system to support organizational learning from technical inconveniences in a military supply chain. The approach is discussed with reference to the Italian context, in line with international and national standards for technical inconvenience reporting. The results of the paper show the benefits of adopting a systematic LFI system for technical inconveniences, providing related exemplar business intelligence dashboards. Further implications for the generalization of the proposed information management system are presented to foster a healthy and effective reporting environment in military scenarios.

Keywords: incidents learning system; technical inconveniences; military supply chain; information management; business intelligence

1. Introduction

Supplying goods or services to the customer is the main target for a sustainable supply chain network that includes manufacturers, distributors, logistics firms, and many other indirect agents (banks, brokers, insurance companies, etc.) [1]. Until the 1950s, in military environments, similarly to any other production domain, business leaders thought of logistics as a combination of procurement, maintenance, transportation of facilities, material, and personnel [2]. In the early 1980s, such perspective extended to the concept of supply chain management (SCM), widening the idea of logistics to the management of suppliers and customers interactions. SCM refers to a combination of activities undertaken within the organizations to encourage the efficient management of their supply chain, and this caught a lot of attention recently both by academics as well as practitioners [3,4]. SCM has become one of the most popular concepts in the management area since the 1980s [5], with a number of journals in manufacturing, procurement, and transportation, information pushing forward the development of the SCM idea in a global competitive environment [6–8]. Specifically in the military context, the annual industrial capabilities report, put out by the Pentagon's Office of Manufacturing and Industrial Base Policy, acknowledges that the industrial base of the weaponry sector is particularly strained, due to the irregular flow of procurement and the lack of new designs being internally developed [9]. Such observations confirm the critical foundation of measuring and managing information on key operational and performance parameters [10].

In a systemic perspective, it is important to highlight how the delivery of a good or a service does not terminate the supply chain. A systemic SCM shall rather include the so-called reverse logistics, which ensure that used, defective and discarded products are managed in order to increase the effectiveness of the network [1]. In the domain of repairable items, reverse logistics is usually regulated by performance-based contracting, i.e., after-sales services aimed at cutting fixed-price costs by ad-hoc interventions [11], following its introduction in the early 1990s [12]. In military contexts, reverse logistics ensure that the material lifecycle is sustainable, facilitating the recycling or reusing of equipment which can be repaired and utilized [13].

Therefore, with the aim of improving SCM sustainability, it has become necessary to adopt structured and effective frameworks for managing reverse streams of the supply chain, both in terms of operations and information management [14]. Good decisions are based on timely, accurate and relevant information, which represent the link between activities and operations [15]. Despite recent significant advances and dramatic improvements in information technology, the discipline of SCM can be further enhanced to address modern practical real-world challenges [16], even more specifically in military supply chains. Available research mostly focuses on the quantitative analysis of detailed aspects of the supply chain. For example, some scholars propose a game model of military reverse logistics based on the Nash equilibrium [17]. Similarly, another work focuses on an optimal model of principal–agent relationships for waste military air materials, stressing the need for provider-specific incentive mechanisms [18]. More recently, a hybrid machine learning model has been developed to improve and predict spare parts reverse flow [19]. A large set of research is also focused on routing problems for reverse logistics or end of life vehicles, exploring multiple facility location problems, e.g., single-facility [20], grouped location problem [21], k-location routing [22], multi-period location routing problems [23]. While these contributions contribute widely on the progress of reverse logistics, they do not present a deep analysis on the management of the reverse flow, especially within military supply chains.

On this side, this paper complements the wide literature relying on mathematical formulation for reverse logistics via a framework to be used for dealing with technical incidents from an organizational perspective. The outcome of the framework allows for an understanding of the strengths and weakness of both the product at hand and the agents involved in its management process.

Based on these premises, it could be possible to relate information on reverse logistics with the theory of learning from incident (LFI), to take maximum advantage from reporting actions.

LFI (or more generally from events) can be defined as a change in the repertoire of behaviors of an organization [24], i.e., a shared understanding of the need for new actions to minimize or prevent negative events [25]. The academic field of LFI is partly fragmented [26], but it is widely acknowledged its potential for both safety and productivity [27,28]. For gathering its benefits, learning has to be set in an organizational environment including the identification of events to be investigated, the application of most suitable analysis techniques, a thorough reflection on the results for developing meaningful repertoires, the sharing of these latter, and the structure of the most advantageous conditions for their applicability [25].

LFI is thus aligned with the idea of a sustainable supply chain, where the application of a systematic learning system may provide savings on input costs such as time, labor and energy, and thus enable profitable outputs and increase customer satisfaction, also in light of environmental dimensions [29]. The relevance of such a proactive learning system has been widely acknowledged in military technical publications, as detailed in the NATO lessons learned handbook [30].

Following the theory of LFI [31,32], this paper aims to present the structure of a database to be used in a military environment for the management of technical inconveniences. By exemplary statistics and dashboards to support decision-making, the paper aims to prove the benefits of a systematic LFI information management system. In summary, the purpose of the paper is two-fold: (i) the definition of concepts and roles for implementing an LFI in military environments; (ii) the development of a database structure for ensuring the implementation of previously mentioned roles and concepts, in line with NATO guidelines.

The remainder of the paper is organized as follows. Section 2 describes the theoretical foundation of an LFI system and describes the relevant military publication both in the international context (i.e., NATO) and for the supply chain of the item at hand (small arms in Italy). Section 3 details the information management system developed in this research and provides exemplar results of the approach. Note that the quantitative results in this section do not refer to the operational situation at hand, but they rather include exemplary anonymized data. Section 4 discusses the obtained results and the advantages of the approach. Lastly, the conclusions summarize the outcome of the approach and provide evidence for further research.

2. Materials and Methods

This section describes the theoretical foundation for the LFI system to be used for information management (Section 2.1), subsequently describing (Section 2.2) the regulatory reporting framework of interest for the approach presented in this document (ILE-NL-1110-0001-12-00B01, ILE-NL-2100-0006-12-00B01), as developed by the entity for logistics (called ILE). Lastly, the section details the as-is reporting framework (Section 2.3).

2.1. The Theoretical Model

In our work, we considered a theoretical model inspired by literature regarding incident learning originating from reliability and safety management [31,32]. In such a model, the components of an Incident Learning System include 8 main phases generally (Figure 1): identification and response; reporting; investigation; identifying the causal structure; making recommendations; communicating; recalling incident learnings; implementing corrective actions.

The first component of the LFI system is the "identification and response", without which no learning, even no business survival, is possible [33]. Such observation is not trivial, since unless the organization is already sensitized about a LFI management policy, deviations from normal behavior may not be noticed or will usually be accepted as "normal deviations" (Dekker, 2011), so it is very important to establish an appropriate identification threshold.

The second component of LFI system is "reporting": no incident can be investigated if it is not duly reported. Here, a proper dimension of reporting has to be arranged, containing relevant information, and excluding those which would require too much efforts, jeopardizing even the credibility of the entire report [34].

The "investigation" is a core component of the LFI system. Starting from the outcomes of "reporting" this phase includes the examination of the report, as well as the involved item/site (if needed), and the interview of users/witnesses. This phase aims to collect and evaluate the available data to establish the sequence of events and establish the basis for subsequent causal analyses. It is often claimed that the purpose of incident investigation is to determine the root causes of the incident [35]. However, since there may be no single root cause, efforts would be better directed towards "identifying the causal structure". For incidents that occur in complex systems, one possible approach is to integrate the techniques of analysis of the root causes with system thinking [36,37]. The work of the investigation team is usually considered as completed with the issuance of an incident report detailing the findings and recommendations ("making recommendations"). The dissemination of this document as well as other communication activities within the organization, i.e., "communication", is a means to enhance organizational learning.

A further inherent phase of the learning process is the "recalling incident learnings", i.e., the application of the learning coming from incidents, and the "failure hypothesizing", i.e., using the investigation report to explore possible failure modes that have not yet occurred [38–40].

Lastly, it is important to implement corrective actions and all the recommendations made by the investigative team in order to obtain a cyclic effective LFI system.

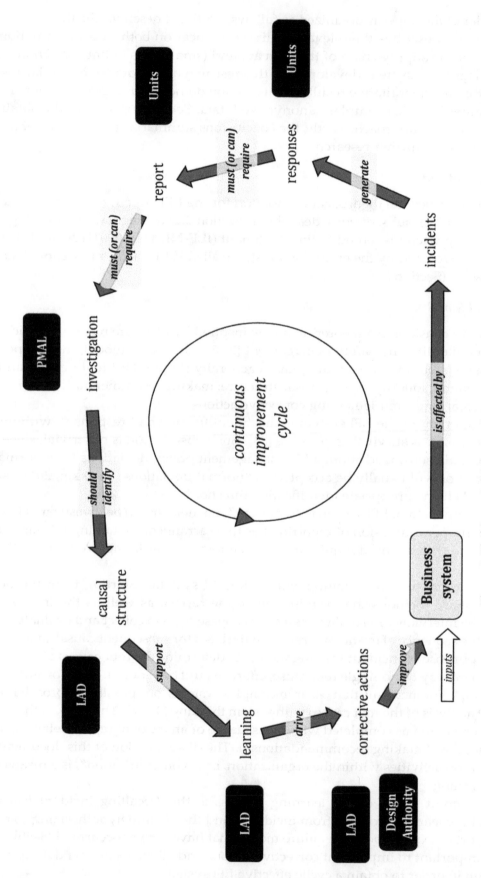

Figure 1. The theoretical learning from incidents (LFI) model.

2.2. The Regulatory Framework

NATO stresses the importance of a LFI model, as established by the Joint Analysis and Lessons Learned Center (JALLC), whose mission is to carry out an inter-force analysis of everyday operations, training, exercises and experiments, including the implementation and management of a single database for all NATO countries regarding lessons learned. The NATO learning doctrine applies to any military activity, even though in real practices it faces the challenges imposed by the lack of a healthy reporting culture. For this purpose, individual armed forces adjust the NATO doctrine on LFI by a set of customized inter-organizations and intra-organization directives, issued by national bodies. On this basis, this paper focused on the regulatory framework implemented in Italy for small arms, as described by two logistics publications which are of interest for sustainable SCM:

– ILE-NL-1110-0001-12-00B01 (see Section 2.2.1), which deals with the management of the different materials supplied to the Italian Army, for the sake of clarity called ILE-MM (ILE—Material Management)
– ILE-NL-2100-0006-12-00B01 (see Section 2.2.2), which derives from the previous one and regulates the management activities and the logistic device related to the armament material, for the sake of clarity called ILE-LM (ILE-Logistics Management).

The regulatory framework is completed by the technical directive TER-50-1000-0007-12-00B000 (see Section 2.2.3), repeatedly recalled by the ILE-NL-2100-0006-12-00B01, which defines the control procedures to ensure the usability of a weapon in safe conditions for the operator and the reliability for operational purposes.

2.2.1. ILE-NL-1110-0001-12-00B01

The publication was issued to maintain the availability of means, materials and weapon systems at the levels set by the Army General Staff, for the effective use of units in operations and training activities. The ILE-MM defines the correct procedures of technical-logistical management so that maintenance interventions and supply activities take place in a harmonious and balanced functional framework, following a cost-effective target. The purpose of the publication is therefore to establish the rules governing the management of the material parks supplied to the Italian Army, for operational, training and logistical needs.

The publication consists of a "general section" and the "park material section". The former provides the main features of the logistic support in all its aspects, and a series of dossiers related to the detailed management rules for homogeneous sets of materials. This section further defines the procedures relating to the main elements of the logistic support, i.e., procurement, supplies, maintenance, transport.

Procurement is at the origin of the material management process and it aims at acquiring the means and materials necessary to achieve or maintain the expected operational capacity.

The Supplies are intended to make the material resources available to the armies, in scheduled times, places and quantities to ensure the operational capabilities necessary for operations. This activity also includes the reverse material handling about replacement of inefficient vehicles and materials.

Maintenance is the activity which seeks to ensure the reliability of the means and materials through checks, revisions, reconfigurations and various types of processing. Furthermore, the ILE-MM specifies the tasks of the Second Level of Maintenance (FLS) institutions, i.e., the Maintenance Poles, which are entrusted with all the corrective actions that fall outside the competence of the First Level of Maintenance (FLA) and the general revision interventions related to the peculiarity of the materials, means and weapon systems. Moreover, the publication establishes, among a series of other activities, that the so-called Maintenance Poles are accountable of carrying out technical investigations on incidents and accidents related to the material of its own competence. For the case under exam, the publication assigns to the Small Arms Maintenance Pole (SAMP) the competence on small arms and light weapons.

The publication defines Transport as an operational activity aimed at transferring personnel, vehicles and materials from a place of origin to a destination, using land, sea and air carriers, through the related infrastructure.

In the second section, the ILE-MM defines the Park Materials as the union of all weapons, artillery, technical means for shooting, rotated and tracked vehicles, machines for earthworks, and aircraft supplied to the Army. It identifies five Park Areas and respective sub-areas, including homogeneous sets of several species of materials, means or weapon systems, having similar technical and employment characteristics, unitarily considered for the purpose of facilitating the material management. For the purposes of this work, the "E Area" concerning armament materials is the one that interests us the most.

2.2.2. ILE-NL-2100-0006-12-00B01

The publication ILE-LM is one of the dossiers of the ILE described in Section 2.2.1 and concerns the materials relating to the "E Area" Park, for which it defines the management activities and the related logistic device. For each material, a specific technical life is indicated in order to allow a correct management of the potentials as well as the planning of maintenance operations. At the end of this life, the material to be sent to the Maintenance Pole is submitted to general revision and, whereas possible, to carry out the resetting of the technical life. The publication then reports a series of tables, for each type of weapon, which detail the preventive interventions, the competent Logistics Area (FLA or FLS), the periodicity of these interventions, the necessary time.

2.2.3. TER-50-1000-0007-12-00B000

This document details the technical inspection procedures aimed at ascertaining, at all levels, the usability of the arms allowing both safety for the human user and reliability for operational purposes. The verifying instruments are a set of artefacts that allow for the checking of significant dimensions for the most important parts of the weapon from the point of view of safety and operation in a simple and rapid manner, as designed by the weapon manufacturer.

2.3. Focus of the Research: Reporting

Following the previous mentioned regulations, the inconveniences constituting technical problems must be reported according to the form in the Annex O of the publication ILE-LM, which defines the roles and the action for each supply chain agent. The reporting form has to be sent to three agents: (i) the Land Armaments Directorate (LAD), which is responsible for technical-administrative issues related to armament, (ii) the Command of Transport and Materials of the Army Logistic Command, (iii) the Logistic Department of the Army General Staff, and (iv) to the Commands on which the report producer unit depends. The report is structured in five sections, which are described following a supply chain information management perspective.

The first section deals with the description of the material and the parts affected by the problem, as well as the applicable technical documentation and the data related to the various types of maintenance interventions carried out. From an information management perspective, it is relevant to prioritize some of fields included in the technical report.

For the material, relevant fields are the Unique Codification Number (NUC), the name and type of the weapon, the Manufacturer, the number plate/frame/serial number (or other identifying element), the date of introduction into service;

For the system: the name, the serial number, the sub-group or the figure number, while for the parts involved in the incident: the name, the catalogue number and the NUC. Additional fields are the relevant Publication or Technical Ordinance; dates and number of hours of operation, and number of shots fired before the last specialized maintenance, the last reliability check, the last technical check, as well as the most recent general revision.

The second section illustrates the purpose of the reporting, highlighting whether it concerns the safety of personnel; regards the functionality of the material; is for information purposes only.

The third section deals with the description of the problem, including shots/hours of usage when incident happened; narrative of the incident; possible causes (if any); taken measures (if any); number of detected cases (if any); previous reports (if any); proposals (if any); any other note.

The fourth section expresses the reporting priority (from high to low): emergency; urgent; normal.

The fifth section (not mandatory) contains a field to report any other data considered to be of interest, and some photos of relevant parts are usually attached, as shown in (e.g.,) Figures 2 and 3.

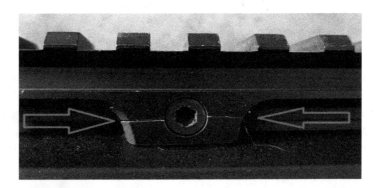

Figure 2. Example of technical inconvenience: mechanical damage in the rail of automatic rifle.

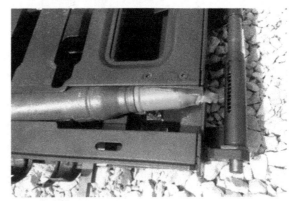

Figure 3. Example of a technical inconvenience for cal. 25 mm machine gun: jammed munitions during the feeding cycle).

Nevertheless, the information management from these reporting activities does not prescribe any systemic data structure and data collection, lacking treats for a completely effective LFI system. Starting from such approach, Section 3 presents a centralized SCM approach in order to maximize the potential of the LFI system, whose results are presented in Section 4.

3. The Proposed Approach

The centralized information management system was developed for the SCM of small arms, and it is here described in terms of data collection (Section 3.1), and database structure (Section 3.2). Then analysis on the dataset are presented in the context of a specific weapon (Section 4), which is supplied to three different Armed Forces. Data and analyses refer to a 6-year interval span, which were manipulated in order not to break the intellectual property of the agents involved, without disclosing any sensitive information.

3.1. Centralized Supply Chain Information Management: Data Collection

The first phase of the work was the data collection from the submitted forms, creating an IT data repository. The report proposed by the ILE-LM should be rigidly structured with well-defined fields to facilitate data entry and allow a simplified information management. Nevertheless, the acquisition, collection, and management of the reports for the weapon of the case study was a long and laborious activity, which lasted for about six weeks. The reason for this process lies in the way in which the messages and the related forms have been transmitted over years, i.e., the oldest reports were in paper format and it was necessary to consult the historical archive and manually enter the data in the various fields of the database. For this reason, a centralized digital repository became necessary and motivated the development of a Business Intelligence (BI) solution to ease dynamic data extraction and data analyses. We want to further stress this point, since it suggests an added value for the paper at hand, clarifying how the contributions.

3.2. Database Structure

Once the reports were gathered, it was necessary to structure the received data in a relational database. Such a database was built to allow an immediate data consultation and support holistic analyses in a multi-variate perspective. This database, whose architecture is represented in Figure 4, is made up of five tables: Reports, Weapons, Units, Contracts, Geographical coordinates. Note that the presented structure is intended as a general data architecture to be used for BI. Figure 4 aims to put emphasis on data organizations in tables, and relationships among tables for the subsequent analyses.

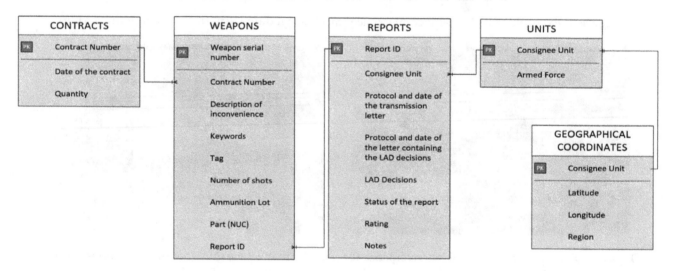

Figure 4. Database architecture using the Crow's foot notation (PK = Primary Key).

The "Reports" table contains all the reports received over a period of six years, theoretically, by units belonging to three different Armed Forces. The key of the table is the couple protocol and date of the reporting message. Other fields of the table are: report identification number (primary key); consignee Unit (or originator of the report); protocol and date of the LAD technical inquiry format letter; protocol and date of the transmission letter of the SAMP technical investigation; protocol and date of the letter containing the LAD determinations; LAD decisions; status of the report; Rating (a score calculated following the rules in Section 4.2); and a free text for notes. The "LAD decisions" field contains the decisions taken by the LAD. In case no investigation is considered necessary, the motivations are reported or, once the investigative process was completed, the corrective actions identified or undertaken are described; The "status of the report" field: it can be "in process" if LAD has still to decide, "in progress", if the technical investigation is being carried out at the SAMP, "closed" when the SAMP closed the investigation and LAD has provided its determinations or the technical investigation is not necessary since the inconvenience is already known or because it is due to the normal use of the weapon;

A "Weapons" table, which shows the data recorded on the forms for each weapon, was also implemented. This table is linked to the previous one using the same key, i.e., the couple protocol-data. Besides the key, its fields are: weapon serial number (primary key); number of the contract; description of the inconvenience; keywords; tag (label used to categorize the incident/accident); number of fired shots; ammunition lot; and part. Note that the ammunition lot is a fundamental information, particularly relevant in cases where an explosion of the weapon has occurred. Unfortunately, the standard reporting form does not provide a dedicated field and, thus this information is not always reported (requiring a successive dedicated information request).

The "Units" table concerns the originators of the reports and includes the following fields: Consignee Unit (primary key); AF (indicating the unit's Armed Force).

The "Geographical Coordinates" table details the latitude and longitude of the unit, to support a graphical representation of the reports in relation to Units. This table comes as a separate table from Unit since it includes data already in place before the development of the LFI system.

The "Contracts" table contains details on the contracts for the supply chain of the analyzed weapon. Relevant fields are: contract number; date of the contract (the date of the contract's approval); quantity (the number of weapons procured with the contract).

3.3. Business Intelligence Framework

Once the data were organized according to the structure described in Section 3.2, statistical analyses were performed to support a holistic and effective supply chain information management. These analyses rely on Business Intelligence (BI), intended as a set of techniques, technologies, systems, practices, methodologies, and applications that transform raw data into meaningful and useful information. BI was adopted in several domains, with recent research developments in aviation safety LFI at European level [41,42]. Similarly, BI becomes relevant for modern supply chains, since it supports a deeper understanding of organization' business values [43]. To this extent, the proposed LFI system, implemented via a BI architecture supports a large number of analytical analyses and a dynamic investigation of the variables included in the dataset, filling a gap in available literature on reverse supply chain in military environments.

4. Results

This section describes the main results obtained from the application of the BI approach based on the LFI perspective to a case study.

4.1. Preliminary Observations on Reporting Activity

As a preliminary observation, the reports of technical incidents/accidents related to the case study originated by Units belonging to two different Armed Forces. Since the weapon at hand is supplied—albeit in minor quantities—even to a third Armed Force, it is questionable that no reports were sent by the latter one.

Another consideration that can be made on reporting activity with reference to the case study, is related to the number of Units that have reported technical problems. This number represents about a third of the Units that actually make use of the weapon at hand. The issue to be investigated should explore if the absence of reporting by approximately sixty percent of units is justified (e.g., particular precautions taken during training or maintenance procedures that allowed preventing incidents), or is due to under-reporting (i.e., in case of an incident, the weapon is sent for repair or replacement, if under warranty, directly to the manufacturer, without reporting the incident following relevant regulations).

4.2. Systematic Analysis of the Reports

Firstly, the analysis showed that just less than 10% of the reports were compiled correctly in each section. More specifically, 35% did not include the shots number; and 90% did not contain any indications on the lot number of ammunitions. It is important to note that this latter information was always reported in cases that presented an explosion of the weapon, or was acquired successively upon explicit request by the LAD. Additionally, 15% of the reports did not include either the name of the item affected by the incident, nor the NUC; the same serial number was reported in six cases, which indicates an error in the reporting form (same weapon uses multiple times).

Starting from these observations, a rating system was calculated for each form to support holistic information management and the goodness estimation of reports. The purpose of this type of analysis consists of identifying the most virtuous reporting Units and taking them as reference examples (best in class, see Figure 5) for the other Units, to push them to produce reporting forms with increasingly complete and accurate information. The rating includes three families (Number of shots reported, Ammunition lot reported, NUC reported) with maximum assigned scores respectively (30, 30, 40).

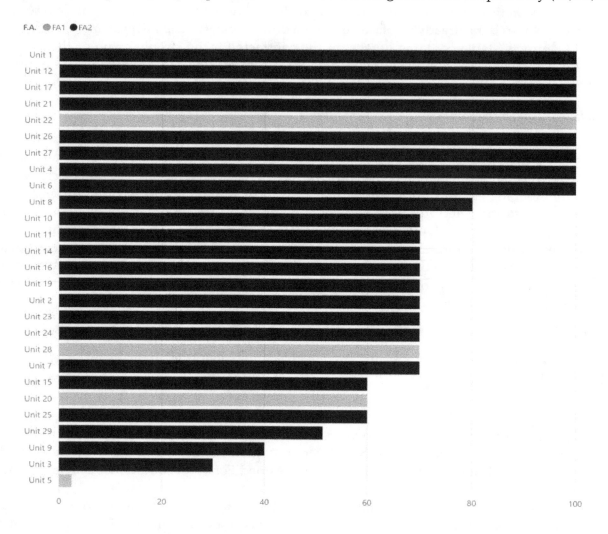

Figure 5. Scores distribution of reports' quality per unit.

4.3. Relationships Between Contracts and Incidents

Subsequently, the six procurement contracts were analyzed in relation to the number of reports to map the contractual supply performance. The relationships were discussed in relative terms, i.e., number of reports vs. number of weapons supplied through the contract. The contract presenting the highest report/quantity ratio is the first contract in chronological order (Contract 1) with a decreasing report/quantity ratio in accordance with the time span (see Figure 6). Such contract refers to a product which was undergoing consolidation, i.e., the first phase of its usage with multiple problems emerging. Over the years, the adoption of mitigating actions defined through the reporting process motivated changes to the configuration of the weapon to improve its technical maturity (Contract 8 and 9).

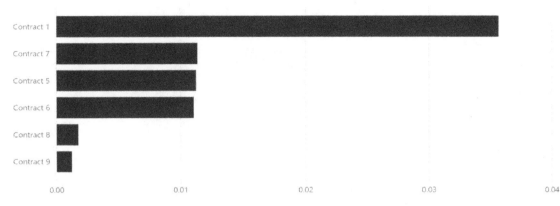

Figure 6. Reported cases over quantities per contract.

4.4. Pareto Analysis

A Pareto analysis is here used as a tool to prioritize some aspects of the phenomenon being investigated out of multiple causes, which compete to gain attention. In more operational terms, firstly, each category of incidents/accidents occurred was tagged: a "tag" was added to each report, containing a three-letter code to link the incidents belonging to the same type (see Table 1).

Table 1. Tag codification for main failure modes.

TAG	DESCRIPTION
GAS	(Gas recovery system failure)—The label identifies cases where it was found or there is a suspicion that the jams occurred on the weapons are due to the non-compliant diameter of the hole in the gas outlet that regulates the recovery system to subtract gas
HDL	(Handle failure)—Tag used to identify all cases that have a defect in the front handle
INV	(To Be Investigated)—Tag used for those cases to be investigated, whose reasons have not yet been clearly identified but have in common the occurrence of an explosion of part of the weapon
MEC	(Mechanical failure)—Tag used to identify mechanical failure of a component, not related to an explosion phenomenon
NCD	(Non-Conformity to Drawing)—Tag used to define the cases in which a non-conformity issue is found with respect to the constructive drawings on some details of the weapon
NUL	(Null)—Tag used to identify cases of minor interest that do not constitute a serious inconvenience
SLD	(Rail slide failure)—Tag used to identify all cases that have a defect in the upper guide of the slide
SPR	(Spring failure)—Tag used to identify all cases where there is a defect in the springs of the ejector-ejector assembly
THM	(Thermo-fusion failure)—Tag used for cases in which a principle of thermo-fusion of the polymer constituting the carcass has occurred.
USC	(Partial Unscrewing failure)—Tag used to identify cases of partial unscrewing

Using the Pareto diagram in Figure 7, it is possible to note that three categories (i.e., SPR, SLD, GAS) out of ten cover more than 75% of the identified technical inconveniences. This type of analysis allows thus isolating the technical inconveniences where priority interventions is required. It also allows for an immediate ex-post verification of the effectiveness of the implemented interventions: by comparing two representations of the same phenomenon, before and after the intervention, there is a clear overview of the progress made and a measure of overall improvement.

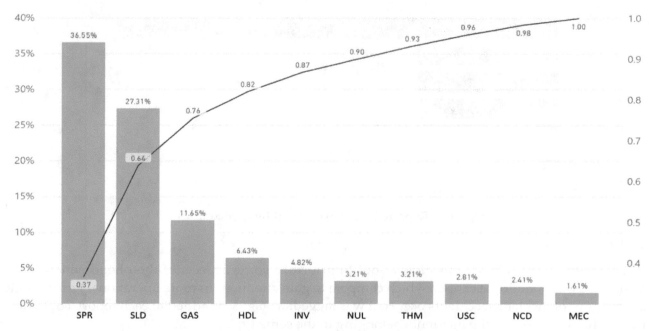

Figure 7. Pareto's diagram applied to most relevant technical components.

In the case study at hand, if a Pareto diagram is re-calculated (see Figure 8) considering only the reports whose status were "in progress "or " in process", it can immediately be observed that the cases relating to the three above-mentioned categories (i.e., SPR, SLD, GAS), are no longer included in the new diagram. This observation confirms that the majority of reports do not represent a current issue and they were solved in more recent contracts.

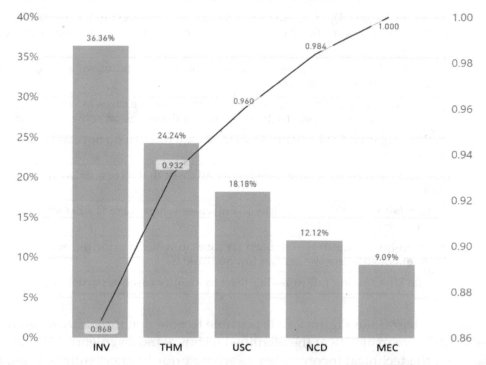

Figure 8. Pareto's diagram applied to most relevant technical components (only "in progress" or "in process" status).

4.5. Dynamic LFI Dashboards

With the purpose of creating a dynamic business intelligence tool for the LFI system, further information was integrated into a dynamic dashboard (see Figures 9 and 10). More specifically, Figure 9 shows some summary data regarding the inconveniences divided into categories: (top left) a histogram depicting the distribution of the incidents by category, (bottom left) a sketch of the same incident categories per involved Unit, (right) a geographical map with a bubble pie chart where the size of the bubble presents the total number of reports, broken down per report tag. The dynamicity is developed through the implementation of the database structure into Microsoft PowerBI, which can be interfaced with the majority of data sources, ranging from MS Excel and MS Access to SQL, IBM database, and more.

Note that the dashboard is not static in the sense that the user can click on any point of any visual to select only one or more elements and automatically query the database to get the respective filtered/combined information.

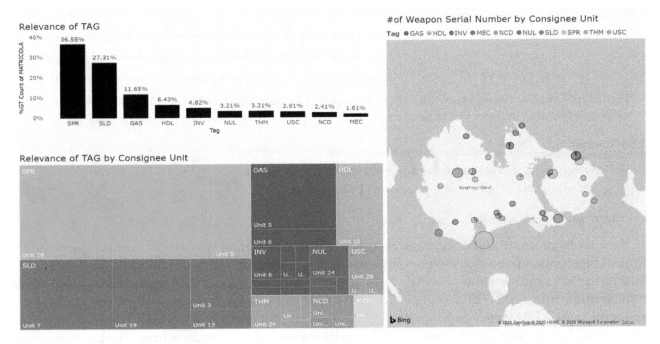

Figure 9. Main dashboard page of the integrated LFI system (quantitative and geographical data were manipulated in order not to break the intellectual property of the units involved).

As a second example, another dashboard page is proposed to show the potential of the framework, and its feasibility to accommodate different type of analysis and different visualizations.

Figure 10 presents a panel where the top right pie chart details the count of Weapon Serial Number by Contract Number, and the respective average rating of technical report. An average target of 90 out of 100 points per report is reported in the gauge (bottom left), while the overall average value is 73. Furthermore, the bottom right graph presents a decomposition tree addressing the count of Weapon Serial Number that were reported in one or more report, and decomposing this number by the different Armed Forces, Contract Numbers, Consignee Unit, and Tag. In the presented case, the analysis stops at Unit 15, clarifying how the reports issued by this unit, referred to Contract 5 involved in descending order Handling failure (HDL), Rail slide failures (SLD), Mechanical failures (MEC) and a small portions of aspects to be further investigated (INV). This dynamic dashboard is intended as a support tool for the decision-maker for managing data for the supply chain at hand.

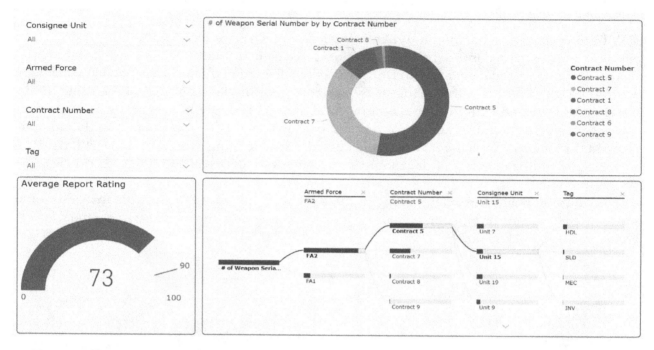

Figure 10. Detailed page on reporting of the integrated LFI system (quantitative and geographical data were manipulated in order not to break the intellectual property of the units involved).

5. Discussion

Following the analysis presented in Section 4, it is possible to outline improvements aimed at ensuring a sustainable SCM via the proposed LFI system.

5.1. *Prioritization of Reporting*

In order to promote and encourage reporting by all the Armed Forces and Armed Corps on the technical incidents related to the weaponry material, it is desirable to issue an inter-forces technical publication that regulates the process. For example, in Italy still, for the aeronautical sector, the technical publication AER (EP).00-01-6a Ed. 2010 "Instructions for the compilation, forwarding and management of inconvenience reports related to aeronautic material", issued by the Aeronautic Armaments Directorate (AAD) is used as a normative example in this direction. The purpose of the AAD publication is to regulate, through the issue of Inconvenience Reports, the activities related to the flow of information and materials so that all the necessary actions are taken and implemented to determine the causes of the occurrence of incidents/accidents related to the aeronautic material. This standard is applicable to all aircraft configuration articles registered in the Register of Military Aircraft of the AAD in relation to the production and use phases.

A similar solution could be adopted in the reporting process concerning the armament material, providing a centralized and unitary management of the incidents related to weapons. In addition, another cue for reflection about the aforementioned AAD publication, is the distinction of the Inconvenient Report in two different categories, which activate two different prioritizations of procedures (based on information, timescale). For the most critical reports (reporting defect or inconveniences of immediate danger that impacts airworthiness and safety for people or things) the AAD publication envisages the immediate involvement of the Design Authority. This shall react immediately within three working days, formulating precautionary and/or definitive measures to ensure that unacceptable operations are protracted over time. Such an approach should undoubtedly be followed when accidents related to weaponry material have a significant impact on safety.

5.2. Improving Digitalization

The data collection phase for the application of the method was an extremely time-consuming phase, since several documents were still paper-based, or there were scans of paper documents hardly processable by automated IT systems (i.e., OCR systems). For this purpose, it could be beneficial to create an IT data entry form, or more suitably, a dedicated web portal on the intranet of relevant military authority. This portal should have a section where one can upload all the information related to the technical problem, by filling out a digital reporting form. It could be possible to have automatic quality check for the report completeness and obtain real-time statistics for the supply chain status. In this phase, a further recommendation would be linked to the formalization of the incident description field, that, being narrative, would benefit from the introduction of a taxonomy.

The taxonomy should allow for the identification of (at least) the affected part of the weapon, the failure mode, its effect, and the use condition. On this path, the taxonomy could be developed in a data-driven approach to reduce the efforts for its development. Such a data-driven approach would lead to the extraction of relevant information from the reports at hand by machine learning techniques for data extraction and text mining, (e.g., Naïve Bayes Classifiers) [44,45]. Once the taxonomy is developed, the "Description of the inconvenience" data field could be potentially structured providing auto-completing text, or even the allowing of the choice only among a determined set of options, based on the data gathered so far that feeds the taxonomy. Obviously, for each field, there should also be an option for an "other" choice that provides the possibility to add information that is not included in the previous list. Such extra data should be revised on a regular basis and, if relevant and significant, added among the permanent selection options, integrating the taxonomy itself. Consequently, the taxonomy could become incrementally wider and more representative, with the advantage of having a uniform database, to allow further text-based analytics.

5.3. A 4.0 LFI System

An additional technology in favor of digitalizing the reporting process could be related to the introduction of an intelligent weapon management system, in line with recent Industry 4.0 notions, propelled by the upsurge and progressive maturity of new information technologies [46]. An intelligent armory management system would facilitate operations through the entire supply chain. Exemplary areas affected by a smart weapon management system would be: (i) the control of access in the armory based on different privileges and the management of the authorization to take arms, providing an undoubted improvement of the process in terms of security; (ii) the logistic and maintenance management of weapons in terms of the potential expressed by the weapon taken from the armory and the management of any maintenance needs following anomalies or malfunctions, as well as the management of preventive maintenance; (iii) the management of accidents/incidents related to the armament material in real-time.

Regarding the latter point, the smart system might be interfaced with the portal discussed in Section 5.2, to feed the underlying database favoring and simplifying the reporting process. A series of data could in fact be acquired directly from the weapon, reducing the efforts for the data entry. This would be possible if each weapon had an electronic device, integrated into the weapon, that allows the recording of the number of shots fired, like the odometer used in cars, and RFID (Radio-frequency identification) tags on which to store information such as the model, the serial number, the contract, the number of shots.

It is easy to picture the improvement that would follow the introduction of such an intelligent armory management system in terms of the weapons maintenance process, since it would guarantee the acquisition of a large number of returns from the operational field, which is an essential starting point to proceed in the studies on reliability and maintainability of the various types of weapons.

5.4. A Healthy Reporting Environment

Incident reporting starts any LFI system. However, other latent factors ensure the LFI initialization even earlier. It is important to observe how an increase in the safety level should not be connected to a decrease in the number of reported incidents, but rather to their lower severity: in other words, few reports do not imply a higher safety level. This situation could be rather a consequence of under-reporting, due to an unhealthy working environment. As for the wide literature in the safety area, the fear of being punished or accused of negligence in managing the weapon could discourage a reporting action. The participation of personnel involved in the investigation activity could be favored in a periodic toolbox meeting at the units responsible for reporting, in order to show the benefits of reporting by means of some significant incidents and recommendations.

On this path, expanding the functionalities of the portal discussed in Section 5.2, the same portal could be further used to gather information on the most significant incidents/accidents, illustrating the investigative activity carried out and the corrective actions (e.g., revision of procedures, emissions of technical notes, execution of retrofit interventions). Such approach may further advance the spreading of the recommended actions, contributing to the overall LFI system via a healthy reporting culture. This latter point puts emphasis on understanding work as actually carried out at organizational level, and on empowering sharp-end operator knowledge [47], ensuring sustainable reverse logistics, and in general, systemic supply chain resilience [48].

6. Conclusions

The literature analysis about LFI emphasizes the importance and the need to implement an effective Incident Learning System in order to achieve higher safety levels within an organization. Through the analysis of the supply chain information management process on military technical inconvenience for armaments, this paper presented an LFI framework valid for military supply chains.

The analysis shows empirical evidence on how technical incident data acquire values that go beyond the technical investigation: a well-structured database can be the basis for effective decision-making, which can be supported by synthetic user-friendly and easily accessible dashboards. Using a Business Intelligence perspective, the developed LFI system shows the benefits of a centralized information management system and supports the identification of future developments beyond the company being analyzed, i.e., the development of an inter-forces reporting regulation, the enhancement of digitalization in the entire process, the adoption of smart systems, and the fostering of a healthy reporting environment. It is important to observe how this paper provides just a subset of the possible indexes to be used for monitoring supply chain sustainability in light of the LFI framework. Furthermore, additional quantitative analyses can be developed to extend the analytical dimension of the proposed framework, e.g., clustering algorithms, trend analyses, multi-dimensional correlations.

Regarding the intelligent data management system, one aspect not considered in this research is related to privacy issues and threats related to cyber-security, which opens the path to future research in the same context [49].

More generally, the proposed LFI system described in this paper could be further enhanced, analyzing the important connections with the world outside of the organization, i.e., exploring how local learning is shared outside the supply chain agents, i.e., providing an external cycle for shared learnings. This cycle could be closed by the benchmarking process that analyses best practices and adapts them to improve the military system in a sustainable perspective.

Note also that the approach refers to the Italian regulatory framework for military reporting, but since it is grounded in the general NATO learning doctrine, it remains flexible enough to accommodate the needs of other settings, as long as they rely on the same NATO foundations for systemic learning. Lastly, even though the proposed case study focuses on small arms, it is worth mentioning how the same logic remains usable for technical inconveniences related to other types of weapons and it could be thus reproduced for the analysis of early phases of the item lifecycle.

Acronyms

AAD	Aeronautic Armaments Directorate
AF	Armed Force
GAS	Gas recovery system failure
HDL	Handle failure
ILE-LM	ILE Material Management (ILE-NL-2100-0006-12-00B01)
ILE-MM	ILE Logistic Management (ILE-NL-1110-0001-12-00B01)
INV	To be Investigated
LAD	Land Armaments Directorate
LFI	Learning from Incident
MEC	Mechanical failure
NCD	Non-Conformity to Drawing
NUC	Unique Codification Number
NUL	Null
SAMP	Small Arms Maintenance Pole
SLD	Rail slide failure
SPR	Spring failure
THM	Thermo-fusion failure
USC	Partial Unscrewing failure

Author Contributions: Conceptualization, G.D.G. and R.P.; methodology, G.D.G., R.C. and R.P.; software, R.C. and R.P.; validation, R.C. and R.P.; formal analysis, R.C. and G.D.G.; investigation, R.C.; resources, R.C. and R.P.; data curation, R.C.; writing—original draft preparation, R.C. and R.P.; writing—review and editing, R.P. and G.D.G.; visualization, R.P. and G.D.G.; supervision, R.P. and G.D.G.; project administration, G.D.G.; funding acquisition, G.D.G. All authors have read and agreed to the published version of the manuscript.

References

1. Kumar, K. Technology for supporting supply chain management. *Commun. ACM* **2001**, *44*, 58–61. [CrossRef]
2. Ballou, R.H. The evolution and future of logistics and supply chain management. *Produção* **2006**, *16*, 375–386. [CrossRef]
3. Iakovou, E. A new framework for supply chain management: Review concepts and examples. In Proceedings of the Third Aegean International Conference on Design and Analysis of Manufacturing Systems, TInos, Greece, 19–22 May 2001; pp. 27–36.
4. Erkan, B.; Mehmet, D.; Koh, S.C.L.; Tatoglu, E.; Zaim, H. A causal analysis of the impact of information systems and supply chain management practices on operational performance: Evidence from manufacturing SMEs in Turkey. *Int. J. Prod. Econ.* **2009**, *122*, 133–149.
5. Habib, M. Supply Chain Management (SCM): Its future implications. *Open J. Soc. Sci.* **2014**, *2*, 238–246. [CrossRef]
6. Cigolini, R.; Cozzi, M.; Perona, M. A new framework for supply chain management: Conceptual model and empirical test. *Int. J. Oper. Prod. Manag.* **2004**, *24*, 7–41. [CrossRef]
7. Matinrad, N.; Roghanian, E.; Rasi, Z. Supply chain network optimization: A review of classification, models, solution techniques and future research. *Uncertain Supply Chain Manag.* **2013**, *1*, 1–24. [CrossRef]
8. Imran, M.; Hamid, S.; Aziz, A.; Hameed, W. The contributing factors towards e-logistic customer satisfaction: A mediating role of information technology. *Uncertain Supply Chain Manag.* **2019**, *7*, 63–72. [CrossRef]
9. Department of Defense. *Fiscal Year 2017 Annual Industrial Capabilities*; Department of Defense: Washington, DC, USA, 2018.
10. Gunasekaran, A.; Ngai, E.W.T. Information systems in supply chain integration and management. *Eur. J. Oper. Res.* **2004**, *159*, 269–295. [CrossRef]
11. Kim, S.; Cohen, M.A.; Netessine, S. Performance contracting in after-sales service supply chains performance contracting in after-sales service supply chains. *Manag. Sci.* **2007**, *53*, 1843–1858. [CrossRef]
12. Stock, J.R. *Reverse Logistics: White Paper*; Council of Logistics Management: Oak Brook, IL, USA, 1992.

13.   Khalili-Damghani, K.; Naderi, H. A mathematical location-routing model of repair centres and ammunition depots in order to support soldiers in civil wars. *Int. J. Manag. Decis. Mak.* **2014**, *13*, 422–450.

14.   Qrunfleh, S.; Tarafdar, M. Supply chain information systems strategy: Impacts on supply chain performance and firm performance. *Int. J. Prod. Econ.* **2014**, *147*, 340–350. [CrossRef]

15.   Hugos, M. *Essentials of Supply Chain Management*, 2nd ed.; Wiley: Hoboken, NJ, USA, 2006.

16.   Fan, C.; Fan, P.; Chang, P. A system dynamics modeling approach for a military weapon maintenance supply system. *Int. J. Prod. Econ.* **2010**, *128*, 457–469. [CrossRef]

17.   Liu, B.-P.; Zhang, K.; Huang, D. Constructing strategy of stable reverse military logistics system based on non-cooperative game. In *Annual Conference Proceedings, Proceedings of the International Conference on Management Science and Engineering*; Nomi, Japan, 17–20 August 2017, Tao, M.A., Zhen, S., Eds.; IEEE Computer Society: Washington, DC, USA, 2018; pp. 33–38.

18.   Wang, K.; Jiang, D.L.; Liu, J.; Zhang, L. Waste military air material reverse logistics system multi-objective incentive and monitoring mechanism. *Adv. Mater. Res.* **2012**, *518–523*, 3631–3640. [CrossRef]

19.   El Garrab, H.; Castanier, B.; Lemoine, D.; Lazrak, A.; Heidsieck, R. Towards hybrid machine learning models in decision support systems for predicting the spare parts reverse flow in a complex supply chain. In *Information system, Logistics & Supply Chain-ILS, Proceedings of the ILS 2020 International Conference on Information Systems, Logistics and Supply Chain, Austin, TX, USA, 22–24 April 2020*; The Center for Direct Scientific Communication (CCSD): Austin, TX, USA, 2020; pp. 188–195.

20.   Mahmoudzadeh, M.; Mansour, S.; Karimi, B. To develop a third-party reverse logistics network for end-of-life vehicles in Iran. *Resour. Conserv. Recycl.* **2013**, *78*, 1–14. [CrossRef]

21.   Glicksman, H.; Penn, M. Approximation algorithms for group prize-collecting and location-routing problems. *Discret. Appl. Math.* **2008**, *156*, 3238–3247. [CrossRef]

22.   Carnes, T.; Shmoys, D.B. Primal-dual schema and Lagrangian relaxation for the k-location-routing problem. *Lect. Notes Comput. Sci. (Incl. Subser. Lect. Notes Artif. Intell. Lect. Notes Bioinform.)* **2011**, *6845*, 99–110.

23.   Guerrero, W.J.; Prodhon, C.; Velasco, N.; Amaya, C.A. Hybrid heuristic for the inventory location-routing problem with deterministic demand. *Int. J. Prod. Econ.* **2013**, *146*, 359–370. [CrossRef]

24.   Wilson, J.M.; Goodman, P.S.; Cronin, M.A. Group learning. *Acad. Manag. Rev.* **2007**, *32*, 1041–1059. [CrossRef]

25.   Ramanujam, R.; Goodman, P.S. The challenge of collective learning from event analysis. *Saf. Sci.* **2011**, *49*, 83–89. [CrossRef]

26.   Le Coze, J.C. What have we learned about learning from accidents? Post-disasters reflections. *Saf. Sci.* **2013**, *51*, 441–453. [CrossRef]

27.   Lukic, D.; Littlejohn, A.; Margaryan, A. A framework for learning from incidents in the workplace. *Saf. Sci.* **2012**, *50*, 950–957. [CrossRef]

28.   Silva, S.A.; Carvalho, H.; Oliveira, M.J.; Fialho, T.; Soares, C.G.; Jacinto, C. Organizational practices for learning with work accidents throughout their information cycle. *Saf. Sci.* **2017**, *99*, 102–114. [CrossRef]

29.   Kaya, E.; Azaltun, M. Role of information systems in supply chain management and its application on five-star hotels in Istanbul. *J. Hosp. Tour.* **2012**, *3*, 138–146. [CrossRef]

30.   NATO JALLC. *The NATO Lessons Learned Handbook*, 3rd ed.; NATO JALLC: Monsanto, Portugal, 2016; ISBN 978-92-845-0188-5.

31.   Cooke, D.L.; Rohleder, T.R. Learning from incidents: From normal accidents to high reliability. *Syst. Dyn. Rev.* **2006**, *22*, 213–239. [CrossRef]

32.   Cooke, D.L.; Dunscombe, P.B.; Lee, R.C. Using a survey of incident reporting and learning practices to improve organisational learning at a cancer care centre. *Qual. Saf. Health Care* **2007**, *16*, 342–348. [CrossRef]

33.   Phimister, J.R.; Oktem, U.; Kleindorfer, P.R.; Kunreuther, H. Near-miss incident management in the chemical process industry. *Risk Anal.* **2003**, *23*, 445–459. [CrossRef]

34.   Hayes, J.; Maslen, S. Knowing stories that matter: Learning for effective safety decision-making. *J. Risk Res.* **2014**, *9877*, 1–13. [CrossRef]

35.   Dekker, S.; Pruchnicki, S. Drifting into failure: Theorising the dynamics of disaster incubation. *Theor. Issues Ergon. Sci.* **2014**, *15*, 534–544. [CrossRef]

36.   Leveson, N. A new accident model for engineering safer systems. *Saf. Sci.* **2004**, *42*, 237–270. [CrossRef]

37.   Hollnagel, E. *FRAM: The Functional Resonance Analysis Method—Modelling Complex Socio-Technical Systems*; Ashgate: Farnham, UK, 2012; ISBN 978-1-4094-4552-4.

38. Pidgeon, N. The limits to safety? Culture, politics, learning and man–made disasters. *J. Contingencies Cris. Manag.* **1997**, *5*, 1–14. [CrossRef]
39. Sagan, S.D. *The Limits of Safety—Organizations, Accidents, and Nuclear Weapons*; Princeton University Press: Princeton, NJ, USA, 1995; ISBN 978-0691021010.
40. Rijpma, J.A. Complexity, tight–coupling and reliability: Connecting normal accidents theory and high reliability theory. *J. Contingencies Cris. Manag.* **1997**, *5*, 15–23. [CrossRef]
41. Patriarca, R.; Cioponea, R.; Di Gravio, G.; Licu, A. Managing safety data: The TOKAI experience for the air navigation service providers. *Transp. Res. Procedia* **2018**, *35*, 148–157. [CrossRef]
42. Patriarca, R.; Di Gravio, G.; Cioponea, R.; Licu, A. Safety intelligence: Incremental proactive risk management for holistic aviation safety performance. *Saf. Sci.* **2019**, *118*, 551–567. [CrossRef]
43. Chen, H.; Chiang, R.H.L.; Storey, V.C. Business intelligence and analytics: From big data to big impact. *MIS Q.* **2012**, *36*, 1165–1188. [CrossRef]
44. Liao, C.; Hiroi, K.; Kaji, K.; Sakurada, K.; Kawaguchi, N. Event locky: System of event-data extraction from webpages based onweb mining. *J. Inf. Process.* **2017**, *25*, 321–330.
45. Usai, A.; Pironti, M.; Mital, M.; Mejri, C.A. Knowledge discovery out of text data: A systematic review via text mining. *J. Knowl. Manag.* **2018**, *22*, 1471–1488. [CrossRef]
46. Diez-Olivan, A.; Del Ser, J.; Galar, D.; Sierra, B. Data fusion and machine learning for industrial prognosis: Trends and perspectives towards Industry 4.0. *Inf. Fusion* **2019**, *50*, 92–111. [CrossRef]
47. Patriarca, R.; Bergström, J.; Di Gravio, G.; Costantino, F. Resilience engineering: Current status of the research and future challenges. *Saf. Sci.* **2018**, *102*, 79–100. [CrossRef]
48. Lam, C.Y. Resilience of logistics network: Analysis and design. In *Proceedings of the 2016 World Congress on Industrial Control Systems Security, WCICSS 2016, London, UK, 12–14 December 2016*; Institute of Electrical and Electronics Engineers Inc.: Piscataway, NJ, US, 2017; pp. 62–66.
49. Chopra, A. Paradigm shift and challenges in IoT security. In *Journal of Physics: Conference Series*; Institute of Physics Publishing: Bristol, UK, 2020; Volume 1432.

Analysis of Variance Amplification and Service Level in a Supply Chain with Correlated Demand

Ahmed Shaban [1], **Mohamed A. Shalaby** [2], **Giulio Di Gravio** [3,*] and **Riccardo Patriarca** [3]

[1] Mechanical Engineering Department, Faculty of Engineering, Fayoum University, Fayoum 63514, Egypt; ahmed.shaban@fayoum.edu.eg

[2] Department of Mechanical Design and Production, Faculty of Engineering, Cairo University, Giza 12613, Egypt; mashalaby@aucegypt.edu

[3] Mechanical and Aerospace Engineering Department, Sapienza University of Rome, Via Eudossiana, 18, 00184 Rome, Italy; riccardo.patriarca@uniroma1.it

* Correspondence: giulio.digravio@uniroma1.it

Abstract: The bullwhip effect reflects the variance amplification of demand as they are moving upstream in a supply chain, and leading to the distortion of demand information that hinders supply chain performance sustainability. Extensive research has been undertaken to model, measure, and analyze the bullwhip effect while assuming stationary independent and identically distributed (i.i.d) demand, employing the classical order-up-to (OUT) policy and allowing return orders. On the contrary, correlated demand where a period's demand is related to previous periods' demands is evident in several real-life situations, such as demand patterns that exhibit trends or seasonality. This paper assumes correlated demand and aims to investigate the order variance ratio (OVR), net stock amplification ratio (NSA), and average fill rate/service level (AFR). Moreover, the impact of correlated demand on the supply chain performance under various operational parameters, such as lead-time, forecasting parameter, and ordering policy parameters, is analyzed. A simulation modeling approach is adopted to analyze the response of a single-echelon supply chain model that restricts return orders and faces a first order autoregressive demand process AR(1). A generalized order-up-to policy that allows order smoothing through the proper tuning of its smoothing parameters is applied. The characterization results confirm that the correlated demand affects the three performance measures and interacts with the operating conditions. The results also indicate that the generalized OUT inventory policy should be adopted with the correlated demand, as its smoothing parameters can be adapted to utilize the demand characteristics such that OVR and NSA can be reduced without affecting the service level (AFR), implying sustainable supply chain operations. Furthermore, the results of a factorial design have confirmed that the ordering policy parameters and their interactions have the largest impact on the three performance measures. Based on the above characterization, the paper provides management with means to sustain good performance of a supply chain whenever a correlated demand pattern is realized through selecting the control parameters that decrease the bullwhip effect.

Keywords: supply chain; generalized Order-up-To inventory policy; autoregressive; correlated demand; bullwhip effect; net stock amplification; service level; simulation; factorial design; sustainable supply chains

1. Introduction

Supply chains consist of multiple partners that collaborate to satisfy customer demand. The demand information flows in the upstream direction of supply chains in the form of replenishment orders so that each partner receives the orders from the immediate downstream partner(s) and places his orders with the adjacent upstream partner(s). Subsequently, the product flows through the downstream direction to satisfy the partner's orders and eventually satisfying the customer demand. This is the common form of coordination in supply chains. The ideal situation is to achieve and sustain the best balance between the supply and demand throughout the supply chain at minimum cost. However, in most situations, the required balance is missing and hard to achieve due to the unpredictability of the supply chain response under various operational conditions [1,2].

Supply chains face a common problem, the so-called the demand information distortion, in which the demand variability is amplified as demand information moves upstream in supply chain. This problem is known as the bullwhip effect, and may also be called 'order variance amplification,' 'demand amplification,' or the 'Forrester effect.' Several studies have empirically confirmed the existence of the bullwhip effect and its negative impacts on supply chain performance and sustainability [3,4]. The bullwhip effect is recognized to cause misalignment between demand and supply, resulting in severe supply chain deficiencies such as excessive production orders, high logistics and inventory costs, and increased inability to meet delivery schedules. The bullwhip effect increases production costs since a highly oscillating order pattern, forces a production plan to change frequently, leading to a higher average production (capacity) costs per period [5]. These consequences of the bullwhip effect affect the balance of the supply chains and hinder their techno-economic sustainability [4,6]. Moreover, as industries are becoming more obliged to greenability [7], the link between bullwhip and the environmental consequences in terms of pollution and carbon emissions have been investigated [8]. Therefore, numerous studies have been conducted to measure and analyze the bullwhip effect (measured as ratio of order variance to demand variance), investigate its causes, and evaluate remedies and mitigation approaches. Different mitigation solutions for the bullwhip effect, such as information sharing mechanisms and order smoothing policies, have been proposed [8,9]. Many other researchers have investigated the effectiveness of the smoothing ordering policies such as smoothing order-up-to (OUT) policy to eliminate the bullwhip effect [10–12].

Most of the previous modeling studies have assumed that demand is an independent and identically distributed (i.i.d) stochastic process, and have provided useful insights regarding the causes of the bullwhip effect and the mitigative solutions for such demand conditions [13]. A correlated demand exists whenever a period's demand is correlated to (or dependent on) the last period's demands, and the 'independence' assumption becomes not valid. Few studies have investigated the bullwhip effect in supply chain models with correlated demand, even though such demand process exists in many real-life supply chains. Several researches have confirmed empirically the existence of correlated demand patterns [14–19]. Lee, So, and Tang [15] reported that the first order autoregressive (AR(1)) demand process was found to match the sales patterns of 150 SKUs (Stock Keeping Units) in a supermarket in UK. In particular, they have analyzed the weekly sales pattern of 165 SKUs over a two-year period. By conducting the Durbin-Watson test, they have found that the sales pattern of 150 SKUs (out of 165 SKUs) have autocorrelation with statistical significance. Moreover, they have found that all of the 150 SKUs have positive autocorrelation coefficients that vary between 0.26 and 0.89. Lee, Padmanabhan, and Whang [14] have also reported that it is common to have positive autocorrelation in the high-tech industry. Erkip, Hausman, and Nahmias [20] have also found that the demands of consumer products are often correlated over time with autocorrelation as high as 0.7. Therefore, most of the obtained results and characteristics of the bullwhip effect for independent demand need to be revised for correlated demand through conducting further research.

Research in correlated demand has attempted to model, measure, and analyze the bullwhip effect in supply chains that employ the classical OUT policy while using different forecasting methods [8,19,21–23]. Most of those studies have been relying upon statistical modeling approaches, and therefore they have been confined to the analysis of the bullwhip effect only and the so-called order variance ratio [18,19]. Moreover, for mathematical tractability, most of the previous studies for both correlated and uncorrelated demand have considered linear supply chains in which negative replenishment orders and open return policy are permitted [8,19,24–28]. Very limited research has been devoted to study the impact of correlated demand on both the bullwhip effect and inventory performance in supply chains that restrict negative replenishment orders. The inventory performance can be measured in terms of net stock amplification ratio (measured as ratio of net stock variance to demand variance), and service level (measured as average fill rate). The net stock variance ratio has an impact on inventory costs since increased inventory variance leads to a higher inventory cost to satisfy a desired service level. Analytical modeling studies have shown that when the demand is i.i.d, then using the smoothing OUT inventory policy will reduce the bullwhip effect. However, this may affect the inventory variance, and thus more inventory will be required to satisfy the desired service level [5,26]. Other studies have indicated that the order rate smoothing can be beneficial to both the bullwhip effect and inventory performance for the sustainability of supply chains of correlated demand [12,28].

The objectives of this paper are two-fold. First, the impact of correlated demand on supply chain performance in terms of order variance ratio, net stock variance ratio, and average fill rate is investigated. Second, the mutual impact of the key supply chain parameters and correlated demand is investigated. Examples of supply chain parameters are the lead-time, forecasting parameters, and ordering policy parameters. Most of the previous research assumes that a supply chain employs the classical OUT inventory policy with a specific forecasting method in response to AR(1). Alternatively, this research investigates the effect of the autoregressive demand under both the classical and generalized OUT ordering policies that are similar to those applied for i.i.d demand in previous studies [11,26]. The generalized policy is a modified version of the classical OUT policy that involves two smoothing parameters (also known as proportional controllers) to regulate the reaction to demand and inventory changes, and thus allowing order smoothing. The two smoothing parameters (Ti and Tw) can be controlled to alter the performance of the ordering policy. Furthermore, this paper investigates the impact of correlated demand not only on the bullwhip effect but also on the inventor stability and service level.

Due to the complexity and stochastic nature of supply chains under correlated demand, a simulation model approach is considered to study the impact of the correlated demand on the three mentioned performance measures. We mainly simulate the response of a single echelon supply chain that employs the generalized OUT policy, and use the exponential smoothing forecasting method to predict demand. A nonlinear supply chain that restricts return orders (negative orders) is assumed. The simulation model is utilized to characterize the supply chain performance in terms of order variance ratio (OVR), net stock amplification ratio (NSA), and average fill rate/service level (AFR), under various operating conditions. Furthermore, a full factorial experiment is conducted to investigate the mutual impact of the other supply chain parameters and their interactions with demand correlation. The characterization results confirm that the correlated demand affects the three performance measures and interacts with the key supply chain parameters. The OVR and NSA results under the classical OUT policy are consistent with the published results in the literature, except when the demand is negatively correlated due to the assumption of return order restriction [23]. Most importantly, the characterization results indicate that the generalized OUT policy should be adopted with the correlated demand, as its smoothing parameters can be tuned to utilize the demand characteristics such that OVR and NSA can be reduced without affecting the service level (AFR). The characterization results are complemented with a full factorial experiment that focused only on the positively correlated demand and the other operational parameters (lead-time, forecasting parameter, and ordering policy parameters). The related ANOVA results indicate that all the investigated factors and their interactions have significant impacts on OVR and NSA. In particular, the ordering policy parameters are found to have the largest impact on OVR, NSA, and AFR. The ANOVA results also confirm that the unmatched smoothing parameters of the OUT inventory control policy will provide better OVR and NSA than the matched case for the positively correlated demand.

This paper contributes to the existing supply chain literature through providing a comprehensive analysis of supply chain performance in the presence of AR(1) demand process. The paper has investigated the impact of the generalized OUT policy on OVR, NSA, and AFR such that the trade-off between bullwhip effect and inventory performance can be analyzed under demand correlation. Previous research has always assumed the presence of independent demand and has indicated that the mitigation of OVR will be coupled with an increase in NSA, and thus a lower AFR will be gained unless safety stock is increased. This paper has provided the evidence that under certain correlated demands, such as AR(1), the mitigation of both OVR and NSA can be achieved. As such, it is expected that the findings of this research shall help management to apply the recommended ordering policies and forecasting methods whenever demand is correlated, and avoid using the classical recommendations for independent demand situations. The application of the proper policies and forecasting methods to control a supply chain should sustain its performance measures at their planned levels.

The paper is structured as follows: Section 2 presents the related literature review. Section 3 describes the supply chain model and the corresponding simulation model. The performance characterization results are presented and discussed in Section 4. The experimental design and the related ANOVA results are presented and analyzed in Section 5. The conclusions and future research direction are provided in Section 6.

2. Literature Review

Several studies have empirically confirmed the existence of the variance amplification of demand in real-life supply chains [3,5,11,14,29–31]. In addition, other studies have resorted to simulation games to prove the existence and to analyze the bullwhip effect [32–36]. Other research is directed to identify and analyze its causes. Research in operational causes of the bullwhip effect includes demand signal processing, batched orders, lead-time, price fluctuations, and rationing and shortage gaming [35].

Extensive modeling research has been conducted to measure and analyze the variance amplification utilizing several modeling methodologies such as analytical modeling [19,22,38,39], control theory modeling [10,11,28,40], and simulation modeling [24,41,42]. Most research in this direction assumes that demand is an independent and identically distributed (i.i.d) stochastic process. Dejonckheere et al. [11] confirmed through a control theoretic modeling approach that the classical OUT inventory policy with exponential smoothing (ES), moving average (MA), or demand signal processing forecasting will produce bullwhip for all demand patterns. However, they also showed that the classical OUT policy can be modified into a smoothing OUT policy, i.e., one that is able to produce replenishment orders with less variance than the demand. Chatfield et al. [40] used simulation to analyze the impact of the stochastic lead time, the information sharing, and the quality of the information on the bullwhip effect, assuming i.i.d normal demand process. Canella [42] used simulation to investigate and compare the behavior of classical and smoothing OUT ordering policies in an information exchange supply chain with i.i.d normal demand process. Several other studies have investigated the effect of forecasting [43], ordering policy [44], lead-time [24], and collaboration [41,44,45], while assuming i.i.d demand process. Those studies have provided useful insights regarding the bullwhip effect causes and mitigation solutions under such demand conditions.

Although the assumption of i.i.d demand has some mathematical advantages, it neglects correlation in a demand time series. Therefore, another research stream has considered correlated demand models such as autoregressive integrated moving average (ARIMA) and its variants [8]. In particular, the first order auto-regressive demand, AR(1), has been the most frequently adopted demand model in the relevant literature [8,19]. In addition, most of these studies have assumed that the supply chain employs the classical OUT policy with the minimum mean squared error (MMSE) forecasting method, and permits the return orders (negative orders) [46–48]. Luong [21] derived a bullwhip effect measure for a single-echelon supply chain that has AR(1) demand process and employs the classical OUT policy with the MMSE forecasting method. Similarly, Luong and Phien [47] quantified the bullwhip effect for AR(2) demand process and extended their results to autoregressive demand processes of higher orders

(AR(q)). Sirikasemsuk and Luong [48] derived a bullwhip effect measure for a first-order bivariate vector autoregression (VAR(1)) demand process in a two-stage supply chain. Those studies have provided useful results concerning the behavior of the bullwhip effect with respect to autoregressive coefficients and lead-time when the supply chain employs the classical OUT policy with MMSE forecasting method and permits the negative orders. In particular, for the AR(1) demand process, they have shown that the bullwhip effect will not exist for the uncorrelated demand (i.i.d. demand, $\rho = 0$, where ρ is the autocorrelation coefficient of demand), negatively correlated demand ($\rho < 0$), or perfect positively correlated demand ($\rho = 1$). They have also shown that the bullwhip effect increases as lead-time increases and there is an upper bound for the bullwhip effect increase that depends on the autocorrelation level. However, these studies have focused only on the bullwhip effect measure and therefore they have been relying on analytical modeling approaches. Further similar studies can be found in Chandra and Grabis [49], and Duc, Luong, and Kim [22].

Unlike the above researches, other correlated demand studies have investigated analytically the performance of the classical OUT policy when integrated with other common forecasting methods such as moving average (MA) and exponential smoothing (ES) [18,28]. Chen, Ryan, and Simchi-Levi [37] and Chen et al. [50] derived analytically the bullwhip effect expressions for both the MA and ES forecasting methods in a supply chain employing the classical OUT policy and facing AR(1). They have also compared the impact of the two forecasting methods on the bullwhip effect. Zhang [46] derived analytical expressions for the bullwhip effect under AR(1) with MA, ES, and MMSE forecasting methods. Ma et al. [51] derived analytically the measures of bullwhip effect and inventory variance for MMSE, MA, and ES under price sensitive AR(1) demand. As stated earlier, these researches have adopted an analytical modeling approach and therefore most of them have focused only on modeling and analyzing the bullwhip effect. They have confirmed that the selected forecasting method has a significant role in determining the effect of lead-time and demand autocorrelation on the bullwhip effect. In particular, they have shown that the impact of reducing lead-time on the bullwhip effect depends on the correlation level and forecasting method, and therefore decision makers should be aware of the underlying demand process and the forecasting method used before making such decisions regarding lead-time reduction.

Other researchers have resorted to simulation modeling to study the impact correlated demand on different measures of supply chain performance. Hussain, Shome, and Lee [23] conducted a simulation study to investigate and compare the impact of ES and MMSE on both the bullwhip effect and inventory variance in a single-echelon supply chain that faces AR(1) demand process, employs the classical OUT policy, and permits return orders. They have concluded that depending on the demand correlation, the appropriate selection of forecasting method can help in controlling the bullwhip effect. However, they have also shown that the inventory variances with ES are greater than inventory variances with MMSE and that the gap increases as lead-time increases. Campuzano-Bolarín et al. [52] also performed a simulation study to compare the impact of six different forecasting methods on the bullwhip effect, net stock amplification, and fill rate. Costantino et al. [53] developed a control chart-based forecasting mechanism and compared its performance with MA and ES in a multi-echelon supply chain that employs the classical OUT policy and faces AR(1) demand process, through a simulation study.

Some other researchers attempted to study the bullwhip effect under correlated demand with different inventory ordering policies other than the classical OUT policy. Bandyopadhyay and Bhattacharya [54] derived analytically bullwhip effect measures for ARMA(p,q) demand process under various inventory replenishment policies. Disney et al. [28] have quantified exactly the bullwhip effect, and the variance of inventory levels over time, for i.i.d. and the weakly stationary autoregressive (AR), moving average (MA), and autoregressive moving average (ARMA) demand processes under the generalized OUT policy. Gaalman and Disney [55] analyzed the behavior of the proportional order-up-to policy for ARMA(2,2) demand with arbitrary lead-times.

The literature review shows that most of the correlated demand research has focused mainly on the modeling, measuring, and analysis of the bullwhip effect in linear supply chains. Most of the previous studies have adopted analytical modeling approach, and therefore their scope has been limited to the analysis of the bullwhip effect for supply chains that allow return orders. Few studies have been directed to the modeling and analysis of both the bullwhip effect and the inventory performance measures (net stock amplification and service level). Moreover, most of the previous research has been devoted to investigating the impact of correlated demand in supply chains that employ the classical OUT policy with different forecasting methods. Limited studies have attempted to investigate the impact of other ordering policies, such as the generalized OUT policy, which is a highly recommended ordering policy to mitigate the bullwhip effect for i.i.d demand. The literature is lacking studies that have attempted to investigate the impact of correlated demand and the mutual impacts of other operational parameters with correlated demand.

3. Model Development

In this section, the single-echelon supply chain model, including ordering policy, forecasting method, demand model, and performance measures, is described. In addition, the simulation model of the considered supply chain model is presented to validate the results.

3.1. Supply Chain Model

A generic single-echelon supply chain that may represent a retailer, distributor, or manufacturer is modeled. This supply chain structure has been widely adopted in related research [23,28]. It is assumed that this supply chain faces a first order autoregressive demand, AR(1), and employs the generalized order-up-to (OUT) policy with the exponential smoothing (ES) forecasting method. The supply chain operations are performed according to the following sequence of events and assumptions that are adapted from the literature. At each time period, the supply chain echelon (e.g., retailer) receives the products/materials from an upstream echelon (e.g., manufacturer), updates the available on-hand inventory, and satisfies the backlogged orders. Afterwards, the downstream echelon observes and updates the on-hand inventory level, and finally places a non-negative replenishment order, if needed. The replenishment order is determined based on the generalized order-up-to (OUT) policy. It is assumed that order returns (negative replenishment orders) are not allowed, and that the upstream echelon can deliver and ship any quantity ordered. Delivery lead-time is assumed deterministic.

3.1.1. Autoregressive Demand

We assume that the supply chain receives a first order autoregressive demand, AR(1), that can be defined as follows:

$$D_t = \mu_d + \rho D_{t-1} + \epsilon_t \tag{1}$$

where D_t is the AR(1) demand at time t, μ_d stands for the mean of the AR(1) demand process, ϵ_t represents the error term which follows a normal distribution with $\mu_\epsilon = 0$ and σ_ϵ^2, and ρ is an autoregressive (autocorrelation) coefficient, where $-1 < \rho < 1$. The variance of AR(1) demand can be approximated as $\sigma_d^2 = \sigma_\epsilon^2/(1-\rho)$, and $\sigma_d^2 = \sigma_\epsilon^2$ when the demand process is independently and identically distributed (i.i.d), i.e., $\rho = 0$ [46].

A demand generator module has been implemented in SIMUL8 to generate AR(1) demand patterns according to Equation (1). In particular, the generator can simulate the AR(1) demand process for any given combination of values of ρ, μ_d, and σ_ϵ^2. After validating the demand generator, several AR(1) demand times series have been simulated at different values of ρ in order to reflect the specific characteristics of each demand process (see Figure 1). It can be observed that for the negatively correlated demand ($\rho < 0$), the demand time series exhibits period-to-period oscillatory behavior. In addition, the negatively correlated demand patterns are almost free of runs and do not develop any trends over time (see Figure 1). On the contrary, the positively correlated demand develops runs and shows trends that materialize as ρ increases (see Figure 1).

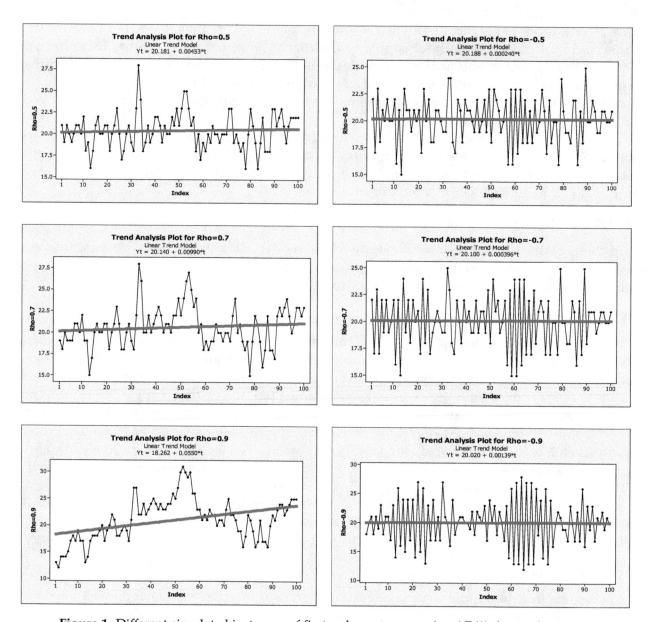

Figure 1. Different simulated instances of first order autoregressive AR(1) demand process.

3.1.2. The Generalized OUT Policy

The generalized order-up-to policy is a modified classical order-up-to (OUT) policy. The later policy is common in the literature of supply chain due to its industrial popularity [56]. In the classical OUT policy, the ordering decision is made at the end of each review period (R) as follows [11]:

$$O_t = Max\{(S_t - InvP_t), 0\} \tag{2}$$

where O_t is a non-negative replenishment order placed at the end of period t, S_t is the order-up-to level considered in period t, and $InvP_t$ is the inventory position which is equal to the net stock (NS_t) plus on-order inventory or work in process (WIP_t). The net stock NS_t represents the on-hand inventory minus backlogged orders. The order-up-to level S_t is updated every period according to

$$S_t = \hat{D}_t^L + SS_t \tag{3}$$

where $\hat{D}_t^L$ is the estimate of mean demand over the risk period ($\hat{D}_t^L = L \times \hat{D}_t$ where $\hat{D}_t$ is an estimate of demand in the next period, and L is the risk period), and SS_t represents the safety stock component which accounts for demand variation over L. The risk period L encompasses the lead-time (Ld) and the review period (R). In this model, the safety stock is included by extending the risk period by a safety stock parameter k [11,28,57]. Accordingly, the order-up-to level S_t is dynamically updated in every review period based on the demand forecast $\hat{D}_t$, and it can be expressed as shown in Equation (4).

$$S_t = (Ld + R + k)\hat{D}_t \qquad (4)$$

The classical OUT policy's ordering rule can be decomposed into several components as shown in Equation (5). In particular, the order decision based on the classical OUT policy consists of three components: A demand forecast term (assuming R = 1), a net stock discrepancy term, and a work in process (on-order inventory) discrepancy term. Thus, both discrepancy terms are completely taken into consideration in replenishment orders (see Equation (5)). However, previous studies have shown that the classical OUT policy with demand forecast updating would always result in a bullwhip effect for any demand process [10,11].

$$
\left.
\begin{aligned}
O_t &= (Ld + R + k)\hat{D}_t - NS_t - WIP_t \\
O_t &= R \times \hat{D}_t + \left(k \times \hat{D}_t - NS_t\right) + \left(Ld \times \hat{D}_t - WIP_t\right) \\
O_t &= R \times \hat{D}_t + (TNS_t - NS_t) + (DWIP_t - WIP_t)
\end{aligned}
\right\} \qquad (5)
$$

A proposed approach to enable order smoothing is to recover only fractions of the two discrepancy terms in each time period through adding the two proportional controllers Ti and Tw. This transforms the classical OUT policy into a generalized OUT policy that is defined as follows:

$$O_t = R \times \hat{D}_t + \frac{TNS_t - NS_t}{Ti} + \frac{DWIP_t - WIP_t}{Tw} \qquad (6)$$

where TNS_t denotes the target net stock level, and $DWIP_t$ denotes the desired work in process at time t. Ti and Tw are two proportional controllers (also known as smoothing parameters).

The parameters Ti and Tw control how much of the discrepancy between actual inventory and target inventory, and how much of the discrepancy between actual work in process and target work in process should be incorporated in the replenishment order [5]. This ordering rule has been adopted as a mitigation solution for the bullwhip effect by tuning the values of Ti and Tw [11]. Most of the previous research has investigated this ordering policy with matched controllers (Ti = Tw) under i.i.d. demand process [12,28,42]. In this study, we allow using unmatched controller and investigate their interaction effect on supply chain performance.

3.1.3. Exponential Smoothing Forecast

The generalized OUT replenishment policy requires an estimate or a forecast of demand over the risk period ($\hat{D}_t^L$) at the end of each time period. The demand forecast $\hat{D}_t^L$ is computed by multiplying the estimate of the next period's demand (D_t) by the risk period L. Exponential smoothing (ES) forecasting method is applied to estimate the expected demand ($\hat{D}_t$). ES has been the most employed forecasting method in the related research [28]. The ES method determines the next period's demand forecast by adjusting this period's forecast error with an exponential smoothing parameter α as follows:

$$\hat{D}_t = \alpha D_t + (1 - \alpha)\hat{D}_{t-1} \qquad (7)$$

where $\hat{D}_t$ is the forecast of next period's demand made in period t, D_t is the received demand at time t, and α represents the exponential smoothing parameter ($0 \leq \alpha \leq 1$). It is known that a larger α implies a greater weight is assigned to the most recent demand observation, while a smaller α implies a greater weight is placed on the demand history in the forecast of next period's demand.

3.1.4. Performance Measures

We consider three performance measures to assess the impact of correlated demand and of the other operational parameters on supply chain performance. The following performance measures are considered: order variance ratio (OVR), net stock amplification ratio (NSA), and average fill rate (AFR). Most of the previous research has considered only the impact of correlated demand on the OVR measure, and a limited research has been devoted to the analysis of NSA and AFR measures [19,23,41]. Thus, analyzing the three performance measures provides a wider perspective about the supply chain performance and its sustainability.

The order variance ratio (OVR) is defined as the ratio of the order rate variance to the demand variance [5]. It can be expressed mathematically as in Equation (8).

$$OVR = \frac{Order\ rate\ variance\ (OV)}{Demand\ variance\ (DV)} \tag{8}$$

The net stock amplification ratio (NSA) refers to the ratio of the net stock variance to the demand variance as in Equation (9) [5,28].

$$NSA = \frac{Net\ stock\ variance\ (NSV)}{Demand\ variance\ (DV)} \tag{9}$$

The service level can be assessed through the measure of average fill rate (AFR) which estimates the proportion of the demand that can immediately be supplied from the on-hand inventory [12,42,57,58]. The proportion of the supplied demand (fill rate) in each time period (FR_t) is calculated as shown in Equation (10), where SR_t represents the released shipment at time T, BL_{t-1} expresses the initial backlog at time t, and D_t is the received demand at time t, and t = 1, ... , T.

$$FR_t = \begin{cases} \frac{FR_t - BL_{t-1}}{D_t} & if\ SR_t - BL_{t-1} > 0 \\ 0 & if\ SR_t - BL_{t-1} \leq 0 \end{cases} \tag{10}$$

The fill rate time series can be used to estimate the average fill rate (AFR), as expressed in Equation (11):

$$AFR = \frac{\sum_{t=1}^{T} FR_t}{T} \tag{11}$$

3.2. Simulation Model Validation

A simulation model for the above-described supply chain model has been implemented in SIMUL8. The complete simulation model includes demand generation module, forecasting module, ordering policy module, and performance measures estimation module. Several verification tests have been performed to ensure that these modules are working properly. Output validation tests have been conducted to ensure the validity and suitability of the simulation model for further analysis. In particular, the simulation model output is compared with the output of the closed form expressions derived by Chen, Ryan, and Simchi-Levi [37], and Disney et al. [28] (see Table 1). Chen, Ryan, and Simchi-Levi [37] derived analytically the OVR measure for a single-echelon supply chain that employs the classical OUT policy with the ES forecasting method, in response to AR(1) demand process. Disney et al. [28] quantified both the OVR and NSA measures for a similar supply chain model that employs the generalized OUT policy with matched smoothing parameters (Ti = Tw = Tn, where Tn is a single smoothing parameter to replace both Ti and Tw in Equation (6) for the matched controller case) under different forecasting methods. We consider their closed form expression for OVR and NSA under the mean demand forecasting method.

Table 1. Closed form expressions for order variance ratio (OVR) and net stock amplification ratio (NSA).

Measure	Mathematical Expressions
Chen, Ryan, and Simchi-Levi [37]	$OVR = 1 + \left(2L\alpha + \frac{2L^2\alpha^2}{2-\alpha}\right)\left(\frac{1-\rho}{1-(1-\alpha)\rho}\right)$
Disney et al. [28]	$OVR = \left(\frac{1}{2Tn-1}\right)\left(\frac{Tn(1+\rho)-\rho}{Tn(1+\rho)+\rho}\right)$
	$NSA = \dfrac{\left(\frac{(Tn^2+Ld(2Tn-1))(Tn(1+\rho)-\rho)}{2Tn-1} + \frac{2\rho\left(Ld(1-\rho)-\rho\left(1-\rho^{Ld}\right)\right)}{(1-\rho)^2}\right)}{Tn(1-\rho)+\rho}$

The validation tests are conducted at different values of ρ that varies in the range of -0.9 and 0.9, while all the other model parameters are kept fixed. It is assumed that negative customer demand is not allowed, i.e., $D_t \geq 0$. Therefore, when simulating AR(1) demand, the mean demand μ_d is set much higher than σ_d to avoid negative demand realizations (e.g., $\mu_d > 4\sigma_d$). In all the validation experiments, the demand pattern is generated with the following parameter settings: $\mu_d = 20$ and $\sigma_\epsilon^2 = 4$. For the validation of OVR with Chen, Ryan, and Simchi-Levi [37] and Disney et al. [28], the simulation experiments are conducted at Ld = 2, k = 1, $\alpha = 0.1$, and Tn = 1 (Ti = Tw = 1). The ES parameter is set to $\alpha = 0$ for the validation with Disney et al. [28] since the demand forecast should be based on the long-term average demand ($\hat{D}_t = \mu_d$). This setting of the ES parameter transforms the ES method's forecast to be the mean demand value. The simulation results are obtained by running the simulation model for five replications, with a replication length of 100,000 periods and a warm-up of 5000 periods. These simulation settings are chosen so that the precision level of the estimated performance measures is less than ±5% [26].

The validation results are summarized in Tables 2 and 3. The simulation results indicate that the behavior of OVR for the positively correlated demand is very consistent with the analytical results. However, the OVR behavior for the negatively correlated demand is less consistent with the analytical results, especially at high correlation values. For the NSA measure, the simulation results are very consistent with those of the analytical results. As such, the existing analytical models for OVR that are based on the assumption of the presence of negative replenishment orders will overestimate the OVR under the negatively correlated demand especially at high correlation values. This result has also been confirmed for the i.i.d demand in multi-echelon supply chains [24,25]. Accordingly, simulation modeling provides an accurate estimation for the performance measures where supply chain nonlinearity can be easily and accurately considered in the simulation model.

Table 2. Simulation model validation for OVR.

OVR	ρ						
	−0.9	**−0.6**	**−0.3**	**0**	**0.3**	**0.6**	**0.9**
Analytical *	2.0166	2.0062	1.9913	1.9684	1.9286	1.8421	1.5097
Simulation Model	2.0170	2.0325	2.0280	2.0103	1.9673	1.8710	1.5206

* Chen, Ryan, and Simchi-Levi [37], and Disney et al. [28].

Table 3. Simulation model validation for NSA.

NSA	ρ						
	−0.9	**−0.6**	**−0.3**	**0**	**0.3**	**0.6**	**0.9**
Analytical *	1.0200	1.3200	1.9800	3.0000	4.3800	6.1200	8.2200
Simulation Model	1.0282	1.3434	2.0012	3.0018	4.3542	6.0761	8.1940

* Disney et al. [28].

4. Performance Characterization under Correlated Demand

Sets of simulation experiments are conducted to investigate the impact of the autoregressive parameter on the three measures of performance (OVR, NSA, and AFR), under various operating conditions. The first set of experiments is conducted to investigate the impact of ρ (the demand correlation coefficient) on the performance measures under the classical OUT policy while considering different combinations of α and Ld. The second set of experiments is devoted to analyzing the impact of ρ under different settings of the ordering policy parameters (Ti and Tw), to allow the comparison between the classical and the smoothing OUT policies. For each simulation experiment, the simulation model is run for five replications with a replication length of 100,000 periods and a warm-up of 5000 periods. The other model parameters are set to $\mu_d = 20$ and $\sigma_\epsilon^2 = 4$, and k = 1. The case of i.i.d. demand is included in each experiment by setting $\rho = 0$.

4.1. Analysis of the OVR Measure

The simulation results of the OVR measure under the classical OUT policy for Ld = 2 and Ld = 4 are depicted in Figure 2. Results confirm that the bullwhip effect will not exist (i.e., OVR = 1), as long as there is no updating of demand forecast ($\alpha = 0$) regardless of the value of ρ or Ld [11,28,37]. The setting of $\alpha = 0$ for the exponential smoothing forecast makes the demand forecast constant, and equals to the long-term average demand ($\hat{D}_t = \mu_d$), for all time periods. On the other hand, the bullwhip effect appears (OVR > 1) when demand forecast is updated ($\alpha > 0$) and it increases as α increases, for all values of ρ. Moreover, the results show that the negatively correlated demand produces a higher bullwhip effect than both the i.i.d demand and the positively correlated demand. The same behavior of OVR for the classical OUT with ES has been reported in Hussain, Shome, and Lee [23], and they have shown that the MMSE forecasting method will result in an increasing pattern of OVR over ρ.

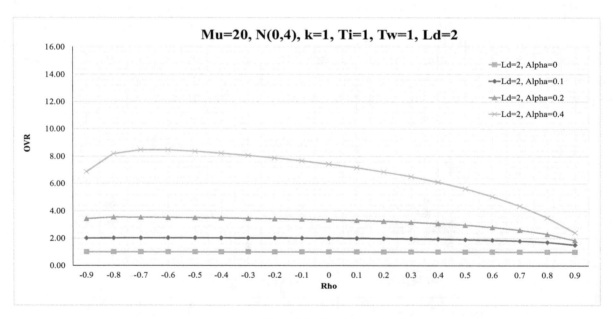

Figure 2. *Cont.*

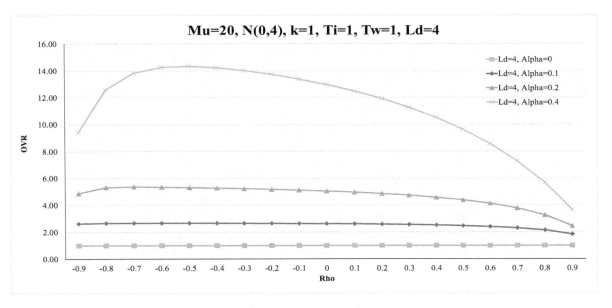

Figure 2. The impact of ρ on OVR under classical OUT policy for Ld = 2 and Ld = 4.

Furthermore, when the demand is positively correlated ($\rho > 0$), the OVR decreases as ρ increases (see Figure 2). Especially for the highly positively correlated demand and when α is large, the forecast shall follow the most recent highly correlated demand, and hence a smaller OVR value is realized as ρ increases. On the contrary, for small ρ, the demand process is stationary and reverses sign around its mean more frequently, and thus a large α will produce higher deviations of the forecasts from the actual demand. For small α ($\alpha = 0$, $\alpha = 0.1$), OVR is not affected by ρ ($-1 < \rho < 1$). However, when the demand is negatively correlated, the OVR increases as ρ increases until it reaches to a maximum level and then decreases. For the highly negative correlation demand ($\rho = -0.7$ to $\rho = -0.9$), the demand variance (σ_d^2) becomes larger, but the order variance increases at a lesser rate, and thus making OVR smaller (see Equation (8)). Moreover, at highly negatively correlated demand, the likelihood of placing negative orders is high, and since it is assumed that all orders should be greater than or equal to zero (no return policy), the order variance is reduced, leading to the shown decline in OVR (see Table 4). The existing analytical models have shown that OVR will be an increasing function of ρ over the negative correlation domain [24,28,37]. Accordingly, these analytical models are not recommended for estimating the OVR measure at highly negatively correlated demand as it will overestimate the actual bullwhip effect for this demand pattern.

Table 4. The OVR under highly negative correlation demand.

Variance Measure	ρ				
	−0.5	**−0.6**	**−0.7**	**−0.8**	**−0.9**
DV	5.4001	6.3104	7.9062	11.1886	21.2177
OV (Ld = 2, α = 0.4)	45.1737	53.4232	66.9546	91.6913	145.9274
OVR (Ld = 2, α = 0.4)	8.3653	8.4659	8.4686	8.1952	6.8782
OV (Ld = 4, α = 0.4)	77.4508	90.0306	109.3083	140.8079	200.0207
OVR (Ld = 4, α = 0.4)	14.3425	14.2672	13.8258	12.5855	9.4281

Figure 2 also shows that the lead-time Ld contributes considerably to the OVR measure (bullwhip) regardless of the autocorrelation level. Moreover, the OVR measure is more sensitive to Ld and α under the negatively correlated demand than under the positively correlated demand. For a given value of ρ, doubling the lead-time (Ld = 4) increases the bullwhip effect almost proportionally. The long lead-time seems to amplify the reaction to demand changes, and thus the forecasting error of the lead-time demand will increase. In addition, as the lead-time increases, the actual demand (D_{t+R+Ld}) will be lagging the actual order size placed based on $\hat{D}_t$, thus, increasing the order variance and increasing the OVR (see Table 4). This is also evident from the closed form expressions for OVR in Table 1 where the effect of lead-time is related to the update of demand forecast.

The impact of the parameters of the inventory ordering policy on OVR is shown in Figure 3. The effect of the ordering policy parameters (Ti and Tw) varies with the value of ρ. In particular, the results confirm that the generalized OUT policy can mitigate and almost eliminate the bullwhip effect by the proper selection of the values of Ti and Tw. In this case, the generalized OUT policy is transformed into a smoothing OUT policy. For the negatively correlated and i.i.d demands, the best bullwhip effect is achieved when Ti = Tw > 1 and that increasing the levels of Ti and Tw leads to a lower OVR. This conclusion is also valid for demands with weak positive correlation. The equality of the two smoothing parameters is called a matched controller, and it has been the most investigated and recommended in the related studies that considered i.i.d. demand process [28]. However, for the highly positively correlated demand, the matched controller (Ti = Tw) is not the preferred setting for lowering the bullwhip effect. It can be seen that the settings "Ti > Tw" provide a lower OVR than "Ti = Tw." These results extend the previous findings of Disney et al. [28] that considered the matched case. However, the results should be extended to investigate the interaction of the ordering policy parameters (Ti and Tw) and their interactions with the other operational parameters (including ρ). This will be accomplished though the factorial design study in Section 5.

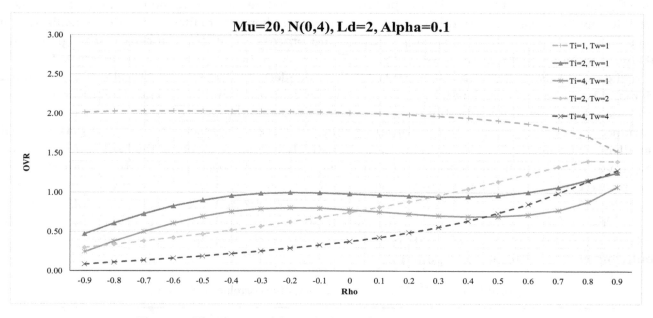

Figure 3. The impact of the ordering policy parameters on OVR.

The results of the OVR measure provide useful insights for the practitioners and decision makers. The practitioners should be aware of the demand pattern (correlated or uncorrelated), and if the demand is correlated, they should identify whether it's positively or negatively correlated. A careful attention should be given to the negatively correlated demand, especially in supply chains that employ the classical OUT policy, since it leads to a higher OVR than the positively correlated demand. In addition, the negatively correlated demand shows a higher sensitivity to lead-time such that reducing the lead-time to improve the OVR measure is highly recommended for the negatively correlated demand. In other words, the benefits gained from reducing the lead-time depend on the demand correlation.

For a practitioner, he is advised to conduct further evaluation before investing in lead-time reduction, especially when the demand is positively correlated. Most importantly, a practitioner is advised to adopt the generalized OUT policy since it can mitigate/eliminate the bullwhip effect. In particular, a practitioner can easily adapt the classical OUT policy (which is commonly applied in real-life supply chains) into a generalized OUT policy by incorporating the two smoothing parameters Ti and Tw. They are also suggested to adapt the matched smoothing parameters for the negatively correlated demand, i.i.d demand and weak positively correlated demand. However, for the highly positively correlated demand, the unmatched smoothing parameters (Ti > Tw) may provide better results than the matched settings (Ti = Tw).

4.2. Analysis of the NSA Measure

The impact of ρ on NSA under the classical OUT policy is depicted in Figure 4. The results show that the positive correlation demand ($\rho > 0$) produces a higher NSA than either the i.i.d. demand or the negatively correlated demand. Moreover, the i.i.d. demand has a higher NSA than the negative correlation demand. For $\rho > 0$, the NSA increases as ρ increases until it reaches to a maximum level and then decreases. However, the NSA becomes an increasing function of ρ when the demand forecast is based on the long-term average demand ($\alpha = 0$). For $\rho < 0$, the NSA decreases as ρ increases. The same behavior of NSA, with respect to the impact of ρ under the classical OUT, is reported in Hussain, Shome and Lee [23] for both the ES and MMSE forecasting methods. Results indicate that the impact of ES forecasting becomes of significant value when the demand process is highly positively correlated ($\rho > 0.7$). The NSA increases with Ld and α consistently but may decline after some cut-off value depending of the value of α. Most likely, this can be explained by the developed trends at highly positively correlated demand (see Figure 1). As such, the over-reaction to demand changes will reduce the gap between the supply and demand and thus the net stock amplification ratio is reduced [28].

The impact of the ordering policy parameters on NSA is shown in Figure 5. The results indicate that the impact of the ordering policy parameters (Ti and Tw) depends on the value of ρ. For the negatively correlated demand, the generalized OUT policy (with the smoothing settings of Ti and Tw) will lead to a lower NSA than the classical OUT policy (Ti = Tw = 1). In general, the effect of the different settings of the ordering policy parameters is within a narrow band for demand with $\rho < 0.5$. For such correlated demand, the results suggest that it is possible to utilize the flexibility of the generalized OUT policy to design inventory ordering policies that can lessen or avoid the bullwhip effect while achieving a comparable NSA. In particular, for the i.i.d and positively correlated demands, the results confirm that the smoothing OUT will result in a higher NSA than the classical OUT policy.

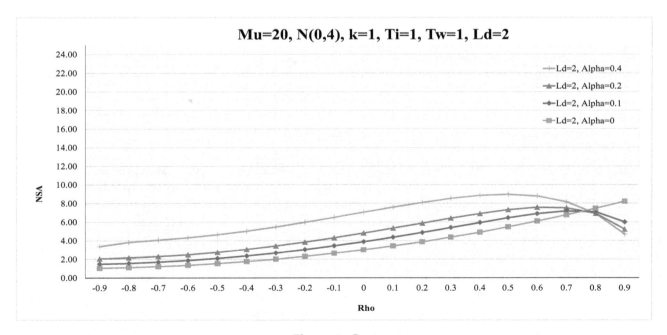

Figure 4. *Cont.*

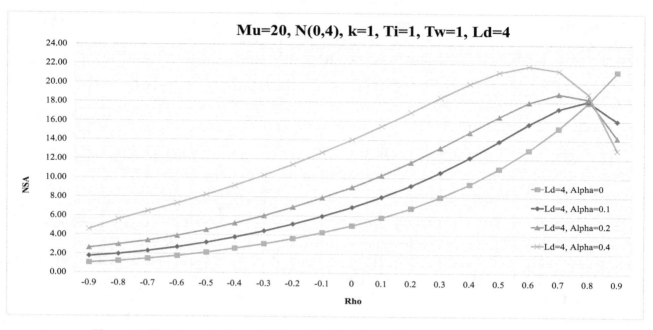

Figure 4. The impact of ρ on NSA under the classical OUT policy (Ti = Tw = 1).

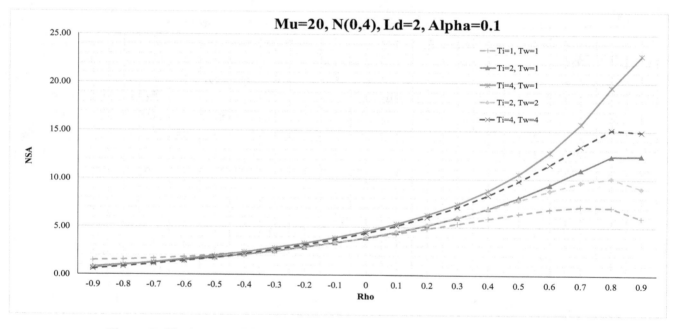

Figure 5. The impact of the ordering policy parameters (Ti and Tw) on NSA.

The results provide useful insights for the supply chain managers regarding the behavior of the inventory under correlated demand. It is known that the increase in NSA implies that the safety stock level should be increased to realize a desired service level (AFR). Therefore, the inventory costs will increase as NSA increases. For the NSA measure, the practitioners are advised to pay more attention to the positively correlated demand as it results in a higher NSA than the negatively correlated demand. They are suggested to use the classical OUT policy with the positively correlated demand while the smoothing OUT policy (with matched smoothing parameters) is highly recommended with the negatively correlated demand. The classical OUT policy will provide a good inventory performance with the positively correlated demand but it has undesirable performance with respect to the order variance ratio as discussed above. On the other side, the smoothing OUT policy will provide a good performance in terms of both OVR and NSA with the negatively correlated demand.

4.3. Analysis of the AFR Measure

The impact of ρ on AFR under the classical OUT policy is shown in Figure 6. The results indicate that AFR is not affected by the change of ρ when the demand is negatively correlated, regardless of the level of Ld and α. Similarly, the AFR is not affected by the change of ρ for the i.i.d and slightly positive correlation demand. However, for the medium and highly positively correlated demand, AFR decreases as ρ increases and that the reduction in AFR will be more for longer lead-time. Furthermore, at this demand structure, the selection of the smoothing parameters of the generalized OUT policy may lead to higher reduction in AFR (see Figure 7). This can be explained by the increase of NSA under such operating conditions as shown above. The results imply that the trade-off between order smoothing and amplification of net stock should be studied carefully when the demand is positively correlated. The higher order smoothing, the higher the safety stock needed to achieve a desired fill rate. Furthermore, the results confirm that the smoothing OUT policy is highly recommended for the negatively correlated demand as it can mitigate/eliminate the bullwhip effect without affecting the inventory performance measures (NSA and AFR) under such demand conditions.

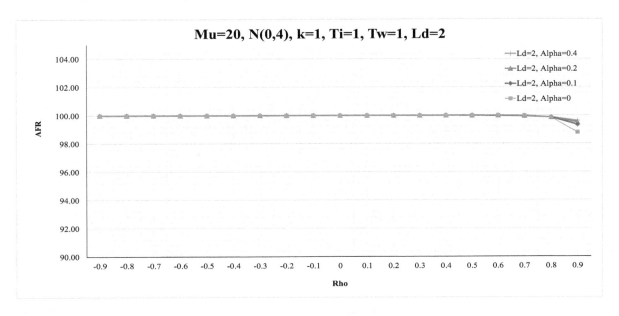

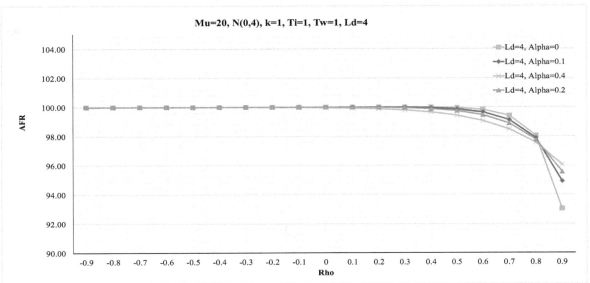

Figure 6. The impact of ρ on AFR under the classical order-up-to (OUT) policy (Ti = Tw = 1).

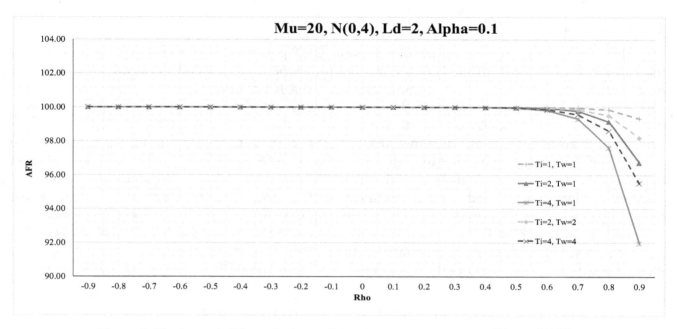

Figure 7. The impact of the ordering policy parameters on average fill rate (AFR).

5. Experimental Design and Analysis

The characterization results have shown that the demand correlation affects the supply chain performance and that its effect varies with the operating conditions: the lead-time (Ld), the ordering policy parameters (Ti and Tw), and the forecasting parameter (α). The results have also revealed that such effects vary with the demand correlation level. To complement the characterization results, a statistically designed experiment is conducted to identify the most important factors and their interactions that significantly affect the studied three performance measures (OVR, NSA, AFR). Furthermore, the experimental design approach facilitates the statistical analysis of the simulation results, thus allowing to identify the statistically significant factors and interactions, and pointing out their relative importance with respect to the different performance measures.

5.1. Investigated Factors

A factorial design approach is considered to investigate the impact of positively correlated demand ($\rho > 0$) with lead-time (Ld), forecasting parameter (α), and ordering policy parameters (Ti and Tw) on the three measures of performance, OVR, NSA, and AFR. The investigated factors and their levels are summarized in Table 5, where two levels are considered for each of the five factors.

Table 5. Investigated factors and their levels.

Factors	Levels	
	Low (−1)	High (+1)
Rho (ρ)	0.3	0.7
Ld	1	3
Alpha (α)	0.2	0.4
Ti	1	3
Tw	1	3

In this experiment, we consider only the case of positively correlated demand since it is the most commonly known in real applications [15,35]. Moreover, the characterization results have shown complex interactions between the operational parameters when the demand is positively correlated.

In particular, the two levels of the autocorrelation parameter ρ 'Rho' are selected to be within 0.3 and 0.7, where the correlated demand becomes nonstationary as Rho gets closer to one. Furthermore, the correlated demand in real supply chains is usually within Rho lower than 0.7 [17,20]. The levels of Ld, α 'Alpha', Ti, and Tw are selected considering the used ranges in related studies [23,42]. Moreover, the low levels of both Ti and Tw are set to one in order to consider the impact of transforming from the classical OUT policy (Ti = Tw = 1) to the generalized OUT policy in this experiment. A full factorial design is run in which all possible combinations of the factors levels are investigated, resulting in 32 simulation scenarios. For each scenario, the simulation model is run for five replications with a simulation run length of 100,000 periods, and a warm-up of 5000 periods, to estimate the performance measures. The estimated performance measures (average responses) for the 32 simulation scenarios are presented in Table 6.

Table 6. Full factorial design and estimated performance measures.

Run	Factors					Performance Measures		
	Rho	Ld	Alpha	Ti	Tw	OVR	NSA	AFR (%)
1	0.3	1	0.2	1	1	2.5160	3.6273	100.00
2	0.3	1	0.2	1	3	5.3611	6.4040	100.00
3	0.3	1	0.2	3	1	1.0053	4.0964	100.00
4	0.3	1	0.2	3	3	0.9111	4.3437	100.00
5	0.3	1	0.4	1	1	4.6327	4.7139	100.00
6	0.3	1	0.4	1	3	9.2888	9.8288	99.99
7	0.3	1	0.4	3	1	2.1224	3.6417	100.00
8	0.3	1	0.4	3	3	1.5111	4.2698	100.00
9	0.3	3	0.2	1	1	3.9103	9.6054	99.99
10	0.3	3	0.2	1	3	66.9747	202.1584	81.70
11	0.3	3	0.2	3	1	2.1973	7.9704	100.00
12	0.3	3	0.2	3	3	1.2658	9.6863	99.99
13	0.3	3	0.4	1	1	8.7397	13.1250	99.95
14	0.3	3	0.4	1	3	66.3925	200.7926	82.62
15	0.3	3	0.4	3	1	6.7739	8.9613	99.99
16	0.3	3	0.4	3	3	2.3617	10.5368	99.98
17	0.7	1	0.2	1	1	2.1196	3.7074	100.00
18	0.7	1	0.2	1	3	3.8702	4.8929	100.00
19	0.7	1	0.2	3	1	1.1697	6.5795	99.98
20	0.7	1	0.2	3	3	1.3344	6.3646	99.98
21	0.7	1	0.4	1	1	3.2204	4.0068	100.00
22	0.7	1	0.4	1	3	6.0879	6.8081	99.97
23	0.7	1	0.4	3	1	1.7462	4.5801	100.00
24	0.7	1	0.4	3	3	1.7977	5.2627	99.99
25	0.7	3	0.2	1	1	3.1573	12.5909	99.65
26	0.7	3	0.2	1	3	38.1882	122.2211	82.68
27	0.7	3	0.2	3	1	1.6287	14.1497	99.51
28	0.7	3	0.2	3	3	1.8007	16.5540	99.21
29	0.7	3	0.4	1	1	5.7269	13.9211	99.51
30	0.7	3	0.4	1	3	39.6230	127.7397	82.79
31	0.7	3	0.4	3	1	3.7065	11.2083	99.77
32	0.7	3	0.4	3	3	2.6806	15.5031	99.33

5.2. Results Analysis

An ANOVA study is conducted to investigate the statistical significance of the key factors and their interactions that impact the three performance measures. ANOVA results are presented in terms of the regression coefficients for a single order model (including the two-way interactions only), and the interaction plots. The regression coefficients tables given in Tables 7–9 convey the same information in the classical ANOVA tables in addition to effect magnitudes of the factors and their interactions.

Table 7. Estimated Effects and Coefficients for OVR (coded units).

Term	Effect	Coef	SE Coef	T	P
Constant		9.494	0.1451	65.44	0.000
Rho	−4.257	−2.128	0.1451	−14.67	0.000
Ld	12.902	6.451	0.1451	44.46	0.000
Alpha	1.813	0.906	0.1451	6.25	0.000
Ti	−14.737	−7.369	0.1451	−50.79	0.000
Tw	12.192	6.096	0.1451	42.02	0.000
Rho*Ld	−3.506	−1.753	0.1451	−12.08	0.000
Rho*Alpha	−0.398	−0.199	0.1451	−1.37	0.173
Rho*Ti	3.971	1.986	0.1451	13.68	0.000
Rho*Tw	−3.079	−1.539	0.1451	−10.61	0.000
Ld*Alpha	0.298	0.149	0.1451	1.03	0.307
Ld*Ti	−11.55	−5.775	0.1451	−39.8	0.000
Ld*Tw	10.739	5.369	0.1451	37.01	0.000
Alpha*Ti	−0.389	−0.195	0.1451	−1.34	0.182
Alpha*Tw	−0.558	−0.279	0.1451	−1.92	0.057
Ti*Tw	−13.028	−6.514	0.1451	−44.9	0.000

Table 8. Estimated Effects and Coefficients for NSA (coded units).

Term	Effect	Coef	SE Coef	T	P
Constant		27.5	1.726	15.93	0.000
Rho	−7.98	−3.99	1.726	−2.31	0.022
Ld	44.6	22.3	1.726	12.92	0.000
Alpha	0.62	0.31	1.726	0.18	0.857
Ti	−38.28	−19.14	1.726	−11.09	0.000
Tw	39.18	19.59	1.726	11.35	0.000
Rho*Ld	−8.14	−4.07	1.726	−2.36	0.020
Rho*Alpha	−0.38	−0.19	1.726	−0.11	0.914
Rho*Ti	11.32	5.66	1.726	3.28	0.001
Rho*Tw	−9.85	−4.93	1.726	−2.85	0.005
Ld*Alpha	0.23	0.12	1.726	0.07	0.946
Ld*Ti	−37.67	−18.84	1.726	−10.91	0.000
Ld*Tw	37.53	18.76	1.726	10.87	0.000
Alpha*Ti	−1.34	−0.67	1.726	−0.39	0.698
Alpha*Tw	0.39	0.2	1.726	0.11	0.910
Ti*Tw	−37.76	−18.88	1.726	−10.94	0.000

Table 9. Estimated Effects and Coefficients for AFR (coded units).

Term	Effect	Coef	SE Coef	T	P
Constant		97.706	0.1791	545.67	0.000
Rho	−0.116	−0.058	0.1791	−0.32	0.746
Ld	−4.576	−2.288	0.1791	−12.78	0.000
Alpha	0.077	0.038	0.1791	0.21	0.831
Ti	4.306	2.153	0.1791	12.02	0.000
Tw	−4.381	−2.19	0.1791	−12.23	0.000
Rho*Ld	−0.106	−0.053	0.1791	−0.3	0.767
Rho*Alpha	−0.031	−0.016	0.1791	−0.09	0.931
Rho*Ti	−0.158	−0.079	0.1791	−0.44	0.660
Rho*Tw	0.075	0.037	0.1791	0.21	0.835
Ld*Alpha	0.076	0.038	0.1791	0.21	0.831
Ld*Ti	4.307	2.154	0.1791	12.03	0.000
Ld*Tw	−4.376	−2.188	0.1791	−12.22	0.000
Alpha*Ti	−0.026	−0.013	0.1791	−0.07	0.942
Alpha*Tw	0.065	0.032	0.1791	0.18	0.857
Ti*Tw	4.287	2.143	0.1791	11.97	0.000

The ANOVA results indicate that most of the investigated factors and their interactions have significant impact statistically on OVR and NSA (see Tables 8 and 9). The investigated factors have similar impacts on both OVR and NSA. In particular, the direction of the change in response is the same for the main and interaction effects (see Figures 8–10). Therefore, we present the analysis of the ANOVA results for both OVR and NSA, followed by a separate section for the analysis of ANOVA results of AFR.

5.2.1. Impact of Factors on OVR and NSA

The ANOVA results confirm that the autocorrelation parameter (Rho) has a notable significant impact on OVR and NSA such that they both decrease as Rho increases (see Tables 8 and 9). This can be clearly observed in the main effect plots shown in Figures 8 and 9. Furthermore, the interaction effect plots show that the OVR and NSA measures are more sensitive to Rho under the classical OUT policy (Ti = 1) (see Figures 8 and 9). However, this sensitivity decreases under the smoothing OUT (Ti > 1). In addition, it can be observed that the impact of Rho is substantial for long lead-times. This has also been shown in the characterization results for a wider range of Rho. The effect of Rho is almost independent of Alpha as can be revealed from the interaction plots. In general, the interaction effect plots indicate that both measures are less sensitive to changes in Rho value when Ti is large, Tw is small, and Ld is short.

Most importantly, the results show that the two smoothing parameters of the generalized OUT policy have the largest effects on both OVR and NSA. The previous research has assumed that both parameters are equal (Ti = Tw) and therefore their results confirm that higher levels of the smoothing parameter are of significant impact on the reduction/elimination of the bullwhip effect [28]. However, the analysis of the main effect plots suggests to select Ti = 3 (high) and Tw = 1 (low) for smaller OVR and NSA under the positively correlated demand. Furthermore, analyzing the interaction effect plots suggests that the combination of Ti = 3 and Tw = 1 also offers the least interaction between Ti and Tw. This confirms that the unmatched case of the smoothing parameters outperforms the matched case. The interaction of the smoothing parameters with the other operational parameters are statistically significant. At low level of Ld (Ld = 1), the OVR and NSA are not affected by the choice of Ti or Tw. However, long lead times (Ld = 3) favors large value of Ti (Ti = 3) and smaller value of Tw (Tw = 1). Low correlated demand (Rho = 0.3) also suggests large Ti and smaller Tw values to decrease OVR. At high correlation parameter (Rho = 0.7), these plots suggest that smaller value of Alpha and Ld, and OUT policy of Ti = 3 and Tw = 1 offers best performance. Therefore, it can be argued that the proper settings of Ti and Tw are of essential importance to control the variance amplification in supply chains with correlated demand.

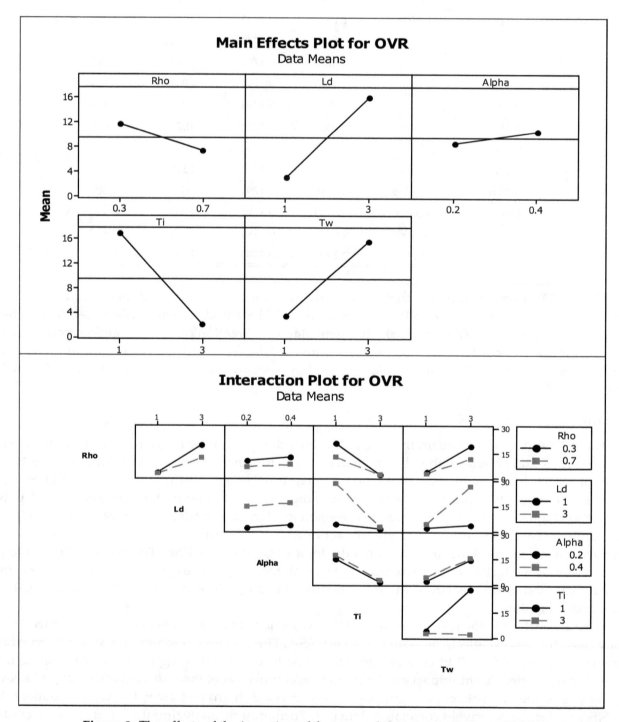

Figure 8. The effects of the investigated factors and their interactions on OVR.

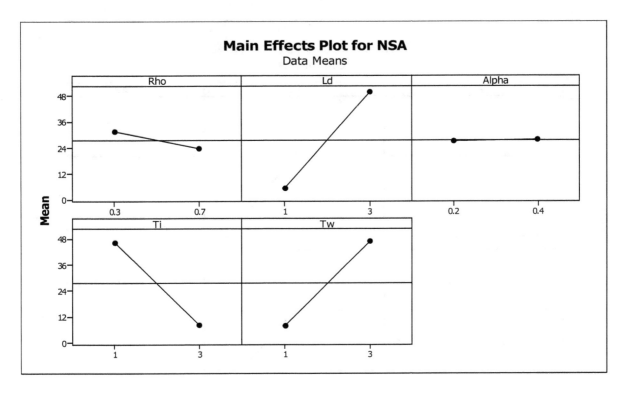

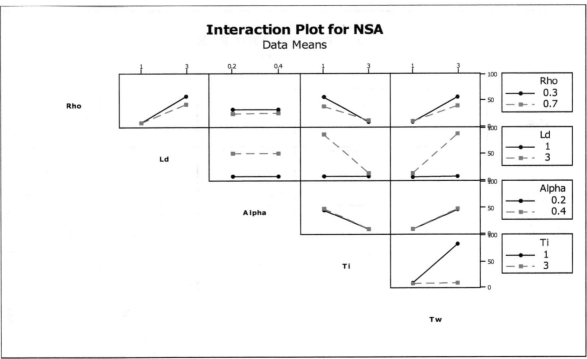

Figure 9. The effects of the investigated factors and their interactions on NSA.

The lead-time has one of the largest effects on OVR and NSA. However, the effect of lead-time can be counteracted by the proper selection of the ordering policy parameters as indicated above. The forecasting parameter (Alpha), in general, has the least impact on OVR and NSA. Its effect is almost independent (no interaction) of the levels of the other factors. This is evident also from the regression coefficients table, where all the interactions between Alpha and the other factors are insignificant.

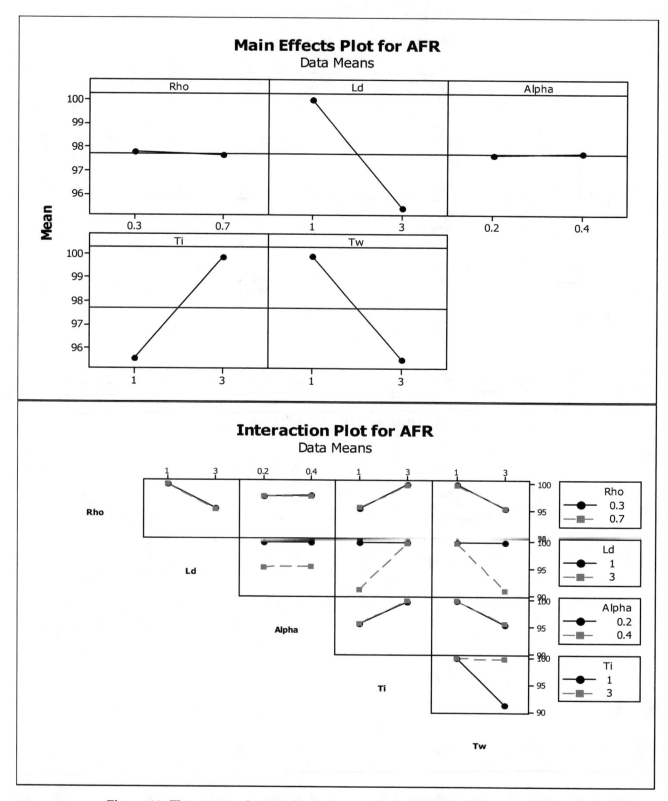

Figure 10. The main and interaction effects of the investigated factors on AFR.

5.2.2. Impact of Factors on AFR

The main and interaction effects plots show that the fill rate is almost insensitive to correlation and forecasting parameters (see Figure 10). This is also evident from the related ANOVA results in Table 9. Changes in AFR are between 95% to 100% as the other factors (Ld, Ti, Tw) are varied in levels. Higher

AFR values favor low Ld, high Ti, and low Tw. This policy is clearly similar to what is recommended for OVR and NSA measures.

6. Conclusions

Supply chains face the variance amplification in replenishment orders and inventory levels, leading to severe inefficiencies at all supply chain partners, such as increased production and inventory costs, and decreased serviceability. Therefore, variability need to be controlled to sustain economic and planned performance of a supply chain. In this regard, extensive modeling studies have been performed to analyze the variance amplification in supply chains while assuming i.i.d demands. Most of the previous studies have investigated the variance amplification in supply chain models that adopt the classical OUT policy, and permit return orders. These studies also have relied upon analytical modeling approaches, and therefore they analyzed the bullwhip effect only. Although supply chains that are subjected to correlated demand are common in reality, not enough attention is devoted to study their characterization and operational performance.

This research has adopted a simulation modeling approach in order to investigate the variance amplification and service level (average fill rate) in a supply chain that faces AR(1) demand, employs the generalized OUT policy, and restricts returns. The generalized OUT policy is a modified version of the classical OUT policy that can be adapted to allow order smoothing and thus mitigating and even eliminating the bullwhip effect. We utilize a simulation model to investigate the impact of correlated demand on order variance ratio (OVR), net stock amplification ratio (NSA), and average fill rate (AFR), under different operating conditions.

The characterization results for OVR and NSA under the classical OUT policy are consistent with the results reported in the literature. Exceptionally, the behavior of OVR over the negatively correlated demand is different from the previous research, due to the different modeling assumption of the allowance of returns. In particular, the results imply that applying the supply chain models that permits return orders will overestimate OVR for the supply chains that restrict returns. Therefore, supply chain practitioners will be misguided if they apply the existing analytical models to estimate the bullwhip effect for the negatively correlated demand. Existing analytical models should be revised to include the proper assumptions that are proved to have significant impact on the estimation of supply chain response.

The characterization results also reveal that the generalized OUT policy should be adopted with the correlated demand since its smoothing parameters can be tuned to produce better OVR and NSA without affecting the service level (AFR). For the negatively correlated demand, the best OVR, NSA, and AFR favors the generalized OUT policy with the matched smoothing parameters (Ti = Tw > 1). The generalized OUT policy can also be utilized to avoid the bullwhip effect (OVR) for both the i.i.d and positively correlated demand. The characterization results are complemented with a factorial design study that focused only on the positively correlated demand and the other operational parameters. The results confirmed that the ordering policy parameters and their interactions have the largest impact on the performance measures. In particular, the results have indicated that the unmatched smoothing parameters are more suitable than the matched settings for the positively correlated demand. The proper settings of the smoothing parameters will alleviate the impact of the lead-time and demand correlation on the performance measures.

This research provides useful managerial recommendations to control the variance amplification in supply chains with AR(1) demand. Supply chain managers have to identify the demand characteristics and determine the performance measures that they need to improve. If the demand is independent or correlated and the objective is to avoid the bullwhip effect, the managers are recommended to use the generalized OUT policy with the proper smoothing parameters according to the demand characteristics. The matched smoothing parameters (Ti = Tw > 1) are recommended for the negatively correlated or independent demand, while the unmatched settings (Ti > Tw) are preferred for the positively correlated demand. These recommended settings provide good inventory performance that can eliminate or minimize the bullwhip effect without affecting the inventory performance. This should lead to considerable savings in supply chain costs while achieving the desired service level, and thus sustaining the economic and planned performance of supply chains. However, managers need to keep track of inventory performance if they apply the generalized OUT policy with the positively correlated demand since it may affect net stock variability and service level. They also need to avoid the generalized OUT policy if inventory performance is their target measure. Moreover, for correlated demand, managers are recommended to trace the long-term average of the AR(1) demand process and use it as their demand forecast for every time period. When the demand is highly correlated, other responsive forecasting methods should be selected, and managers are advised to counteract the impact of lead-time through tuning the ordering policy parameters. These managerial implications are essential to achieve the techno-economic sustainability of supply chains with correlated demand.

For future research, forecasting methods other than the most industrially popular methods should be investigated, such as the time series forecasting methods and new adaptive forecasting methods that can comply with the nature of correlated demand. Also, the development of new ordering policies that cope with correlated demand is an interesting future research direction. The variance amplification under mixed and higher order correlated demand processes, such as ARIMA models and its variants, need to be characterized. The optimization of the forecasting and ordering policy parameters under correlated demand should be considered in future work. In general, performance of multi-echelon supply chains under correlated demand conditions is a highly viable research area of practical importance.

Author Contributions: Conceptualization, A.S., M.A.S. and G.D.G.; methodology, A.S. and M.A.S.; software, A.S., G.D.G. and R.P.; validation, A.S. and M.A.S.; formal analysis, A.S. and M.A.S.; investigation, A.S., M.A.S. and G.D.G.; resources, G.D.G. and R.P.; data curation, A.S., G.D.G. and R.P.; writing—original draft preparation, A.S.; writing—review and editing, A.S., M.A.S. and R.P.; visualization, A.S., G.D.G. and R.P.; supervision, M.A.S.; project administration, A.S., M.A.S. and G.D.G; funding acquisition, G.D.G. and R.P. All authors have read and agreed to the published version of the manuscript.

References

1.   Priore, P.; Ponte, B.; Rosillo, R.; de la Fuente, D. Applying machine learning to the dynamic selection of replenishment policies in fast-changing supply chain environments. *Int. J. Prod. Res.* **2019**, *57*, 3663–3677. [CrossRef]

2.   Costantino, F.; Di Gravio, G.; Patriarca, R.; Petrella, L. Spare parts management for irregular demand items. *Omega (UK)* **2018**, *81*, 57–66. [CrossRef]

3.   Pastore, E.; Alfieri, A.; Zotteri, G. An empirical investigation on the antecedents of the bullwhip effect: Evidence from the spare parts industry. *Int. J. Prod. Econ.* **2019**, *209*, 121–133. [CrossRef]

4.   Alvarado-Vargas, M.J.; Kelley, K.J. Bullwhip severity in conditions of uncertainty: Regional vs global supply chain strategies. *Int. J. Emerg. Mark.* **2019**, *15*, 131–148. [CrossRef]

5.   Lambrecht, M.R.; Disney, S.M. On replenishment rules, forecasting, and the bullwhip effect in supply chains. *Found. Trends Technol. Inf. Oper. Manag.* **2008**, *2*, 1–80.

6.   Huang, J.; Shuai, Y.; Liu, Q.; Zhou, H.; He, Z. Synergy Degree Evaluation Based on Synergetics for Sustainable Logistics Enterprises. *Sustainability* **2018**, *10*, 2187. [CrossRef]

7.   Qu, Y.; Yu, Y.; Appolloni, A.; Li, M.; Liu, Y. Measuring Green Growth Efficiency for Chinese Manufacturing Industries. *Sustainability* **2017**, *9*, 637. [CrossRef]

8.   Wang, X.; Disney, S.M. The bullwhip effect: Progress, trends and directions. *Eur. J. Oper. Res.* **2016**, *250*, 691–701. [CrossRef]

9.   Shaban, A.; Costantino, F.; Di Gravio, G.; Tronci, M. Coordinating of multi-echelon supply chains through the generalized (R, S) policy. *Simulation* **2020**. [CrossRef]

10.   Dejonckheere, J.; Disney, S.M.; Lambrecht, M.R.; Towill, D.R. Measuring and avoiding the bullwhip effect: A control theoretic approach. *Eur. J. Oper. Res.* **2003**, *147*, 567–590. [CrossRef]

11. Dejonckheere, J.; Disney, S.; Lambrecht, M.; Towill, D. The impact of information enrichment on the Bullwhip effect in supply chains: A control engineering perspective. *Eur. J. Oper. Res.* **2004**, *153*, 727–750. [CrossRef]

12. Costantino, F.; Di Gravio, G.; Shaban, A.; Tronci, M. A real-time SPC inventory replenishment system to improve supply chain performances. *Expert Syst. Appl.* **2015**, *42*, 1665–1683. [CrossRef]

13. Dominguez, R.; Ponte, B.; Cannella, S.; Framinan, J.M. On the dynamics of closed-loop supply chains with capacity constraints. *Comput. Ind. Eng.* **2019**, *128*, 91–103. [CrossRef]

14. Lee, H.; Padmanabhan, V.; Whang, S. The Bullwhip Effect in Supply Chains. *Sloan Manag. Rev.* **1997**, *38*, 93–102. [CrossRef]

15. Lee, H.L.; So, K.C.; Tang, C.S. The Value of Information Sharing in a Two-Level Supply Chain. *Manag. Sci.* **2000**, *46*, 626–643. [CrossRef]

16. Mahajan, S.; Venugopal, V. Value of Information Sharing and Lead Time Reduction in a Supply Chain with Autocorrelated Demand. *Technol. Oper. Manag.* **2011**, *2*, 39–49. [CrossRef]

17. Boute, R.N.; Disney, S.M.; Lambrecht, M.; Van Houdt, B. Coordinating Lead-Time and Safety Stock Decisions in a Two-Echelon Supply Chain with Autocorrelated Consumer Demand. *SSRN Electron. J.* **2020**. [CrossRef]

18. Michna, Z.; Disney, S.M.; Nielsen, P. The impact of stochastic lead times on the bullwhip effect under correlated demand and moving average forecasts. *Omega* **2019**, *93*, 102033. [CrossRef]

19. Tai, P.D.; Duc, T.T.H.; Buddhakulsomsiri, J. Measure of bullwhip effect in supply chain with price-sensitive and correlated demand. *Comput. Ind. Eng.* **2019**, *127*, 408–419. [CrossRef]

20. Erkip, N.; Hausman, W.H.; Nahmias, S. Optimal Centralized Ordering Policies in Multi-Echelon Inventory Systems with Correlated Demands. *Manag. Sci.* **1990**, *36*, 381–392. [CrossRef]

21. Luong, H.T. Measure of bullwhip effect in supply chains with autoregressive demand process. *Eur. J. Oper. Res.* **2007**, *180*, 1086–1097. [CrossRef]

22. Duc, T.T.H.; Luong, H.T.; Kim, Y.-D. A measure of bullwhip effect in supply chains with a mixed autoregressive-moving average demand process. *Eur. J. Oper. Res.* **2008**, *187*, 243–256. [CrossRef]

23. Hussain, M.; Shome, A.; Lee, D.M. Impact of forecasting methods on variance ratio in order-up-to level policy. *Int. J. Adv. Manuf. Technol.* **2012**, *59*, 413–420. [CrossRef]

24. Chatfield, D.C.; Pritchard, A.M. Returns and the bullwhip effect. *Transp. Res. Part E Logist. Transp. Rev.* **2013**, *49*, 15–175. [CrossRef]

25. Dominguez, R.; Cannella, S.; Framinan, J.M. On returns and network configuration in supply chain dynamics. *Transp. Res. Part. E Logist. Transp. Rev.* **2015**, *73*, 152–167. [CrossRef]

26. Shaban, A.; Shalaby, M.A. Modeling and optimizing of variance amplification in supply chain using response surface methodology. *Comput. Ind. Eng.* **2018**, *120*, 392–400. [CrossRef]

27. Jakšič, M.; Rusjan, B. The effect of replenishment policies on the bullwhip effect: A transfer function approach. *Eur. J. Oper. Res.* **2008**, *184*, 946–961. [CrossRef]

28. Disney, S.M.; Farasyn, I.; Lambrecht, M.; Towill, D.R.; de Velde, W. Van Taming the bullwhip effect whilst watching customer service in a single supply chain echelon. *Eur. J. Oper. Res.* **2006**, *173*, 151–172. [CrossRef]

29. Zotteri, G. An empirical investigation on causes and effects of the Bullwhip-effect: Evidence from the personal care sector. *Int. J. Prod. Econ.* **2013**, *143*, 489–498. [CrossRef]

30. Klug, F. The Internal Bullwhip Effect in Car Manufacturing. *Int. J. Prod. Res.* **2013**, *51*, 303–322. [CrossRef]

31. Chiang, C.-Y.; Lin, W.T.; Suresh, N.C. An empirically-simulated investigation of the impact of demand forecasting on the bullwhip effect: Evidence from U.S. auto industry. *Int. J. Prod. Econ.* **2016**, *177*, 53–65. [CrossRef]

32. Sterman, J.D. Modeling Managerial Behavior: Misperceptions of Feedback in a Dynamic Decision Making Experiment. *Manag. Sci.* **1989**, *35*, 321–339. [CrossRef]

33. Shovityakool, P.; Jittam, P.; Sriwattanarothai, N.; Laosinchai, P. A Flexible Supply Chain Management Game. *Simul. Gaming* **2019**, *50*, 461–482. [CrossRef]

34. Wu, D.Y.; Katok, E. Learning, communication, and the bullwhip effect. *J. Oper. Manag.* **2006**, *24*, 839–850. [CrossRef]

35. Lee, H.L.; Padmanabhan, V.; Whang, S. Information Distortion in a Supply Chain: The Bullwhip Effect. *Manag. Sci.* **1997**, *43*, 546–558. [CrossRef]

36. Nienhaus, J.; Ziegenbein, A.; Duijts, C. How human behaviour amplifies the bullwhip effect—A study based on the beer distribution game online. *Prod. Plan. Control.* **2006**, *17*, 547–557. [CrossRef]

37. Chen, F.; Ryan, J.K.; Simchi-Levi, D. The Impact of Exponential Smoothing Forecasts on the Bullwhip Effect. *Nav. Res. Logist.* **2000**, *47*, 269. [CrossRef]

38. Kim, J.G.; Chatfield, D.; Harrison, T.P.; Hayya, J.C. Quantifying the bullwhip effect in a supply chain with stochastic lead time. *Eur. J. Oper. Res.* **2006**, *173*, 617–636. [CrossRef]

39. Disney, S.M.; Towill, D.R. On the bullwhip and inventory variance produced by an ordering policy. *Omega* **2003**, *31*, 157–167. [CrossRef]

40. Chatfield, D.C.; Kim, J.G.; Harrison, T.P.; Hayya, J.C. The Bullwhip Effect-Impact of Stochastic Lead Time, Information Quality, and Information Sharing: A Simulation Study. *Prod. Oper. Manag.* **2004**, *13*, 340–353. [CrossRef]

41. Shaban, A.; Costantino, F.; Di Gravio, G.; Tronci, M. A new efficient collaboration model for multi-echelon supply chains. *Expert Syst. Appl.* **2019**, *128*, 54–66. [CrossRef]

42. Cannella, S. Order-Up-To policies in Information Exchange supply chains. *Appl. Math. Model.* **2014**, *38*, 5553–5561. [CrossRef]

43. Jaipuria, S.; Mahapatra, S.S. An improved demand forecasting method to reduce bullwhip effect in supply chains. *Expert Syst. Appl.* **2014**, *41*, 2395–2408. [CrossRef]

44. Hussain, M.; Saber, H. Exploring the bullwhip effect using simulation and Taguchi experimental design. *Int. J. Logist. Res. Appl.* **2012**, *15*, 231–249. [CrossRef]

45. Dominguez, R.; Cannella, S.; Barbosa-Póvoa, A.P.; Framinan, J.M. OVAP: A strategy to implement partial information sharing among supply chain retailers. *Transp. Res. Part E Logist. Transp. Rev.* **2018**, *110*, 122–136. [CrossRef]

46. Zhang, X. The impact of forecasting methods on the bullwhip effect. *Int. J. Prod. Econ.* **2004**, *88*, 15–27. [CrossRef]

47. Luong, H.; Phien, N. Measure of bullwhip effect in supply chains: The case of high order autoregressive demand process. *Eur. J. Oper. Res.* **2007**, *183*, 197–209. [CrossRef]

48. Sirikasemsuk, K.; Luong, H.T. Measure of bullwhip effect in supply chains with first-order bivariate vector autoregression time-series demand model. *Comput. Oper. Res.* **2017**, *78*, 59–79. [CrossRef]

49. Chandra, C.; Grabis, J. Application of multi-steps forecasting for restraining the bullwhip effect and improving inventory performance under autoregressive demand. *Eur. J. Oper. Res.* **2005**, *166*, 337–350. [CrossRef]

50. Chen, F.; Drezner, Z.; Ryan, J.K.; Simchi-Levi, D. Quantifying the Bullwhip Effect in a Simple Supply Chain: The Impact of Forecasting, Lead Times, and Information. *Manag. Sci.* **2000**, *46*, 436–443. [CrossRef]

51. Ma, Y.; Wang, N.; Che, A.; Huang, Y.; Xu, J. The bullwhip effect on product orders and inventory: A perspective of demand forecasting techniques. *Int. J. Prod. Res.* **2013**, *51*, 281–302. [CrossRef]

52. Campuzano-Bolarín, F.; Frutos, A.G.; Ruiz Abellón, M.D.C.; Lisec, A. Alternative Forecasting Techniques that Reduce the Bullwhip Effect in a Supply Chain: A Simulation Study. *Prsomet–Traffic Transp.* **2013**, *25*, 177–188. [CrossRef]

53. Costantino, F.; Di Gravio, G.; Shaban, A.; Tronci, M. SPC forecasting system to mitigate the bullwhip effect and inventory variance in supply chains. *Expert Syst. Appl.* **2015**, *42*, 1773–1787. [CrossRef]

54. Bandyopadhyay, S.; Bhattacharya, R. A generalized measure of bullwhip effect in supply chain with ARMA demand process under various replenishment policies. *Int. J. Adv. Manuf. Technol.* **2013**, *68*, 963–979. [CrossRef]

55. Gaalman, G.; Disney, S. On bullwhip in a family of order-up-to policies with ARMA (2, 2) demand and arbitrary lead-times. *Int. J. Prod. Econ.* **2009**, *121*, 454–463. [CrossRef]

56. Pacheco, E.D.O.; Cannella, S.; Lüders, R.; Barbosa-Povoa, A.P. Order-up-to-level policy update procedure for a supply chain subject to market demand uncertainty. *Comput. Ind. Eng.* **2017**, *113*, 347–355. [CrossRef]

57. Costantino, F.; Di Gravio, G.; Shaban, A.; Tronci, M. The impact of information sharing and inventory control coordination on supply chain performances. *Comput. Ind. Eng.* **2014**, *76*, 292–306. [CrossRef]

58. Patriarca, R.; Costantino, F.; Di Gravio, G.; Tronci, M. Inventory optimization for a customer airline in a Performance Based Contract. *J. Air Transp. Manag.* **2016**, *57*, 206–216. [CrossRef]

3

Multi-Product Production System with the Reduced Failure Rate and the Optimum Energy Consumption under Variable Demand

Shaktipada Bhuniya [1], Biswajit Sarkar [2],* and Sarla Pareek [1]

[1]   Department of Mathematics and Statistics, Banasthali Vidyapith, Banasthali, Rajasthan 304 022, India; shakti13math@gmail.com (S.B.); spareek13@gmail.com (S.P.)

[2]   Department of Industrial & Management Engineering, Hanyang University, Ansan Gyeonggi-do 15588, Korea

*   Correspondence: bsbiswajitsarkar@gmail.com.

Abstract: The advertising of any smart product is crucial in generating customer demand, along with reducing sale prices. Naturally, a decrease in price always increases the demand for any smart product. This study introduces a multi-product production process, taking into consideration the advertising- and price-dependent demands of products, where the failure rate of the production system is reduced under the optimum energy consumption. For long-run production systems, unusual energy consumption and machine failures occur frequently, which are reduced in this study. All costs related with the production system are included in the optimum energy costs. The unit production cost is dependent on the production rate of the machine and its failure rate. The aim of this study is to obtain the optimum profit with a reduced failure rate, under the optimum advertising costs and the optimum sale price. The total profit of the model becomes a complex, non-linear function, with respect to the decision variables. For this reason, the model is solved numerically by an iterative method. However, the global optimality is proved numerically, by using the Hessian matrix. The numerical results obtained show that for smart production, the maximum profit always occurs at the optimum values of the decision variables.

Keywords: inventory; smart production; variable demand; advertisement; energy; rework; system reliability

---

1. Introduction

Any production system may produce both perfect and imperfect products. During the long-run production process of a smart production system, there may be a chance of machine failure, due to machine breakdown, unskilled laborers, or interrupted energy suppliers, and so on. Due to these reasons, a defective product may be produced in two ways: at a constant rate or at a random rate. For a constant defect rate, the total number of defective items is constant and, for a random defect rate, the total number of defective products is a random variable. Many studies based on constant defect rates in single-item production systems have been carried out (see, for instance, [1]); however, very little research based on random defect rates (see, for instance, [2]) is available. Sarkar [3] proposed a model for a multi-item production system with a random defect rate and budget and space constraints. There has been no research, to our knowledge, on multi-item smart production systems with the optimum consumption of energy and a random defect rate for smart products, with advertisement, price-dependent demand patterns, and reduced failure rates. Therefore, this proposed model gives a new direction for production systems with budget and space constraints under the effect of energy.

For this type of (perfect and imperfect) production system, rework has a vital role in smart production, where the production system becomes out-of-control (from an in-control state) within a random time interval. It provides a reliable system by reworking the defective items. Some studies of imperfect production systems with deterioration are already available in the literature, such as Rossenblat and Lee [4], who discussed imperfect production systems; which was extended by Kim and Hog [5] by considering the deterioration of products in a production system to find the optimal production length. They indicated three types of deterioration methods—constant deterioration, linearly increasing deterioration, and exponentially increasing deterioration—for system moving from an in-control to an out-of-control state. Giri and Dohi [6] proposed a model which highlights random machine failure rates for single-item production systems, where the machine breakdown is stochastic and the preventive maintenance time for machine failure is also a random variable.

Sana et al. [7] gave an idea for a research model of an imperfect production system, by considering defective products with reduced prices, although this type of idea is now common in the market. Chiu et al. [8] proposed a model which assumes a rework policy of the defective products, using extra costs for the reworking of imperfect products. In the literature, there are few models based on energy in an imperfect smart production system. No study, to our knowledge, has considered the optimum energy consumption and its profit for a smart production system, under advertising- and price-dependent demands. Egea et al. [9] expressed, in a model, how to measure energy during the loading of a smart machine. González et al. [10] proposed a model for turbo-machinery components, using a total energy consideration.

Sarkar [11] considered an inventory model involving stock-dependent demand with delayed payments. This model indicated the replenishment policy for an imperfect production system with a finite replenish rate. A production-inventory model with deterioration and a finite replenishment rate was developed by Sarkar [12]. In this model, to maximize the profit, several discount offers for customers, to attract a large order size, were considered. Generally, imperfect product production depends on the production system reliability. Sarkar [13] developed an economic manufacturing quantity (EMQ) model with an investment in the production system for the development of a high system reliability with lower imperfect production. This model first considered an advertisement policy, where the demand depends on the price of products. An imperfect production model was considered by Chakraborty and Giri [14] with some imperfect products produced in an out-of-control system during preventive maintenance. An inspection was considered in this model to detect the defective items for the reworking process, although some defective products cannot be repaired.

Sarkar [15] investigated an economic production quantity (EPQ) model with imperfect products, where a back-ordering policy was included in the model, along with a reworking policy. To calculate the rate of defective items, three different distribution functions were used and the results are compared in this model. Sarkar and Saren [16] introduced a production model in an imperfect production system with an inspection policy. In their model, the production system becomes out-of-control in a random time interval. This model considered a quality inspector for choosing falsely an imperfect product and making a decision about quality, and vice versa. Over a fixed time period, the warranty policy also makes this model more realistic.

Pasandideh et al. [17] extended a production model for multiple products in a single-machine imperfect production system, where the imperfect products were classified by their nature, to consider whether to rework or scrap them. To make this model more realistic, they considered fully backlogging all shortages. An inventory model for a system with a non-stationary stochastic demand with a detailed analysis of the lot-size problem was developed by Purohit et al. [18]; a carbon-emissions mechanism was included with this model to make it a more generalized study. This model discussed labor issues with the training required involving work related to the machine. Sana [19] considered an EPQ lot-size model for imperfect production with defective items when the system becomes out-of-control. An optimal inventory for a repair model was initiated by Cárdenas-Barrón et al. [20].

Another two research models, based on deterioration and partial backlogging, were developed by Tiwari et al. [21,22]

Storage capacity for an inventory system plays an important role in any production house. Limited storage makes increasing production problematic. Due to this reason, shortages may occur. Huang et al. [23] developed an inventory model in which a rental warehouse was considered, with an associated cost, for fulfilling the required capacity in addition to the available warehouse. This inventory model investigated optimal retailer lot-size policies with delayed payments and space constraints. An inventory model for multiple products with limited space was proposed by Pasandideh and Niaki [24]. This model contained a non-linear integer programming problem and found an optimal solution for the available warehouse by adding space constraints. Through a genetic algorithm with a non-linear cost function and space constraint, a multi-stage inventory model was discussed by Hafshejani et al. [25]. An inventory model considering demand and limited space availability, where reliability depends on the unit production costs, was introduced by Mahapatra et al. [26].

In a production model, the budget for a production system is initially required for the manufacturer. Instead of a periodic budget, a limited budget is preferable. There is some on-going research into budget constraints, such as Taleizadeh et al. [27], who proposed a model, in a multi-item production system, for a reworking of defective items policy. They found the global minimum of the total cost by considering a service level and a budget constraint. Minimizing the total annual cost with a limited capital budget and calculating the optimal lot size and capital investment in a setup-costs model was explained by Hou and Lin [28]. Mohan et al. [29] introduced an inventory model, considering delayed payments, budget constraints, and permissible partial payment (with penalty) for a multi-item production system with a replenishment policy. Todde et al. [30] and Du et al. [31] published the basic energy models, based on energy consumption and energy analysis. Cárdenas-Barrón et al. [32] proposed an inventory model with an improved heuristic algorithm solving method for a just-in-time (JIT) system with the maximum available budget. Xu et al. [33] presented a bio-fuel model for the pyrolysis products of plants. Tomić and Schneider [34] discussed a method for recovering energy from waste using a closed-loop supply chain. Haraldsson and Johansson [35] developed an energy model, based on different energy efficiencies during production. Similarly, Dey et al. [36] and Sarkar et al. [37–39] developed their models based on energies, but did not consider advertising for smart products, reducing the sale price of products, or reducing the failure rate of a production system. Yao et al. [40] and Gola [41] put forth the valuable idea of formulating a model considering the reliability of a manufacturing system.

The world becomes smarter every day. Several researchers have discussed imperfect production processes, such as Tayyab et al. [42], Sarkar [43], Kim et al. [44], and Sarkar et al. [45], but the effect of a smart manufacturing system in any production model has not been discussed. The effects of energy and failure rate in a multi-item smart production system was first discussed by Sarkar et al. [3]. In reality, the demand for a particular product depends on various key factors, with advertisement of a particular product being one of them. Ideally, advertisement of a particular product increases the demand for that product. Thus, the total profit can be optimized when the demand depends on the advertisement of products. The relationship between product quality and advertising, in an analytical model, was developed by Chenavaz and Jasimuddin [46]; they also explained the positive and negative advertising–quality relationships. A two-level supply chain model was developed by Giri and Sharma [47], where the demand depends on the advertising cost. In this model, they considered a single-manufacturer, two-retailer system, where the retailers compete. In the same direction, Xiao et al. [48] formulated a two-echelon supply chain model for a single manufacturer and multiple retailers. In this model, they studied co-operative issues in advertising. Recently, Noh et al. [49] developed a two-echelon supply chain model, where the demand depends on the advertisement. They used the Stackelberge game policy to solve this model. Sale price, also, has a great impact on the demand for a product. The demand for a product gradually increases if the sale price is less, and vice versa. Constant demand is a business service that helps customers to find new consumers and penetrate new markets, which can optimize the inside-sales and marketing activities to achieve high-quality sales. Variable demand can predict and quantify changes that are caused by transportation conditions on the demand. As a high price negatively affects how likely clients are to buy products or services, assuming the demand to be price-dependent is more realistic. Karaoz et al. [50] considered an inventory model with price- and time-dependent demand, under the influence of complementary and substitute product sale prices. The finite replenishment inventory model was developed by considering the demand to be sensitive to changes in time and sale price. Sana [51] introduced the price-sensitive demand for perishable items in an inventory model. The demand for any inventory system is not always constant and may depend on time, sale price, and inventory. Pal et al. [52] developed a multi-item inventory model where the demand was sensitive to the sale price and price-break. Sarkar et al. [53] developed an EMQ model with price- and time-dependent demand, under the effects of reliability and inflation. Sarkar and Sarkar [54] established an inventory model, where the demand was inventory-dependent, and an algorithm was developed to maximize the profit. To maximize the vendor profit, the optimal ordering quantity and sale price were optimized by an analytical procedure. An integrated model, with development lead time and production rate, was discussed by Azadeh and Paknafs [55]. Several researchers have developed many models where the demand depends on the sale price of the products or advertising-dependent demand; however, price- and advertising-dependent demand in a smart production system has still not been considered, to our knowledge. Thus, this new direction is considered in this research. Table 1 shows the contribution of previous author(s).

Table 1. Author(s) contribution table.

Author(s)	Development Cost	Inspection	Demand	Advertisement	Energy	Rework	Reliability
Cárdenas-Barrón [1]			√			√	
Sana et al. [2]			√				
Sarkar et al. [3]	√	√	√		√	√	√
Rosenblatt and Lee [4]			√				
Sarkar [12]	√		√				√
Sarkar and Saren [16]			√				
Sana [19]	√		√				√
Taleizadeh et al. [27]			√				√
Mohan et al. [29]	√		√				
Cárdenas-Barrón [32]			√			√	√
This Paper	√	√	√	√	√	√	√

2. Problem Definition, Notation, Assumptions

2.1. Problem Definition

Smart production systems are modern production systems, in which the main aim is to produce smart products (such as mobile phones, computers, and so on) through some smart machines by some smart, skilled labors. The whole smart production process is controlled under the optimum energy consumptions. For example, a smart machine can produce more woolen clothes than an expert labor; in this case, quality and quantity will also be more developed than in simple production systems. An imperfect production system is a production system in which a defective product is produced in a long-run process, due to machine breakdown or any other problem. Energy consumption has an important role in imperfect production systems. In smart production systems, production of imperfect products can be controlled with sufficient consumption of energy. Our model is based on a smart production system for multiple products, where machine failure occurs in random time intervals, γ_i, in which there is an unusual amount of energy consumption and less reliable conditions and production completed in random time intervals, T_i. For this situation, the development cost used in this model is reliability-dependent, to reduce the machine failure rate and to minimize the consumption of energy. An inspection cost is used to detect defective items. For the popularity of the products in this model, advertisement costs and price-dependent demand patterns are used. To obtain more reliability, there are a several possibilities for the reworking of defective items before being sold to the customer. The aim of this model is to obtain the maximum profit for a multi-item production system with the conditions of energy consumption and a random defect rate, under the effects of advertisement and sale price. Process flow for multi-product production system are shown in the following Figure 1.

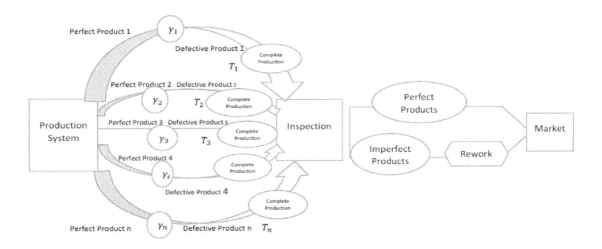

Figure 1. Complex production management with system reliability.

2.2. Assumptions

In developing the proposed model, the following assumptions are considered:

1. This is a multi-item production model, where defective products are produced after a random time. The system moves to an out-of-control state at a random time, γ_i, at a failure rate of α, and produces defective items. These items are then reworked to make them as new products.
2. This system is controlled, under energy consumption, for completely finished products only.
3. No shortages are allowed for this multi-item smart production system, as variable production rate is greater than the demand and the lead time is considered to be negligible.
4. The demand is assumed to be advertising- and price-dependent, to increase the demand pattern. It is taken as $D(S,y) = \frac{S_{max}-S}{S-S_{min}} + xy^\mu$, where x is the scaling parameter and μ is the shape parameter.
5. If the failure rate α decreases, then the system will be more reliable, and vice versa.
6. The system contains multiple items and, thus, there will be a possibility for space problems for the products, which affects the total budget. Thus, to make this model more realistic under the sufficient energy consumption, space, and budget constraints are considered in this model.

3. Model Formulation

The model studies about a smart production system for multi-item. During the time $t_i = 0$ to $t_i = t_{1i}$, the production continues with upward direction graph and for the time $[t_{1i}, T]$, there is no production, thus, the holding inventories positions are downstream direction with demand D. The production system becomes out-of-control from in-control in random time interval γ_i. See Figure 2 for the description of the production system. The governing differential equation of the inventory is

$$\frac{dI_{1i}(t_i)}{dt_i} = p_i - D, 0 \le t_i \le t_{1i} \qquad (1)$$

with initial condition $I_{1i}(0) = 0$ and

$$\frac{dI_{2i}(t_i)}{dt_i} = -D, t_{1i} \leq t_i \leq T \tag{2}$$

with initial condition $I_{2i}(T) = 0$.

Solving the above differential equations, one can obtain

$$I_{1i} = (p_i - D)t_i, 0 \leq t_i \leq t_{1i} \tag{3}$$

$$I_{2i} = D(T - t_i), t_{1i} \leq t_i \leq T \tag{4}$$

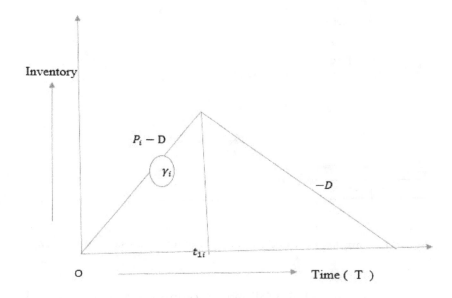

Figure 2. Economic Production quantity.

Considering the following costs in a multi-item smart production system, we must optimize for those which have a low failure rate and maximum profit.

Setup Cost (SC)

In this model, setup cost for product i is S_{ci} per setup and per setup energy consumption cost be S'_{ci}. Then, the average setup cost per cycle is

$$SC = \sum_{i=1}^{n}(S_{ci} + S'_{ci})\frac{D}{q_i}. \tag{5}$$

Holding Cost (HC)

For this production system, to calculate the holding cost it is necessary to find the total inventory by summation from $i = 1$ to $i = n$; further, to get the average inventory, the total inventory can be divided by cycle length. Thus, the total inventory can be calculated as

$$\text{Total Inventory} = \sum_{i=1}^{n}\left[\int_{0}^{t_{1i}} I_{1i}(t_i)dt_i + \int_{t_{1i}}^{T} I_{2i}(t_i)dt_i\right]$$

$$= \sum_{i=1}^{n}\left[\int_{0}^{t_{1i}} (p_i - D)t_i dt_i + \int_{t_{1i}}^{T} D(T - t_i)dt_i\right]. \tag{6}$$

Hence, the total holding cost, with sufficient consumption of energy, can be calculated, as follows:

$$
\begin{aligned}
\mathrm{HC} &= \sum_{i=1}^{n} \frac{(H_{ci} + H'_{ci})D}{2q_i} \left[\int_0^{t_{1i}} (p_i - D)t_i dt_i + \int_{t_{1i}}^{T} ((p_i - D)\frac{q_i}{p_i} - Dt_i) dt_i \right] \\
&= \sum_{i=1}^{n} \frac{(H_{ci} + H'_{ci})q_i}{2} \left(1 - \frac{D}{p_i} \right).
\end{aligned}
\tag{7}
$$

Development Cost (DC)

The system becomes more reliable based on development costs. A high investment in the production system, in terms of development costs, makes for a low failure rate, and vice versa. The labor cost and energy resources cost are included in the development cost. Thus, the total development cost per unit time is

$$
\mathrm{DC} = G + Z e^{r \frac{\alpha_{max} - \alpha}{\alpha - \alpha_{min}}}.
\tag{8}
$$

Inspection Cost (IC)

A multi-item smart production system is considered to be a long-run process, where the process is imperfect. Thus, an inspection cost plays an important role in detecting defective items, such that the defective products can be reworked easily. Thus, the inspection cost per unit cycle, under energy consumption, is

$$
\begin{aligned}
\mathrm{IC} &= \sum_{i=1}^{n} (I_c + I'_c)q_i \times \frac{D}{q_i} \\
&= \sum_{i=1}^{n} (I_c + I'_c)D.
\end{aligned}
\tag{9}
$$

Rework Cost (RC)

For reworking the defective products, at first, inspection is needed for all defective products. To find the RC, it is important to know how many defective products there are, and how much the RC is for defective items. The rate of defective items is considered (see, for instance, [3]) to be $\beta P_i^{\delta}(t_i - \gamma_i)^{\gamma}$, where $\delta \geq 0, \tau \geq 0$, and $t_i \geq \gamma_i$. Hence, the number of imperfect items produced by the machine is

$$
\begin{aligned}
E(K) &= \sum_{i=1}^{n} \left(\frac{\beta}{\tau + 1} \right) p_i^{\delta+1} \int_0^{t_{1i}} (t_{1i} - \gamma_i)^{\gamma+1} dH(\gamma_i) \\
&= \sum_{i=1}^{n} p_i^{\delta+1} \left(\frac{\beta}{\tau + 1} \right) e^{\frac{-\alpha q_i}{p_i}} \chi\left(\alpha, \frac{q_i}{p_i} \right), \quad \text{as } t_{1i} = \frac{q_i}{p_i}.
\end{aligned}
\tag{10}
$$

For reworking the defective products to perfect state, a RC is needed, along with a consumption of energy cost. The rework cost (RC) per cycle can, thus, be calculated as

$$
\mathrm{RC} = \sum_{i=1}^{n} (R_{ci} + R'_{ci}) \frac{D}{q_i} E(K).
\tag{11}
$$

Unit Production Cost (UPC)

The production cost depends on the raw material costs, the development cost, and the tool/die cost. It is proportional to the cost of the previous indicated costs. The quality of the raw materials affects the reliability of the products. In this model, the unit production cost is considered to be as follows:

$$
\mathrm{UPC} = \sum_{i=1}^{n} [M_c + \frac{\mathrm{DC}}{p_i} + \sigma p_i^{\xi}].
\tag{12}
$$

Advertisement Cost (AC)

The multi-item production system based on advertisement, and demand gradually increased due to huge amount investment on advertisement.This model consider advertisement cost to make popular of the smart products.

$$\text{AC} = \frac{hy^2}{2}. \tag{13}$$

Total Expected Profit (TEP)

The TEP per cycle is

$$
\begin{aligned}
\text{TEP}(q_i, p_i, S, \alpha, Y) &= \text{Revenue} - \text{HC} - \text{SC} - \text{IC} - \text{RC} - \text{AC} \\
&= \sum_{i=1}^{n} \left[D(S - \text{UPC}) - \frac{(H_{ci} + H_{ci}')q_i}{2}\left(1 - \frac{D}{p_i}\right) - (S_{ci} + S_{ci}')\frac{D}{q_i} - (I_c + I_c')D - (R_{ci} + R_{ci}')\frac{D}{q_i}E(K) \right] - \frac{hy^2}{2} \\
&= \sum_{i=1}^{n} \left[\left(\frac{S_{max}-S}{S-S_{min}} + xy^\mu\right)(S - P_{ci}) - \frac{(H_{ci}+H_{ci}')q_i}{2}\left(1 - \frac{\left(\frac{S_{max}-S}{S-S_{min}}+xy^\mu\right)}{p_i}\right) \right. \\
&\quad - (S_{ci} + S_{ci}')\frac{\left(\frac{S_{max}-S}{S-S_{min}}+xy^\mu\right)}{q_i} - (I_c + I_c')\left(\frac{S_{max}-S}{S-S_{min}} + xy^\mu\right) \\
&\quad \left. - (R_{ci} + R_{ci}')\frac{\left(\frac{S_{max}-S}{S-S_{min}}+xy^\mu\right)}{q_i}p_i^{\delta+1}\left(\frac{\beta}{\tau+1}\right)e^{\frac{-\alpha q_i}{p_i}}\chi\left(\alpha, \frac{q_i}{p_i}\right) \right] - \frac{hy^2}{2},
\end{aligned} \tag{14}
$$

where

$$t_{2i} = \frac{\left(p_i - \left(\frac{S_{max}-S}{S-S_{min}} + xy^\mu\right)\right)q_i}{p_i\left(\frac{S_{max}-S}{S-S_{min}} + xy^\mu\right)}, \tag{15}$$

and

$$
\begin{aligned}
\chi\left(\alpha, \frac{q_i}{p_i}\right) &= \frac{t_1^{\tau+2}}{\tau+2} + \frac{\alpha t_1^{\tau+3}}{\tau+3} + \frac{\alpha^2 t_1^{\tau+4}}{\tau+4} + \frac{\alpha^3 t_1^{\tau+5}}{\tau+5} + \cdots\cdots \\
&= \sum_{i=1}^{\infty} \frac{t_1^{\tau+j+1}\alpha^{j+1}}{(j-1)!(\tau+j+1)} \\
&= \sum_{i=1}^{\infty} \frac{\left(\frac{q_i}{p_i}\right)^{\iota+j+1}\alpha^{j+1}}{(j-1)!(\tau+j+1)}.
\end{aligned} \tag{16}
$$

Constraints

Capital investment in a smart production system plays an important role, although the amount is limited. A sufficient amount of investment gives an opportunity to choose good-quality raw materials within a required time. Although in this model, defective items are produced and a rework facility is available, this may differ in other situations, with different investment budgets. This model considers a budget constraint and, to separate the imperfect products, managers define a specific quality level, which may or may not be chosen for reworking. Considering A for maximum space available for storing in square feet and B for maximum budget available. Sufficient spaces are allotted for storing good-quality products and for reworking imperfect products. Therefore, the profit function, including budget and space constraints, becomes

$$
\begin{aligned}
\text{TEP}(q_i, p_i, S, \alpha, Y) &= \sum_{i=1}^{n} \left[\left(\frac{S_{max}-S}{S-S_{min}} + xy^\mu\right)(S - P_{ci}) - \frac{(H_{ci}+H_{ci}')q_i}{2}\left(1 - \frac{\left(\frac{S_{max}-S}{S-S_{min}}+xy^\mu\right)}{p_i}\right) \right. \\
&\quad - (S_{ci} + S_{ci}')\frac{\left(\frac{S_{max}-S}{S-S_{min}}+xy^\mu\right)}{q_i} - (I_c + I_c')\left(\frac{S_{max}-S}{S-S_{min}} + xy^\mu\right) \\
&\quad \left. - (R_{ci} + R_{ci}')\frac{\left(\frac{S_{max}-S}{S-S_{min}}+xy^\mu\right)}{q_i}p_i^{\delta+1}\left(\frac{\beta}{\tau+1}\right)e^{\frac{-\alpha q_i}{p_i}}\chi\left(\alpha, \frac{q_i}{p_i}\right) \right] - \frac{hy^2}{2},
\end{aligned} \tag{17}
$$

$\sum_{i=1}^{n} \phi_i q_i \leq A$, and $\sum_{i=1}^{n} \psi_i q_i \leq B$.

The model cannot be solved analytically. Thus, this model is solved through a numerical tool. The global maximum values of the decision variables are proved numerically.

4. Numerical Examples

We use three numerical examples to validate the model.

4.1. Example 1

In this section, numerical examples are provided to validate this model. In Table 2, for Example 1, the parametric values of the material, holding, rework, and inspection costs; maximum and minimum sale prices; maximum and minimum failure rate; energy costs due to different materials; and other shifting and scaling parameters are shown, which are used in the model and solved using the Mathematica 9.0 software (Wolfram Research, Champaign, IL, USA). The output values of the decision variables (production rate, production lot size, average sale price, advertising variable, and failure rate) are shown in Table 3.

Table 2. Input parameters of Example 1.

I_c ($/unit)	I'_c ($/unit)	H_{c1} ($/unit)	H_{c2} ($/unit)	M (Square Feet)
6	4	2	3.05	130
S_{ci} ($/unit)	S'_{ci} ($/unit)	R_{ci} ($/ defective items)	R'_{ci} ($/defective items)	β (unit)
1000	1100	110	120	5.9
S_{max} ($/unit)	S_{min} ($/unit)	α_{max} (unit)	α_{min} (unit)	δ (unit)
2000	100	0.90	0.10	0.8
ζ	h ($/year)	r	σ	G ($/item)
0.7	20,000	0.85	0.02	200
τ	x	μ	M_c ($/unit)	Z ($)
3	10	1.85	100	30

Table 3. Optimum results of Example 1.

p_1	p_2	q_1	q_2	S	y	α	Total Profit
598.50 (units/year)	530.29 (units/year)	60.17 (units)	51.70 (units)	565.31 ($/unit)	0.25 ($/year)	0.50 (unit)	2619.20 ($/unit)

The TEP is maximum, as the values of the Hessian at the optimal values of the decision variables are $H_{11} = -0.0388796 < 0$; $H_{22} = 0.00254255 > 0$; $H_{33} = -1.01444 \times 10^{-7} < 0$; $H_{44} = 4.75811 \times 10^{-12} > 0$; $H_{55} = -1.5627 \times 10^{-10} < 0$; $H_{66} = 2.66536 \times 10^{-13} > 0$; $H_{77} = -1.87583 \times 10^{-8} < 0$.

4.2. Example 2

In Table 4, for Example 2, the parametric values of the material, holding, rework, and inspection costs; maximum and minimum sale prices; maximum and minimum failure rate; energy costs due to different materials; and other shifting and scaling parameters are shown, which are used in the model and solved using the Mathematica 9 software. The output values of the decision variables (production rate, production lot size, average sale price, advertising variable, and failure rate) are shown in Table 5

Table 4. Input parameters of Example 2.

I_c (\$/unit)	I_c' (\$/unit)	H_{c1} (\$/unit)	H_{c2} (\$/unit)	M (Square feet)
8	5	3	5.05	120
S_{ci} (\$/unit)	S_{ci}' (\$/unit)	R_{ci} (\$/defective items)	R_{ci}' (\$/defective items)	β (unit)
1100	1300	110	120	3.8
S_{max} (\$/unit)	S_{min} (\$/unit)	α_{max} (unit)	α_{min} (unit)	δ (unit)
2000	250	0.50	0.10	0.65
ξ	h (\$/year)	r	σ	G (\$/item)
0.7	5000	0.75	0.01	350
τ	x	μ	M_c (\$/unit)	Z (\$)
4	9	1.35	150	60

Table 5. Optimum results of Example 2.

p_1	p_2	q_1	q_2	S	y	α	Total Profit
707.48	596.59	125.82	106.539	379.61	1.04	0.50	6133.76
(units/year)	(units/year)	(units)	(units)	(\$/unit)	(\$/year)	(unit)	(\$/unit)

The TEP is maximum, as the values of the Hessian at the optimal values of the decision variables are $H_{11} = -0.0267288 < 0$; $H_{22} = 0.00137255 > 0$; $H_{33} = -1.37276 \times 10^{-7} < 0$; $H_{44} = 1.88938 \times 10^{-11} > 0$; $H_{55} = -8.46171 \times 10^{-10} < 0$; $H_{66} = 2.25542 \times 10^{-10} > 0$; $H_{77} = -1.21061 \times 10^{-6} < 0$.

4.3. Example 3

In Table 6, for Example 3, the parametric values of the material, holding, rework, and inspection costs; maximum and minimum sale prices; maximum and minimum failure rate; energy costs due to different materials; and other shifting and scaling parameters are shown, which are used in the model and solved using the Mathematica 9 software. The output values of the decision variables (production rate, production lot size, average sale price, advertising variable, and failure rate) are shown in Table 7.

Table 6. Input parameters of Example 3.

I_c (\$/unit)	I_c' (\$/unit)	H_{c1} (\$/unit)	H_{c2} (\$/unit)	M (Square Feet)
8	5	2	4.05	120
S_{ci} (\$/unit)	S_{ci}' (\$/unit)	R_{ci} (\$/defective items)	R_{ci}' (\$/defective items)	β (unit)
1100	1400	110	120	4.8
S_{max} (\$/unit)	S_{min} (\$/unit)	α_{max} (unit)	α_{min} (unit)	δ (unit)
1600	400	0.50	0.10	0.25
ξ	h (\$/year)	r	σ	G (\$/item)
0.7	6000	0.65	0.01	350
τ	x	μ	M_c (\$/unit)	Z (\$)
4	10	1.35	150	60

Table 7. Optimum results of Example 3.

p_1	p_2	q_1	q_2	S	y	α	Total Profit
689.67	547.70	193.80	156.36	508.92	1.96	0.50	11914.6
(units/year)	(units/year)	(units)	(units)	($/unit)	($/year)	(unit)	($/unit)

The TEP is maximum, as the values of the Hessian at the optimal values of the decision variables are $H_{11} = -0.0119313 < 0$; $H_{22} = 0.000332921 > 0$; $H_{33} = -5.68341 \times 10^{-8} < 0$; $H_{44} = 1.57781 \times 10^{-11} > 0$; $H_{55} = -9.86172 \times 10^{-10} < 0$; $H_{66} = 8.62069 \times 10^{-10} > 0$; $H_{77} = -4.44002 \times 10^{-6} < 0$.

Table 8 compares the total expected profits (TEP) of the three given examples. There is are another scope to maximize the TEP—by increasing sale price, which depends on the total cost of making the products; although production rate and production lot size also give opportunity to maximize the TEP. Setup cost and energy consumption costs due to setup also have impacts on the TEP. Furthermore, advertising plays an important role; due to increased investment into advertisement, the examples show how the total profit can be extended.

Table 8. Comparative Study.

	Example 1	Example 2	Example 2
TEP	2619.20 $/unit	6133.76 $/unit	11914.6 $/unit

The following three dimension Figures 3–9 are total expected profit (TEP) versus different pair decision variables. The concavity of the figures indicated the profit of the model in different cases.

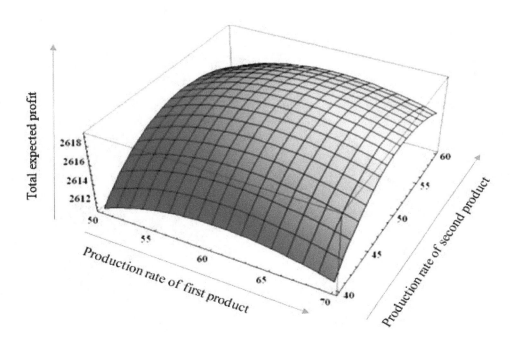

Figure 3. The total expected profit versus the production rate of two products (P_1, P_2).

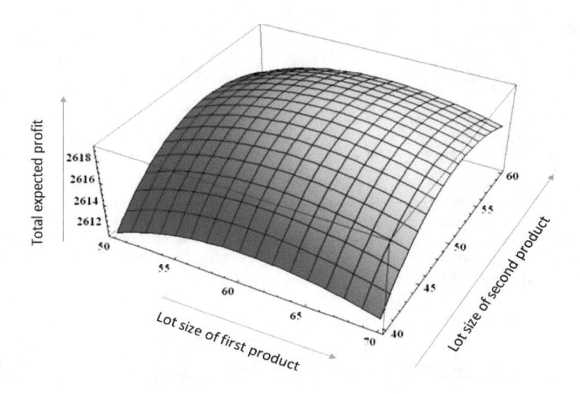

Figure 4. The total expected profit versus lot size of two products (q_1, q_2).

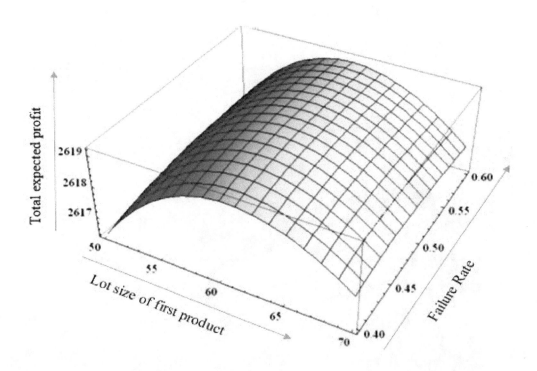

Figure 5. The total expected profit versus the production rate P_1 and the failure rate α.

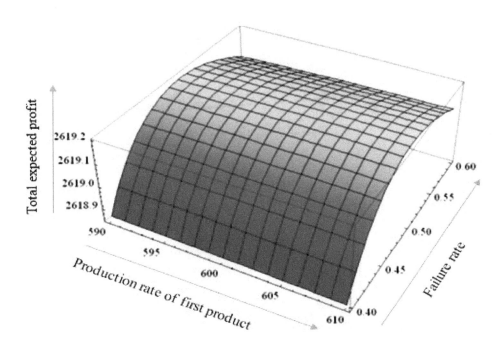

Figure 6. The total expected profit versus the production lot size q_1 and failure rate α.

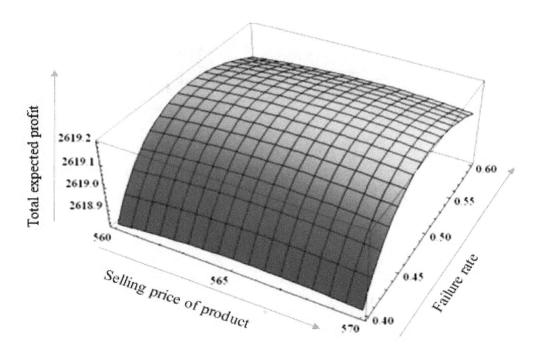

Figure 7. The total expected profit versus the advertising variable quantity and failure rate α of two products.

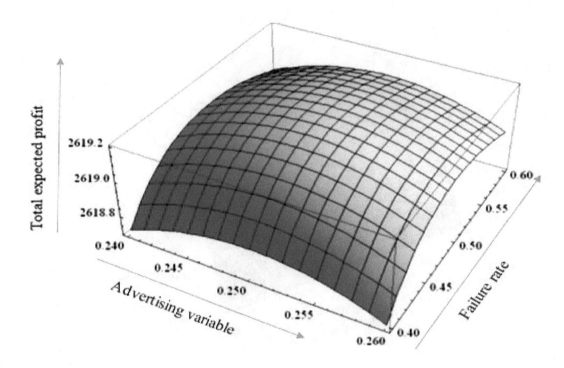

Figure 8. The total expected profit versus the selling price and the failure rate α.

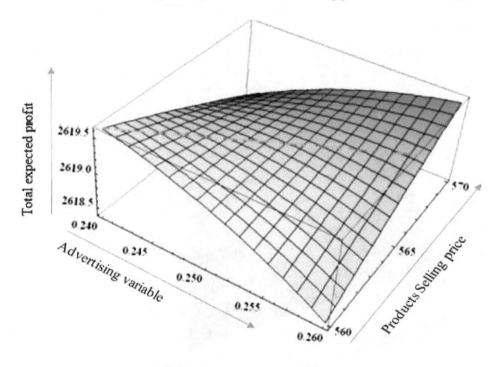

Figure 9. The total expected profit versus the advertising variable and the sale price.

5. Sensitivity Analysis

A sensitivity analysis of the cost and scaling parameters was conducted, and the major changes are summarized in Table 9 and Figure 10.

Table 9 shows how changes by certain percentages ($-50\%, -25\%, +25\%, +50\%$) in the cost and scaling parameters affect the total profit. Here NF indicates that the numerical result is not feasible. We can conclude the following from the sensitivity analysis.

Table 9. Sensitivity analysis of the key parameters.

Parameters	Changes (%)	TEP (%)	Parameters	Changes (%)	TEP (%)
I_c	-50	$+0.44$	I_c'	-50	$+0.29$
	-25	$+0.22$		-25	$+0.15$
	$+25$	-0.22		$+25$	-0.15
	$+50$	-0.44		$+50$	-0.29
H_{c1}	-50	$+1.32$	H_{c2}	-50	$+1.73$
	-25	$+0.61$		-25	$+0.18$
	$+25$	-0.54		$+25$	-0.70
	$+50$	-1.03		$+50$	-1.34
S_{ci}	-50	$+1.43$	S_{ci}'	-50	$+1.84$
	-25	$+0.66$		-25	$+0.84$
	$+25$	-0.58		$+25$	-0.74
	$+50$	-1.10		$+50$	-1.40
R_{ci}	-50	$+0.03$	R_{ci}'	-50	$+0.02$
	-25	$+0.01$		-25	$+0.01$
	$+25$	-0.01		$+25$	-0.01
	$+50$	-0.02		$+50$	-0.02
M_c	-50	$+16.18$	x	-50	-30.70
	-25	$+7.71$		-25	-9.36
	$+25$	-7.03		$+25$	$+4.74$
	$+50$	-13.49		$+50$	$+7.24$
σ	-50	$+0.13$	h	-50	NF
	-25	$+0.27$		-25	$+5.44$
	$+25$	-0.23		$+25$	-6.30
	$+50$	-0.12		$+50$	-13.06

1. That changes in energy cost due to inspection and energy cost per setup has low effects on the total optimal profit as, in a smart production system, there is an optimum consumption of energy for different purposes. Some industries do not consider inspection on the final product, due to the value-added process. Due to an increase of inspection, the reworking cost and other costs also increase, which has a large impact on the total optimal profit. On the other hand, inspection maintains the quality and correctness of the products produced in a smart production system.

2. Changes in holding cost had little impact on the total profit of the smart production system. This result can be justified, as the products are not held for a long time. Similarly, variation of the setup cost also has a lesser, but significant, effect on the total optimal profit. Increasing the value of the cost parameters decreases the total optimal profit, which is clearly shown in the sensitivity analysis table and agrees with reality.

3. On the other hand, the material costs in a multi-item smart production system has a great impact on the total profit. With an increase in material costs, all other production costs will increase and, thus, the profit decreases.

4. The value of the scaling parameters for advertising and the tool/die cost function also had effects on the total profit. These parameters behave similarly to other cost parameters for controlling the total optimal profit.

5. The effect of advertisement has a sensitive impact on the total profit. The advertisement of a product is very much important for generating a high popularity and increasing the market demand for the product. Due to increases in sales, the total optimal profit gradually increases. As in Table 9, it is found that eventually, an increasing value of advertising will reduce the total profit.

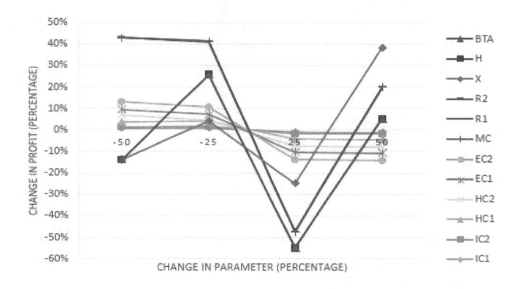

Figure 10. Change of total expected profit (TEP) in percentage versus parametric values in percentage.

6. Managerial Insights

Some recommendations for the industry are as follows:

1. The industry manager must concentrate on the matter of advertisement. This paper clearly shows the impact of advertisement on the total profit. To increase the popularity of products and, in turn, the demand for products, the industry manager should invest some costs into advertisement. In the competitive modern market, this matter plays a significant role for a smart production system. However, no research has considered the advertisement concept, until now, in the field of smart production system. Thus, the result of this study will help the industry manager to increase their profits.

2. Another support that industry managers of smart production systems can use are the strategies, obtained by this research, regarding energy consumption. If a smart production system uses a machine, instead of labor, energy consumption will be present and there will, subsequently, be energy costs to bear. Thus, this model will help the industry to maximize the profit.

3. This model considers random machine breakdowns. Using this idea, the industry manager can pay attention to the previous data of machine failures. This way, the failure rate can be reduced by using smart machines with optimum energy consumptions, and by optimizing development-cost investments.

7. Conclusions

The advertising of smart products has a large impact on the market demand, in addition to the reduction of sale prices, which has an important influence on the profit made from smart products. This study used these two ideas, along with the effects of the optimum use of energy consumption, random machine failures, and optimization of profit, in order to design a model for investigating the optimal decision variables for smart production systems, which gave strong benefits regarding the quality of the smart products. The profit equation of the model was a non-linear equation, and thus could not be solved with an analytical approach. A numerical tool was used to obtain the results, and the numerical findings gave a global optimum solution. The main limitation of the model is that the setup cost in the model is considered to be constant, which can be reduced by an initial investment. In this direction, the model can be extended (refer to the references Malik and Sarkar, [56]; Sarkar and Moon, [57]; Sarkar et al. [58]; Sarkar and Majumdar, [59]; Sarkar et al. [60]; and Majumdar et al. [61]). This model may also be extended by incorporating inspection errors, as the inspection may be done by human beings.

Author Contributions: Conceptualization, B.S. and S.B.; methodology, B.S. and S.B.; software, S.B.; validation, B.S., S.B. and S.P.; formal analysis, S.B.; investigation, B.S.; resources, B.S. and S.P.; data curation, S.B., B.S. and S.P.; writing—original draft preparation, S.B.; writing—review and editing, B.S., S.B. and S.P.; visualization, B.S. and S.B.; supervision, B.S. and S.P.

Acknowledgments: The authors are happy to acknowledge the support from two reviewers for revising the earlier versions of the paper.

Notations

Index

i — number of product ($i = 1, 2, 3, \ldots\ldots, n$)

Model Decision Variables

p_i — production rate for item i per cycle (unit/year)

q_i — production lot size for item i per cycle (units)

S — average selling price of the product ($/unit)

y — advertising variable ($/year)

α — failure rate, indicates reliability, known as system design variable

Input Parameters

N — available maximum budget ($/planning period)

M — available maximum space for sorting in square feet

α_{max} — maximum system failure rate

α_{min} — minimum system failure rate

T — production length per cycle (year)

t_{1i} — required time for maximum inventory (year)

D_c — development cost per unit item ($/unit)

P_c — production cost per unit item ($/unit)

S_{max} — maximum selling price ($/unit)

S_{min} — minimum selling price ($/unit)

ψ_i — consumed budget of item i ($/unit)

ϕ_i — occupied space for the unit item i (square feet per item)

K — number of defective items per cycle

I_c — inspection cost per item ($/item)

D — demand for item i

$E(K)$ — per unit production system expected number of defective items

H_{ci} — holding cost for item i ($/unit/unit time)

S_{ci} — setup cost for item i per setup ($/setup)

M_C — material cost for item i ($/unit)

R_{ci} — rework cost for item i ($/defective item)

R'_{ci} — energy consumption cost due to rework for item i ($/item)

x — scaling parameter for the products

μ — shape parameter for the products

Z — resources fixed cost ($)

G — fixed energy and labor cost, independent of reliability α ($/item)

TEP — total expected profit per unit time ($/year)

I'_c — energy consumption due to Inspection per unit cycle ($/cycle)

S'_{ci} — energy consumption cost per setup ($/setup)

r — shape parameter for development cost function

β — scaling parameter for defective item function

σ — scaling parameter for tool/die cost function

δ — shape parameter for defective item function

h — investment cost for advertisement

ξ — shape parameter for tool/die cost function

Random Variable

γ_i — system random time to move to an out-of-control state from an in-control situation, for item i.

References

1.   Cárdenas-Barrón, L.E. Economic production quantity with rework process at a single-stage manufacturing system with planned backorders. *Comput. Ind. Eng.* **2009**, *57*, 1105–1113. [CrossRef]
2.   Sana, S.S. A production-inventory model in an imperfect production process. *Eur. J. Oper. Res.* **2010**, *200*, 451–464. [CrossRef]
3.   Sarkar, M.; Sarkar, B.; Iqbal, M.W. Effect of energy and failure rate in a multi-item smart production system. *Energies* **2018**, *11*, 2958. [CrossRef]
4.   Rosenblatt, M.J.; Lee, H.L. Economic production cycles with imperfect production processes. *IIE Trans.* **1986**, *18*, 48–55. [CrossRef]
5.   Kim, C.H.; Hong, Y. An optimal production run length in deteriorating production processes. *Int. J. Prod. Econ.* **1999**, *58*, 183–189.
6.   Giri, B.; Dohi, T. Exact formulation of stochastic EMQ model for an unreliable production system. *J. Oper. Res. Soc.* **2005**, *56*, 563–575. [CrossRef]
7.   Sana, S.S.; Goyal, S.K.; Chaudhuri, K. An imperfect production process in a volume flexible inventory model. *Int. J. Prod. Econ.* **2007**, *105*, 548–559. [CrossRef]
8.   Chiu, Y.-S.P.; Chen, K.-K.; Cheng, F.-T.; Wu, M.-F. Optimization of the finite production rate model with scrap, rework and stochastic machine breakdown. *Comput. Math. Appl.* **2010**, *59*, 919–932. [CrossRef]
9.   Egea, A.J.S.; Deferrari, N.; Abate, G.; Martínez Krahmer, D.; Lopez de Lacalle, L.N. Short-cut method to assess a gross available energy in a medium-load screw friction press. *Metals* **2018**, *8*, 173. [CrossRef]
10. González, H.; Calleja, A.; Pereira, O.; Ortega, N.; Lopez de Lacalle, L.N.; Barton, M. Super abrasive machining of integral rotary components using grinding flank tools. *Metals* **2018**, *8*, 24. [CrossRef]
11. Sarkar, B. An EOQ model with delay in payments and stock dependent demand in the presence of imperfect production. *Appl. Math. Comput.* **2012**, *218*, 8295–8308. [CrossRef]
12. Sarkar, B. An EOQ model with delay in payments and time varying deterioration rate. *Math. Comput. Model.* **2012**, *55*, 367–377. [CrossRef]
13. Sarkar, B. An inventory model with reliability in an imperfect production process. *Appl. Math. Comput.* **2012**, *218*, 4881–4891. [CrossRef]
14. Chakraborty, T.; Giri, B. Lot sizing in a deteriorating production system under inspections, imperfect maintenance and reworks. *Oper. Res.* **2014**, *14*, 29–50. [CrossRef]
15   Sarkar, B.; Cárdenas-Barrán, L.E.; Sarkar, M.; Singgih, M.L. An economic production quantity model with random defective rate, rework process and backorders for a single stage production system. *J. Manuf. Syst.* **2014**, *33*, 423–435. [CrossRef]
16. Sarkar, B.; Saren, S. Product inspection policy for an imperfect production system with inspection errors and warranty cost. *Eur. J. Oper. Res.* **2016**, *248*, 263–271. [CrossRef]
17. Pasandideh, S.H.R.; Niaki, S.T.A.; Nobil, A.H.; Cárdenas-Barrán, L.E. A multi-product single machine economic production quantity model for an imperfect production system under warehouse construction cost. *Int. J. Prod. Econ.* **2015**, *169*, 203–214. [CrossRef]
18. Purohit, A.K.; Shankar, R.; Dey, P.K.; Choudhary, A. Non-stationary stochastic inventory lot-sizing with emission and service level constraints in a carbon cap-and-trade system. *J. Clean. Prod.* **2016**, *113*, 654–661. [CrossRef]
19. Sana, S.S. An economic production lot size model in an imperfect production system. *Eur. J. Oper. Res.* **2010**, *201*, 158–170. [CrossRef]
20. Cárdenas-Barrán, L.E.; Chung, K.-J.; Kazemi, N.; Shekarian, E. Optimal inventory system with two backlog costs in response to a discount offer: Corrections and complements. *Oper. Res.* **2018**, *18*, 97–104. [CrossRef]
21. Tiwari, S.; Jaggi, C.K.; Gupta, M.; Cárdenas-Barrón, L.E. Optimal pricing and lot-sizing policy for supply chain system with deteriorating items under limited storage capacity. *Int. J. Prod. Econ.* **2018**, *200*, 278–290. [CrossRef]
22. Tiwari, S.; Cárdenas-Barrón, L.E.; Goh, M.; Shaikh, A.A. Joint pricing and inventory model for deteriorating items with expiration dates and partial backlogging under two-level partial trade credits in supply chain. *Int. J. Prod. Econ.* **2018**, *200*, 16–36. [CrossRef]
23. Huang, Y.-F.; Lai, C.-S.; Shyu, M.-L. Retailer's EOQ model with limited storage space under partially permissible delay in payments. *Math. Prob. Eng.* **2007**, *2007*, 90873. [CrossRef]

24. Pasandideh, S.H.R.; Niaki, S.T.A. A genetic algorithm approach to optimize a multi-products EPQ model with discrete delivery orders and constrained space. *Appl. Math. Comput.* **2008**, *195*, 506–514. [CrossRef]

25. Hafshejani, K.F.; Valmohammadi, C.; Khakpoor, A. Retracted: Using genetic algorithm approach to solve a multi-product EPQ model with defective items, rework, and constrained space. *J. Ind. Eng. Int.* **2012**, *8*, 1–8. [CrossRef]

26. Mahapatra, G.; Mandal, T.; Samanta, G. An EPQ model with imprecise space constraint based on intuitionists fuzzy optimization technique. *J. Mult.-Valued Log. Soft Comput.* **2012**, *19*, 409–423.

27. Taleizadeh, A.; Jalali-Naini, S.G.; Wee, H.-M.; Kuo, T.-C. An imperfect multi-product production system with rework. *Sci. Iran.* **2013**, *20*, 811–823.

28. Hou, K.-L.; Lin, L.-C. Investing in setup reduction in the EOQ model with random yields under a limited capital budget. *J. Inf. Optim. Sci.* **2011**, *32*, 75–83. [CrossRef]

29. Mohan, S.; Mohan, G.; Chandrasekhar, A. Multi-item, economic order quantity model with permissible delay in payments and a budget constraint. *Eur. J. Ind. Eng.* **2008**, *2*, 446–460. [CrossRef]

30. Todde, G.; Murgia, L.; Caria, M.; Pazzona, A. A comprehensive energy analysis and related carbon footprint of dairy farms, Part 2: Investigation and modeling of indirect energy requirements. *Energies* **2018**, *11*, 463. [CrossRef]

31. Du, Y.; Hu, G.; Xiang, S.; Zhang, K.; Liu, H.; Guo, F. Estimation of the diesel particulate filter soot load based on an equivalent circuit model. *Energies* **2018**, *11*, 472. [CrossRef]

32. Cárdenas-Barrón, L.E.; Treviño-Garza, G.; Widyadana, G.A.; Wee, H.-M. A constrained multi-products EPQ inventory model with discrete delivery order and lot size. *Appl. Math. Comput.* **2014**, *230*, 359–370. [CrossRef]

33. Xua, L.; Cheng, J.-H.; Liu, P.; Wang, Q.; Xu, Z.-X.; Liu, Q.; Shen, J.-Y.; Wang, L.-J. Production of bio-fuel oil from pyrolysis of plant acidified oil. *Renew. Energy* **2018**, *130*, 910–919. [CrossRef]

34. Tomic, T.; Schneider, D.R. The role of energy from waste in circular economy and closing the loop concept-Energy analysis approach. *Renew. Sustain. Energy Rev.* **2018**, *98*, 268–287. [CrossRef]

35. Haraldsson, J.; Johansson, M.T. Review of measures for improved energy efficiency in production-related processes in the aluminium industry-from electrolysis to recycling. *Renew. Sustain. Energy Rev.* **2018**, *93*, 525–548. [CrossRef]

36. Dey, B.; Sarkar, B.; Sarkar, M.; Pareek, S. An integrated inventory model involving discrete setup cost reduction, variable safety factor, selling-price dependent demand, and investment. *Rairo-Oper. Res.* **2019**, in press. [CrossRef]

37. Sarkar, B.; Sarkar, S.; Yun, W.Y. Retailer's optimal strategy for fixed lifetime products. *Int. J. Mach. Learn. Cybern.* **2016**, *7*, 121–133. [CrossRef]

38. Sarkar, B.; Majumder, A.; Sarkar, M.; Dey, B.K.; Roy, G. Two-echelon supply chain model with manufacturing quality improvement and setup cost reduction. *J. Ind. Manag. Opt.* **2017**, *13*, 1085–1104. [CrossRef]

39. Sarkar, B.; Chaudhuri, K.S.; Moon, I. Manufacturing setup cost reduction and quality improvement for the distribution free continuous-review inventory model with a service level constraint. *J. Manuf. Syst.* **2015**, *34*, 74–82. [CrossRef]

40. Yao, X.; Zhou, J.; Zhang, J.; Boer, C.R. From intelligence manufacturing to smart manufacturing for industry 4.0 driven by next generation artificial intelligence and further on. In Proceedings of the 2017 5th International Conference on Enterprise Systems (ES), Beijing, China, 22–24 September 2017. [CrossRef]

41. Gola, A. Reliability analysis of reconfigurable manufacturing system structures using computer simulation methods. *Eksploatacja I Niezawodnosc—Maintaience Reliab.* **2019**, *21*, 90–102. [CrossRef]

42. Tayyab, M.; Sarkar, B.; Yahya, B. Imperfect Multi-Stage Lean Manufacturing System with Rework under Fuzzy Demand. *Mathematics* **2019**, *7*, 13. [CrossRef]

43. Sarkar, B. Mathematical and analytical approach for the management of defective items in a multi-stage production system. *J. Clean. Prod.* **2019**, in press. [CrossRef]

44. Kim, M.S.; Kim, J.S.; Sarkar, B.; Sarakr, M.; Iqbal, M.W. An improved way to calculate imperfect items during long-run production in an integrated inventory model with backorders. *J. Manuf. Syst.* **2018**, *47*, 153–167. [CrossRef]

45. Sarkar, B.; Sett, B.K.; Sarkar, S. Optimal production run time and inspection errors in an imperfect production system with warranty. *J. Ind. Manag. Opt.* **2018**, *14*, 267–282. [CrossRef]

46. Chenavaz, R.Y.; Jasimuddin, S.M. An analytical model of the relationship between product quality and advertising. *Eur. J. Oper. Res.* **2017**, *263*, 295–307. [CrossRef]

47. Giri, B.C.; Sharma, S. Manufacturer's pricing strategy in a two-level supply chain with competing retailers and advertising cost dependent demand. *Econ. Model.* **2014**, *38*, 102–111. [CrossRef]

48. Xiao, D.; Zhou, Y.W.; Zhong, Y.; Xie, W. Optimal cooperative advertising and ordering policies for a two-echelon supply chain. *Comp. Ind. Eng.* **2018**, in press. [CrossRef]

49. Noh, J.S.; Kim, J.S.; Sarkar, B. Two-echelon supply chain coordination with advertising demand under Stackelberg game policy. *Eur. J. Ind. Eng.* **2019**, in press. [CrossRef]

50. Karaöz, M.; Erçlu, A.; Sütçü, A. An EOQ model with price and time dependent demand under the influence of complement and substitute product's selling-prices. *J. Alanya Fac. Bus.—Alanya Isletme Fakültesi Dergisi* **2011**, *3*, 21–32.

51. Sana, S.S. Price-sensitive demand for perishable items—An EOQ model. *App. Math. Mod.* **2011**, *217*, 6248–6259.

52. Pal, B.; Sana, S.S.; Chaudhuri, K. Multi-item EOQ model while demand is sales price and price break sensitive. *Eco. Mod.* **2012**, *29*, 2283–2288. [CrossRef]

53. Sarkar, B.; Mandal, P.; Sarkar, S. An EMQ model with price and time dependent demand under the effect of reliability and inflation. *Appl. Math. Comput.* **2014**, *231*, 414–421. [CrossRef]

54. Sarkar, B.; Sarkar, S. Variable deterioration and demand-An inventory model. *Econ. Mod.* **2013**, *31*, 548–556. [CrossRef]

55. Azadeh, A.; Paknafs, B. Integrated simulation modeling of business, maintenance and production systems for concurrent improvement of lead time, cost and production rate. *Ind. Eng. Manag. Syst.* **2017**, *15*, 403–431.

56. Malik, I.A.; Sarkar, B. Optimizing a Multi-Product Continuous—Review Inventory Model With Uncertain Demand, Quality Improvement, Setup Cost Reduction, and Variation Control in Lead Time. *IEEE Access* **2018**, *6*, 36176–36187. [CrossRef]

57. Sarkar, I.; Moon, I. Improved quality, setup cost reduction, and variable backorder costs in an imperfect production process. *Int. J. Prod. Econ.* **2014**, *155*, 204–213. [CrossRef]

58. Sarkar, B.; Mondal, B.; Sarkar, S. Quality improvement and backorder price discount under controllable lead time in an inventory model. *J. Manuf. Syst.* **2015**, *35*, 26–36. [CrossRef]

59. Sarkar, B.; Majumdar, A. Integrated vendor–buyer supply chain model with vendor's setup cost reduction. *Appl. Math. Comput.* **2013**, *224*, 362–371. [CrossRef]

60. Sarkar, B.; Saren, S.; Sinha, D.; Hur, S. Effect of unequal lot sizes, variable setup cost, and carbon emission cost in a supply chain model. *Math. Probl. Eng.* **2015**, *2015*, 1–13. [CrossRef]

61. Majumdar, A.; Guchhait, R.; Sarkar, B. Manufacturing quality improvement and setup cost reduction in an integrated vendor-buyer supply chain model. *Eur. J. Ind. Eng.* **2017**, *13*, 588–612. [CrossRef]

4

The Quantitative Analysis of Workers' Stress Due to Working Environment in the Production System of the Automobile Part Manufacturing Industry

Muhammad Omair [1], Misbah Ullah [2], Baishakhi Ganguly [3], Sahar Noor [2], Shahid Maqsood [2] and Biswajit Sarkar [4,*]

[1] Department of Industrial Engineering, Jalozai Campus, University of Engineering and Technology, Peshawar 25000, Pakistan
[2] Department of Industrial Engineering, University of Engineering and Technology, Peshawar 25000, Pakistan
[3] Department of Mathematics & Statistics, Banasthali University, Rajasthan 304022, India
[4] Department of Industrial and Management Engineering, Hanyang University, Ansan 15588, Korea
[*] Correspondence: bsbiswajitsarkar@gmail.com.

Abstract: Production now requires the management of production processes and operations on the basis of customers' demand to ensure the best combination of technology and humans in the system. The role of the humans in the production process is very significant for the production and quality of the product. The production system depends upon technology and human factors and is highly influenced by the working conditions of the workers, that is, work load, physical, dealings, job timings and so forth. In the current global economy, minimizing production costs is a serious priority for the industries. However, the costs of bad working conditions increase the intensity of the average stress among employees to cause extra costs by affecting the workers' efficiency and products' quality, which is invisible in the eyes of decision makers. This research identifies the cost of workers' stress by developing a linkage between the economic benefits of the firms and the social upgrading of the workers. A numerical example of a production based system is performed to represent the real-time application of the proposed model. A sensitivity analysis is also carried out to quantify the impact of average stress among workers on the production system. Sequential quadratic programming is used to optimize the given nonlinear model for production planning. The optimal results influence ergonomics awareness and the relationship with the safety culture among managers in a firm. It is concluded that efficient and effective production cannot be possible without considering the working conditions of humans in the firm. Managerial insights are also generated from the implications of the results and sensitivity analysis.

Keywords: production; imperfect production; defective rate; workplace stress; workers' efficiency

---

1. Introduction

The production industry is considered one of the key indicators for the development of a nation. Human resources are a significant approach to a firm's performance and it is believed that the most important assets of the firm are its people. The workforce has been an important variable for management to maximize the revenues [1]. Despite these assessments, managers are giving a relatively low priority to workers. That is the reason why, when a firm needs to cut costs, they first look to the investments in the worker, that is, wages, training and firing [2]. Human workers require social development and deserve a good working environment to avoid workplace stress. It is the responsibility of the firm to provide a safe and healthy environment for the workers for better performance and productivity.

Work-related stress and workplace violence are widely recognized as major challenges to occupational health and safety [3–5]. Most injuries at work occur from physical stress and the strain to perform repetitive and overused tasks, over a long time, which results in damaged joints, muscles, and tendons [6]. Job stress can be defined as the occurrence of harmful physical and emotional response when the requirement of the work does not fulfil the capability of worker [7]. It is considered as a major challenge to the individual on the basis of mental and physical health, and it also damages the organizational health [8]. Job insecurity and physical exertion at the workplace also cause stress. Stressed workers are more likely to be unhealthy, less motivated, poor productivity and a less safe working environment, which ultimately produces a bad impact on the success factor of the firm in a competitive market [9]. It is estimated that job stress costs the state economy, health care and lost productivity. The latest figures state that the estimated cost of work-related stress costs the UK economy are £7 billion a year in sick pay and lost production [10].

Even in advanced high-technology based industries, the physical demands of work are still high, which is directed to produce the environment of physical hazards and work injuries [11]. However, limited work has been done on the impact of stresses on work performance. Similarly, many factors can reduce the impact of work stress during work, but also a very little work has been done to cover these individual and organizational factors. An important source of stress is job strain, which is faced by workers at the workplace. Job insecurity and physical exertion at workplace also cause stress. Even in advanced high-technology based industries, the physical demands of work are still high, which is directed to produce an environment of physical hazards and work injuries [12].

Traditionally decision makers consider common costs, that is, manufacturing, labor cost, holding cost and maintenance cost to take decisions in inventory and production systems. Despite the significant importance of non-ergonomic working conditions and work injuries, these are ignored. Managers cannot justify the investments in any project regarding the working environment unless it is economically feasible and beneficial to the firm. Accordingly, to manage the workplace, it is extremely significant to understand the costs and economic benefits of breakeven time [13]. This study represents the significance of controlling workplace stress due to the working environment through a mathematical model. The inclusion of stress level among workers is anticipated in considering effective and efficient production. The mathematical analysis of average stress is a big contribution, which is inversely related to the worker's efficiency and product's quality. The contribution of this research is extended to quantify the production loss and required labor due to the stress. The analysis provides a platform for production managers to make investments in favor of workers and can be utilized to support the research with the objective to determine the factors that bring awareness and a safety culture in the firm.

This paper is structured as follows: Section 2 present a literature survey regarding stress level, and imperfect production. Furthermore, Section 3 is related to the verbal problem statement to discuss the imperfect production system and drawbacks in the form of workplace stress. The formulation of a mathematical model considering notation, assumptions along with solution methodology is given in Section 4. Section 5 depict the numerical experiment for the practical implication of the mathematical model including data collection and data analysis. Section 6 is related to the numerical results of the experiment performed in the automobile part manufacturing firm. Section 7 presents the sensitivity analysis of the model to determine the effect of workers' stress on the production system. The directions and recommendations for the support of management firms are also given. Finally, Section 8 finds the conclusions of this study.

2. Literature Survey

Effective and efficient production systems rely on the working conditions of the worker. The objective is to improve the working environment by optimising the effort of workers to enhance the firm's performance and promote human well-being. Most of the ergonomic-related work in developing countries is based in the industrial sector. Researchers also worked to create a link between working environment and cost. But the problem arises of how to quantify the invisible average costs of work-related injuries [14]. There is no specific and unique methodology in the literature, which could understand and calculate the cost of displeasure due to bad work conditions and the average cost of pain due to work-related injuries.

Most of the researchers have worked on the economic and environmental aspect of the production system i.e., [15–18]. However, now a work has been started to encourage the social dimension of the system, and in this direction several authors contributed to measure the cost associated in such cases. The cost of work injuries due to bad working environment is calculated by using the friction method, capital method, and willingness to pay method [19]. Furthermore, it also observed that working hours have a huge impact on work-related injuries because longer shift timings increase the probability of an accident [20]. Ruhm (2000) observes a good relationship between macroeconomic conditions and mortality, which he attributes to bad working conditions, the physical exertion of the worker, and work stress when job hours are extended [21]. Work stressors are environmental factors at work that lead to individual strain, that is, potentially harmful reactions of the individual [22].

The most common job stressors considered by researchers are chronic, for example, job conflict. Few researchers also focus on the shorter-term stressors, also called acute stressors. Examples of acute stressors might include something as annoying as a research assistant encountering computer shutdowns [23]. Chronic stressors are usually conceptualized and measured generically (i.e., the same for all jobs), while measures of events or acute stressors tend to be more job-specific, both conceptually and operationally [24]. This study considers the chronic stressors. The questionnaire and the data collection are based on the chronic stressors among the workers. The consequences of high stress among workers are production loss, bad quality work, work injuries, hiring new workers, time lost, legislation, legal expenses, lost jobs and training.

Knauth (1998) [25] discussed the effect of different attributes of working hours on fatigue. Early morning shifts, night shifts, extended working hours, and short recesses are the significant factors, which may cause accidents at work and reduce productivity. The concept behind the risk of fatigue among workers due to shift schedule is to keep it simple [26]. Inconvenient working environments cause stress, which does not allow the maximum utilization of personal ability to perform well [27]. A global survey estimated that due to high stress levels, 90% of the workers were disengaged and among 57% were absolutely disconnected from their work [28]. Another issue caused by increase stress level among worker is production loss. If a worker is normal, then he can work efficiently and effectively to achieve his target production, on the other hand if he feel any stress or pressure then definitely it will cause production loss [29]. Abraham Maslow imagined the categorized employee behaviour patterns in five levels of survival, security, social, stability and satisfaction for the knowledge-based global economy [30].

The effect of intangible cost on production and inventory can be analysed in various production and supply chain models. Most of the researchers ([31–36]) worked on imperfect production systems to help the managers in planning and controlling the bad quality items. However, very few researchers analyzed the cause to reduce the imperfect production in the system. There are many factors affecting the production flow to produce imperfection in the form of reworks, rejections and scraps. Errors can be generated by man, machine or material. This research covers the imperfect production occurring due to the average stress among unskilled workers caused by non-ergonomic working conditions. Previous studies analyzed the effect of stress on the efficiency of the workers and still its effect on the production system was missing. Mansour (2016) [26] only related the stress among workers due to bad working conditions and injuries to the efficiency of the systems. However, this research paper considers the stress level among workers that not only affects the efficiency of the system but also the defective rate. The contribution of this study is to incorporate the workplace depending efficiency and defective rate in the production model as an extension. The impact of stress on the production system is valid theoretically but still there is a gap to find it in tangible dimensions. The production model is developed to analyze the quantitative effect of stress on the total cost and required workers in the production system. The mathematical analysis of the proposed production model is evident to provide the importance of the good working environment, where there is less human stress to avoid the economic loss due to degraded efficiency and high defective rate.

3. Verbal Problem Statement

The research is performed by converting the theoretical idea into the mathematical model and be analysed by the nonlinear programming technique. The model considered an optimization problem to minimize the total cost of production system provided with the limitation of budget, production, and inventory space. The launch of a new product by the combination of human and technology is a big challenge for production planning and control. The developing countries are mainly concerned about manpower as compared to technology because the firms can easily acquire cheap labor against expensive high tech machines. That is the reason, in such scenarios the efficiency and the performance of unskilled labor is highly dependent upon ergonomic conditions and other moral support from the firm, which may result in a high stress level among workers in typical production firms. The issue can be clearly highlighted by considering a mass production system of automobile spare part industry, where there is a need to manage the resources in the form of unskilled workers and machines. The machines are performing the same operation of mass production and worker is working on it. The task might be repetitive or time consuming with an effect of bad working conditions. A single machine problem is considered to experiment the research idea represented in this paper. The flow diagram of imperfect quality production system of three automobile parts A, B, and C parts is illustrated in Figure 1.

The raw material from the inventory transported to the production department, where operators are working on machines for manufacturing of a automobile parts. A production planing and control decisions are looking to find the resources in terms of machines and labor required in production department, which depends upon the production rate and demand rate. The efficiency of operators is influenced by the average stress. The finished parts are shifted to quality department for inspection, where reworked parts are backtracked to machines while the scrapped items are recycled. After managing the imperfect products, the finished goods are transported to the final inventory. The defective items (bad quality items) are produced due to errors caused by man, machine or material, that is the reason the total defective rate is introduced to be the sum of the initial and variable defective rate. The former is the result of machine errors while the latter depends upon the average stress among workers. The main reasons for psychological stress among workers are injuries, moral degradation and so forth.

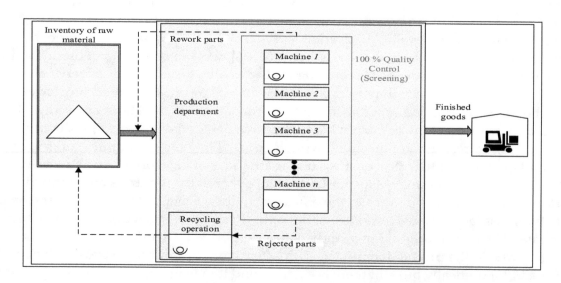

Figure 1. Representation of imperfect quality production system.

Let x_i represents a scaled input qualitative variable. The relationship between these qualitative input variables can be mapped into a single value to represent an average stress level among employees. Accordingly, the stress can be expressed as given in Equation (1).

$$s \quad = \quad \sum_{i=1}^{n}(w_i.x_i) \tag{1}$$

where s is stress level; x_i is the scaled elements of the work conditions that cause stress; w_i is the normalized weights.

3.1. Stress Level and Efficiency

The stressed worker cannot provide his best utilization according to his capabilities. The affiliation of the worker's stress level with efficiency can be formulated as given in Equation (2), where ρ is efficiency of the workers. The efficiency is directly proportional to the average stress (s) and the relationship is drawn by a curve as shown in Figure 2 [26].

$$\rho(s) \quad = \quad e^{-s/m} \tag{2}$$

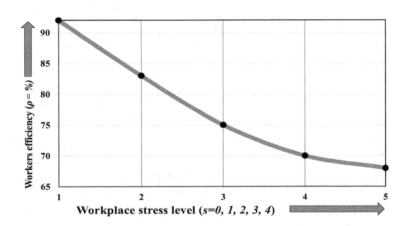

Figure 2. Relation between workers' stress and efficiency.

3.2. Stress Level and Defective Rate

The expression for defective rate includes variable defective rate depending upon the average stress with initial defective rate to cover the rest of factors, that is, machine, material and so forth, is given as in Equation (3). The Initial defective rate is considered to follow a uniform distribution. A direct relationship between stress and defective rate can be shown as in Figure 3, where μ is the total defective rate of the production system, μ_0 is the initial defective rate, τ and ϵ are the scaling factors and s is average stress among worker.

$$\mu(s) \quad = \quad \mu_0 + \tau \times s^{\epsilon} \tag{3}$$

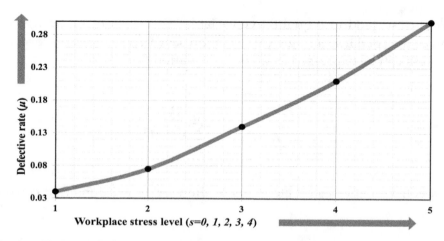

Figure 3. Relation between workers' stress and defective rate.

4. Formal Problem Statement

4.1. Assumptions

There are following assumptions for the proposed model.

1. The model is considered for multiple type items.
2. All products are screened and screening cost is incurred on each item [37].
3. Defective rate is stress level-dependent and the initial defective rate is considered as uniformly distributed.
4. Average efficiency of workers is also a function of stress level.
5. The defective items are reworked to make the perfect quality products.
6. Some parts are rejected after reworking the operation, which is recycled [38].

4.2. Notation

The research is based on the optimization of the decision variables to provide significant support to the managers and experts in production planing and control phase. Indeed this research provides a production resource planing for any production system with given data. There are three decision variables proposed in the mathematical modelling, that is, cycle time (T), number of machines required (K_j), and number of workers required (L_j). The cycle time provides data regarding the total time of the production system to process all the required parts with respect to the given demand. There are K_j number of machines working similar operations, the capacity of the system depends on the number of machines. Similarly, the number of workers L_j depend upon number of machines. The proposed research based on mathematical model will be effectively and efficiently providing information to the managers regarding exact number of machines and number of workers required to process parts by fulfilling the annual demand. The notations of the parameters and decision variables of the proposed imperfect production model are enlisted comprehensively as.

4.3. Mathematical Modelling

A mathematical model based on a single-stage production system with defective in the form of reworked and rejected items include fixed and variable costs, that is, capital cost, labor cost, setup cost, manufacturing cost, inventory carrying cost, reworking cost, energy cost and recycling cost. The capital cost is time-related, which consists of initial investment for purchasing and installing machine units. Cost of manufacturing in this model is associated with the machine/workstation used to manufacture the product. The total inventory of the production system is holding as given in Figure 4, where P is the production rate of the system, D is the demand, $I(t)$ is the total inventory of the system, the cycle time T is divided into small time fractions (i.e., t_1, t_2, and, t_3), h_1 and h_2 are the parameters used to represent the heights of the inventories during production and reworking process respectively. It is a continuous production scenario for one production cycle T. The model is based on pure production system where the production is going on and the demand D is also fulfilling simultaneously during t_1 and t_2. The reworking operations are done during time interval t_2. The production stopped at t_2, then there will be no production and inventory is going down to zero during t_3. Theocratically, the total cost of production is the sum of capital cost, setup cost, manufacturing cost, holding, backorder cost, energy, inspection, reworking and recycling cost. Mathematically, these fractions of the total cost can be mathematically calculated as given in Appendix A for the support of managers and industries.

By considering the interaction between the labors and machines, the total cost function is the sum of the fixed costs to represent the capital cost and variable costs in terms of labor cost. The objective function is to minimize the total cost of production as given in Equation (4).

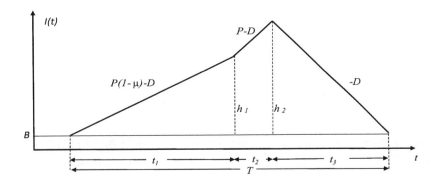

Figure 4. Economic production Quantity model with variable defective rate and backorders.

$$
\begin{aligned}
\text{Minimize cost} \quad = \quad & \text{Capital cost} + \text{Setup cost} + \text{Manufacturing cost} + \text{Labor cost} + \\
& \text{Holding cost} + \text{Backorder cost} + \text{Energy cost} + \text{Reworking cost} + \\
& \text{Screening cost} + \text{Recycling cost}
\end{aligned}
\tag{4}
$$

The mathematical form of the objective function to minimize the total cost of production can be given as in Equation (5). The model is limited by the budget, production, and capacity constraints.

$$
\begin{aligned}
Min\ TC \ = \ \sum_{j=1}^{J} \Bigg[& \frac{K_j V_j}{T} + \frac{S_j}{T} + M_j D_j + \frac{\rho(s) L_j W_j}{T} + \left(\frac{H_j D_j T \left(1 - \left(1 + \mu(s) + \mu(s)^2 \right) \frac{D_j}{P_j} \right)}{2} \right) + \frac{H_j B_j^2 (1-\mu(s))}{2 D_j T (1-\mu(s) - \frac{D_j}{P_j})} \\
& - H_j B_j \Bigg) + \left(\frac{F_j B_j}{T} + \frac{y_j B_j^2 (1-\mu(s))}{2 D_j T (1-\mu(s) - \frac{D_j}{P_j})} \right) + \pi U_j D_j + \mu(s) M_j D_j + \frac{\theta_j}{T} + D_j \psi_j + \eta u_j \mu(s) D_j \Bigg]
\end{aligned}
\tag{5}
$$

Subject to

Budget constraint: The budget constraint is the limitation given by the management on the availability of the resources. There is a cost associated with the machines and number of workers. The addition or removal of the machine or worker in the production plan will effect the cost budget and balance. That is the reason the combination of the workers and machines should by utilized in this way to not exceed than the total budget as represented by Equation (6).

$$ K_j V_j + W_j L_j \ = M_j \tag{6} $$

Production function constraint: The production function provides a constraint to relate the production quantity with the number of workers and number of machines. Where there is a combine effect of availability factor A_f (%) for machines and workers, and an efficiency (ρ) of the workers is multiplied with the number of workers. The α and β are the respective shares of machines and workers in the production system depending upon the level of automation.

$$D_j T = A_f K_j^{\alpha} \left(\rho(s) L_j \right)^{\beta} \tag{7}$$

Space constraint: The inventory of the production system is also controlled depending upon the capacity of the storage system or warehouse. Therefore, the space constrain (volume based) is very important to limit the maximum quantity depending on the size of each part.

$$c_j D_j T \leq C_j \tag{8}$$

Non-negative constraint: All the decision variable i.e., T, K_j, and L_j are non negative.

$$T, K_j, L_j \geq 0 \tag{9}$$

5. NumericaL Experiment

Most of the data used for analysis of the proposed mode has been taken from the numerical experiment done by Sarkar et al., (2014) [39] except the data related to the average stress among workers in a production system.

5.1. Data Collection

The average stress is measured by the workplace stress scale on the basis of a questionnaire as given in Appendix B. The scale was designed and made by the Marlin Company, North Haven, CT, USA, and the American Institute of Stress (AIS) in 1978, Yonkers, NY, USA [40]. There are two basic type of stressors, that is, chronic and acute. Chronic stressors are usually conceptualized and measured generically (i.e., the same for all jobs), while measures of events or acute stressors tend to be more job-specific, both conceptually and operationally [23]. The chronic stressors are considered to collect the data from the workers because the research covered basic but not specific working conditions and the production system rely on long term data for making decisions. That is the reason a questionnaire is considered to reflect the data from the workers facing generic stresses throughout their job. The questionnaire is standard and general, which can be applied to any circumstances to find the average stress among workers. Each question indicates the specific performance factor of the worker chronically and in generic, that is, job satisfaction, safe working conditions, deadlines, job pressure, skills utilization and so forth. Responses of the workers are collected by using a five-point scale starting from one to five representing never, rarely, sometimes, often and very often, respectively [41]. This scale of questionnaires was utilized to evaluate the function of occupational stress among workers [42]. A survey was conducted among five automobile spare parts industries. A Total of 150 questionnaires were distributed among unskilled workers. The demographics of the participating workers are as follows.

1.   All workers are participated in the survey irrespective of the age and health.
2.   They are working on the production floor as an operator or helper.
3.   The respondent unskilled workers are performing manual activities, e.g., loading, unloading, helping, operating, heavy working, manual forging, cutting etc.

The survey was conducted during fall 2018. It was performed at an Industrial estate in Pakistan. The data was collected from the workers in two ways—those who could understand filled the questionnaire by themselves, otherwise most of them were interviewed for collecting the data. The workers were chosen randomly to avoid bias. Almost five general manufacturing industries related to the automobile part were selected for the collection of data for workplace stress to reflect the general conditions of workers. These industries are working as a separate firms to manufacture automobile spare parts, each consist of almost 400–500 workers. 150 workers were selected randomly among total 2200 workers from five industries (at the rate of 6%), where 130 workers returned the questionnaires and among which 12 were rejected due to incomplete and unreliable information. Therefore, a total 118 questionnaires were considered for the analysis of this research work and the response rate was about 78.7%. The sample size of 118 is enough to reflect the population of the workers among manufacturing industries.

5.2. Data Analysis

For the reliability and adequacy of the data, a Cronbach's reliability test was performed. The objective of the test is to check the average differences among each data. The test value for each question is calculated, which was more than 0.7 and is commonly recommended for the validation and reliability of the data. As all values result were above 0.70, a good reliability resulted for data sets, and these data sets were accepted for further analysis [43]. The value of stress among workers was found to be 2.6 as a normal average on a five-point Likert scale. The formula for central tendency (mean) was utilized to find the mean average of the workplace stress among workers. The value 2.6 value was considered as a general average stress existed among unskilled workers on the production floor of manufacturing system. The value of workplace stress above 2.6 will be assumed as "High Stressed" and lower value will be considered as a "Low stressed". The five-point Likert scale had qualitative levels from 1 to 5, tagged as never, rarely, sometimes, often, and very often respectively. The never and very often stress levels are the ideal situations for industry. The sensitivity analysis is performed on the basis of these mentioned stress levels to find the changing cost of production and number of labor required.

The data related to the production of each automobile part on the basis of demand, production rate, backorders and, energy utilization are given as in Table 1. The data related to the production rate, setup, holding, demand and manufacturing cost are taken from the work done by Sarkar et al., (2014) [39]. The data related to the energy, machine cost, defective rate, recycling cost, and labor costs are considered directly from the industry because these are depending on the industrial conditions and state regulations. The inspection data is collected from the research study of Sarkar (2016) [44]. The data related to stress are incorporated by the detailed survey using the questionnaire as discussed in the data collection section.

Table 1. Data related to the production and demand.

Item Type	Demand (Units)	Production Rate (Units/Year)	Backorders (Units)	Scrap (%)	Energy (KWh)
A	180	450	25	0.2	0.45
B	200	550	30	0.3	0.5
C	210	580	35	0.4	0.58

The data related to the cost of production are given in Table 2, that is, manufacturing, holding, setup, backorder, labor and machine costs. Manufacturing costs includes running costs incurred on each item. The backorder cost is applied for extra resources when shortages are occurred to fulfill the demand. When parts are transported from production department to quality department, imperfection is produced.

Table 2. Data related to the production costs.

Item Type	Manufacturing Cost ($/Unit)	Setup Cost ($)	Holding Cost ($/Unit/Year)	Fixed Backorder ($)	Variable Backorder ($/Unit)	Machine Cost ($)	Labor Cost ($/Unit)
A	6	45	47	9	0.9	450	1.7
B	7	50	50	10	1	500	2
C	8	55	56	10.5	1.25	580	2.2

The cost related to imperfect production is given as in Table 3. Inspection is carried out after production at quality department, where all parts are checked for defective and sorted the pass, rework and rejected parts. Inspection process acquire cost to perform some visual as well as lab testing. Recycling include process of converting the semi-finished item into raw material to reduce the waste and carry a cost.

Table 3. Data related to the imperfect production.

Item Type	Variable Inspection Cost ($/Unit)	Fixed Inspection Cost ($)	Recycling Cost ($/Unit)	Energy Cost ($/Unit)	Initial Defective Rate (%)
A	0.01	9.5	1.8	5	2.5
B	0.02	10	2	5	2.5
C	0.03	10.5	2.5	5	2.5

6. Results and Discussions

The model is nonlinear and complex enough to solve by using any analytical method. However, there are many iterative methods available to find the optimal solution of nonlinear optimization model with many decision variables and more constraints. The sequential quadratic programming (SQP) are the most effective methods to solve nonlinear equations [45]. The method of SQP is based on Newton's method in the best way to deal with the unconstrained optimizations [46]. The SQP deals with the quadratic programming problems, to find an optimal solution. SQP methods represent the state of the art in nonlinear programming methods. Schittkowski [47] has implemented and tested a version that outperforms every other tested method in terms of efficiency, accuracy, and percentage of successful solutions, over a large number of test problems. The method closely mimics Newton's method for unconstrained optimization. At each major iteration, an approximation is made of the Hessian using a quasi-Newton updating method. This is then used to generate a QP subproblem whose solution is used to form a search direction for a line search procedure.

The proposed production model in the form of nonlinear problem was coded in MATLAB for the analysis and by using the methodology of SQP, optimal solution and results are obtained [48]. The optimal solution of the production model is given as in Table 4, which is a complete production plan for the manufacturing of three items A, B and C. To meet the target in the form of demand rate and by the capability of the production system in term of production rate, the required machines and labor for each item is calculated. The cycle time of the complete production plan is almost three months (0.329 years). The optimal solution of the imperfect production model, that is, total cost (TC) considering the impact of workers' stress is found as $428,248.

Table 4. Optimal solution of the production model.

Sr. No.	Item Type	Decision Variable	Optimal Result	Objective Function (TC)
1		(T)	0.329 years	
2	A	K_1	56 machines	
3	B	K_2	60 machines	
4	C	K_3	60 machines	\$428,248
5	A	L_1	111 workers	
6	B	L_2	123 workers	
7	C	L_3	131 workers	

The optimal results and solutions have been found to support the production planning phase of the manufacturing firm. Optimal requirements of resources in the form of workers and machines are quantified with the minimum expense of total cost (TC). This paper presents the impact of average stress on the production system with defective rate and workers' efficiency as a function of workers' stress. However, stress elements are generated among worker, whatever their cost, such stress factors have personal as well as economic consequences and can cause poor productivity and unavailability. Stress factors are required to be calculated economically for the benefit of decision makers. That is the reason, further analysis is required to find the sensitivity of the model by the effect of stress levels.

7. Sensitivity Analysis

Stresses can be divided into chronic and acute [23]. Given the differences between acute and chronic stressors, they may differ in their relations with individual strains and performance [24]. Stressors that are more job specific (whether chronic or acute) may have the greatest impact on individual strains and performance, because they are most salient to employees in a particular job. The chronic job stressors are considered. The stress factor is a variable function and it depends upon various aspects of the production system for example, repetitive and cyclic work type are common in mass production systems to make the job more boring and tedious, which is one of the causes of high stress. However, workers feel less stress in case of job production where the management invested on the training and development for handling a variety of tasks. Similarly, stress also depending upon the firm's policies regarding workers' health care and safety. Sometimes, there are a lot of medical facilities and insurances available for labors in low-income management firms and on the other hand, a very few incentives are available in high-quality firms.

There is a need to check the model on different levels of stress existed across various production firms. The stress factor negatively affects the workers' performance and efficiency, which is directed to lessen the workforce and increase the number of rejections. Hence there are two changes occur, firstly the actual number of labor will be reduced from the standard requirements due to the decreased performance level and secondly, the output production will be reduced to meet the target level. Therefore, to compensate the loss efficiency and maintain the output quantity at a certain level, the amount of labor should be increased. This can be done either by hiring extra labor in terms of cost or increasing the production schedule time. In both cases, the total cost (TC) will be increased. The detailed analysis and variations of TC and labors at each level of stress are given as in Table 5. These cases are given as following.

1. The scale can divided into five values of s levels from never, rarely, sometimes, often, and very often. An analysis is carried to quantify the exact amount of labor required by increasing the level of workers' stress ranging from $s = 0$ to $s = 4$ as given in Table 5. In first case, by considering L_1 it is observed that when stress is increasing then there is no changes occurs. The reason is the demand for first part A is almost 180, which can be easily fulfilled by the same number of workers, that is, 111. The change in average stress would not create any variation in the production system to disturb the manual workers.

2. By comparing the status of the labors required for part B and C, that is, L_2 and L_3 respectively at extreme levels of the stress, the labors required at $s = 0$ and $s = 4$ are 119 and 126 for item B while 124 and 137 for item C respectively. Indeed, the analysis is providing a quantitative impact of the stress level on the number of workers required in the production system.

3. Since the stress is a variable factor and there is also a need to analyze the sensitivity of the proposed model for the TC by changing the stress among workers. It is clear that the model is sensitive to the stress on the basis of TC and labors required for each part, that is, the total cost of production and labor requirements are increased by increasing the stress from level to level. However, the mathematical calculations are required. When comparing the extreme levels of the workplace stress, it is found that at $s = 0$, the total cost of production is around \$420,601, and at $s = 4$, the value increased to \$432,410.

4. The machines (K_1, K_2, and K_3) are not changing by increasing the average stress among the workers because the capital cost is enough that it cannot be effected by the average stress among workers. The efficiency $\rho(s)$ of the workers is inversely proportional whereas the defective rate $\mu(s)$ is directly proportional to the workplace stress.

Hence the mathematical analysis for the impact of the stress on the workers required and TC is providing an evidence to think and plan for the good working environment to the workers. Where, there is less chances to induce stress among workers due to which the efficiency of the workers is at a maximum level and there are less chances to create rejections due to workers. These meaningful results in different scenarios are beneficial to understand the economic loss (almost \$40,000) and consequences of the production system due to high-level stress among workers, which will pressurize the managers to improve the safety culture and working environment.

Table 5. Sensitivity analysis of the model with respect to the stress level of worker.

Parameter	Stress Level					
	$s = 0$	$s = 1$	$s = 2$	$s = 2.6$	$s = 3$	$s = 4$
				(This Paper)		
TC	420,601	422,469	426,464	428,248	429,438	432,410
L_1	111	111	111	111	111	111
L_2	119	120	123	123	123	126
L_3	124	126	131	131	132	137
K_1	56	56	56	56	56	56
K_2	60	60	60	60	60	60
K_3	60	60	60	60	60	60
$\rho(s)$	1	0.93	0.875	0.84	0.818	0.765
$\mu(s)$	0.025	0.035	0.053	0.066	0.076	0.105

8. Conclusions

This paper investigates the meaningful hidden costs, which are not considered by management in the planning phase of the production system. The injuries and the poor working conditions are the causes of the high workers' stress. The stress exists among workers in every environment, but the intensity and level of stress are different. Poor work conditions will amplify the stress among employees, which will significantly influence the production system. On the other hand, a more ergonomic workplace and safer practices will benefit the corporations. In-depth, the stress affects the efficiency of the workers and production rate causes the management to hire more workers and material for compensation causes more cost. The average stress among workers of traditional spare part industries is calculated by the detailed survey for practical application of the model. The incorporation of stress level in production enhances the quality of decision making to consider for the optimal solution. To get the optimal solution, the solution methodology of sequential quadratic programming (SQP) is selected, which uses Langrage multiplier directly and is based on the equations of Karush-Kuhn-Tucker (KKT). The sensitivity analysis provides a detailed analysis of the stress at each level in different scenarios for the sensitivity of the proposed imperfect production model. The results addressed the increased amount of invested labor and defective rate due to the increased stress level. These increments affect the total cost of production, which are not estimated and are ignored. The objective value of this research is to create awareness among production managers by calculating the tangible cost of workplace stress to control.

A set of recommendations are drawn from the optimal results obtained by the numerical analysis of production model. In case of high stress, almost 3, 11, and 21 extra workforce required for part A, B, and C respectively ($15,020) and overall economic loss is in the production cost is almost $47,000. The study motivates the decision makers to also include the quantitative factor of workplace stress in the production planing and control phase. The managers need to aware about the causing factors of stress among workers to minimize the economic loss (almost $47,000). The data collection and data analysis from the detailed questionnaire provide a better understanding of each performance factor related to the worker stress, which can be analysed for improving the average efficiency of the workers. It is one of the social responsibility of the production system to improve and maintain the workers' job satisfaction, safe working conditions, work deadlines, job pressure and skills utilization to avoid inducing stress. Furthermore, by this research the managers are required to calculate tangibly the average stress among workers quarterly or bimonthly for efficient and effective production with minimum rejections.

The understanding and the extensions of the proposed model can be extended into a socially responsible production model, one of the significant and major areas, but unfortunately it has less value in the eyes of managers. Future extensions of the models are also possible under certain conditions. Demand as a function of a sustainable product can be incorporated for better results. The purposed model concluded that stress among workers affects the production system due to the efficiency of workers and defective items. There is a need to make production more reliable by considering intangible costs, which seem invisible but ultimately affect the total cost of production under variable production quantity. A long-term strategic analysis is also necessary to represent the stress affecting capital units (machines). In addition, the detailed validation of the quantitative impact of workplace stress on the production is also required, which might include a survey based on questionnaires. The respondents will be the industrial managers, experts, and academicians. The objective is to validate the changes occurred in the production cost due to change in the workplace stress as an outcome of this research. Furthermore the proposed model can be compared against the research work done by Sarkar et al. (2014) [39] on the basis of the total cost by considering the same assumptions. The data collected from the manufacturing firms can be utilized to find the stress levels of the industries on the basis of the collected data. The analysis could be helpful for industries to identify the weak areas and the potential to improve their stress levels to achieve fewer rejections and higher efficiency in the production system. Overall, this research creates an awareness among managers to understand the economic value of workers' stress level in production.

Author Contributions: All the authors contributed equally at every stage of this research work. However, the individual contributions in the research study are as following i.e., writing–original draft preparation and methodology, M.O.; writing–review and editing, S.N.; resources and investigation, M.U.; software, S.M.; data curation and formal analysis, B.G.; supervision and conceptualization, B.S.

Indices

j the index used to indicate the number of items, $j = 1, 2, ..., J$

Decision variables

n number of cycles (number)

T	Cycle time of production (years)
L_j	Number of labors work to manufacture jth item (numbers)
K_j	Number of capital units utilized to manufacture jth item (numbers)

Parameters

W_j	average wage of labor to manufacture jth item (\$/labor)
B_j	backorder of jth item (\$/unit/year)
F_j	fixed backorder cost to fulfill the shortages of jth item (\$/year)
y_j	variable backorder cost to fulfill the shortages of item jth (\$/unit)
H_j	holding cost of each item per cycle (\$/unit/year)
P_j	production rate (units/year)
V_j	cost of each machine unit require to manufacture jth item (\$/machine/year)
D_j	demand rate, units per planning period (unit/year)
U_j	units of energy utilised to manufacture jth item (kwh/unit)
s	average stress among workers (number)
m	scale element for stress level of worker (constant)
S_j	setup cost for jth item (\$/year)
R_j	reworking cost of jth item (\$/unit)
α	labor share (%)
β	capital share (%)
A_f	availability factor (%)
θ_j	fixed inspection cost of item jth (\$/year)
ψ_j	variable inspection cost of item jth (\$/unit)
π_j	cost of energy per unit required for jth item (\$/kWh/unit)
η_j	scrap rate for recycling (%)
ν_j	recycling cost of item jth (\$/unit)
$\mu(s)$	total defective rate (percentage)
μ_0	initial defective rate (percentage)
τ	scaling parameter (positive constant)
ϵ	shape parameter (positive constant)
c	capacity of each item (%)
C	total capacity of inventory (%)
$\rho(s)$	the average efficiency of workers (%)
$I(t)$	total inventory of the production system (units)
TC	total cost of production model(\$/cycle)

Appendix A

Generally, managers are facing complexities to calculate the total cost of production. Therefore, a mathematical expressions of all the costs i.e., setup, manufacturing, labor, energy, inspection, reworking, recycling, and holding cost as a part of production system are represented from Equations (A1)–(A8).

Capital cost (CC)

This cost is an independent of the production quantity. It is time related, which consists of initial investment and setup cost of production as given in Equation. Cost of capital in this model is associated with the machine/workstation used to manufacture product.

$$CC = \sum_{j=1}^{J} \frac{K_j V_j}{T} \tag{A1}$$

Setup cost (SC)

The fixed cost including initial cost for each setup of the production system.

$$SC = \sum_{j=1}^{J} \frac{S_j}{T} \tag{A2}$$

Manufacturing cost (MC)

The basic cost depending on the production quantity of the system to meet the targeted demand.

$$MC = \sum_{j=1}^{J} M_j D_j \tag{A3}$$

Labor cost (LC)

The labor cost includes the wages and salaries of the workers depending on the production cycle time.

$$LC = \sum_{j=1}^{J} \frac{\rho(s) L_j W_j}{T} \tag{A4}$$

Energy cost (EC)

Energy cost incurred on all the production quantity due to the energy consumed by the machines, equipments, and utilities etc.

$$EC = \sum_{j=1}^{J} \pi U_j D_j \tag{A5}$$

Inspection cost (IC)

The insepction cost is incurred on all the items to check whether the parts are correct, rejected, or should move towards reworking operations.

$$IC = \sum_{j=1}^{J} \frac{\theta_j}{T} + D_j \psi_j \tag{A6}$$

Reworking cost (RWC)

The reworking cost also affects the total cost for reworking operations on a fraction of defective items.

$$RWC = \sum_{j=1}^{J} \mu(s) M_j D_j \tag{A7}$$

Recycling cost (RC)

The rejected items are move towards recycling process for the regeneration of the raw material.

$$RC = \sum_{j=1}^{J} \eta u_j \mu(s) D_j \tag{A8}$$

Holding cost and Backorder cost

The holding cost is referred to the cost of carrying inventory in the production house, which includes rents, salaries, insurance etc. It also depends on the time during which the final product will be held in inventory. The backorder cost is also incurred on the items produced to fulfill the shortages. Both the holding and backorder costs are taken from the work of Sarkar et al., (2014) [39].

Appendix B

Table A1. Questionnaire from the American Institute of Stress.

Sr.	Questions	Never	Rarely	Sometimes	Often	Very Often
1	In general, I am not particularly proud or satisfied with my job.	1	2	3	4	5
2	Conditions at work are unpleasant or sometimes even unsafe.	1	2	3	4	5
3	I feel that my job is negatively affecting my physical or emotional well-being.	1	2	3	4	5
4	I have too much work to do and/or too many unreasonable deadlines.	1	2	3	4	5
5	I find it difficult to express my opinions or feelings about my job conditions to my superiors.	1	2	3	4	5
6	I feel that job pressures interfere with my family or personal life.	1	2	3	4	5
7	I don't have adequate control or input over my work duties.	1	2	3	4	5
8	I do not receive appropriate appreciation or rewards for good performance.	1	2	3	4	5
9	I cannot utilize my skills and talents fully at work.	1	2	3	4	5
10	I tend to have frequent arguments with superiors, co-workers, or customers.	1	2	3	4	5

References

1. Perla, A.; Nikolaev, A.; Pasiliao, E. Workforce management under social link based corruption. *Omega* **2018**, *78*, 222–236. [CrossRef]
2. Barney, J.B. *Gaining and Sustaining Competitive Advantage*; Addison-Wesley Pub. Co.: Boston, MA, USA, 1997.
3. Choudhry, R.-M.; Fang, D. Why operatives engage in unsafe work behavior: Investigating factors on construction sites. *Saf. Sci.* **2008**, *46*, 566–584. [CrossRef]
4. Leka, S.; Jain, A.; Zwetsloot, G.; Cox, T. Policy-level interventions and work-related psychosocial risk management in the European Union. *Work Stress* **2010**, *24*, 298–307. [CrossRef]
5. EU-OSHA–European Agency for Safety and Health at Work. *Expert Forecast on Emerging Psychosocial Risks Related to Occupational Safety and Health*; European Agency for Safety and Health at Work: Bilbao, Spain, 2007.
6. Kumar, S. Theories of musculoskeletal injury causation. *Ergonomics* **2001**, *44*, 17–47. [CrossRef] [PubMed]
7. NIOSH. *Stress...at Work*; National Institute for Occupational Safety and Health (NIOSH): Washington, DC, USA, 1999; Volume 20, pp. 99–101.
8. Karasek, R. Demand/control model: A social-emotional, and psychological approach to stress risk and active behavior development. In *ILO Encyclopedia of Occupational Health and Safety*; ILO: Paris, France, 1998.
9. Leka, S.; Griffiths, A.; Cox, T.; World Health Organization (WHO). *Work Organisation and Stress: Systematic Problem Approaches for Employers, Managers and Trade Union Representatives*; WHO: Geneva, Switzerland, 2003.

10. Palmer, S.; Cooper, C.; Thomas, K. A Model of Work Stress. Counselling at Work-Winter. Available online: https://s3.amazonaws.com/academia.edu.documents/31468591/acw_winter04_a.pdf?response-content -disposition=inline%3B%20filename%3DPalmer_S._Cooper_C._and_Thomas_K._2004_..pdf&X-Amz-Alg orithm=AWS4-HMAC-SHA256&X-Amz-Credential=AKIAIWOWYYGZ2Y53UL3A%2F20190714%2Fus-east-1%2Fs3%2Faws4_request&X-Amz-Date=20190714T064506Z&X-Amz-Expires=3600&X-Amz-Signed Headers=host&X-Amz-Signature=99276df961605f827720de490055880ce6bf5eefbf248336ac81476d42ddf3d 9 (accessed on 6 April 2019).

11. Dollard, M.-F.; Metzer, J.-C. Psychological research, practice, and production: The occupational stress problem. *Int. J. Stress Manag.* **1999**, *6*, 241–253. [CrossRef]

12. Park, J. Work stress and job performance. *Perspect. Labour Income* **2008**, *20*, 7.

13. Hendrick, H.-W. Determining the cost–benefits of ergonomics projects and factors that lead to their success. *Appl. Ergon.* **2003**, *34*, 419–427. [CrossRef]

14. Mrozek, J.-R.; Taylor, L.-O. What determines the value of life? A meta-analysis. *J. Policy Anal. Manag.* **2002**, *21*, 253–270. [CrossRef]

15. Habib, M.-S.; Sarkar, B.; Tayyab, M.; Saleem, M.-W.; Hussain, A.; Ullah, M.; Omair, M.; Iqbal, M.-W. Large-scale disaster waste management under uncertain environment. *J. Clean. Prod.* **2019**, *212*, 200–222. [CrossRef]

16. Omair, M.; Noor, S.; Hussain, I.; Maqsood, S.; Khattak, S.-B.; Akhtar, R.; Haq, I.-U. Sustainable development tool for Khyber Pakhtunkhwa's dimension stone industry. *Technol. J.* **2015**, *20*, 160–165.

17. Omair, M.; Noor, S.; Maqsood, S.; Nawaz, R. Assessment of Sustainability in Marble Quarry of Khyber Pakhtunkhwa Province Pakistan. *Int. J. Eng. Technol.* **2014**, *14*, 84–89.

18. Kang, C.-W.; Imran, M.; Omair, M.; Ahmed, W.; Ullah, M.; Sarkar, B. Stochastic-Petri Net Modeling and Optimization for Outdoor Patients in Building Sustainable Healthcare System Considering Staff Absenteeism. *Mathematics* **2019**, *7*, 499. [CrossRef]

19. Amador-Rodezno, R. An overview to cersss self evaluation of the cost-benefit on the investment in occupational safety and health in the textile factories: A step by step methodology. *J. Saf. Res.* **2005**, *36*, 215–229.

20. Boone, J.; van Ours, J.-C. Are recessions good for workplace safety? *J. Health Econ.* **2006**, *25*, 1069–1093. [CrossRef] [PubMed]

21. Ruhm, C.-J. Are recessions good for your health? *Q. J. Econ.* **2000**, *115*, 617–650. [CrossRef]

22. Beehr, T.A.; Johnson, L.B.; Nieva, R. Occupational stress: Coping of police and their spouses. *J. Organ. Behav.* **1995**, *16*, 3–25. [CrossRef]

23. Caplan, R.D.; Jones, K.-W. Effects of work load, role ambiguity, and type A personality on anxiety, depression, and heart rate. *J. Appl. Psychol.* **1975**, *60*, 713–719. [PubMed]

24. Motowidlo, S.-J.; Packard, J.-S.; Manning, M.-R. Occupational stress: Its causes and consequences for job performance. *J. Appl. Psychol.* **1986**, *71*, 618–629. [CrossRef]

25. Knauth, P. Innovative worktime arrangements. *Scand. J. Work Environ. Health* **1998**, *24*, 13–17.

26. Mansour, M. Quantifying the intangible costs related to non-ergonomic work conditions and work injuries based on the stress level among employees. *Saf. Sci.* **2016**, *82*, 283–288. [CrossRef]

27. Wilkinson, J. Shift work and fatigue-and the possible consequences. *Occup. Health Wellbeing* **2013**, *65*, 27–30.

28. Dyble, J. Workplace stress linked to lower productivity. *Empl. Benefits* **2014**, *9*, 2014.

29. Locke, E.-A. Toward a theory of task motivation and incentives. *Organ. Behav. Hum. Perform.* **1968**, *3*, 157–189. [CrossRef]

30. Harvard, P.-S. Maslow, mazes, minotaurs; updating employee needs and behavior patterns in a knowledge-based global economy. *J. Knowl. Econ.* **2010**, *1*, 117–127. [CrossRef]

31. Wee, H.-M.; Yu, J.; Chen, M.-C. Optimal inventory model for items with imperfect quality and shortage backordering. *Omega* **2007**, *35*, 7–11. [CrossRef]

32. Ganguly, B.; Pareek, S.; Sarkar, B.; Sarkar, M.; Omair, M. Influence of controllable lead time, premium price, and unequal shipments under environmental effects in a supply chain management. *RAIRO-Operations Research.* **2018**.://doi.org/10.1051/ro/2018041. [CrossRef]

33. Goyal, S.-K.; Cárdenas-Barrón, L.-E. Note on: Economic production quantity model for items with imperfect quality–a practical approach. *Int. J. Prod. Econ.* **2002**, *77*, 85–87. [CrossRef]

34. Wook Kang, C.; Ullah, M.; Sarkar, M.; Omair, M.; Sarkar, B. A Single-Stage Manufacturing Model with Imperfect Items, Inspections, Rework, and Planned Backorders. *Mathematics* **2019**, *7*, 446. [CrossRef]

35. Bouslah, B.; Gharbi, A.; Pellerin, R. Integrated production, sampling quality control and maintenance of deteriorating production systems with AOQL constraint. *Omega* **2016**, *61*, 110–126, doi:10.1016/j.omega.2015.07.012. [CrossRef]

36. Jeang, A. Simultaneous determination of production lot size and process parameters under process deterioration and process breakdown. *Omega* **2012**, *40*, 774–781, doi:10.1016/ j.omega.2011.12.005. [CrossRef]

37. Sarkar, B.; Omair, M.; Choi, S.-B. A multi-objective optimization of energy, economic, and carbon emission in a production model under sustainable supply chain management. *Appl. Sci.* **2018**, *8*, 1744. [CrossRef]

38. Omair, M.; Sarkar, B.; Cárdenas-Barrón, L.-E. Minimum quantity lubrication and carbon footprint: A step towards sustainability. *Sustainability* **2017**, *9*, 714. [CrossRef]

39. Sarkar, B.; Cárdenas-Barrón, L.-E.; Sarkar, M.; Singgih, M.-L. An economic production quantity model with random defective rate, rework process and backorders for a single stage production system. *J. Manuf. Syst.* **2014**, *33*, 423–435. [CrossRef]

40. The Marlin Company and American Institute of Stress (AIS). *The Workplace Stress Scale*; The Marlin Company and American Institute of Stress: North Haven, CT, USA and Yonkers, NY, USA, 1978.

41. Aghilinejad, M.; Zargham Sadeghi, A.-A.; Sarebanha, S.; Bahrami-Ahmadi, A. Role of occupational stress and burnout in prevalence of musculoskeletal disorders among embassy personnel of foreign countries in Iran. *Iran. Red Crescent Med. J.* **2014**, *16*, e9066. [CrossRef] [PubMed]

42. McCalister, K.-T.; Dolbier, C.-L.; Webster, J.-A.; Mallon, M.-W.; Steinhardt, M.-A. Hardiness and support at work as predictors of work stress and job satisfaction. *Am. J. Health Promot.* **2006**, *20*, 183–191. [CrossRef] [PubMed]

43. Idrees, M.; Hafeez, M.; Kim, J.-Y. Workers' age and the impact of psychological factors on the perception of safety at construction sites. *Sustainability* **2017**, *9*, 745. [CrossRef]

44. Sarkar, B. Supply chain coordination with variable backorder, inspections, and discount policy for fixed lifetime products. *Math. Probl. Eng.* **2016**, *2016*. [CrossRef]

45. Birgin, E.-G.; Haeser, G.; Ramos, A. Augmented lagrangians with constrained subproblems and convergence to second-order stationary points. *Comput. Optim. Appl.* **2018**, *69*, 51–75. [CrossRef]

46. Mostafa, N.; Khajavi, M. Optimization of welding parameters for weld penetration in FCAW. *J. Achiev. Mater. Manuf. Eng.* **2006**, *16*, 132–138.

47. Schittkowski, K. NLPQL: A fortran subroutine solving constrained nonlinear programming problems. *Ann. Oper. Res.* **1986**, *5*, 485–500. [CrossRef]

48. Theodorakatos, N.-P.; Manousakis, N.-M.; Korres, G.-N. A sequential quadratic programming method for contingency-constrained phasor measurement unit placement. *Int. Trans. Electr. Energy Syst.* **2015**, *25*, 3185–3211. [CrossRef]

5

How does a Radio Frequency Identification Optimize the Profit in an Unreliable Supply Chain Management?

Rekha Guchhait [1,2], Sarla Pareek [1] and Biswajit Sarkar [2,*]

[1] Department of Mathematics & Statistics, Banasthali Vidyapith, Rajasthan 304022, India; rg.rekhaguchhait@gmail.com (R.G.); psarla13@gmail.com (S.P.)

[2] Department of Industrial & Management Engineering, Hanyang University, Ansan, Gyeonggi-do 15588, Korea

* Correspondence: bsarkar@hanyang.ac.kr.

Abstract: Competition in business is higher in the electronics sector compared to other sectors. In such a situation, the role of a manufacturer is to manage the inventory properly with optimized profit. However, the problem of unreliability within buyers still exists in real world scenarios. The manufacturer adopts the radio frequency identification (RFID) technology to manage the inventory, which can control the unreliability, the inventory pooling effect, and the investment on human labor. For detecting RFID tags, a reasonable number of readers are needed. This study investigates the optimum distance between any two readers when using the optimum number of readers. As a vendor managed inventory (VMI) policy is utilized by the manufacturer, a revenue sharing contract is adopted to prevent the loss of buyers. The aim of this study is to maximize the profits of a two-echelon supply chain management under an advanced technology system. As the life of electronic gadgets is random, it may not follow any specific type of distribution function. The distribution-free approach helps to solve this issue when the mean and the standard deviation are known. The Kuhn-Tucker methodology and classical optimization are used to find the global optimum solution. The numerical analysis demonstrates that the manufacturer can earn more profit in coordination case after utilizing revenue sharing and the optimum distance between readers optimizing cost related to the RFID system. Sensitivity analysis is performed to check the sensibility of the parameters.

Keywords: supply chain management; inventory control; distribution-free approach; revenue sharing; radio frequency identification; information asymmetry

1. Introduction

Instead of a traditional business system, supply chain management (SCM) provides different kinds of business policies in terms of inventory management. The vendor managed inventory (VMI) is one of these in which the manufacturer takes full responsibility of the existing inventory at the buyer's position. Dong and Xu [1] found opportunities where buyers received more profit than the manufacturer. The manufacturer's profit may vary according to the business policy, where the short-term and long-term VMI affects the SCM, which were decided by them. They concluded that the short-term VMI can be a competitor for coordination business policy. In any business, the forecasting uncertainty is a major issue and Guo et al. [2] developed a method to reduce the supply chain forecasting uncertainty through information sharing via macro prediction which can reduce the system robustness. However, it is possible that not all information is shared by both parties. Then, unreliability occurs in the business system due to information asymmetry (Mukhopadhyay et al. [3];

Yan and Pei [4]; Xiao and Xu [5]). An information basically flows in the upward direction of SCM. The lack of information of the manufacturer may cause insufficient supply of products which can affect the inventory and production process. The situation is even more complicated when an imperfect production process takes place (Sarkar [6]). The rework of defective products was considered by Cárdenas-Barrón et al. [7] for an imperfect production process. They developed an improved algorithm to find the optimum lot size and replenish the defective production system. Cleaner production can be formed by discarding defective products, which was established by Tayyab and Sarkar [8]. Those defective products were reworked up to good quality through additional investment. This work was extended by multi-stage cleaner production by Kim and Sarkar [9] using budget constraints. There are several researchers who worked on imperfect products, reworking, and deterioration (Guchhait et al. [10], Majumder et al. [11], Tiwari et al. [12]). Finally, Sarkar [13] introduced an exact duration for reworking within a multi-stage multi-cycle production system. However, there is a lack of literature regarding RFID, i.e., RFID was not used to maintain the inventory pooling effect. Reworking was considered by Sarkar et al. [14] in a material requirement planning (MRP) system.

Production quantity mainly depends upon the market demand. In reality, it cannot always be the case that data related with demand are available. If no known distribution function is followed by the demand or no data are available, then instead of taking any arbitrary probability distribution, the distribution-free (DF) approach is used (Gallego and Moon [15], Sarkar et al. [16], Guchhait et al. [17]). This method was invented by Scarf [18]. Due to the complex calculations, it was not understandable to people in the industry at that time. Later, this approach was simplified by Gallego and Moon [15]. This method is used by Sarkar et al. [19] for a consignment stock-based newsvendor model. They allowed a fixed-fee payment technique to prevent loss from any participant. There are multiple manufacturers and retailers available for a single-type of products. Based on advertisements given by the manufacturer, retailers opted to choose their manufacturers. For the random demand, the variable production rate is useful (Sarkar et al. [20]) for modeling uncertain demand. A service level can help avoid shortages (Moon et al. [21]) and backorder (Sarkar [22]) due to the uncertain random demand. Partial trade credit for deteriorating items in the inventory model was discussed by Tiwari et al. [23]. For any industry, it may be that they need to analyze their previous data. Tiwari et al. [24] provided a big data analysis of SCM from 2010 to 2016.

Competitive markets in the business industry becoming more intense everyday. To handle this situation, companies prefer to adopt smart technologies within the SCM. The fast movement of products for the electronic industry is a key feature since competition is very high in the electronics sector. The implementation of technology instead of labor-based production is helpful not only for fast production, but also to profit gain. The use of RFID technology in SCM for managing inventory has been studied by several researchers. A wireless sensing problem for coverage was first studied by Meguerdichian et al. [25]. Zhang and Hou [26] investigated how many readers need to be implemented to provide a complete coverage of a search area. The coverage area sensing radius and transmitting radius were discussed by Hefeeda and Ahmadi [27]. They established that probabilistic sensing coverage can function as deterministic coverage. Dias [28] implemented RFID for a multi-agent system. Sarac et al. [29] surveyed the literature and found several implementation and usages of RFID in different sectors of SCM. They found that inventory loss can be reduced with increased efficiency of the system and real-time information of the inventory. Kim and Glock [30] investigated the effectiveness of an RFID tracking system for container management and found that the return rate of container was increased after using RFID. A four-echelon SCM was studied by Sari [31] to examine the effects of collaboration. They found through simulation that the integrated RFID technology is more beneficial for good collaboration between participants. Besides SCM, warehouse efficiency can be improved using RFID technology (Biswal et al. [32]). In the production sector, RFID improves the efficiency and maintenance, as investigated by Chen et al. [33]. They established that operation time can be increased by up to 89% and that the labor cost is reduced significantly by using RFID. Even, remanufacturing companies can get benefit from RFID via just-in-time (JIT) features or transiting towards a closed-loop SCM (Tsao et al. [34]).

From literature, it is found in most of the studies that RFID is used in SCM to prevent inventory shrinkage as well as minimize the operation time of the system, reduction of lead time, and labor consumption (Ustundag and Tanyas [35]; Jaggi et al. [36]) and improve the efficiency. However, the reason behind this efficiency improvement by RFID is not discussed in the literature. This study introduces for the first time the RFID distance function $f(d)$ based on the sensing and transmitting radii. The distance between two readers can be optimized and thus, the number of RFID readers can be found to increase the efficiency. Based on the transmitting and sensing radii, two types of readers are used by the manufacturer, namely Type 1 and Type 2. To understand the complete search capacity of a Type 1 reader, the area is divided into sub-areas that are under the coverage of Type 2 readers. This combined system may enhances the system accuracy and provides strong coverage of the sensing and transmitting areas. Table 1 gives the contribution of different authors in the literature. This study shows benefits for the buyer in the optimum order quantity, optimizes distance the between two readers, and optimizes the service given by the buyers. The rest of the study is designed as Section 2 gives the details about the mathematical model. Section 3 gives the results of the numerical experiment and Section 4 provides a discussion of results. Section 5 concludes this study. Associated references are attached in the References section.

Table 1. Comparison of author's contribution.

Author(s)	Model Type	Business Policy	Unreliability	RFID
Dong and Xu [1]	stochastic	VMI	NA	NA
Guo et al. [2]	stochastic	macro prediction market	NA	NA
Mukhopadhyay et al. [3]	deterministic	mixed channel	information	NA
Yan and Pei [4]	deterministic	mixed channel	information	NA
Xiao and Xu [5]	deterministic	VMI	NA	NA
Sarkar [6]	stochastic	production model	reliable	NA
Guchhait et al. [10]	deterministic	traditional	NA	NA
Majumder et al. [11]	deterministic	traditional	NA	NA
Gallego and Moon [15]	stochastic (DF)	inventory model	NA	NA
Scarf [18]	stochastic (DF)	inventory model	NA	NA
Sarkar et al. [19]	stochastic (DF)	CP	NA	NA
Moon et al. [21]	stochastic (DF)	inventory model	NA	NA
Tiwari et al. [23]	deterministic	SCM	NA	NA
Meguerdicihian et al. [25]	networking	NA	NA	sensing
Zhang and Hou [26]	networking	NA	NA	sensing
Hefeeda and Ahmadi [27]	networking	NA	NA	coverage
Dias et al. [28]	survey	SCM	NA	survey
Sarac et al. [29]	value chain	survey	NA	survey
Kim and Glock [30]	stochastic	closed-loop	NA	tracking
Shin et al. [37]	stochastic (DF)	inventory	NA	NA
This model	stochastic (DF)	VMI	information	distance and readers

2. Problem Definition, Notation, and Assumptions

This section describes the problem definition for this study. Associated assumptions and notation are given here.

2.1. Problem Definition

A two-echelon supply chain model is considered under the newsvendor framework where participants are in a VMI contract. The inventory of the whole system is controlled by the manufacturer. Controlling the inventory manually by human labor is a time consuming task, as the manufacturer takes full responsibility of the full business of all buyers. To do this, the manufacturer installs smart RFID technology. The number of RFID readers is needed by the manufacturer such that the inventory can be controlled in a proper way within a minimum time duration. The number of readers depends on the sensing distance between two readers. Thus, the distance between readers is optimized for RFID investment. Buyers are not reliable with respect to the manufacturer's business. Buyers provide services to the customers, and therefore an unreliable SCM is formed as a single-manufacturer multi-buyer. The goal of the newsvendor model is to maximize profit for the buyer without incurring any storage or redundancy costs. However, the buyer is unable to decide on the optimum order quantity, where there should not be any understock or overstock costs. For that, the manufacturer takes the full responsibility of the buyers to for profits through the VMI strategy. Even though the manufacturer tries their best to help the buyer, the buyer is unreliable in nature and may provide wrong information regarding the demand to manufacturer. To mitigate this matter, the RFID technology is installed allowing the manufacturer to obtain more profit.

2.2. Notation

The following notation (Table 2) is used in the present study.

Table 2. Notation in this study.

Index	
i	number of buyers i, $i = 1, 2, ..., n$
Decision variables	**description**
δ_i	service by buyer i
q_i	order quantity of buyer i per cycle (units/cycle), $Q = \sum_{i=1}^{n} q_i$
d	distance between two RFID readers
Parameters	**description**
p_i	selling price of buyer i per unit under RFID effect ($/unit)
d_i	demand of buyer i per cycle (unit/cycle)
μ_i	mean value of demand d_i, $\mu = \sum_{i=1}^{n} \mu_i$
σ_i	standard deviation
l, b	length and breadth of the search area (m)
S_t	transmission radius of Type 1 reader (m)
S_s	sensing radius of Type 1 reader (m)
ρ	decay parameter for sensing
c_1, c_2	costs of Type 1 and Type 2 reader per unit ($/unit)
λ	maximum threshold value of Type 1 reader
θ	threshold parameter $(0 < \theta < 1)$
w	purchasing/wholesale cost per unit under the RFID effect ($/unit)
π_m	goodwill lost cost of manufacturer per unit with RFID ($/unit)
π_{ri}	buyer i's goodwill lost cost per unit under consideration of RFID ($/unit)
η_i	service investment of buyer i ($)
δ_i	service by buyer i
ζ_i	customer satisfaction cost of buyer i ($/unit)
h_m	holding cost of manufacturer under RFID effect ($/unit/unit time)
h_{ri}	buyer i's holding cost with RFID ($/unit/unit time)
Others	**description**
$f(d)$	cost of RFID per cycle ($/cycle)
$E(\cdot)$	expected value
ETP	expected total profit of the coordinate case per cycle ($/cycle)
ETP_r	buyer's expected total profit per cycle ($/cycle)
ETP_m	manufacturer's expected total profit per cycle ($/cycle)

2.3. Assumptions

The following assumptions are used for this model.

1. A two-echelon SCM is considered for a single-type of electronic products, where the inventory is managed by a manufacturer through a VMI contract. To ensure the profit of the buyers, a revenue sharing policy for coordination case is used by the manufacturer. The finished products are sent to the n buyers.

2. Buyers are not reliable enough and they are not sharing data to the manufacturer. It forms an information asymmetry in the business system. The manufacturer losses some information about market and installs the RFID system to solve the unreliability issue.

3. As VMI recommends that the supreme controlling authority is the manufacturer and the manufacturer decides to use RFID technology for controlling the unreliability issues. Hence, the manufacturer decides the whole deployment for the design of installing RFID reader, which can be done by the third-party. As the manufacturer cannot reach to the retailer's place in each and every moment, the technology will support to solve the issue of the unreliability. Those support will be taken from the third-party by investing some fixed cost. That fixed cost is inserted within the cost of Type 1 and Type 2 reader. Therefore, the RFID reader deployment cannot be specified within the modelling part of the manufacturer. However, the design of RFID reader can be added for the entering gate or any other place, but it depends on the third-party who is dealing with the whole area for covering the RFID. Therefore, through VMI, it is not the responsibility for the manufacturer to check the design for the installed RFID readers as this is a paid service from the third-party. Two types of reader are used to give a complete coverage of the search area. The total search area is divided into subareas and each subarea is covered by Type 1 readers, based on a disk sensing model. Each subarea is again divided into small search areas that are covered by Type 2 readers, based on an exponential coverage protocol. The frequency range of the readers is measured for usual road transport.

4. It may not be possible that the demand pattern always follows some distribution function. As data are random, it is assumed that the market demand is uncertain and does not follow any particular type of distribution. The known mean is μ_i and the standard deviation is σ_i (Shin et al. [37]).

5. The planning horizon is [0,T] and the lead time is negligible.

3. Mathematical Modelling

A VMI contract policy for the electronic industry is discussed for a single-manufacturer and multi-buyer newsvendor model. The optimum number of RFID readers, which can cover the optimized distance, can provide maximum profit to the supply chain for a long time. As implementation of RFID requires a huge investment, a reasonable demand rate is expected for the manufacturer. However, the market demand (d_i) for buyer i is uncertain, it cannot be predicted. The demand (d_i) for buyer i can be represented by a random variable where the mean is (μ_i) and (σ_i) is the standard deviation which both are known. As d_i does not follow any specific distribution function, this problem can be solved using the DF approach. The surplus and shortage amount can be calculated by the lemma of Gallego and Moon [15]. The required surplus amount is

$$E(q_i - d_i)^+ \leq \frac{1}{2}\left[\sqrt{\sigma_i^2(\mu_i - q_i)^2} + (q_i - \mu_i)\right], \mu_i < q_i \tag{1}$$

and the shortage amount is

$$E(d_i - q_i)^+ = \frac{1}{2}\left[\sqrt{\sigma_i^2(\mu_i - q_i)^2} + (\mu_i - q_i)\right], q_i < \mu_i, \text{ for } F \in \mathbb{F}. \tag{2}$$

3.1. Structure of the Proposed RFID System

The total search area is covered by the RFID tracking system. The cost regarding RFID depends on the number of readers. The concept of VMI is that the manufacturer will manage the whole inventory of the retailer as some unreliable issues are coming from retailer's side. To overcome these issues, the manufacturer introduces RFID technology with the minimum investment for it. Therefore, within the total area of the retailer, how much inventory are these, that should be verified by RFID readers. Therefore, it is not essential to use always powerful RFID readers like as Type 1 or similarly it is not recommended also that always low powerful Type 2 reader should be used. Hence, an optimization is needed to optimize the optimum number of Type 1 and Type 2 reader within the whole area. That is why, this model recommended two types of RFID reader for the sensing and coverage model: the disk sensing model and the exponential coverage model. The entire search area is divided into subareas which are covered by the Type 1 reader. This Type 1 reader has a higher sensing power for coverage, which uses the disk sensing model. Each subarea is divided into subareas those are covered by two Type 2 readers. Type 2 readers have low sensing power and use an exponential coverage protocol system. The connectivity between the sensing radius and transmitting radius is given by the condition $2S_s \leq S_t$ (for instance, see Zhang and Hou [26]).

If l_1 is the length and b_1 is the breadth of each subdivided area, then from the properties of right-angled triangle (Figure 1), it is follows that

$$l_1^2 + b_1^2 = c^2, \text{ i.e., } l_1^2 + b_1^2 = 4S_t^2, \text{ i.e., } S_t = \sqrt{\frac{l_1^2 + b_1^2}{4}}.$$

For each square foot area, $l_1 = b_1$, which implies that

$$S_t = \frac{l_1}{\sqrt{2}}, \text{ i.e., } l_1 = \sqrt{2}S_t.$$

Therefore, if the length and the breadth of the total search area are l and b, respectively, the total number of Type 1 reader is $\left\lceil \frac{l}{\sqrt{2}S_t} \right\rceil \left\lceil \frac{b}{\sqrt{2}S_t} \right\rceil$.

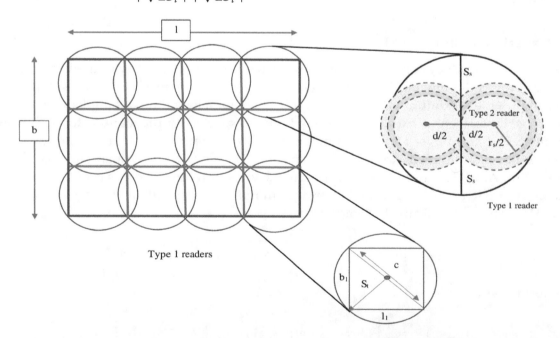

Figure 1. Execution of Type 1 and Type 2 readers for a search area.

Now, each subdivided area of sensing radius S_s is divided into two areas with sensing radius r_s. The maximum distance between two Type 2 readers is d, i.e., $r_s = \dfrac{d}{2}$. Now, from the exponential coverage protocol (Hefeeda and Ahmadi [27]), the maximum distance d between two Type 2 readers is smaller than $\sqrt{3}\left(\lambda - \dfrac{Log\left[1 - \sqrt[3]{1-\theta}\right]}{\rho}\right)$, i.e.,

$$d \leq \sqrt{3}\left(\lambda - \frac{Log\left[1 - \sqrt[3]{1-\theta}\right]}{\rho}\right).$$

The area of the circle for sensing radius S_s is πS_s^2. The area of circle of sensing radius r_s is $\pi r_s^2 = \dfrac{\pi d^2}{4}$. Therefore, the number of Type 2 readers for each subdivided area of Type 1 reader is $\left\lceil \dfrac{\pi S_s^2}{\dfrac{\pi d^2}{4}} \right\rceil = \left\lceil \dfrac{4S_s^2}{d^2} \right\rceil$. Hence, the total number of Type 2 readers for all Type 1 readers is

$$\left\lceil \frac{4S_s^2}{d^2} \right\rceil \left\lceil \frac{l}{\sqrt{2}S_t} \right\rceil \left\lceil \frac{b}{\sqrt{2}S_t} \right\rceil.$$

3.2. Manufacturer's Model

In reality, it is not always the case that all buyers are reliable enough to share all information to the manufacturer. To prevent the piracy on the inventory inaccuracy, the manufacturer invests in RFID technology even though this may reduce the profit margins. However, there may be long-term benefits compensate the shrinkage of inventory. Still, there may be some ambiguity regarding information due to information asymmetry.

3.2.1. RFID Cost

The total area is covered by $\left\lceil \dfrac{l}{\sqrt{2}S_t} \right\rceil \left\lceil \dfrac{b}{\sqrt{2}S_t} \right\rceil$ Type 1 readers. This area is again subdivided and is covered by Type 2 readers. If c_1 is the cost of each Type 1 reader and c_2 is for each Type 2. A fixed cost is included within c_1 and c_2 which the manufacturer pays as an investment. Then the required RFID cost is given by

$$f(d) = c_1 \left\lceil \frac{l}{\sqrt{2}S_t} \right\rceil \left\lceil \frac{b}{\sqrt{2}S_t} \right\rceil + c_2 \left\lceil \frac{4S_s^2}{d^2} \right\rceil \left\lceil \frac{l}{\sqrt{2}S_t} \right\rceil \left\lceil \frac{b}{\sqrt{2}S_t} \right\rceil$$

subject to the conditions

$$d \leq \sqrt{3}\left(\lambda - \frac{Log\left[1 - \sqrt[3]{1-\theta}\right]}{\rho}\right)$$

$$(3)$$

$$S_t \geq 2S_s.$$

Therefore, the RFID cost per cycle is $\dfrac{f(d)\mu}{Q}$, where $D = \sum_i d_i$ and $\mu = E(D)$.

3.2.2. Production Cost and Wholesale Price

If the manufacturer produces a lot size Q per cycle then the production cost of those products is given by cQ. When the manufacturer sells products as a wholesale price w per unit, then the wholesale price is given by wQ.

3.2.3. Holding Cost

The situation of holding products is created when the demand (d_i) is less than the ordered quantity wq_i. If h_{ri} is the unit holding cost of buyer i, the holding cost is $h_{ri}E(q_i - d_i)^+$, $d_i \leq q_i$. As the manufacturer pays both the holding cost of the buyers and the manufacturer (h_m), the total holding cost of the manufacturer is given by $\sum_i E(q_i - d_i)^+ \left(h_{ri} + h_m \right)$, $d_i \leq q_i$.

3.2.4. Goodwill Lost Cost

A goodwill lost cost (π_m) is allowed since the manufacturer takes the responsibility for the products for the whole supply chain, where shortage affects the goodwill of manufacturer. The cost expression for goodwill loss is given by $\sum_i \pi_m E(q_i - d_i)^+$, $q_i < d_i$.

Including the RFID cost, the expected total profit of the manufacturer is given by the following expression

$$ETP_m(q_i, d) = (w - c)Q - \sum_i \frac{1}{2}(h_{r_i} + h_m)\left[\sqrt{\sigma_i^2 + (\mu_i - q_i)^2} + (q_i - d_i) \right] - \frac{\pi_m}{2}\sum \left[\sqrt{\sigma_i^2 + (\mu_i - q_i)^2} \right. $$
$$\left. + (d_i - q_i) \right] - \frac{f(d)\mu}{Q} \tag{4}$$

subject to the conditions

$$d \leq \sqrt{3}\left(\lambda - \frac{Log\left[1 - \sqrt[3]{1-\theta}\right]}{\rho} \right)$$

$$S_t \geq 2S_s.$$

3.3. Buyer's Model

Buyers are unreliable resulting in information asymmetry. As this is a dependent business policy and the manufacturer is responsible for both inventory supervision and holding inventory for buyers, all information should be known to the manufacturer. However, today's business systems are very complex and buyers are unreliable at sharing information their own business strategy. Buyer i buys the electronic products from the manufacturer and sells them in the market. To increase market demand, the buyers provide facilities to the customers without telling the manufacturer meaning that an unreliable supply chain system is formulated.

3.3.1. Revenue

p_i is the unit selling price of the electronic products. Now, two types of situation may arise, where the demand (d_i) is more than the ordered quantity (q_i) or vice-versa. Then the selling price can be found as

$$\begin{cases} p_i d_i & d_i \leq q_i \\ p_i q_i & q_i < d_i. \end{cases}$$

3.3.2. Purchasing Cost and Goodwill Lost Cost

If w is the unit purchasing cost for the ordered quantity q_i, then the purchasing cost is given by wq_i. When the reverse situation arises i.e., the demand is more than the ordered quantity, backordering occurs, meaning that some goodwill for buyer i is lost. The goodwill lost cost is given by $\pi_{ri}E(d_i - q_i)^+$, $q_i < d_i$ where π_{ri} is the unit goodwill lost cost of buyer i.

3.3.3. Service Cost

The buyer provides extra services (δ_i) to attract customers, which requires extra money to invests (η_i). Customer satisfaction is involved in this situation. If the service is appropriate and satisfactory to the customers, the purpose of giving service is fulfilled. On the other hand, if some customers are not happy with the given service or buyer is incapable to give the standard service, customers may not want to buy products from that buyer as customers have multiple choices to buy the same product. This is the opposite situation of the service, i.e., $(1 - \delta_i)$. Thus, it creates some monetary loss to the buyer, which is indicated as customer satisfaction cost. It has the inverse relation with the provided service. Whenever the service increases, the customer satisfaction increases and thus the cost $(1 - \delta_i)^2 \zeta_i$, related to the customer satisfaction decreases. If η_i is the service cost and ζ_i is the customer satisfaction cost, the relative cost is given by $\dfrac{\eta_i \delta_i^2}{2} + (1 - \delta_i)^2 \zeta_i$. Therefore, the expected total profit of buyer i is

$$
ETP_{ri} = \begin{cases} p_i \mu_i - wq_i - \dfrac{\eta_i \delta_i^2}{2} - (1 - \delta_i)^2 \zeta_i, & d_i \le q_i \\[3mm] p_i q_i - wq_i - \pi_{ri} E(d_i - q_i)^+ - \dfrac{\eta_i \delta_i^2}{2} - (1 - \delta_i)^2 \zeta_i, & q_i < d_i. \end{cases} \tag{5}
$$

The total profit of buyer is given by

$$
ETP_r(q_i, \delta_i) = \sum p_i(\mu_i + q_i) - wQ - \frac{1}{2}\sum \pi_{ri}\left(\sqrt{\sigma i^2 + (\mu_i - d_i)^2} + \mu_i - q_i\right) - \sum \frac{\eta_i \delta_i^2}{2} - \sum(1 - \delta_i^2)\zeta_i. \tag{6}
$$

Therefore, the expected total profit of SCM is given by

$$
ETP(q_i, \delta_i, d) = \sum_i p_i(\mu_i + q_i) - cQ - \frac{1}{2}\sum_i (h_{ri} + h_m)\left[\sqrt{\sigma_i^2 + (\mu_i - q_i)^2} + (q_i - \mu_i)\right] - \frac{1}{2}\sum_i (\pi_{ri} + \pi_m)
$$
$$
\left[\sqrt{\sigma_i^2 + (\mu_i - q_i)^2} + (\mu_i - q_i)\right] - \sum_i \frac{\eta_i \delta_i^2}{2} - \sum_i (1 - \delta_i)^2 \zeta_i - \frac{f(d)\mu}{Q} \tag{7}
$$

subject to the conditions

$$
d \le \sqrt{3}\left(\lambda - \frac{Log\left[1 - \sqrt[3]{1 - \theta}\right]}{\rho}\right)
$$

$$
S_t \ge 2S_s.
$$

3.4. Solution Methodology

The solution is found for both the coordination and non-coordination cases. The model is solved by using classical optimization techniques. The necessary conditions give the optimum results for the corresponding decision variables and the sufficient conditions give the stability of the solutions. The constraint function of the manufacturer is modified and transferred into an unconstrained function using the Kuhn-Tucker (KT) method. The modified function is given by

$$
LETP_m = (w - c)Q - \sum_i (h_{ri} + h_m)E(q_i - d_i)^+ - \pi_m \sum_i E(d_i - q_i)^+ - \frac{\mu}{Q}\left(c_1\left[\frac{l}{\sqrt{2S_t}}\right]\left[\frac{b}{\sqrt{2S_t}}\right]\right.
$$
$$
\left. + c_2\left[\frac{4S_s^2}{d^2}\right]\left[\frac{l}{\sqrt{2S_t}}\right]\left[\frac{b}{\sqrt{2S_t}}\right]\right) + \lambda_1\left[\sqrt{3}\left(\lambda - \frac{\log(1 - \sqrt[3]{1 - \theta})}{\rho}\right) - d\right] + \lambda_2(2S_s - S_t). \tag{8}
$$

Then, the total profit of the entire SCM is

$$
LETP = \sum_i p_i(\mu_i + q_i) - cQ - \sum_i (h_{r_i} + h_m) E(q_i - d_i)^+ - \sum_i (\pi_m + \pi_{ri}) E(d_i - q_i)^+ - \frac{\mu}{Q}\left(c_1\left[\frac{l}{\sqrt{2}S_t}\right]\right.
$$
$$
\left.\left[\frac{b}{\sqrt{2}S_t}\right] + c_2\left[\frac{4S_s^2}{d^2}\right]\left[\frac{l}{\sqrt{2}S_t}\right]\left[\frac{b}{\sqrt{2}S_t}\right]\right) + \lambda_1\left[\sqrt{3}\left(\lambda - \frac{\log(1-\sqrt[3]{1-\theta})}{\rho}\right) - d\right]
$$
$$
+ \lambda_2(2S_s - S_t). \tag{9}
$$

3.4.1. Non-Coordination Case

The necessary conditions of optimization provide the optimum values of the decision variable for the manufacturer. The value of the decision variable (q_i) is computed by

$$
\frac{\partial LETP_m}{\partial q_i} = (w-c) + \frac{\mu_i - q_i}{2\sqrt{\sigma_i^2 + (\mu_i - q_i)^2}}(h_{r_i} + h_m + \pi_m) - \frac{1}{2}(h_{r_i} + h_m - \pi_m) + \frac{f(d)\mu}{Q^2} = 0,
$$
$$
\text{i.e., } q_i = \mu_i \pm \frac{\sigma_i \Gamma_1}{\sqrt{1 - \Gamma_1^2}}, \tag{10}
$$

where

$$
\Gamma_1 = \frac{2\left(w - c + \frac{f(d)\mu}{Q^2}\right) - h_{r_i} - h_m + \pi_m}{h_{r_i} + h_m + \pi_m}.
$$

Therefore, $Q = \sum_i q_i$ (from Equation (10)) gives the optimum order quantity for the manufacturer. The optimum distance is given by the following value of d.

$$
\frac{\partial LETP_m}{\partial d} = -\lambda_1 + \frac{8c_2 S_s^2}{d^3}\left[\frac{l}{\sqrt{2}S_t}\right]\left[\frac{b}{\sqrt{2}S_t}\right]\frac{\mu}{Q} = 0,
$$
$$
\lambda_1 = \frac{8\mu c_2 S_s^2\left[\frac{l}{\sqrt{2}S_t}\right]\left[\frac{b}{\sqrt{2}S_t}\right]}{Qd^3\left(\lambda - \frac{\log(1-\sqrt[3]{1-\theta})}{\rho}\right)}.
$$
$$
\frac{\partial LETP_m}{\partial \lambda_1} = \sqrt{3}\left(\lambda - \frac{\log(1-\sqrt[3]{1-\theta})}{\rho}\right) - d = 0, \tag{11}
$$
$$
\text{i.e., } d = \sqrt{3}\left(\lambda - \frac{\log(1-\sqrt[3]{1-\theta})}{\rho}\right).
$$

Equation (11) provides the optimum distance between readers. The sufficient conditions prove that the above results represent global solutions.

$$
\frac{\partial^2 LETP_m}{\partial q_i^2} = -\frac{1}{2}\frac{(h_{r_i} + h_m + \pi_m)\sigma_i^2}{\left(\sigma_i^2 + (\mu_i - q_i)^2\right)^{\frac{3}{2}}} - \frac{2f(d)\mu}{Q^3} < 0,
$$
$$
\frac{\partial^2 LETP_m}{\partial d^2} = -\frac{24c_2 S_s^2 \mu}{Qd^4}\left[\frac{l}{\sqrt{2}S_t}\right]\left[\frac{b}{\sqrt{2}S_t}\right] < 0,
$$
$$
\frac{\partial^2 LETP_m}{\partial q_i d_i} = -\frac{\mu\lambda_1}{Q^2} < 0,
$$

$$\text{and} \quad \begin{pmatrix} \dfrac{\partial LETP_m}{\partial q_i^2} & \dfrac{\partial LETP_m}{\partial q_i d_i} \\[3mm] \dfrac{\partial LETP_m}{\partial d_i q_i} & \dfrac{\partial LETP_m}{\partial d_i^2} \end{pmatrix} = \left(\dfrac{1}{2} \dfrac{(h_{r_i} + h_m + \pi_m)\sigma_i^2}{\left(\sigma_i^2 + (\mu_i - q_i)^2\right)^{\frac{3}{2}}} + \dfrac{2f(d)\mu}{Q^3} \right) \left(\dfrac{24c_2 S_s^2 \mu}{Qd^4} \left[\dfrac{l}{\sqrt{2S_t}} \right] \left[\dfrac{b}{\sqrt{2S_t}} \right] \right)$$

$$+ \dfrac{\mu \lambda_1}{Q^2} > 0.$$

All criterion for the sufficient conditions of a Hessian matrix are satisfied proving the stability of the optimum solution. Therefore, the values of the decision variables are the optimum for the manufacturer.

The optimum values of the decision variables for the buyer are given by the following necessary conditions for optimization.

$$\frac{\partial ETP_r}{\partial q_i} = 0,$$

$$\text{i.e., } q_i = \mu_i \pm \frac{\sigma_i \Gamma_2}{\sqrt{1 - \Gamma_2^2}}, \tag{12}$$

where

$$\Gamma_2 = \frac{2(p_i - w) + \pi_{r_i}}{\pi_{r_i}}.$$

The optimum order quantity for the buyer i is given by Equation (12). Equation (13) gives the optimum service provided by the buyer i to customers.

$$\frac{\partial ETP_r}{\partial \delta_i} = -\eta_i \delta_i + 2\zeta_i(1 - \delta_i) = 0,$$

$$\text{i.e., } \delta_i = \frac{2\zeta_i}{\eta_i + 2\zeta_i}. \tag{13}$$

This sufficient condition proves the global nature of the solution.

$$\frac{\partial ETP_r}{\partial q_i^2} = -\frac{\pi_{r_i}\sigma_i^2}{2\left(\sigma_i^2 + (\mu_i - q_i)^2\right)^{\frac{3}{2}}} < 0,$$

$$\frac{\partial ETP_r}{\partial \delta_i^2} = -\eta_i - 2\zeta_i < 0,$$

$$\frac{\partial^2 ETP_r}{\partial \delta_i q_i} = 0,$$

$$\text{i.e., } \begin{pmatrix} \dfrac{\partial ETP_r}{\partial q_i^2} & \dfrac{\partial ETP_r}{\partial q_i \delta_i} \\[3mm] \dfrac{\partial ETP_r}{\partial \delta_i q_i} & \dfrac{\partial ETP_r}{\partial \delta_i^2} \end{pmatrix} = \frac{\pi_{r_i}\sigma_i^2 (\eta_i + 2\zeta_i)}{2\left(\sigma_i^2 + (\mu_i - q_i)^2\right)^{\frac{3}{2}}} > 0.$$

The Algorithm 1 is developed to find the numerical results from theory. The following steps help to solve the model numerically.

Algorithm 1:	
Step 1	Input all values of all relevant parameters. Set the value of i.
Step 2	Set the initial values of q_i for manufacturer and buyers.
Step 3	Write down the values of q_i from the Equation (10) and d from the Equation (11) for manufacturer.
	For buyers, the values of q_i and δ_i are given by Equation (12) and (13), respectively.
Step 4	Find the value of q_i, δ_i, and d using the values from Step 1 and Step 2.
Step 4.a	If $q_i \geq q_{i+1}$ and $\delta_i \geq \delta_{i+1}$, then terminate the process. The optimum values are obtained as $q_i{}^*$, $\delta_i{}^*$, and d^*.
Step 4.b	Else if $q_i < q_{i+1}$ and $\delta_i < \delta_{i+1}$, go to Step 4.
Step 4.c	Increment of i as $i = i + 1$.
Step 5	Stop.

3.4.2. Coordination Case

The results for the joint profit of the entire SCM are given by the following necessary conditions.

$$\frac{\partial ETP}{\partial q_i} = p_i - c + \frac{f(d)\mu}{Q^2} + \frac{\mu_i - q_i}{2\sqrt{\sigma_1^2 + (\mu_i - q_i)^2}}(h_{r_i} + h_m + \pi_{r_i} + \pi_m) = 0$$

$$- \frac{1}{2}(h_{r_i} + h_m - \pi_{r_i} - \pi_m), \qquad (14)$$

$$\text{i.e., } q_i = \mu_i \pm \frac{\sigma_i \Gamma_3}{\sqrt{1 - \Gamma_3^2}},$$

where

$$\Gamma_3 = \frac{2\left(p_i - c + \dfrac{f(d)\mu}{Q^2}\right) - h_{r_i} - h_m + \pi_{r_i} + \pi_m}{h_{r_i} + h_m + \pi_{r_i} + \pi_m},$$

$$\text{and } \frac{\partial ETP}{\partial \delta_i} = -\eta_i \delta_i - 2(1 - \delta_i)\zeta_i(-1) = 0, \qquad (15)$$

$$\text{i.e., } \delta_i = \frac{2\zeta_i}{\eta_i + 2\zeta_i}.$$

The optimum order quantity is given by Equation (14) and service is given by Equation (15). Using the necessary conditions, one has

$$\frac{\partial LETP}{\partial \lambda_1} = \sqrt{3}\left(\lambda - \frac{\log(1 - \sqrt[3]{1 - \theta})}{\rho}\right) - d = 0,$$

$$\text{i.e., } d = \sqrt{3}\left(\lambda - \frac{\log(1 - \sqrt[3]{1 - \theta})}{\rho}\right),$$

$$\frac{\partial LETP}{\partial d} = -\lambda_1 + \frac{8c_2 S_s^2}{d^3}\left[\frac{l}{\sqrt{2S_t}}\right]\left[\frac{b}{\sqrt{2S_t}}\right]\frac{\mu}{Q} = 0, \qquad (16)$$

$$\text{i.e., } \lambda_1 = \frac{8c_2 S_s^2 \mu\left[\dfrac{l}{\sqrt{2S_t}}\right]\left[\dfrac{b}{\sqrt{2S_t}}\right]}{Qd^3}.$$

Equation (16) gives the optimum distance between two RFID readers. From the sufficient conditions, it can be concluded that since the second order derivatives are negative definite and the values of the Hessian matrix alternate, the required values of the decision variables are global.

$$\frac{\partial^2 ETP}{\partial q_i^2} = -\frac{1}{2} \frac{(h_{r_i} + h_m + \pi_{r_i} + \pi_m)\sigma_i^2}{\left(\sigma_i^2 + (\mu_i - q_i)^2\right)^{\frac{3}{2}}} - \frac{2f(d)\mu}{Q^3} < 0,$$

$$\frac{\partial^2 ETP}{\partial \delta_i^2} = -\eta_i^2 - 2\zeta_i < 0,$$

$$\frac{\partial^2 ETP}{\partial d^2} = -\frac{24c_2 S_s^2}{d^4} \left[\frac{l}{\sqrt{2}S_t}\right]\left[\frac{b}{\sqrt{2}S_t}\right]\frac{\mu}{Q} < 0.$$

Now, the calculation of the principal minors gives

$$H_1 = \begin{pmatrix} \frac{\partial^2 ETP}{\partial q_i^2} & \frac{\partial^2 ETP}{\partial q_i \partial \delta_i} \\ \frac{\partial^2 ETP}{\partial \delta_i \partial q_i} & \frac{\partial^2 ETP}{\partial \delta_i^2} \end{pmatrix} = \left[\frac{\left(h_{r_i} + h_m + \pi_{r_i} + \pi_m\right)\sigma_i^2}{2(\sigma_i^2 + (\mu_i - q_i)^2)^{\frac{3}{2}}} + \frac{2f(d)\mu}{Q^3}\right]\left[\eta_i^2 + 2\zeta_i\right] > 0,$$

$$H_2 = \begin{pmatrix} \frac{\partial^2 ETP}{\partial q_i^2} & \frac{\partial^2 ETP}{\partial q_i \partial \delta_i} & \frac{\partial^2 ETP}{\partial q_i \partial d} \\ \frac{\partial^2 ETP}{\partial \delta_i \partial q_i} & \frac{\partial^2 ETP}{\partial \delta_i^2} & \frac{\partial^2 ETP}{\partial \delta_i \partial d} \\ \frac{\partial^2 ETP}{\partial d \partial q_i} & \frac{\partial^2 ETP}{\partial d \partial \delta_i} & \frac{\partial^2 ETP}{\partial d^2} \end{pmatrix} = -(\eta_i + 2\zeta_i)\left[\left(\frac{\left(h_{r_i} + h_m + \pi_{r_i} + \pi_m\right)\sigma_i^2}{2\left(\sigma_i^2 + (\mu_i - q_i)^2\right)^{\frac{3}{2}}} + \frac{2f(d)\mu}{Q^3}\right)\right.$$

$$\left.\frac{24c_2 S_s^2}{d^4}\left[\frac{l}{\sqrt{2}S_t}\right]\left[\frac{b}{\sqrt{2}S_t}\right] - \left\{\frac{8\mu c_2 S_s^2}{Q^2 d^3}\left[\frac{l}{\sqrt{2}S_t}\right]\left[\frac{b}{\sqrt{2}S_t}\right]\right\}^2\right] < 0.$$

Lemma 1. *The values of the coordinated case are optimum if the Hessian matrix of third order (H_2) has a value less than zero, i.e., $H_2 < 0$. The required criteria is given by*

$$\left(\frac{(h_{r_i} + h_m + \pi_{r_i} + \pi_m)Q^2 \sigma_i^2}{2\mu\left(\sigma_i^2 + (\mu_i - q_i)^2\right)^{\frac{3}{2}}} + \frac{2f(d)}{Q}\right)\frac{3}{d} > \left[\frac{l}{\sqrt{2}S_t}\right]\left[\frac{b}{\sqrt{2}S_t}\right].$$

This Algorithm 2 helps to find the numerical results. The following steps are required as follows.

Algorithm 2:

Step 1	Input all parametric values. Set the value of i.
Step 2	Set the initial values of q_i.
Step 3	Write down the values of q_i from the Equation (14), δ_i from Equation (15), and d from the Equation (16).
Step 4	Find the value of q_i, δ_i, and d using the values from Step 1 and Step 2.
Step 4.a	If $q_i \geq q_{i+1}$ and $\delta_i \geq \delta_{i+1}$, then terminate the process. The optimum values are obtained as q_i^*, δ_i^*, and d^*.
Step 4.b	Else $q_i < q_{i+1}$ and $\delta_i < \delta_{i+1}$, go to Step 4.
Step 4.c	i as $i = i + 1$.
Step 5	Stop.

3.5. Revenue Sharing (RS)

Instead of a traditional policy, the manufacturer and multiple buyers are involved in a VMI contract. It is the manufacturer's role to support buyer such that the buyers so that they do not face losses due to the contract. Thus, a revenue sharing policy for coordinated supply chain is incurred by the manufacturer. If α ($0 < \alpha < 1$) is the sharable revenue by the manufacturer from the total profit, then the sharing mechanism for the coordinated case is αETP. The rest of the profit is accounted for by the manufacturer as he invests more in the business.

4. Numerical Experiment

Numerical experiments are used to validate this study numerically. Supportive data are taken from Sarkar et al. [19] and Xiao and Xu [5]. Some data are taken from an industry visit in West Bengal, India, which justifies the industry using this policy for their business. Two examples are provided here.

Example 1. *Table 3 gives all input values of the related parameters and Table 4 provides the optimum results for Example 1.*

Table 3. Input values of the parameters for Example 1.

Parameters	Values	Parameters	Values	Parameters	Values
n	2	(π_{r_1}, π_{r_2})	\$(10, 11)/unit	π_m	\$20/unit
(p_1, p_2)	\$(33, 34)/unit	(σ_1, σ_2)	(200, 202)	h_m	\$0.33c/unit/year
(μ_1, μ_2)	(200, 210)unit/year	(η_1, η_2)	\$(2, 3)	c	\$19/unit
(h_{r_1}, h_{r_2})	\$(0.21c, 0.23c)/unit/year	(ζ_1, ζ_2)	(0.7, 0.8)	w	\$30/unit
(c_1, c_2)	\$(140, 90)/reader	ρ	0.032	λ	10
l	200 m	b	200 m	S_s	50 m

Table 4. Optimum results from the numerical analysis for Example 1.

Coordination Case					
Variables	**Optimum Values**	**Number of Readers**	**Optimum Values**	**Results**	**Optimum Values**
(q_1^*, q_2^*)	(201.05, 210.82) unit	Type 1	4	d^*	85.56 m
(s_1^*, s_2^*)	(0.41, 0.35)	Type 2	8	ETP	\$19,783.46/cycle
				RFID cost	\$293.48/cycle
Non-Coordination Case					
Manufacturer					
(q_1^*, q_2^*)	(212.86, 251.57) unit	Type 1	4	d^*	85.56 m
RFID cost	\$82.62/cycle	Type 2	8	ETP_m	\$4431.10/cycle
Buyers					
(q_1^*, q_2^*)	(200, 210) unit	(s_1, s_2)	(0.41, 0.35)	ETP_r	\$15,179.07/cycle

Therefore, \$19,783.46 is the total profit of the entire supply chain. After gaining profit from the business, the manufacturer shares the revenue $\alpha = 0.45$ (Xiao and Xu [5]) of the total profit with the buyers, i.e., the manufacturer shares \$8902.56 with the two buyers. Thus, a (\$19,783.46 − \$8902.56) = \$10,880.90 profit is earned by the manufacturer from the VMI contract policy. The required number of Type 1 readers is 4 and the number of Type 2 readers is 8, which cover the total search area.

Example 2. *Table 5 gives all input values of the related parameters and Table 6 provides the optimum results for Example 2.*

Table 5. Input values of the parameters for Example 2.

Parameters	Values	Parameters	Values	Parameters	Values
n	2	(π_{r_1}, π_{r_2})	\$(6, 8)/unit	π_m	\$12/unit
(p_1, p_2)	\$(32, 30) /unit	(σ_1, σ_2)	(200, 202)	h_m	\$0.30c/unit/year
(μ_1, μ_2)	(190, 195) unit/year	(η_1, η_2)	\$(1.8, 1.5)	c	\$18/unit
(h_{r_1}, h_{r_2})	\$(0.18c, 0.19c)/unit/year	(ζ_1, ζ_2)	(0.6, 0.5)	w	\$27/unit
(c_1, c_2)	\$(138, 100)/reader	ρ	0.059	λ	12
l	210 m	b	190 m	S_s	45 m

Table 6. Optimum results from the numerical analysis for Example 2.

Coordination Case

Variables	Optimum Values	Number of Readers	Optimum Values	Results	Optimum Values
$(q_1{}^*, q_2{}^*)$	(190.07, 195.19) unit	Type 1	4	d^*	63.37 m
$(s_1{}^*, s_2{}^*)$	(0.40, 0.40)	Type 2	12	ETP	\$17,122.01/cycle
				RFID cost	\$434.65/cycle

Non-Coordination Case

Manufacturer

$(q_1{}^*, q_2{}^*)$	(216.36, 277.90) unit	Type 1	4	d^*	63.37 m
RFID cost	\$82.45/cycle	Type 2	12	ETP_m	\$3439.95/cycle

Buyers

$(q_1{}^*, q_2{}^*)$	(190, 195) unit	(s_1, s_2)	(0.40, 0.40)	ETP_r	\$13,464.34/cycle

$17,122.01 is the total profit of the entire supply chain for Example 2. The manufacturer shares the revenue $\alpha = 0.45$ (Xiao and Xu [5]) of the total profit with the buyers, i.e., the manufacturer shares \$7704.90 with the two buyers for the coordination business policy. Thus, a (\$17,122.01 − \$7704.90) = \$9417.11 profit is earned by manufacturer from the VMI contract policy. The total search area is covered by 4 number of Type 1 readers and 12 number of Type 2 readers.

Comparative Study of the Coordination and Non-Coordination Cases

From Table 7, it is seen that, manufacturer and buyer's profit in the coordination case are higher than the non-coordination case for both of the examples. The results conclude that the coordination VMI is more beneficial for both business participants. It is seen that the coordination policy is beneficial for both the manufacturer and the total supply chain profit, whereas buyers get more profit in the non-coordination policy than then coordination case. The shared revenue to the buyers in the coordinated case is less than the profit earned from the non-coordination case. As in the non-coordination policy, buyers can move freely according to their surrounding phenomenon, but in the coordination policy, the joint profit for the entire supply chain is more important for a long-term business rather than an individual one. Even though the profit of buyers is less in the coordination case, they do not face any loss from the business. In both cases of coordination and non-coordination policy, the manufacturer needs same number of readers as the area of the manufacturer is fixed for both of the cases.

Table 7. Comparative study between the coordination and non-coordination cases.

Participant(s)	Example 1		Example 2	
	Coordination Case	Non-Coordination Case	Coordination Case	Non-Coordination Case
Manufacturer	$10,880.90	$4431.10	$9417.11	$3439.95
Buyers	$8902.56	$15,179.07	$7704.9	$13,464.34
SCM	$19,783.46	$19,610.17	$17,122.01	$16,904.29

5. Discussion

Service is provided to the customers by buyers. This extra service makes an effect to the customers of satisfaction that they are happy and satisfied after buying products from that buyer. Whenever the service level increases, the satisfaction increases.

The sensitivities of the cost parameters of Example 1 over the total profit are depicted in Table 8. It is found that the manufacturing cost c is the most profit sensitive parameter relative to the others. Positive percentage changes of the parameter are more sensitive than negative changes, i.e., profit loss will be more whenever the cost increases. For the holding cost of the manufacturer (h_m), whenever h_m decreases and increases, the total profit decreases and increases, respectively. Negative percentage changes of h_m result in a smaller q_i, which leads to an increased RFID cost, i.e., decreasing h_m increases the radio frequency cost per cycle. The holding cost of the buyers and the shortage costs of the manufacturer and buyers have the same type of positive and negative changes. The service investment of the buyers has the usual impact on total profit, where increasing the investment causes less profit and vice-versa.

Table 8. Sensitivity analysis of the key parameters of Example 1.

Parameters	Percentage Changes	Changes in Profit (%)	Parameters	Percentage Changes	Changes in Profit (%)
h_{r_1}	−20	0.008	h_{r_2}	−20	0.02
	−10	0.005		−10	0.011
	+10	−0.008		+10	−0.13
	+20	−0.02		+20	−0.03
	−20	−2.52		−20	0.002
h_m	−10	−2.41	π_m	−10	0.001
	+10	−0.04		+10	−0.002
	+20	−0.09		+20	−0.005
	−20	0.002		−20	0.0008
π_{r_1}	−10	0.001	π_{r_2}	−10	0.0003
	+10	−0.001		+10	−0.0001
	+20	−0.002		+20	−0.0003
	−20	0.0002		−20	0.0002
η_1	−10	0.00007	η_2	−10	0.00008
	+10	−0.0001		+10	−0.0001
	+20	−0.0002		+20	−0.0002
	−20	4.75			
c	−10	1.14			
	+10	−4.29			
	+20	−26.88			

6. Conclusions and Future Recommendations

The measurement of the distance between two RFID readers could lead an SCM towards sustainability, which not only helps to prevent inventory shrinkage, but also helps to collect used products via RFID tags and readers. The distance between two readers was optimized, and based on this an industry manager can decide how many readers are needed to cover the whole search area. Results confirmed that RFID could be profitable for a VMI contract. This business policy was shown to be beneficial for the entire supply chain for the coordinated case. Besides that, a non-coordinated business policy provided profit to both the manufacturer and the buyers. This study ensured that the manufacturer need not be worried about the installation of smart technology by themselves. The manufacturer was benefited from a third-party provider and can mitigate the problems of unreliability within the SCM. Implementation of an RFID system was beneficial for the electronics industry by reducing e-waste and reusing products and parts.

However, this study did not consider the reuse of tags of used products, which can be an immediate extension for waste reduction. Within this study, it was assumed that the coverage area for Type 1 and Type 2 readers is perfectly circular. In general, it may not be circular always. Using any other geometrical shape or any non-geometrical shape, the number of the readers can be increased or decreased. Those will be further extensions of this model. This study did not consider any obstacles and interference sources within the range of the RFID readers. Therefore, using one or more obstacles or interference can change the number of Type 1 and Type 2 readers as Type 1 readers are more powerful than Type 2 readers. This study can be extended by optimizing the utilization of human labor and a comparative study can be made of human labor over autonomation. Another realistic scenario is imperfect production for which an autonomation policy can help reduce the unclear scarp faster than human labor.

Author Contributions: Conceptualization, methodology, software, validation, writing—original draft preparation, R.G.; formal analysis, data curation, visualization, supervision, S.P. and B.S.; investigation, resources, writing—review and editing, B.S.

Abbreviations

The following abbreviations are used in this manuscript:

SCM	Supply chain management
VMI	Vendor managed inventory
RFID	Radio frequency identification
DF	Distribution-free
RS	Revenue sharing
JIT	Just-in-time

References

1. Dong, Y.; Xu, K. A supply chain model of vendor managed inventory. *Trans. Res. Part E Logist. Trans. Rev.* **2002**, *38*, 75–95. [CrossRef]
2. Guo, Z.; Fang, F.; Whinston, A.B. Supply chain information sharing in a macro prediction market. *Decis. Support Syst.* **2006**, *42*, 1944–1958. [CrossRef]
3. Mukhopadhyay, S.K.; Yao, D.Q.; Yue, X. Information sharing of value-adding retailer in a mixed channel hi-tech supply chain. *J. Bus. Res.* **2008**, *61*, 950–958. [CrossRef]
4. Yan, R.; Pei, Z. Information asymmetry, pricing strategy and firm's performance in the retailer- multi-channel manufacturer supply chain. *J. Bus. Res.* **2011**, *64*, 377–384. [CrossRef]
5. Xiao, T.; Xu, T. Coordinating price and service level decisions for a supply chain with deteriorating item under vendor managed inventory. *Int. J. Prod. Econ.* **2013**, *145*, 743–752. [CrossRef]
6. Sarkar, B. An inventory model with reliability in an imperfect production process. *App. Math. Comput.* **2012**, *218*, 4881–4891. [CrossRef]
7. Cárdenas-Barrón, L.E.; Sarkar, B.; Treviño-Garza, G. Easy and improved algorithms to joint determination of the replenishment lot size and number of shipments for an EPQ model with rework. *Math. Comput. Appl.* **2013**, *18*, 132–138. [CrossRef]

8.   Tayyab, M.; Sarkar, B. Optimal batch quantity in a cleaner multi-stage lean production system with random defective rate. *J. Clean. Prod.* **2016**, *139*, 922–934. [CrossRef]

9.   Kim, M.S.; Sarkar, B. Multi-stage cleaner production process with quality improvement and lead time dependent ordering cost. *J. Clean. Prod.* **2017**, *144*, 572–590. [CrossRef]

10.   Guchhait, R.; Sarkar, M; Sarkar, B.; Pareek, S. Single-vendor multi-buyer game theoretic model under multi-factor dependent demand. *Int. J. Invent. Res.* **2018**, *4*, 303–332. [CrossRef]

11.   Majumder, A.; Guchhait, R.; Sarkar, B. Manufacturing quality improvement and setup cost reduction in a vendor-buyer supply chain model. *Eur. J. Ind. Eng.* **2017**, *11*, 588–612. [CrossRef]

12.   Tiwari, S.; Cárdenas-Barrón, L.E.; Goh, M.; Shaikh, A.A. Joint pricing and inventory model for deteriorating items with expiration dates and partial backlogging under two-level partial trade credits in supply chain. *Int. J. Prod. Econ.* **2018**, *200*, 16–36. [CrossRef]

13.   Sarkar, B. Mathematical and analytical approach for the management of defective items in a multi-stage production system. *J. Clean. Prod.* **2019**, *218*, 896–919. [CrossRef]

14.   Sarkar, B.; Guchhait, R.; Sarkar, M.; Cárdenas-Barrón, L.E. How does an industry manage the optimum cash flow within a smart production system with the carbon footprint and carbon emission under logistics framework? *Int. J. Prod. Econ.* **2019**, *213*, 243–257. [CrossRef]

15.   Gallego, G.; Moon, I. The distribution free newsboy problem: Review and extensions. *J. Oper. Res. Soc.* **1993**, *44*, 825–834. [CrossRef]

16.   Sarkar, B.; Guchhait, R.; Sarkar, M.; Pareek, S.; Kim, N. Impact of safety factors and setup time reduction in a two-echelon supply chain management. *Robot. Comput.-Integr. Manuf.* **2019**, *55*, 250–258. [CrossRef]

17.   Guchhait, R.; Pareek, S.; Sarkar, B. *Application of Distribution-Free Approach in Integrated and Dual-Channel Supply Chain under Buyback Contract*; IGI Global: Hershey, PA, USA, 2018; Chapter 21, pp. 303–332.

18.   Scarf, H. A min-max solution of an inventory problem. In *Studies in the Mathematical Theory of Inventory and Production*; Arrow, K.J., Karlin, S., Scarf, H.E., Eds.; Standford University Press: Redwood City, CA, USA, 1958, p. 910.

19.   Sarkar, B.; Zhang, C.; Majumder, A.; Sarkar, M.; Seo, Y.W. A distribution free newsvendor model with consignment policy and retailer's royalty reduction. *Int. J. Prod. Res.* **2018**, *56*, 5025–5044. [CrossRef]

20.   Sarkar, B.; Majumder, A.; Sarkar, M.; Kim, N.; Ullah, M. Effects of variable production rate on quality of products in a single-vendor multi-buyer supply chain management. *Int. J. Adv. Manuf. Technol.* **2018**, *99*, 567–581. [CrossRef]

21.   Moon, I.; Shin, E.; Sarkar, B. Min–max distribution free continuous-review model with a service level constraint and variable lead time. *Appl. Math. Comput.* **2014**, *229*, 310–315. [CrossRef]

22.   Sarkar, B. Supply chain coordination with variable backorder, inspections, and discount policy for fixed lifetime products. *Math. Probl. Eng.* **2016**, *2016*, 6318737. [CrossRef]

23.   Tiwari, S.; Jaggi, C.K.; Gupta, M.; Cárdenas-Barrón, L.E. Optimal pricing and lot-sizing policy for supply chain system with deteriorating items under limited storage capacity. *Int. J. Prod. Econ.* **2018**, *200*, 278–290. [CrossRef]

24.   Tiwari, S.; Wee, H.M.; Daryanto, Y. Big data analytics in supply chain management between 2010 and 2016: Insights to industries. *Comput. Ind. Eng.* **2018**, *115*, 319–330. [CrossRef]

25.   Meguerdichian, S.; Koushanfar, F.; Potkonjak, M.; Srivastava, M.B. Coverage problems in wireless ad-hoc sensor networks. In Proceedings of the IEEE INFOCOM 2001, Anchorage, AK, USA, 22–26 April 2001; pp. 1380–1387. [CrossRef]

26.   Zhang, H.; Hou, J.C. Maintaining sensing coverage and connectivity in large sensor networks. *Ad Hoc Sens. Wirel. Netw.* **2005**, *1*, 89–124. [CrossRef]

27.   Hefeeda, M.; Ahmadi, H. A probabilistic coverage protocol for wireless sensor networks. In Proceedings of the 2007 IEEE International Conference on Network Protocols, Beijing, China, 16–19 October 2007; pp. 41–50. [CrossRef]

28.   Dias, J.C.Q.; Calado J.M.F.; Luís Osório, L.F.; Morgado, L.F. RFID together with multi-agent systems to control global value chains. *Annu. Rev. Control* **2009**, *33*, 185–195. [CrossRef]

29.   Sarac, A.; Absi, N.; Dauzère-Pérès, S. A literature review on the impact of RFID technologies on supply chain management. *Int. J. Prod. Econ.* **2010**, *128*, 77–95. [CrossRef]

30. Kim, T.; Glock, C.H. On the use of RFID in the management of reusable containers in closed-loop supply chains under stochastic container return quantities. *Trans. Res. Part E Logist. Trans. Rev.* **2014**, *64*, 12–27. [CrossRef]

31. Sari. K. Exploring the impacts of radio frequency identification (RFID) technology on supply chain performance. *Eur. J. Oper. Res.* **2010**, *217*, 174–183. [CrossRef]

32. Biswal. A.K.; Jenamani, M.; Kumar, S.K. Warehouse efficiency improvement using RFID in a humanitarian supply chain: Implications for Indian food security system. *Trans. Res. Part E Logist. Trans. Rev.* **2018**, *109*, 205–224. [CrossRef]

33. Chen. J.C.; Cheng, C.H.; Huang, P.B. Supply chain management with lean production and RFID application: A case study. *Exp. Syst. Appl.* **2013**, *40*, 3389–3397. [CrossRef]

34. Tsao. Y.C.; Linh, V.T.; Lu, J.C. Closed-loop supply chain network designs considering RFID adoption. *Comput. Ind. Eng.* **2017**, *113*, 716–726. [CrossRef]

35. Ustundag. A.; Tanyas, M. The impacts of radio frequency identification (RFID) technology on supply chain costs. *Trans. Res. Part E Logist. Trans. Rev.* **2009**, *45*, 716–726. [CrossRef]

36. Jaggi. A.S.; Sawhney, R.S.; Balestrassi, P.P.; Simonton, J.; Upreti, G. An experimental approach for developing radio frequency identification (RFID) ready packaging. *J. Clean. Prod.* **2014**, *85*, 371–381. [CrossRef]

37. Shin, D.; Guchhait, R.; Sarkar, B.; Mittal, M. Controllable lead time, service level constraint, and transportation discounts in a continuous review inventory model. *RAIRO Oper. Res.* **2016**, *50*, 921–934. [CrossRef]

6

A Model and an Algorithm for a Large-Scale Sustainable Supplier Selection and Order Allocation Problem

Jong Soo Kim [1,*], Eunhee Jeon [1], Jiseong Noh [1] and Jun Hyeong Park [2]

[1] Department of Industrial and Management Engineering, Hanyang University, Erica Campus, Ansan 15588, Korea; jackiejeh@naver.com (E.J.); slaylina@naver.com (J.N.)
[2] KPMG Samjong Accounting Corp., Gangnam Finance Center, 152 Teheran-ro, Gangnam-gu, Seoul 06236, Korea; common123@nate.com
* Correspondence: pure@hanyang.ac.kr

Abstract: We consider a buyer's decision problem of sustainable supplier selection and order allocation (SSS & OA) among multiple heterogeneous suppliers who sell multiple types of items. The buyer periodically orders items from chosen suppliers to refill inventory to preset levels. Each supplier is differentiated from others by the types of items supplied, selling price, and order-related costs, such as transportation cost. Each supplier also has a preset requirement for minimum order quantity or minimum purchase amount. In the beginning of each period, the buyer constructs an SSS & OA plan considering various information from both parties. The buyer's planning problem is formulated as a mathematical model, and an efficient algorithm to solve larger instances of the problem is developed. The algorithm is designed to take advantage of the branch-and-bound method, and the special structure of the model. We perform computer experiments to test the accuracy of the proposed algorithm. The test result confirmed that the algorithm can find a near-optimal solution with only 0.82 percent deviation on average. We also observed that the use of the algorithm can increase solvable problem size by about 2.4 times.

Keywords: optimization; integer linear programming; sustainable; supplier selection; order allocation

---

1. Introduction

Supplier evaluation and selection are important decisions in the management of a supply network [1,2]. After determining suppliers to fill orders, the subsequent decision to allocate orders to chosen suppliers follows. Recent awareness in sustainable supply chain management frequently integrates these decisions with sustainability factors. The concept of sustainability plays an essential role in many organization and industries with respect to environmental protection and social responsibility [3]. As a consequence, sustainable supplier selection and order allocation (SSS & OA) emerges as a hot issue in the area of production and logistics. Huge number of papers have been published for this important decision problem. For example, Kuo et al. [4] developed a supplier selection system through fuzzy AHP and DEA. Their method was successfully applied to an auto lighting system company in Taiwan. The SSS & OA can be included in green supply chain management to improve the performance of a supply chain. Roehrich et al. [5] did such a study for a globalized German-based aircraft interior manufacturer and six key suppliers. There are a few commercial systems having supplier selection and evaluation functions. eSourcing Capability Models developed by ITSqc and CMMI-ACQ, made by SEI, are useful systems in the business area for acquiring products and services [6,7].

This paper studies an SSS & OA problem for a buyer who performs regular replenishment activities with heterogeneous suppliers who sell a few types of items. The system analyzed here is a two-stage supply chain system, which consists of a single buyer controlling inventories using a periodic order-up-to inventory control policy, and multiple heterogeneous suppliers who can supply items in response to orders from the buyer. The buyer sells items to end customers and replenishes items regularly based on the inventory status and future demand forecasts. In response to an order from the buyer, the suppliers transport the ordered amount after a constant lead time.

The problem analyzed in this paper is a buyer's decision problem of selecting suppliers and, at the same time, order allocation for selected suppliers. Based on such replenishment decisions, the buyer considers various system variables and several contract terms, including minimum order quantity (MOQ) and minimum purchase amount (MPA) requirements. The MOQ and MPA specify that suppliers accept only those orders that exceed a predetermined minimum order quantity and minimum order value [8–10]. Additional factors the buyer considers in the decision process include working capital requirement and sustainability factors.

Even though several optimization model variants have been introduced for systems similar to the one analyzed in this paper, a detailed model representing all the important characteristics of the SSS & OA process has not yet been analyzed. To handle larger instances of real decision processes requiring big data and excessive computational capacity, an efficient new solution methodology is also desired to make full use of a developed model. Considering this research need, the current paper introduces a mathematical model and solution methodology, which are constructed by relaxation and ideas from the branch-and-bound method.

2. Literature Review

A large number of studies dealing with the supplier selection problem have been published. A recent survey paper reviewed 370 works in this area [11]. As stated in their review, the subjects of supplier selection problems are very wide, ranging from criteria analysis for supplier selection to multiple criteria inventory control problems. Among numerous topics studied in this area, our review of previous research is narrowly focused on the supplier selection and order allocation problem of a single buyer dealing with multiple items, as well as multiple suppliers requiring MOQ and MPA constraints, working capital requirement constraint, and sustainability features. Thus, the basic forms of research related to this paper can be classified into two sub-areas. The first sub-area is about supplier selection and order allocation, while the second area is the sustainable supplier selection and order allocation. Previous research on the two sub-areas are presented followed by a discussion on the research gaps and contribution of this paper.

2.1. Supplier Selection and Order Allocation

To solve the supplier selection and order allocation problem, Ghorbani et al. [12] proposed a two-phased model. At first, suppliers are evaluated according to both quantitative and qualitative criteria resulting from SWOT analysis. Shannon entropy is used to calculate criteria weights. Then, the results are used as an input for an integer linear programming model to allocate orders to suppliers. Nazari-Shirkouhi et al. [13] provided an integrated linear programming model that aimed to minimize total ordering costs and defective items. Jadidi et al. [14], [15] modeled the supplier selection as a multi-objective optimization model where minimization of price, rejects, and lead-time were considered as three objectives. Sodenkamp et al. [16] proposed a novel meta-approach for collaborative multi-objective supplier selection and order allocation (SSOA)decisions by combining multi-criteria decision analysis and linear programming. The proposed model accounted for suppliers' performance synergy effects within a hierarchical decision-making process. Shabanpour et al. [17]

proposed efficiency improvement plans for supplier selection, including goal programming and data envelopment analysis applications to rank sustainable suppliers.

In addition to usual constraints included in the previous research on SSOA, our model includes two other kinds of features practiced in the real world. The first constraint is MOQ/MPA-related practices, and the second is limitation caused by working capital management. Research concerning an SSOA considering the MOQ/MPA requirements was initiated by Robb and Silver [18]. Afterward, several researchers, including Kiesmüller et al. [9], Zhao and Katehakis [19], Zhou et al. [20], and Meena and Sarmah [21] have studied several variants of the SSOA problems with associated requirements. All of these studies could be categorized a basic model, because all studied a single-item problem. More realistic multi-item problems were first analyzed by Zhou [22], and Aktin and Gergin [23]. Recently, Park et al. [10] considered an order allocation problem with the MOQ/MPA requirements and proposed a rolling-horizon implementation strategy for solving a formulated optimization model more efficiently. Their model, however, did not contain a sustainability feature or working capital requirements.

Supply chain models typically only consider the physical transformation activities and disregard the financial implications of those activities. Recently, however, the literature on supply chain management (SCM) became aware of the real-world situation that financing and operational problems are closely connected and, thus, optimizing the two problems jointly could improve the entire performance of a supply chain [24,25]. However, only a few related papers were found on an SSOA with a working capital requirement (WCR). Chao et al. [26] developed recursive equations for a replenishment (order size determination) problem with a cash flow constraint. The problem was for a single item without considering supplier's perspectives, and thus could be categorized as the primitive type of research compared with our current problem. Bendavid et al. [27] studied a buyer's replenishment problem with a single type of item using a more sophisticated flow balance equation for the working capital constraint. Bian et al. [24] presented a new generic working capital requirement model for a single-item lot sizing problem. They presented a mixed integer programming model, including a flow balance equation, for operating working capital requirement (OWCR). To the best of our knowledge, there is no prior work addressing the SSOA problem that also directly considered WCR or OWCR.

2.2. Sustainable Supplier Selection and Order Allocation

The traditional supplier selection and order allocation problem has now been changed to an SSS & OA, where sustainability triple bottom line (3BL) attributes (environmental, economic, and social) are integrated into the selection and allocation processes [28]. The environmental factors can also be evaluated in terms of political, economic, social, technological, and environmental aspects, as can be seen in the well-known method named PESTEL [29]. The literature on sustainable supplier selection is quite rich. A few prior studies include [30–48]. These studies used various kinds of methods, including the AHP, DEMATEL, ANP, TOPSIS, multi-objective GA, DEA, and VIKOR for evaluating and selecting desirable sustainable suppliers. All the above referenced research deals with the question of which sustainable supplier to select. Research dealing with order allocation together with sustainable supplier selection is in its early stages. Only five papers on SSS & OA have been noted during the literature review. Kannan et al. [49] introduced a fuzzy TOPSIS method for supplier selection and a bi-objective model for order allocation. Govindan et al. [50] analyzed a five-echelon supply chain for assigning suppliers for a single product. Aktin and Gergin [23] introduced a mixed integer programming model using 3BL index scores. Problems analyzed in these three papers can be categorized as basic SSS & OA because they considered a single product and single period case with a deterministic demand. Recently, more sophisticated models have been offered by Gören [51] and Ghadimi et al. [1]. The former solved a problem with multiple products and suppliers, and formulated a bi-objective optimization model for a single period decision. The latter analyzed a similar system, but formulated it as a multi-period bi-objective model. However, both of these studies assumed a deterministic demand and did not consider other realistic features, such as transportation lead time or MOQ requirement.

2.3. Research Gap and the Contribution of This Paper

As can be found in the discussion of previous research and also in Table 1, our study is the first attempt to analyze the most realistic and complicated SSS & OA problem representing various important features of a real system, including transportation features (transportation lead times and capacity of the suppliers) and buyer monetary limitations (multi-period working capital flow balances and limitation, time value of money). Given the various aspects we are considering for this analysis, the optimization model introduced in this paper is the most sophisticated of any existing models representing SSS & OA activities. One of the challenges we experienced during the development of such a large-scale model is that none of the existing methods can solve our model to a desired accuracy within a practical time limit. For example, a problem with 20 items and 12 time periods cannot be solved within 24 h time limit. When we consider that real-world problems can include more than 100 items, it is necessary to fill this research gap. In response to this research challenge, a new algorithm specifically aimed to solve such a big model is developed. During a computational experiment, the algorithm is capable of solving such a model within a reasonable computational time with desired accuracy.

Table 1. Comparison of the contributions of different authors.

Author(s)	Problem Type		Model Type		Demand Process			Number of Items		Number of Periods		New Solution Method	Constraints			Transportation Lead Time
			Supplier			Stochastic										
	Supplier Selection	Order Allocation	Single Supplier	Multiple Supplier	Determi-nistic	Stationary	Non-Stationa-ry	Single Item	Multi-Item	Single Period	Multi-Period		MOQ/MPA	WCM	Sustainability	
Zhao and Katehakis [19]		✓	✓			✓					✓					
Zhou et al. [20]		✓	✓			✓		✓			✓					
Chao et al. [26]		✓	✓			✓		✓			✓	✓		✓		
Zhou [22]		✓	✓			✓			✓		✓		✓			
Kiesmüller et al. [9]		✓	✓			✓		✓			✓		✓			✓
Kannan et al. [49]	✓	✓		✓	✓			✓		✓					✓	
Meena and Sarmah [21]	✓	✓		✓	✓			✓		✓			✓			
Govindan et al. [38]	✓	✓		✓	✓			✓		✓		✓			✓	
Ayhan and Kilic [52]	✓	✓		✓	✓				✓	✓					✓	
Trapp and Sarkis [43]	✓			✓					✓	✓		✓				
Aktin and Gergin [23]	✓	✓		✓	✓				✓	✓					✓	
Bendavid et al. [27]	✓	✓	✓			✓		✓			✓			✓		
Gören [51]	✓	✓		✓	✓				✓		✓				✓	
Ghadimi et al. [1]	✓	✓		✓	✓				✓	✓					✓	
Bian et al. [24]	✓	✓	✓		✓			✓			✓	✓		✓		
Park et al. [10]	✓	✓		✓			✓		✓		✓		✓			✓
This model	✓	✓		✓			✓		✓		✓	✓	✓	✓	✓	✓

3. System Description and Assumptions

The system analyzed in this paper involves two or more heterogeneous suppliers and a single buyer. The suppliers are distinguished from each other by the type and selling prices of the items they carry, delivery lead times, and minimum order quantity requirements. The buyer carries multiple types of items which are sold to end customers. The items are replenished to minimize related inventory costs based on a periodic order-up-to inventory control policy. Previous research on inventory control frequently assumed that the end customer demand can be described by a known probability distribution. However, since the future demand for a product can be influenced by unforeseeable events, complete information on future demand distribution may not be available [53]. Considering this kind of real-world situation, this paper assumes that the demand of the end customers may not belong to a theoretical probability distribution. Other assumptions are as follows:

- There is a planned allocation schedule of money for each period during a planning horizon.
- Money remaining at the end of a period is inflated by interest rate and carried forward to the next period.
- Payment for purchase and transportation costs are made as an order is placed.
- Nonzero transportation lead time exists between an order placement and the arrival of the ordered amount.
- Major and minor ordering costs occur when an order is placed.
- The major ordering cost occurs as a fixed amount when an order is placed.
- The minor ordering cost occurs in proportion to an order size.
- A supplier has limited production capacity and thus has an order size limit per order.
- A supplier has a limited number of transportation vehicles.
- Any amount of an item can be purchased at a price higher than supplier's regular price from a spot market.
- 3BL factor scores of each potential supplier are prepared for input to an SSS & OA decision.

Considering the characteristics of each supplier, the buyer must make an SSS & OA decision at the beginning of each period. The objective that the buyer is trying to achieve is to minimize the net present value of the related costs occurring throughout the planning horizon. Required notations are as follows.

Indices:

i	item number, $i = 1, 2, \cdots, I$,
j	3BL index, $j = \text{env}, \text{eco}, \text{soc}$,
k	supplier number, $k = 1, 2, \cdots, K$,
t	period, $t = 1, 2, \cdots, T$, where T denotes the end period of the planning horizon.

Parameters:

$K(i)$	set of suppliers who sell item i, $\forall i$,
$I(k)$	set of items sold by supplier k, $\forall k$,
d_{it}	demand forecast of item i during future period t, $\forall i, t$,
ξ_{it}	standard deviation of error of $d_{i,t}$, $\forall i, t$,
v_i	volume of item i, $\forall i$,
wc_t	warehouse capacity of the buyer during period t, $\forall t$,
h_i	holding cost of item i, $\forall i$,
b_i	shortage cost of item i, $\forall i$,
p_{ikt}	unit purchase price for item i paid by the buyer to supplier k during period t, $\forall i, k \in K(i), t$,
p_{it}^s	unit spot market price during period t for item i, $\forall i, t$,
$owcl_t$	operating working capital limit in period t, $\forall t$,
$capt_t$	capital originally allocated to period t, $\forall t$,
ic_t	inventory control related cost (holding plus shortage costs) in period t, $\forall t$,

rc_t replenishment related cost in period t, $\forall t$,

r per-period discount (interest) rate.

moq_{ik} per-period minimum order quantity specified by supplier k for item i, $\forall i, k$,

mpa_k per-period minimum purchase amount set by supplier k, $\forall k$,

mpl_{ik} per-period maximum purchase limit for item i specified by supplier k, $\forall i, k \in K(i)$,

ma_k major ordering cost for supplier k, $\forall k$,

mi_{ik} minor ordering cost for item i for supplier k, $\forall i, k \in K(i)$,

sc_{jk} jth 3BL factor score of supplier k, $\forall j, k$,

$target_{jt}$ jth 3BL factor target score of period t, $\forall j, t$,

l_k supplier k's lead time, $\forall k$,

f_{kt} freight fair per vehicle of supplier k during period t, $\forall t, k$,

vc_k volume capacity per vehicle of supplier k, $\forall k$,

nv_{kt} number of vehicles available for transportation of supplier k in period t, $\forall k$,

$\widetilde{x}_{ikt}$ purchase already made at the start of past period t and in delivery of item i from supplier k, $\forall i, k \in K(i)$, $t = -1, -2, \cdots, 1 - l_k$,

IP_{i0} inventory position of item i at the start of planning, $\forall i$,

M very large number.

Decision variables:

IP_{it} inventory position of item i at the end of period t, $\forall i, t$,

IP_{it}^+ positive part of $IP_{i,t}$, $\forall i, t$,

IP_{it}^- negative part of $IP_{i,t}$, $\forall i, t$,

x_{ik1} purchase amount of item i from supplier k during the present period (period 1), $\forall i, k \in K(i)$,

x_{ikt} planned purchase amount of item i from supplier k during future period t, $\forall i, k \in K(i)$, $t = 2, \cdots, T$,

x_{i1}^s purchase quantity of item i from the spot market for the present period, $\forall i$,

x_{it}^s planned purchase quantity of item i from the spot market for period t, $\forall i$, $t = 2, \cdots, T$,

RL_{it} replenishment level of item i after the arrival of orders scheduled to arrive at the start of period t, $\forall i, t$,

o_{jt} positive deviation from target $_{jt}$ in period t,

α_{ikt}^{moq} binary integer for controlling the minimum order quantity requirement, $\forall i, k, t$,

α_{kt}^{mpa} binary integer for controlling the minimum purchase amount requirement, $\forall k, t$,

β_{kt}^{MA} binary integer for controlling major ordering cost, $\forall k, t$,

β_{ikt}^{MI} binary integer for controlling minor ordering cost, $\forall i, k, t$,

θ_i safety factor of item i, $\forall i$.

4. Model Formulation

4.1. Relevant Costs

Cost factors included in the total cost of our model are inventory-related costs (holding and shortage costs) and replenishment-related costs (major and minor ordering costs, transportation, and purchase costs). Inventory-related costs are the sum of inventory holding and shortage costs incurred during the planning horizon, and are expressed as in Equation (1).

$$ic_t = \sum_{i=1}^{I} \left(\frac{1}{2} h_i (RL_{it} + IP_{it}^+) + b_i IP_{it}^- \right), \quad \forall t. \tag{1}$$

Transportation cost of period t is

$$\sum_{k=1}^{K} f_{kt} NV_{kt}.$$

Purchase cost is the sum of the payment to suppliers and spot market.

$$\sum_{i=1}^{I} \sum_{k \in K(i)} p_{ikt} x_{ikt} + \sum_{i=1}^{I} s p_{it} x_{it}^s.$$

Major and minor ordering costs are as follows:

$$\sum_{k=1}^{K} ma_k \beta_{kt}^{MA} + \sum_{i=1}^{I} \sum_{k \in K(i)} mi_{ik} \beta_{ikt}^{MI}.$$

Replenishment-related cost is the sum of the cost factors in Equation (2).

$$
rc_t = \sum_{k=1}^{K} (ma_k \beta_{kt}^{MA} + f_{kt} nv_{kt}) + \sum_{i=1}^{I} \sum_{k \in K(i)} (p_{ikt} x_{ikt} + mi_{ik} \beta_{ikt}^{MI})
$$
$$
+ \sum_{i=1}^{I} s p_{it} x_{it}^s, \quad \forall t.
\tag{2}
$$

The total cost function of the model (*TC*) is the present value of inventory control cost plus replenishment-related cost incurred during the planning horizon. When we use a discounting factor *r* to account for the time value of money, the cost function can be written as

$$TC = \sum_{t=1}^{T} \frac{1}{(1+r)^t} (ic_t + rc_t).$$

4.2. Operating Working Capital Requirement

In practice, many firms are financially constrained; therefore, their ability to manage their inventories is directly affected by many factors, including their operating working capitals. To represent this financial constraint, the following equations are included.

$$ic_t + rc_t \leq owcl_t, \quad \forall t, \tag{3}$$

$$owcl_t = capt_t + (1 + \gamma)(owcl_{t-1} - rc_{t-1} - ic_{t-1}), \quad \forall t. \tag{4}$$

Equation (3) specifies that the cost occurring during period *t* is limited by an operating working capital limit (OWCL) in that period. The equation was based on the cash-to-cash methodology found in Theodore Farris and Hutchison [54], and Hofmann and Kotzab [55]. Consequently, we assumed that the OWCR for replenishing a unit of product depends on the money invested in the related operations, for example, purchasing, setup, transportation, inventory holding, and shortage costs. Also, as in Bian et al. [24], it is assumed that the profit portion of the sales revenue is not accounted for in the OWCR. Profit can be allocated to other higher priority objectives of the firm (e.g., debt reduction, dividend payments, or internal and external investment). Thus, the profit portion of a firm's activities was not represented in our model (e.g., Equations (3) and (4)). Equation (4) models monetary flow during two adjacent periods and ensures that the OWCL in period *t* equals the sum of the operating working capital (OCM) allocated to period t and the money left in the previous period inflated by interest and forwarded to the current period.

4.3. 3BL Target Constraints

$$\sum_{i=1}^{I} \sum_{k=1}^{K} sc_{jk} \beta_{ikt}^{MI} - o_{jt} = target_{jt}, \quad \forall j, t. \tag{5}$$

As stated in Aktin and Gergin [23], corporate sustainability is concerned with the integration of environmental, economical, and social dimensions, called the triple-bottom-line (3BL), into the company processes. In response to this need, SSS & OA decisions try to combine the 3BL sustainability factors into supplier selection and order allocation activities. A practical way to find good sustainable procurement strategies is to measure sustainability scores for all potential suppliers. Then, the completed 3BL factor scores of each supplier are input to a mathematical model formulated for supplier selection and order allocation. Equation (5) performs this kind of function. It states that all selected suppliers' combined 3BL score should at least equal to a preset target score for environmental, economical, and social dimensions.

4.4. Mathematical Programming Model

In this section, we define a mixed integer programming model to solve the SSS & OA problem. The proposed MIP model can be defined as follows:

MIP1: Min TC
s.t.

$$IP_{it-1} + \sum_{k \in K(i) | l_k = 0} x_{ikt} + \sum_{\substack{k \in K(i) | l_k \geq 1 \\ t - l_k \leq 0}} \widetilde{x}_{ik,t-l_k} + \sum_{\substack{k \in K(i) | l_k \geq 1 \\ t - l_k > 0}} x_{ik,t-l_k} + x_{it}^s = RL_{it}, \tag{6}$$
$$\forall i, t,$$

$$RL_{it} - d_{it} = IP_{it}, \ \forall i, t, \tag{7}$$

$$IP_{it} = IP_{it}^+ - IP_{it}^-, \quad \forall i, t, \tag{8}$$

$$\sum_{k=1}^{K} (ma_k \beta_{kt}^{MA} + f_{kt} nv_{kt}) + \sum_{i=1}^{I} \sum_{k \in K(i)} (p_{ikt} x_{ikt} + mi_{ik} \beta_{ikt}^{MI}) + \sum_{i=1}^{I} p_{it}^s x_{it}^s \\ = rc_t, \ \forall t, \tag{9}$$

$$\sum_{i=1}^{I} \left(\frac{1}{2} h_i (RL_{it} + IP_{it}^+) + b_i IP_{it}^- \right) = ic_t, \ \forall t, \tag{10}$$

$$ic_t + rc_t \leq owcl_t, \ \forall t, \tag{11}$$

$$owcl_t = capt_t + (1 + \gamma)(owcl_{t-1} - rc_{t-1} - ic_{t-1}), \ \forall t, \tag{12}$$

$$IP_{it} \geq \theta_i \xi_{it}, \ \forall i, t, \tag{13}$$

$$x_{ikt} \leq mpl_{ik}, \ \forall i, k \in K(i), t, \tag{14}$$

$$x_{ikt} \leq M\alpha_{ikt}^{moq}, \ \forall i, k \in K(i), t, \tag{15}$$

$$x_{ikt} \geq moq_{ik} - M(1 - \alpha_{ikt}^{moq}), \ \forall i, k \in K(i), t, \tag{16}$$

$$\sum_{i \in I(k)} p_{ikt} x_{ikt} \leq M\alpha_{kt}^{mpa}, \ \forall k, t, \tag{17}$$

$$\sum_{i \in I(k)} p_{ikt} x_{ikt} \geq mpa_k - M(1 - \alpha_{kt}^{mpa}), \ \forall k, t, \tag{18}$$

$$\sum_{i=1}^{I} \sum_{k=1}^{K} sc_{jk} \beta_{ikt}^{MI} - o_{jt} = target_{jt}, \ \forall j, t, \tag{19}$$

$$\sum_{i \in I(k)} x_{ikt} \leq M\beta_{kt}^{MA}, \ \forall k, t, \tag{20}$$

$$x_{ikt} \leq M\beta_{ikt}^{MI}, \ \forall i, k \in K(i), t, \tag{21}$$

$$\sum_{i=1}^{I} v_i RL_{it} \leq wc_t, \ \forall t, \tag{22}$$

$$\sum_{i \in K(i)} v_i x_{ikt} \leq vc_k nv_{kt}, \ \forall k, t, \tag{23}$$

$$x_{ikt} \geq 0, \quad \alpha_{ikt}^{moq}, \quad \beta_{ikt}^{MI} \text{ 0 or 1}, \quad \forall i, k \in K(i), t, \tag{24}$$

$$\alpha_{kt}^{mpa}, \quad \beta_{kt}^{MA}, \text{ 0 or 1}, \quad nv_{kt}, \text{ nonnegative integer}, \quad \forall k, t, \tag{25}$$

$$x_{it}^s, \quad RL_{it}, \quad IP_{it}^+, \quad IP_{it}^- \geq 0, \quad IP_{it}, \text{ unrestricted}, \quad \forall i, t, \tag{26}$$

$$o_{jt} \geq 0, \quad \forall j, t, \tag{27}$$

$$\theta_i, \text{ unrestricted}, \quad \forall i, \tag{28}$$

$$M, \quad \text{large number.} \tag{29}$$

The objective function in Equation (1) is to minimize the present value of the expected total cost, which is the sum of the inventory and replenishment-related costs. Equation (6) enforces that the replenishment level of item i is the sum of the initial inventory, spot market purchases, and orders scheduled to arrive from each supplier during the period. Equation (7) regulates that the net inventory of item i at the end of period t is equal to the inventory position at the start of the period, minus the depletion due to the demand of item i during period t. Equation (8) sets that, at the end of period t, the net inventory of item i, $IP_{i,t}$, is equal to the on-hand inventory level of item i at the end of period t, $IP_{i,t}^+$, minus the shortage level of item i at the end of period t, $IP_{i,t}^-$.

Equations (9)–(12) enforce the operating working capital limit. Equations (13) and (14) describe the customer service level and maximum purchase limit set by a supplier, respectively. Equations (15) and (16) are for the minimum order quantity requirement. Term moq_{ik} in the constraint is the minimum order size of supplier k, and α_{ikt}^{moq} is a binary variable used to enforce the relationship as planned. The variable M is a very large number used to activate the minimum order constraint only when an order is placed. As a consequence, if the buyer purchases item i from supplier k, the term α_{ikt}^{moq} will become 1 in Equation (15), thereby validating Equation (16) and enforcing the minimum order size requirement. The next constraints, described by Equations (17) and (18), concern the minimum purchase amount requirement. If the buyer purchases an item from supplier k, Equation (17) makes the term α_{kt}^{mpa} equal to 1. Equation (18), in this case, forces the purchase amount to be at least the minimum purchase amount (mpa_k). Equation (19) concerns the 3BL target constraint. Equations (20) and (21) control the major and minor ordering occurrences. The following Equations (22) and (23) address the buyer's warehouse capacity and supplier's transportation capacity, respectively.

MIP1 has $5IKT + 3IT + 4KT + JT + 5T$ constraints and $3IKT + 5IT + 3KT + JT + I$ variables. If a contract problem has a weekly planning grid with a one year planning period (52 weeks) and 10 suppliers with 20 items, 58,136 constraints and 37,086 variables are present. It is possible to solve the size of MIP1 using commercially available software tools (GAMS, LINGO etc.). However, if the size of MIP1 grows considerably large for real-world applications, a prohibitive computational burden will result. In other words, expanding the size of the system requires an excessive computational resource. Considering this difficulty, a faster and reasonably accurate algorithm is needed for real life problems. The next section discusses such an algorithm.

5. Solution Method

5.1. Conceptual View of the Proposed Algorithm

The algorithm introduced in this section is referred to as the branch-and-freeze (BF) algorithm. The logical idea behind the BF algorithm is to solve relaxed problems (sub-problems) of the original problem in a manner similar to the branch-and-bound method. We observed that the MOQ and MPA constraints in Equations (15)–(18) are computationally burdensome because of the binary variables involved and the large number of constraints, amounting to the total $2IKT + KT$. Based on this observation, the sub-problems are created by removing the MOQ and MPA constraints of the original problem, MIP1. When the sub-problem is solved, one of three cases can occur, as illustrated in Figure 1.

The first of the three cases is that a solution to a sub-problem also satisfies the MOQ and MPA constraints of all suppliers, which we call complete feasibility (CF) case. In Figure 1 below, the CF case is represented by the left-most branch. In this case, the solution is also optimal to MIP1. Since, the original problem is solved optimally, the algorithm stops. The second case occurs when the MOQ and MPA constraints are satisfied partially, which is the situation where the solution to a sub-problem satisfies the two constraints of all suppliers up to a certain intermediate period, but not to the end of the planning horizon. This case is named partial feasibility (PF). When PF occurs, the algorithm stores the current output up to the satisfied period, which is called freezing. For the remaining periods that are not frozen, a new condensed problem is generated by adding the MOQ and MPA constraints of the supplier(s) whose constraints were violated in the previous run. In Figure 1 below, this process is denoted by the circle with FC (freezing and condensing). When the condensed problem is solved afterwards, it results in one of the three cases already explained above.

The final case, which is in the right most side of Figure 1, is the complete infeasibility (CI) case, where the sub-problem's output can satisfy none of the suppliers' MOQ and MPA constraints, even at the starting period. If this happens, a new sub-problem is created by adding all of the removed constraints. This process is denoted by a circle with an R (restoring) inside. When a restored problem is solved, one of the same three cases can occur. A node is fathomed when the stop condition is met after CF, or no additional constraint is available for addition after PF or CI. The best feasible solution to the original problem is the best feasible solution found until all end nodes are fathomed. If there is no feasible solution found up to that point, the original problem is infeasible.

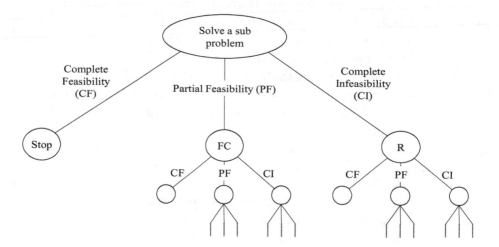

Figure 1. Conceptual view of the branch-and-freeze (BF) algorithm.

5.2. Branch-and-Freeze (BF) Algorithm

The BF algorithm can be described formally as follows:

Step 1: (Initialize)

Let the current period be period 1.
Set the current inventory level, $z_{i,0} = 0$ for $i = 1, 2, \cdots, I$.
Forecast demand for all future periods, $d_{i,t}$ for $t = 1, 2, \cdots, T$.

Step 2: (Generate sub-problem for the first run)

Construct the sub-problem by removing the MOQ and MPA constraints (Equations (15)–(18) from MIP1).

Step 3: (Run sub-problem)

Run the current sub-problem.

Step 4: (Check status and branch)

> Step 4.1 Check the output of Step 3. If status is PF or CF, go to Step 4.3.
> Step 4.2 (Complete feasibility case)
> Algorithm found a feasible solution. Stop.
> Step 4.3 (Partial feasibility or complete infeasibility case)
> If there is no constraint to add, the given problem is infeasible. Stop.
> Go to Step 5 if status is PF. Otherwise, go to Step 6.

Step 5: (Partial feasibility case)

> Step 5.1 (Freeze the output)
> Freeze the output for the feasible periods.
> Step 5.2 (Re-initialize)
> Let the starting period be the first infeasible period.
> Reset the current inventory level to the net inventory level of the last feasible period.
> Reset the forecast of demand from the starting to the end periods of the planning horizon.
> Step 5.3 (Prepare a sub-problem)
> Prepare a new sub-problem by adding the MOQ or MPA constraints of the supplier(s), which caused infeasibility during the previous run. Go to Step 3.

Step 6: (Complete Infeasibility case)

> Prepare a new sub-problem by adding the MOQ or MPA constraints of the supplier(s), which caused infeasibility during the previous run. Go to Step 3.

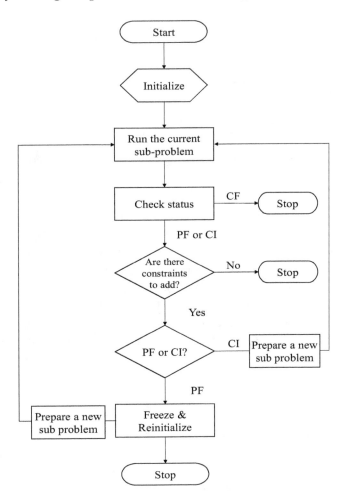

Figure 2. Flow chart of the BF algorithm.

Step 1 is for the initialization required for the first planning run. The constraint relaxation that is required to solve MIP1 without the MOQ and MPA constraints is done in Step 2. After initialization and relaxation, a relaxed version of MIP1 (sub-problem) is solved in Step 3. In Step 4, the output of the previous run is evaluated for status. Based on the status, the algorithm stops or proceeds to Steps 5 or 6 when there is (are) a constraint(s) to add. Figure 2 shows the flow of the algorithm. Figure 3 illustrates an implementation of the algorithm.

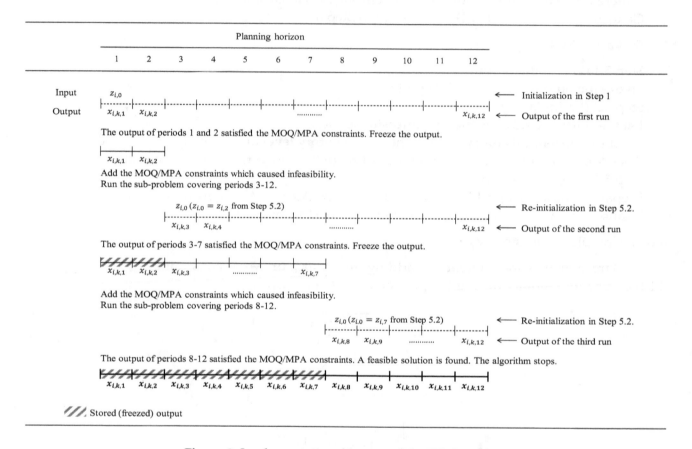

Figure 3. Implementation diagram of the BF algorithm.

6. Numerical Experiments

In this chapter, numerical experiments are carried out with two objectives in mind. The first objective of the numerical experiment is to test the accuracy of the BF algorithm by comparing it with a commercially available software tool (GAMS/XPRESS solver). The second experiment explores the maximum size of MIP1 that can be solved by the BF algorithm and by commercial software tools (GAMS/XPRESS and GAMS/COINGLPK solvers). The results of these two numerical experiments will determine the effectiveness of the BF algorithm. The GAMS used in the numerical experiment is a very popular modeling language containing many powerful solvers. Thus, it is a suitable competitor for verifying the accuracy and identifying the maximum solvable problem size of the BF algorithm. The experiments were performed on a PC with Microsoft 7 OS, 3.4GHz Intel i5 CPU, and 16 GB RAM.

6.1. Accuracy Test of the BF Algorithm

The purpose of this experiment is to identify the accuracy of the BF algorithm by comparing the results obtained using our algorithm with those of the GAMS/XPRESS solver. The comparative experiment is performed with the assumption that the item's demand is generated from a stationary demand process. Most previous studies on inventory management performed experiments by assuming that demand follows a stationary demand process, such as a Poisson or normal distribution [56]. For our problem, many relevant studies, including Robb and Silver [18],

Chen et al. [57], and Zhou [22], also assumed a normal distribution. This experiment is also carried out similarly by assuming a normal distribution assumption. The number of item types is set to five. The actual demand data for each item were generated from five different normal distributions $(N(400, 20^2), N(600, 30^2), N(700, 40^2), N(800, 40^2), N(900, 50^2))$. Each item's demand forecast is prepared using the forecasting module of SPSS.

To obtain the average total cost, the experiment was repeated 10 times for each setting. The average cost obtained in this manner is plugged into the following percent deviation measure to identify the accuracy of the BF algorithm.

$$\text{Percent deviation} = \frac{\text{BF algorithm' cost} - \text{GAMS' cost}}{\text{GAMS' cost}} \times 100.$$

The experimental design is as follows:

- There are 10 suppliers in the system.
- Transportation lead time is zero.
- Each supplier can deliver all five types of items.
- The unit period length is four weeks.
- The planning horizon length is sized to 48 weeks, which amounts to 1 year.

Other input parameters were prepared as shown in Tables 2–6.

Table 2. Input parameters for the comparative experiment.

Warehouse Capacity of Buyer (wc_t)	Very Large Number (M)	Discount Factor (r)	Initial Inventory Level (IP_{i0})
5000.00	10^7	0.01	0

Table 3. Input parameters for each item.

Item	Holding Cost (h_i)	Shortage Cost (b_i)	Volume (v_i)	Spot Market Price (p_{it}^s)
All items	$N(2, 0.1^2)$	$N(15, 1^2)$	2.00	$N(27, 1^2)$

N denotes a normal distribution.

Table 4. Input parameters for each supplier.

Supplier	Minimum Purchase Amount (mpa_k)	Major Ordering Cost (ma_k)
All suppliers	$20 \times 1.0 \times \hat{d}$	$N(250, 10^2)$

$\hat{d}$ is the forecast average for the planning horizon.

Table 5. Input parameters for each item of each supplier.

Supplier	Minimum Order Quantity (mpa_{ik})	Minor Ordering Cost (mi_{ik})
	Item 1 to 5	Item 1 to 5
All suppliers	$N(1, 0.2^2) \times \hat{d}_i$	$N(1.5, 0.2^2)$

$\hat{d}_j$ denotes the average of forecasts for item j at the planning horizon.

Table 6. Input parameters for each period.

Supplier	Purchase Price (p_{ikt}) for All Period	Maximum Purchase Limit (mpl_{ik}) for All Period
	Item 1 to 5	Item 1 to 5
All suppliers	$N(20, 1^2)$	$N(3, 0.5^2) \times \hat{d}_i$

The results of the first experiment are summarized in Table 7. Using the BF algorithm instead of commercial solvers (GAMS/XPRESS solver), the average total discounted cost increased by 0.82%. The reason for this was the inventory and shortage appearing at the end of the planning horizon. However, the proposed BF algorithm can offer a result very close to the optimum solution. Thus, it seems that the BF algorithm is able to find a near-optimal solution, even though it is a heuristic algorithm mainly developed to solve larger instances of the problem which cannot be solved by any other existing tools.

Table 7. Summary of the accuracy test results.

Method	Average Annual Discounted Cost	Average Percent Deviation (%)	Standard Deviation of Percent Deviation	Average CPU Time	Average Number of Sub-Problems Solved
GAMS	$805,041.43	-	-	1.467 s	-
BF algorithm	$811,630.50	0.82%	0.34%	2.920 s	5.5

6.2. Experiment to Estimate the Maximum Solvable Problem Size of the BF Algorithm

Various software tools developed to solve optimization models have a maximum size limit on the problem which can be solved within a reasonable computational time. Considering this limitation, we attempted to estimate the maximum problem size that can be solved by the BF algorithm. More specifically, the maximum size of problems that can be solved by commercial software tools and the BF algorithm was estimated for comparison. In the experiment, GAMS/XPRESS and GAMS/COINGLPK solvers were selected for comparison. The planning horizon of the problem was fixed to 12 time periods, and the number of suppliers was set to 10 times the number of items. The maximum computational time limit was set to 24 h. We increased the number of items until each method could not find a solution within the time limit. Other input parameters were set as shown in Section 5.1 (Tables 2–6), and demand data were generated using a normal distribution.

Table 8. Summary of the results for the maximum problem size test.

GAMS Solver	Size of the Problem That Can Be Solved (Number of Items, Number of Constraints, and Number of Variables)	
	GAMS Solver	BF Algorithm
COINGLPK	(12, 92,688, 56,928)	(17, 182,268, 111,233)
XPRESS	(69, 2,892,300, 1,743,045)	(108, 7,054,224, 4,244,544)

The results of the experiment are summarized in Table 8, and show that the BF algorithm could considerably increase the solvable problem size. The BF algorithm using the COINGLPK to solve sub-problems can double the solvable problem size compared with a naive use of the COINGLPK. Moreover, for the XPRESS case, the size increased approximately 2.4 times in terms of the number of constraints. Thus, it is expected that buyers will be aided in effective decision-making upon using this method for solving real-world complex problems.

7. Managerial Implications

7.1. Academic Implications

In this paper, we studied a sustainable supplier selection and order allocation problem. This is the first attempt to develop a model for the most realistic and complicated SSS & OA problem representing various important features of a real system. A new algorithm specifically designed to solve such a large-scale model is developed. The algorithm performed as expected by increasing solvable problem size considerably. In this way, we have done some initiating academic research in SSS & OA that will help researchers study related follow-up problems.

7.2. *Managerial Implications*

This study provides valuable insights for firms that regularly make a supplier selection and order allocation decisions. The model and solution method of this paper helps managers to make the SSS & OA decision more systematically. They can prepare a cost-minimizing plan quickly and easily after they complete a computerized planning system. The model is flexible and customizable, and can be modified based on the actual needs of a firm. Output of the developed system provides an efficient SSS & OA plan and, also, some useful additional information, which can be used for many what-if analyses. For example, the dual price of Equation (19) is an incremental cost for raising the 3BL target value by one unit. A firm trying to achieve more stringent sustainability performance can use the estimated cost to make an investment decision for improving a production or logistics system for better sustainability. Thus, good implementation of the model and algorithm of this research will result in better decisions on reducing costs, increasing profitability, and improving customer service sustainability. The final result will be enhanced competitiveness and improved financial status.

8. Conclusions

This paper presents models representing an SSS & OA problem for a buyer replenishing from two or more heterogeneous suppliers with MOQ and MPA constraints, operating working capital limits, and a 3BL sustainability target requirement. A mixed-integer programming model can find a cost-minimizing SSS & OA plan of choosing order-fulfilling suppliers and allocate the order amount for each select supplier. Since the size of a completed model for a real-life application is too big to implement it naively, a fast heuristic algorithm, called a BF algorithm, was also developed for such a large-scale implementation.

The logical idea behind the BF algorithm is two-fold, relaxation and branching. Observing that the MOQ and MPA constraints of the model are very computationally burdensome because of the binary variables included and large number of constraints involved, the algorithm creates sub-problems by relaxing (removing) the MOQ and MPA constraints of the original problem. When the sub-problem is created, a procedure similar to the branch-and-bound method is employed to solve the sub-problems efficiently. Several types of experiments were conducted using the GAMS solvers and IBM SPSS statistics package to verify the validity of the proposed model and to test the accuracy of the developed algorithm. The test result confirmed that the algorithm can find a near-optimal solution with only 0.82 percent deviation on average.

Another test was done to find how much larger a model can be solved when using the proposed algorithm compared with a direct one-time use of popular commercial solvers. The test result showed that the use of the BF algorithm can increase solvable problem size by as much as 2.4 times. It was verified that a model with 7 million constraints and 9 million variables can be handled by our algorithm. All in all, the test results can be summarized as the BF algorithm is an effective tool for handling complex real-life applications. Buyers faced with a large-scale system will, thus, be able to handle such large-scale decision problems without much difficulties.

There are some related research topics that require exploration. Further research may incorporate the supplier's perspective into the current problem to extend to a supplier–buyer problem. Also, the single objective of the current model can be extended to allow bi- or multi-objective functions to consider quantitative targets and qualitative preferences at the same time. Then, another kind of solution methodology should be developed to solve such a multi-objective optimization model of realistic size. Finally, the current model describes SSS & OA activities in a two-stage supply chain composed of a single buyer and several suppliers. These simple stages can be extended to a more complex case, such as a three-stage model, including another layer of suppliers or manufacturers.

Author Contributions: Writing and methodology, J.K. and J.P.; Data preparation and experiments, E.J. and J.N.

Acknowledgments: The authors would like to thank the editors and referees for their valuable comments to enhance the clarity of this paper.

References

1.   Ghadimi, P.; Toosi, F.G.; Heavey, C. A multi-agent systems approach for sustainable supplier selection and order allocation in a partnership supply chain. *Eur. J. Oper. Res.* **2018**, *269*, 286–301. [CrossRef]
2.   Fazlollahtabar, H. An integration between fuzzy promethee and fuzzy linear program for supplier selection problem: Case study. *J. Appl. Math. Model. Comput.* **2016**, *1*. Available online: http://www.lawarencepress.com/ojs/index.php/JAMMC/article/download/30/543 (accessed on 10 December 2018).
3.   Kannan, D. Role of multiple stakeholders and the critical success factor theory for the sustainable supplier selection process. *Int. J. Prod. Econ.* **2018**, *195*, 391–418. [CrossRef]
4.   Kuo, R.; Lee, L.; Hu, T.-L. Developing a supplier selection system through integrating fuzzy ahp and fuzzy dea: A case study on an auto lighting system company in taiwan. *Prod. Plan. Control* **2010**, *21*, 468–484. [CrossRef]
5.   Roehrich, J.K.; Hoejmose, S.U.; Overland, V. Driving green supply chain management performance through supplier selection and value internalisation: A self-determination theory perspective. *Int. J. Oper. Prod. Manag.* **2017**, *37*, 489–509. [CrossRef]
6.   CMMI Product Team. *Cmmi for Acquisition*; Version 1.3.; Software Engineering Institute: Pittsburgh, PA, USA, 2010.
7.   ITSqc. Available online: http://www.itsqc.org (accessed on 10 December 2018).
8.   Musalem, E.P.; Dekker, R. Controlling inventories in a supply chain: A case study. *Int. J. Prod. Econ.* **2005**, *93*, 179–188. [CrossRef]
9.   Kiesmüller, G.P.; De Kok, A.; Dabia, S. Single item inventory control under periodic review and a minimum order quantity. *Int. J. Prod. Econ.* **2011**, *133*, 280–285. [CrossRef]
10. Park, J.H.; Kim, J.S.; Shin, K.Y. Inventory control model for a supply chain system with multiple types of items and minimum order size requirements. *Int. Trans. Oper. Res.* **2018**, *25*, 1927–1946. [CrossRef]
11. Yao, M.; Minner, S. Review of multi-supplier inventory models in supply chain management: An update. 2017. Available online: https://papers.ssrn.com/sol3/papers.cfm?abstract_id=2995134 (accessed on 10 December 2018).
12. Ghorbani, M.; Bahrami, M.; Arabzad, S.M. An integrated model for supplier selection and order allocation; using shannon entropy, swot and linear programming. *Procedia Soc. Behav. Sci.* **2012**, *41*, 521–527. [CrossRef]
13. Nazari-Shirkouhi, S.; Shakouri, H.; Javadi, B.; Keramati, A. Supplier selection and order allocation problem using a two-phase fuzzy multi-objective linear programming. *Appl. Math. Model.* **2013**, *37*, 9308–9323. [CrossRef]
14. Jadidi, O.; Cavalieri, S.; Zolfaghari, S. An improved multi-choice goal programming approach for supplier selection problems. *Appl. Math. Model.* **2015**, *39*, 4213–4222. [CrossRef]
15. Jadidi, O.; Zolfaghari, S.; Cavalieri, S. A new normalized goal programming model for multi-objective problems: A case of supplier selection and order allocation. *Int. J. Prod. Econ.* **2014**, *148*, 158–165. [CrossRef]
16. Sodenkamp, M.A.; Tavana, M.; Di Caprio, D. Modeling synergies in multi-criteria supplier selection and order allocation: An application to commodity trading. *Eur. J. Oper. Res.* **2016**, *254*, 859–874. [CrossRef]
17. Shabanpour, H.; Yousefi, S.; Saen, R.F. Future planning for benchmarking and ranking sustainable suppliers using goal programming and robust double frontiers dea. *Transp. Res. Part D Transp. Environ.* **2017**, *50*, 129–143. [CrossRef]
18. Robb, D.J.; Silver, E.A. Inventory management with periodic ordering and minimum order quantities. *J. Oper. Res. Soc.* **1998**, *49*, 1085–1094. [CrossRef]
19. Zhao, Y.; Katehakis, M.N. On the structure of optimal ordering policies for stochastic inventory systems with minimum order quantity. *Probab. Eng. Inf. Sci.* **2006**, *20*, 257–270. [CrossRef]
20. Zhou, B.; Zhao, Y.; Katehakis, M.N. Effective control policies for stochastic inventory systems with a minimum order quantity and linear costs. *Int. J. Prod. Econ.* **2007**, *106*, 523–531. [CrossRef]
21. Meena, P.; Sarmah, S. Multiple sourcing under supplier failure risk and quantity discount: A genetic algorithm approach. *Transp. Res. Part: Logist. Transp. Rev.* **2013**, *50*, 84–97. [CrossRef]
22. Zhou, B. Inventory management of multi-item systems with order size constraint. *Int. J. Syst. Sci.* **2010**, *41*, 1209–1219. [CrossRef]

23. Aktin, T.; Gergin, Z. Mathematical modelling of sustainable procurement strategies: Three case studies. *J. f Clean. Prod.* **2016**, *113*, 767–780. [CrossRef]
24. Bian, Y.; Lemoine, D.; Yeung, T.G.; Bostel, N.; Hovelaque, V.; Viviani, J.-L.; Gayraud, F. A dynamic lot-sizing-based profit maximization discounted cash flow model considering working capital requirement financing cost with infinite production capacity. *Int. J. Prod. Econ.* **2018**, *196*, 319–332. [CrossRef]
25. Chen, T.-L.; Lin, J.T.; Wu, C.-H. Coordinated capacity planning in two-stage thin-film-transistor liquid-crystal-display (tft-lcd) production networks. *Omega* **2014**, *42*, 141–156. [CrossRef]
26. Chao, X.; Chen, J.; Wang, S. Dynamic inventory management with cash flow constraints. *Nav. Res. Logist.* **2008**, *55*, 758–768. [CrossRef]
27. Bendavid, I.; Herer, Y.T.; Yücesan, E. Inventory management under working capital constraints. *J. Simul.* **2017**, *11*, 62–74. [CrossRef]
28. Azadnia, A.H.; Saman, M.Z.M.; Wong, K.Y. Sustainable supplier selection and order lot-sizing: An integrated multi-objective decision-making process. *Int. J. Prod. Res.* **2015**, *53*, 383–408. [CrossRef]
29. Oxford. What Is a Pestel Analysis? Available online: https://blog.oxfordcollegeofmarketing.com/2016/06/30/pestel-analysis/ (accessed on 10 December 2018).
30. Handfield, R.; Walton, S.V.; Sroufe, R.; Melnyk, S.A. Applying environmental criteria to supplier assessment: A study in the application of the analytical hierarchy process. *Eur. J. Oper. Res.* **2002**, *141*, 70–87. [CrossRef]
31. Lu, L.Y.; Wu, C.; Kuo, T.-C. Environmental principles applicable to green supplier evaluation by using multi-objective decision analysis. *Int. J. Prod. Res.* **2007**, *45*, 4317–4331. [CrossRef]
32. Lee, A.H.; Kang, H.-Y.; Hsu, C.-F.; Hung, H.-C. A green supplier selection model for high-tech industry. *Expert Syst. Appl.* **2009**, *36*, 7917–7927. [CrossRef]
33. Hsu, C.-W.; Hu, A.H. Applying hazardous substance management to supplier selection using analytic network process. *J. Clean. Prod.* **2009**, *17*, 255–264. [CrossRef]
34. Kannan, G.; Pokharel, S.; Kumar, P.S. A hybrid approach using ism and fuzzy topsis for the selection of reverse logistics provider. *Resour. Conserv. Recycl.* **2009**, *54*, 28–36. [CrossRef]
35. Yeh, W.-C.; Chuang, M.-C. Using multi-objective genetic algorithm for partner selection in green supply chain problems. *Expert Syst. Appl.* **2011**, *38*, 4244–4253. [CrossRef]
36. Büyüközkan, G.; Çifçi, G. A novel hybrid mcdm approach based on fuzzy dematel, fuzzy anp and fuzzy topsis to evaluate green suppliers. *Expert Syst. Appl.* **2012**, *39*, 3000–3011. [CrossRef]
37. Shaw, K.; Shankar, R.; Yadav, S.S.; Thakur, L.S. Supplier selection using fuzzy ahp and fuzzy multi-objective linear programming for developing low carbon supply chain. *Expert Syst. Appl.* **2012**, *39*, 8182–8192. [CrossRef]
38. Govindan, K.; Khodaverdi, R.; Jafarian, A. A fuzzy multi criteria approach for measuring sustainability performance of a supplier based on triple bottom line approach. *J. Clean. Prod.* **2013**, *47*, 345–354. [CrossRef]
39. Shen, L.; Olfat, L.; Govindan, K.; Khodaverdi, R.; Diabat, A. A fuzzy multi criteria approach for evaluating green supplier's performance in green supply chain with linguistic preferences. *Resour. Conserv. Recycl.* **2013**, *74*, 170–179. [CrossRef]
40. Dobos, I.; Vörösmarty, G. Green supplier selection and evaluation using dea-type composite indicators. *Int. J. Prod. Econ.* **2014**, *157*, 273–278. [CrossRef]
41. Kannan, D.; Govindan, K.; Rajendran, S. Fuzzy axiomatic design approach based green supplier selection: A case study from singapore. *J. Clean. Prod.* **2015**, *96*, 194–208. [CrossRef]
42. Awasthi, A.; Kannan, G. Green supplier development program selection using ngt and vikor under fuzzy environment. *Comput. Ind. Eng.* **2016**, *91*, 100–108. [CrossRef]
43. Trapp, A.C.; Sarkis, J. Identifying robust portfolios of suppliers: A sustainability selection and development perspective. *J. Clean. Prod.* **2016**, *112*, 2088–2100. [CrossRef]
44. Qin, J.; Liu, X.; Pedrycz, W. An extended todim multi-criteria group decision making method for green supplier selection in interval type-2 fuzzy environment. *Eur. J. Oper. Res.* **2017**, *258*, 626–638. [CrossRef]
45. Gupta, H.; Barua, M.K. Supplier selection among smes on the basis of their green innovation ability using bwm and fuzzy topsis. *J. Clean. Prod.* **2017**, *152*, 242–258. [CrossRef]
46. Luthra, S.; Govindan, K.; Kannan, D.; Mangla, S.K.; Garg, C.P. An integrated framework for sustainable supplier selection and evaluation in supply chains. *J. Clean. Prod.* **2017**, *140*, 1686–1698. [CrossRef]
47. Yu, F.; Yang, Y.; Chang, D. Carbon footprint based green supplier selection under dynamic environment. *J. Clean. Prod.* **2018**, *170*, 880–889. [CrossRef]

48. Banaeian, N.; Mobli, H.; Fahimnia, B.; Nielsen, I.E.; Omid, M. Green supplier selection using fuzzy group decision making methods: A case study from the agri-food industry. *Comput. Oper. Res.* **2018**, *89*, 337–347. [CrossRef]

49. Kannan, D.; Khodaverdi, R.; Olfat, L.; Jafarian, A.; Diabat, A. Integrated fuzzy multi criteria decision making method and multi-objective programming approach for supplier selection and order allocation in a green supply chain. *J. Clean. Prod.* **2013**, *47*, 355–367. [CrossRef]

50. Govindan, K.; Jafarian, A.; Nourbakhsh, V. Bi-objective integrating sustainable order allocation and sustainable supply chain network strategic design with stochastic demand using a novel robust hybrid multi-objective metaheuristic. *Comput. Oper. Res.* **2015**, *62*, 112–130. [CrossRef]

51. Gören, H.G. A decision framework for sustainable supplier selection and order allocation with lost sales. *J. Clean. Prod.* **2018**, *183*, 1156–1169. [CrossRef]

52. Ayhan, M.B.; Kilic, H.S. A two stage approach for supplier selection problem in multi-item/multi-supplier environment with quantity discounts. *Comput. Ind. Eng.* **2015**, *85*, 1–12. [CrossRef]

53. Yang, Y.H.; Kim, J.S. An adaptive joint replenishment policy for items with non-stationary demands. *Oper. Res.* **2018**, 1–20. [CrossRef]

54. Theodore Farris, M.; Hutchison, P.D. Cash-to-cash: The new supply chain management metric. *Int. J. Phys. Distrib. Logist. Manag.* **2002**, *32*, 288–298. [CrossRef]

55. Hofmann, E.; Kotzab, H. A supply chain-oriented approach of working capital management. *J. Bus. Logist.* **2010**, *31*, 305–330. [CrossRef]

56. Agrawal, N.; Smith, S.A. Estimating negative binomial demand for retail inventory management with unobservable lost sales. *Nav. Res. Logist.* **1996**, *43*, 839–861. [CrossRef]

57. Chen, J.; Zhao, X.; Zhou, Y. A periodic-review inventory system with a capacitated backup supplier for mitigating supply disruptions. *Eur. J. Oper. Res.* **2012**, *219*, 312–323. [CrossRef]

7

A Meta-Model-Based Multi-Objective Evolutionary Approach to Robust Job Shop Scheduling

Zigao Wu [1,*], Shaohua Yu [2] and Tiancheng Li [3,*]

[1] Department of Industrial Engineering, Northwestern Polytechnical University, Xi'an 710072, China
[2] Laboratoire Genie Industriel, CentraleSupélec, Université Paris-Saclay, 91190 Saint-Aubin, France; shaohua.yu@centralesupelec.fr
[3] Key Laboratory of Information Fusion Technology (Ministry of Education), School of Automation, Northwestern Polytechnical University, Xi'an 710072, China
* Correspondence: zgwu@mail.nwpu.edu.cn (Z.W.); t.c.li@mail.nwpu.edu.cn or t.c.li@usal.es (T.L.)

Abstract: In the real-world manufacturing system, various uncertain events can occur and disrupt the normal production activities. This paper addresses the multi-objective job shop scheduling problem with random machine breakdowns. As the key of our approach, the robustness of a schedule is considered jointly with the makespan and is defined as expected makespan delay, for which a meta-model is designed by using a data-driven response surface method. Correspondingly, a multi-objective evolutionary algorithm (MOEA) is proposed based on the meta-model to solve the multi-objective optimization problem. Extensive experiments based on the job shop benchmark problems are conducted. The results demonstrate that the Pareto solution sets of the MOEA are much better in both convergence and diversity than those of the algorithms based on the existing slack-based surrogate measures. The MOEA is also compared with the algorithm based on Monte Carlo approximation, showing that their Pareto solution sets are close to each other while the MOEA is much more computationally efficient.

Keywords: scheduling; evolutionary algorithm; robustness; multi-objective; machine breakdown

1. Introduction

Production scheduling is of great significance in both scientific study and engineering applications [1–5]. Generally, the aim of the job shop scheduling problem (JSS) is to find a schedule that minimizes certain performance objective, given a set of machines and a set of jobs. However, in practice, the execution of a schedule is usually confronted with disruptions and unforeseen events, such as random machine breakdowns (RMDs), which make the actual performance of a schedule hard to predict. Against this background, we will focus on the multi-objective robust JSS under RMDs with the goal of optimizing the makespan and the robustness simultaneously.

In the last few decades, the JSS problems have been extensively studied, most of which have addressed the JSS with makespan as the objective [6–8], such as the hybrid genetic algorithm [9], the genetic algorithm [10] with search area adaptation [11], the global optimization technique which combines tabu search with the ant colony optimization [12], and the memetic algorithm conditioned on a limited set of human operators [13]. However, it is often assumed that the problem parameters about jobs and machines are known and deterministic. This makes it difficult to generate a good schedule for a real-world job shop which is subjected to various uncertainties [14], such as machine breakdowns, variable processing times, and due date changes. Mehta et al. [15] had classified the uncertainties in the practical manufacturing into three main categories: complete unknowns, suspicions about the future, and known uncertainties. Complete unknowns are those unpredictable events, e.g. a sudden strike, about which no a-priori information is available, while suspicions about the future arise from the intuition and experience of the human scheduler. On the other hand, known uncertainties are those events about which some information is available in advance, such as machine breakdowns [16–18] whose frequency and duration may be characterized by probability distributions. Under these uncertainties, a schedule will be difficult to execute as planned, and finally the actual performance of the schedule will deteriorate.

Recently, robust optimization has gained intensive interest [19], where most of existing studies focus on addressing the scheduling problems under known uncertainties. The robustness of a schedule indicates the ability of the schedule to preserve a specified level of solution quality in the presence of uncertainties [20], which is generally measured by the expected deviation of the performance from its initial performance under uncertainties [21]. Liu et al. [22] defined the robust schedule as a schedule that is insensitive to uncertainties, such as that a schedule may degrade its performance to a very small degree under disruptions. Thus, in addition to the makespan, the robustness of a schedule will also be taken as one of the objectives in the robust scheduling. Xiao et al. [23] addressed the stochastic JSS problem with uncertain processing times, and the robustness took the expected relative deviation between the realized makespan and the predictive makespan. Zuo et al. [24] considered both the expectation and standard deviation of the performance of a schedule. Ahmadi et al. [25] defined the robustness of a schedule as the expected deviation of starting and completion time of each job between preschedule and realized schedule under RMD.

With simultaneous consideration of the performance and the robustness of a schedule, the JSS under uncertainties holds a multi-objective nature. Usually, the two objectives are combined by the weight sum, and then the problem with two objectives will be transferred into a single-objective problem, such as that described in [26,27]. However, providing a wide range of solutions to decision-makers might be more useful [20], since decision-makers can make a better trade-off between the performance and the robustness for their schedules. The multi-objective evolutionary algorithm (MOEA), such as NSGA II [28–30], has been successfully solved the classic JSS without considering uncertainties [31]. In addition, Hosseinabadi, et al. [32] proposed a TIME_GELS algorithm that uses the gravitational emulation local search [33] for solving the multiobjective flexible dynamic job-shop scheduling problem. But, when the robustness is considered, a MOEA should further be able to solve the problems in the presence of uncertainties [34].

Because of the intractable complexity of JSS with uncertainties, it is difficult to evaluate the effects of uncertainties on a schedule, and thus the robustness is not available in a closed form. In this case, approximation methods should be applied for fitness evaluation in the MOEA. The simplest way is to employ the Monte Carlo method [35,36] to estimate the robustness, by averaging the objective values over a few randomly sampled uncertainty scenarios. The Monte Carlo method is based on random sampling and has been proven to be a powerful method for estimation [37–39]. However, it may cause potentially expensive fitness evaluations and reduce the computing efficiency. For this reason, the problem approximation that tends to replace the original statement of a problem by one which is simple but easier to solve, has been applied. Mirabi, et al. [40] simplified the machine breakdown by assuming the repair time is constant, while Liu et al. [41] assumed that all possible machine breakdowns during a scheduling horizon are aggregated as one. However, this may lead to a large mismatch between the model and the actual problem. In contrast, the meta-model which is an approximate function of the real fitness, also known as the surrogate measure, may be preferred. However, the design of a meta-model for the robustness is challenging. So far, the available surrogate measures for the robustness measured by the expected makespan delay (EMD) only include the average total slack time of operations in [42] and the sum of free slack times of operations in [26]. Since these surrogate measures ignored uncertainties, their estimation accuracy will be reduced [43].

In comparison with the existing research, the main contributions of our approach are as follows:

- The robustness of a schedule is considered jointly with the makespan and is defined as EMD, for which a meta-model is designed by using a data-driven response surface method.
- A MOEA is proposed based on the meta-model, gaining excellent performance and efficiency.

The remainder of this paper is organized as follow. The multi-objective optimization model for the JSS under RMD is defined in the next section. In Section 3, a meta-model-based MOEA is proposed. The performance of the proposed algorithm is presented in Section 4, with comparison with the Monte Carlo method. In Section 5, we conclude the whole study.

2. Problem Definition

We consider the JSS problem with n jobs ($J = \{J_j | j = 1, 2, \ldots, n\}$) to be processed on m machines ($M = \{M_i | i = 1, 2, \ldots, m\}$). All jobs and machines are available at time zero. The processing of job j on machine i is called operation O_{ij}, $i \in [1, m]$, $j \in [1, n]$, and its processing time p_{ij} is constant and known. Each job includes m operations ($O_j = \{O_{ij} | i = 1, 2, \ldots, m\}$, $j \in [1, n]$) that must be processed in a specified sequence through each machine. A feasible schedule that specifies the starting and completion time of all operations should satisfy the constraints: (1) job splitting is not allowed; (2) an operation is not allowed to be preempted by the others; (3) each operation is performed only once on one machine; and (4) each machine performs only one operation at a time.

In this study, the operation-based machine breakdown model presented in [21] will be applied. More specifically, the machine breakdown is modeled by two parameters: the downtime required to repair the machine after its breakdown, and the breakdown probability during a time interval. The machine breakdown probability Pr_{ij} when processing operation O_{ij} can be calculated by Equation (1), where λ_0 is the machine failure rate of each machine.

$$\mathrm{Pr}_{ij} = \min\{\lambda_0 p_{ij}, 1\} \tag{1}$$

The downtime D_{ij} of a machine after a breakdown when processing operation O_{ij} is modeled as an exponential distribution, as shown in Equation (2), where β_0 is the expectation of the downtime.

$$f(D_{ij}) = \begin{cases} \frac{1}{\beta_0} e^{-\frac{1}{\beta_0} D_{ij}} & D_{ij} > 0 \\ 0 & D_{ij} \leq 0 \end{cases} \tag{2}$$

In the classic JSS problems without considering uncertainties, the aim of scheduling is generally to find a schedule that minimizes the makespan. The makespan of a schedule is equal to the maximum completion time of all operations in the schedule, which can be determined by Equation (3), where ct_{ij} is the completion time of operation O_{ij}.

$$C_{\max}^0 = \max_{i \in M}\{\max_{j \in J}\{ct_{ij}\}\} \tag{3}$$

However, the makespan of a schedule will be affected by RMDs in practice [16–18]. Since RMDs postpone the completion time of operations, the actual makespan $C_{\max}^r$ of a schedule will be delayed. As shown in Figure 1a, the makespan $C_{\max}^0$ of the schedule before execution is equal to 10. If a machine breakdown with one unit of downtime occurring on the operation O_{21}, as shown in Figure 1b, its completion time is directly postponed by one unit of time. Then, all the completion times of its subsequent operations $\{O_{22}, O_{11}, O_{23}, O_{12}, O_{31}\}$ are also delayed by one unit of time. Finally, the actual makespan $C_{\max}^r$ of the schedule is equal to 11, which has been delayed by one unit of time.

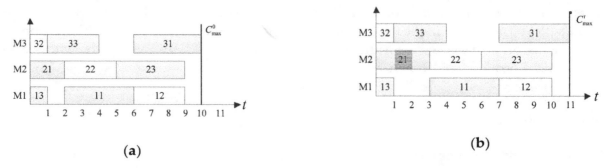

Figure 1. An example for a schedule with 3 machines and 3 jobs under a machine breakdown. (**a**) The schedule before a machine breakdown; (**b**) the schedule after a machine breakdown.

According to the analysis above, the influence of machine breakdowns on the makespan of a schedule can be given by the makespan delay δ_c in Equation (4).

$$\delta_c = \max(C^r_{max} - C^0_{max}, 0) \tag{4}$$

Since machine breakdowns take place randomly, the makespan delay of a schedule will vary with the actual scenario of machine breakdowns, which makes the actual makespan very instability. The stochastic change of the actual makespan will reduce the performance of a schedule, such as that it may lead to the products cannot be delivered on time and lose the customer good will. Therefore, it is preferred that the makespan of a schedule is robust under RMDs. To measure the robustness of makespan, the EMD will further be applied, as the Δ_c shown in Equation (5).

$$\Delta_c = E(\delta_c) = \int_0^{+\infty} \delta_c f(\delta_c) d\delta \tag{5}$$

However, a schedule with the minimum makespan is generally very compact, which means that it may be very sensitive to RMD and with a large EMD. Thus, the makespan C^0_{max} of a schedule will conflict with the EMD. Since different decision-makers have various preferences for the makespan and the makespan delay, it is worth providing a wide range of schedules for decision-makers to make the best trade-off. When consider the makespan and the EMD of a schedule at the same time, the JSS under RMD can be modeled as a multi-objective optimization problem. Let A be the set of precedence constraints (O_{ij}, O_{kj}) that require job j to be processed on machine i before it is processed on machine k, the multi-objective optimization model can be provided as follows:

Minimize:

$$\mathbf{F} = (C^0_{max}, \Delta_c) \tag{6}$$

Subject to:

$$st_{kj} - st_{ij} \geq p_{ij}, \text{ for all } (O_{ij}, O_{kj}) \in A \tag{7}$$

$$st_{ij} - st_{il} \geq p_{il} \text{ or } st_{il} - st_{ij} \geq p_{ij}, \text{ for all } O_{ij} \text{ and } O_{il} \tag{8}$$

$$st_{ij} \geq 0, \text{ for all } O_{ij} \tag{9}$$

$$\lambda_i = \lambda_0, \text{ for all } i \in M \tag{10}$$

$$D_{ij} \sim Exp(1/\beta_0), \text{ for all } O_{ij} \tag{11}$$

3. The Meta-Model Based MOEA

When solving the multi-objective optimization model in Section 2 by a MOEA, the primary task is to evaluate the fitness of each individual in a population. However, the EMD in Equation (5) cannot be analytically calculated for the intractable complexity of JSS under RMD. Although the commonly-used Monte Carlo simulation can be used to approximate the EMD, it will make the MOEA inefficient for it is very time-consuming to evaluate each single individual, especially for the problems with larger scales. In view of this, a meta-model-based MOEA will be proposed to solve the multi-objective optimization model for the robust JSS.

3.1. Framework of The Algorithm

The meta-model-based MOEA is designed according to the basic framework of the classic NSGA-II [28]. As shown in Figure 2, the algorithm begins with an initial population P_0 with N randomly generated individuals. Before executing the following genetic operators, the meta-model Δ_c^a of the Δ_c will be constructed based on the initial population P_0. Then, the selection, crossover, and mutation operators will be applied on the current population P_k to generate new individuals and construct a combined population R_{k+1}. The fitness of individuals in the combined population R_{k+1} will first be evaluated by the makespan C_{max}^0 and the proposed meta-model Δ_c^a, and then the individual-based evolution control will be applied to update the fitness of some individuals. Finally, the next generation population P_{k+1} will be generated according to the ranks of individuals. When the maximum generation number is reached, the algorithm will stop and return the obtained Pareto solution set.

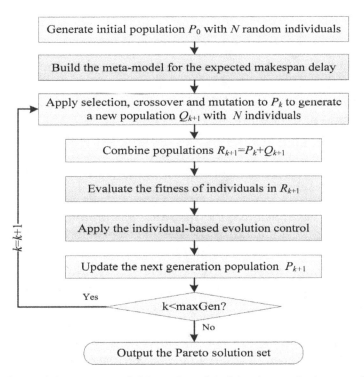

Figure 2. The flow chart of the meta-model-based multi-objective evolutionary algorithm (MOEA).

3.2. Meta-Model of The EMD

The meta-model for the EMD will be constructed based on the response surface methodology. As shown in Equation (12), this method applies a quadratic polynomial $\hat{f}(x)$ to approximate the function relation between the input x and the output y of a system,

$$y \approx \hat{f}(x) = a_0 + Bx + xCx^T, \tag{12}$$

where, x is the input variant vector with v variables as shown in Equation (13), a_0 is the constant term, B is the coefficient vector of the linear term as shown in Equation (14), and C is the coefficient matrix of the quadratic term as shown in Equation (15).

$$x = (x_1, x_2, \ldots, x_v) \tag{13}$$

$$B = (b_1, b_2, \ldots, b_v) \tag{14}$$

$$C = \begin{bmatrix} c_{11} & c_{12} & \cdots & c_{1v} \\ & c_{22} & \cdots & c_{2v} \\ & & \ddots & \vdots \\ & & & c_{vv} \end{bmatrix} \tag{15}$$

However, a schedule cannot be directly taken as an input variant of the EMD, since it cannot be quantified. Therefore, to construct a meta-model by the response surface method for the EMD, the primary task is to extract features related to the EMD from the schedule. To this end, we will further analyze how RMDs affect the makespan of a schedule. As we all know, a feasible job shop schedule is decided by the process constraints and the resource constraints. As a result, machines may have some idle time during a schedule period, as shown in Figure 3a. In the classic JSS problems, we are devoted to reducing the idle time to minimize the makespan for improving the utilities of machines. However, when RMDs are considered, the idle time may be useful for an operation to control the influence of machine breakdowns on the makespan of a schedule and then improve the robustness of the makespan.

The available idle time of operations in a schedule can be classified into two types: the free slack time and the total slack time. The former is the time that an operation can be delayed without delaying the starting of its very next operations, while the latter is the difference between the earliest and latest starting times of an operation without delaying the makespan. Take the schedule in Figure 3a as an example, the free slack time of operations $\{O_{13}, O_{11}, O_{12}, O_{21}, O_{22}, O_{23}, O_{32}, O_{33}, O_{31}\}$ are $\{0, 0, 1, 0, 0, 1, 0, 1, 0\}$, respectively. The earliest and latest starting time of operations $\{O_{13}, O_{11}, O_{12}, O_{21}, O_{22}, O_{23}, O_{32}, O_{33}, O_{31}\}$ without delaying the makespan is $\{0, 2, 6, 0, 2, 5, 0, 1, 6\}$ and $\{1, 2, 7, 0, 3, 6, 2, 3, 6\}$, respectively. Therefore, the total slack time of each operation is $\{1, 0, 1, 0, 1, 1, 2, 2, 0\}$, respectively.

It is clear that not all operations have the free/total slack time. For an operation without slack time, the makespan of a schedule will be directly delayed, when an RMD takes place on it. As shown in Figure 3b, when a RMD with one unit of downtime takes places on the operation O_{11}, the actual makespan C_{max}^r is changed to 11, which is directly delayed by one unit of time. However, when an RMD takes places on an operation with slack time, the makespan will not be delayed until the slack time of this operation is used up. As shown in Figure 3c, after a RMD with one unit of downtime takes place on the operation O_{33} with two units of free slack time, the makespan is still equal to 10, for the free slack time of this operation is larger than the downtime of the breakdown. On the other hand, although the operation O_{22} has no free slack time, the makespan can also be protected by the total slack time of the operation, as shown in Figure 3d.

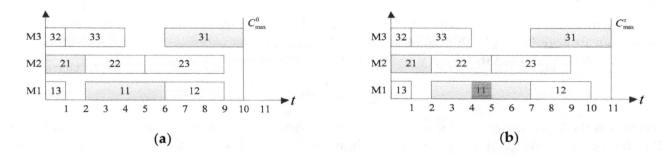

(a)   **(b)**

Figure 3. *Cont.*

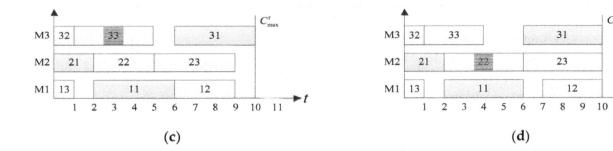

Figure 3. The relationship between the makespan delay and the machine breakdowns on different operations. (**a**) No machine breakdown; (**b**) a machine breakdown on operation O_{11}; (**c**) a machine breakdown on operation O_{33}; (**d**) a machine breakdown on operation O_{22}.

According to the analysis above, it can be found that the makespan delay of a schedule depends on the machine breakdown level, the free slack time and total slack time of each operation. In view of this, we will extract the mathematical features for the schedule under RMDs from these three aspects: the RMDs, the set O_y of operations with slack time and the set O_n of operations without slack time. For the RMDs, the machine failure rate λ_0 and the expected downtime β_0 after a breakdown will be taken. For the operations in the set O_y, all their processing time p_{ij}, free slack time fs_{ij} and total slack time ts_{ij} will be taken. As for the operations in the set O_n, only their processing time p_{ij} will be taken.

However, it is practically impossible to consider all the processing time, free slack time, and total slack time of operations as the input variants of the EMD. To reduce the number of input variants, we will further generalize these basic features into some comprehensive features. Formally, the sum of processing time p_s^y and p_s^n will be used to represent the processing time of operations in the sets O_y and O_n, respectively. For the slack time, the average free slack time fs_a and the average total slack time ts_a of operations in the set O_y will be applied.

Finally, the input variants of the EMD can be listed as follows: the machine failure rate λ_0, the expected downtime β_0, the sum of processing time p_s^n, the sum of processing time p_s^y, the average free slack time fs_a, and the average total slack time ts_a. Then, the input variant vector x of the EMD can be set as $x = (x_1, x_2, x_3, x_4, x_5, x_6) = (\lambda_0, \beta_0, p_s^n, p_s^y, fs_a, ts_a)$, and then the meta-model Δ_c^a of Δ_c can be defined by Equation (16).

$$\Delta_c \approx \Delta_c^a = a_0 + \sum_{i=1}^{6} b_i x_i + \sum_{i=1}^{5} \sum_{j=1}^{6} c_{ij} x_i x_j \tag{16}$$

Then, the coefficients should further be determined to finalize the meta-model Δ_c^a. As shown in Algorithm 1, it takes the initial population P_0 and the input variant vector x as the inputs, and outputs the meta-model Δ_c^a with the determined coefficients. First, a training data set D_c which includes N data instances will first be generated based on the initial population P_0. A data instance $I_i = (x_i, \Delta_c^i)$ is composed of the values of the input variant vector x_i and the corresponding Δ_c^i. The values of the input variant vector x_i can be determined once a schedule s_i is generated based on the ith individual in the initial population P_0. Since the EMD cannot be analytically calculated, it will be evaluated by the Monte Carlo approximation Δ_c^{sim} as shown in Equation (17). After the training data set D_c is constructed, the Multiple Linear Regression will be used to determine the coefficients of the meta-model Δ_c^a for the EMD,

$$\Delta_c^{sim} = \frac{1}{N_s} \sum_{i=1}^{N_s} (C_{max}^i - C_{max}^0), \tag{17}$$

where N_s is the simulation times and C_{max}^i is the makespan of a schedule under the ith simulation.

Algorithm 1 The pseudo-code to finalize the meta-model.

Inputs: the initial population P_0 and the input variant vector x
Outputs: the meta-model Δ_c^a with the determined coefficients

---

1:   Set the training data set $D_c = \varnothing$;
2:   Generate N_s machine breakdown scenarios with the machine failure rate λ_0 and the expected downtime β_0;
3:   for $i = 1$ to N
4:        Generate the schedule s_i based on the ith individual in P_0;
5:        Determine the makespan C_{max}^0 of the schedule s_i by Equation (3);
6:        Calculate the free slack time fs_{ij} and the total slack time ts_{ij} in schedule s_i;
7:        Calculate the sum of processing time p_s^n and p_s^y;
8:        Calculate the average free slack time fs_a and the average total slack time ts_a;
9:        Determine the values x_i of the input variant vector $x = (\lambda_0, \beta_0, p_s^n, p_s^y, fs_a, ts_a)$;
10:       Determined the EMD $\Delta_c^a = \Delta_c^{sim}$ by Equation (17);
11:       Generate the ith data instance $I_i = (x_i, \Delta_c^i)$;
12:       Update the training data set $D_c = D_c \cup I_i$;
13:   end for
14:   Based on the training data set D_c, apply the multiple linear regression to determine the coefficients of the meta-model Δ_c^a in Equation (16);
15:   Return the finalized meta-model Δ_c^a.

3.3. Fitness Evaluation

To compare the fitness of different individuals, the makespan and the EMD of each individual in a population should be evaluated. Once a schedule is generated, the makespan can be directly determined by Equation (3). However, the EMD cannot be analytically calculated for the complexity of the JSS. Although it can be effectively approximated by the time-consuming Monte Carlo approximation in Equation (17), the efficiency of the algorithm will be significantly reduced. In view of this, we will apply the proposed meta-model Δ_c^a in Equation (16) to approximate the EMD. The basic motivation for using the meta-model in the fitness evaluation is to reduce the number of expensive fitness evaluations without degrading the quality of the obtained optimal solution.

Based on the proposed meta-model Δ_c^a, Algorithm 2 can be used to provide the fitness set $F_{k+1} = \left\{ (C_{max}^0(s_0), \Delta_c^a(s_0)), \ldots, (C_{max}^0(s_i), \Delta_c^a(s_i)), \ldots, (C_{max}^0(s_i), \Delta_c^a(s_i)) \right\}$ of the individuals in the combined population P_{k+1}, where $F_{k+1}^i = (C_{max}^0(s_i), \Delta_c^a(s_i))$ represents the fitness of the ith individual in the combined population P_{k+1} with the makespan $F_{k+1}^i(1) = C_{max}^0(s_i)$ and the EMD $F_{k+1}^i(2) = \Delta_c^a(s_i)$.

Algorithm 2 Fitness evaluation for the combined population

Inputs: the combined population R_{k+1}
Outputs: the fitness set F_{k+1} of the individuals in R_{k+1}

1:   Set the fitness set $F_{k+1} = \varnothing$;
2:   for $i = 1$ to $2N$
3:        Select the ith individual chm_i from the population R_{k+1};
4:        Generate the schedule s_i based on the individual chm_i;
5:        Evaluate the makespan $C_{max}^{0,i}$ of the schedule s_i by Equation (3);
6:        Get machine failure rate λ_0 and expected downtime β_0;
7:        Calculate the free slack time fs_{ij} and the total slack time ts_{ij} in the schedule s_i;
8:        Calculate the sum of processing time p_s^n and p_s^y;
9:        Calculate the average free slack time fs_a and the average total slack time ts_a;
10:       Determine the values x_i of the input variant vector $x = (\lambda_0, \beta_0, p_s^n, p_s^y, fs_a, ts_a)$
11:       Evaluate the EMD by $\Delta_c^a(s_i)$ in Equation (16) with the values of x_i;
12:       Update the fitness set $F_{k+1} = F_{k+1} \cup F_{k+1}^i = F_{k+1} \cup (C_{max}^0(s_i), \Delta_c^a(s_i))$;
13:   end for
14:   Return the fitness set F_{k+1};

3.4. Individual-Based Evolution Control

Generally, the approximate model is assumed to be of high fidelity and, therefore, the real fitness function will be not at all used in the evolution [20]. However, an evolutionary algorithm using meta-models without controlling the evolution using the real fitness function can run the risk of an incorrect convergence [28]. For this reason, the meta-model is combined with the real fitness function in our algorithm, which is often known as evolution control or model management.

As shown in Algorithm 3, the individual-based evolution control framework will be applied, which chooses the best individuals according to the pre-evaluation using the meta-model Δ_c^a for reevaluation using the real fitness function. For this purpose, the fitness set F_{k+1} will first be ranked by the fast non-dominated sorting. And then, the individuals with the rank $rank(F_{k+1}^i) = 1$ will further be reevaluated by the Monte Carlo approximation Δ_c^{sim} in Equation (17). In addition, to avoid the unnecessary simulation computational time, the repeated individuals will only be evaluated once.

Algorithm 3 Individual-based evolution control framework

Inputs: the fitness set F_{k+1} of the combined population R_{k+1}
Outputs: the modified fitness set $\hat{F}_{k+1}$

1:   Generate N_s scenarios with the machine failure rate λ_0 and the expected downtime β_0;
2:   Rank the fitness set F_{k+1} by the fast non-dominated sorting;
3:   Sort the fitness set F_{k+1} in the ascending lexicographic order of the rank, the makespan and the EMD;
4:   Set $\hat{F}_{k+1} = F_{k+1}$;
5:   for $i = 1$ to $2N$
6:      if $rank(F_{k+1}^i) > 1$
7:         Break;
8:      else if $F_{k+1}^i(1) = F_{k+1}^{i-1}(1)$ and $F_{k+1}^i(2) = F_{k+1}^{i-1}(2)$
9:         Update the fitness $\hat{F}_{k+1}^i$ by $\hat{F}_{k+1}^i(2) = \hat{F}_{k+1}^{i-1}(2)$;
10:     else
11:        Generate the schedule s_i of the individual associated by F_{k+1}^i in the R_{k+1};
12:        Evaluate the EMD by the Monte Carlo method Δ_c^{sim} in Equation (17);
13:        Update the fitness $\hat{F}_{k+1}^i$ by $\hat{F}_{k+1}^i(2) = \Delta_c^{sim}$;
14:     end if
15: end for
16: Return the modified fitness set $\hat{F}_{k+1}$.

3.5. Evolutionary Operators

In our algorithm, the preference list representation is applied to code the chromosomes. The chromosome built by this coding method is made up of m substrings corresponding to m machines. Every substring is a preference list of n jobs on the corresponding machine. Supposing the chromosome is [(2 3 1) (1 3 2) (2 1 3)], the substring (2 3 1) is the preference list for machine 1, the substring (1 3 2) for machine 2 and the substring (2 1 3) for machine 3. When decoding, the job the first to appear in every precedence list will be selected firstly. If a selected operation meets the process constraint, the operation will be scheduled, and then it is removed from corresponding preference list. If there are more than one operation can be scheduled, then select one randomly.

The main genetic operators include selection, crossover and mutation. The usual binary tournament selection is used to select parent individuals for generating child solutions. Namely, randomly select two individuals from the population, and choose one of them with better fitness for the subsequent genetic operators. In the crossover operator, the substring crossover which exchanges the substrings of parents between two randomly selected machine numbers is applied. For the mutation operator, the swap-mutation operator to a randomly selected substring is applied.

Before updating the next generation population, the fast non-dominated sorting approach is applied to ranking the solutions in the combined population. Then, the population will be updated by choosing the individuals in the order of their ranks. Since all the previous and current population members are included in the combined population, the elitism can also be ensured.

4. Experimental Analysis

In this section, the performance of the meta-model in evaluating the EMD will first be presented, and then the meta-model-based MOEA will be used to solve the robust JSS problem.

4.1. Experiment Setting

The algorithm is implemented using C++ and run on a 2.8 GHz PC with an Intel Pentium dual-core CPU and 2 GB of RAM. The parameters are listed as follows: the population size is 1024; the generation number is 64; the crossover rate is 0.95; the mutation rate is 0.05; the machine breakdown ratio is 0.005; the expected downtime is 20; and the simulation times are 600.

In the literature, many benchmark problems have been generated by different researchers to test the performance of different algorithms, which are also very useful for this research for they include a wide range of problem instances. In this study, the problem instances La01-La40 with sizes from 10×5 to 30×10 in the benchmark problem set LA (Lawrence in 1984) and the problem instances Ta01-Ta40 with sizes from 15×15 to 30×15 in the benchmark problem set TA (Taillard in 1994) will be applied. In total, there are 80 benchmark problem instances will be used to test the performance of the proposed algorithm.

4.2. Evaluation Performance of The Proposed Mete-Model

To distinguish the robustness of different schedules, an effective meta-model must have high evaluation accuracy and perform a strong linear correlation to the real value of the robustness. To show the accuracy of the proposed meta-model Δ_c^a in evaluating the EMD, the average $\bar{\chi}$ in Equation (18) and standard variance $\sigma(\chi)$ in Equation (19) of the absolute relative deviation $\chi(\Delta_c^a, \Delta_c^{sim})$ from the Monte Carlo approximation Δ_c^{sim} will be applied. In addition, a correlation study will be conducted using IBM SPSS. For each test problem, the R^2 statistic and the significance level $Sig.$ of the linear model ANOVA are recorded. The value of R^2 is used to measure the fitting degree of the meta-model, while the significance level $Sig.$ is used to test whether there is a significant linear correlation between the meta-model and the EMD. Therefore, a good meta-model should be with a large value of R^2 and a small value of $Sig.$ for each test problem.

$$\bar{\chi} = \frac{1}{N}\sum_{i=1}^{N}\chi(\Delta_c^a, \Delta_c^{sim}) = \frac{1}{N}\sum_{i=1}^{N}\left|\frac{\Delta_c^a - \Delta_c^{sim}}{\Delta_c^{sim}}\right| \qquad (18)$$

$$\sigma(\chi) = \sqrt{\frac{\sum_{i=1}^{N}\left(\chi(\Delta_c^a, \Delta_c^{sim}) - \bar{\chi}\right)^2}{N-1}} \qquad (19)$$

The experimental results have been processed and recorded in Tables 1 and 2 for the problem sets LA and TA, respectively. It can be found that the maximum and minimum values of $\bar{\chi}$ for all problems in LA are equal to 0.041 and 0.020, respectively. And, the maximum and minimum values of $\bar{\chi}$ for all problems in TA are equal to 0.026 and 0.017, respectively. That is, the values of $\bar{\chi}$ for all test problems are less than 0.05 in average. Therefore, the values of the meta-model are very close to that of the Monte Carlo approximation, which indicate that the proposed meta-model have high accuracy in evaluating the EMD for the JSS under RMD. On the other hand, the maximum and minimum values of $\sigma(\chi)$ for all problems in LA are equal to 0.031 and 0.015, respectively. The maximum and minimum values of $\sigma(\chi)$ for all problems in TA are equal to 0.020 and 0.013, respectively. All these results show that the meta-model have a small variance in the absolute relative deviation, which indicate that the performance of the meta-model is also robust in evaluating the EMD.

Table 1. The experimental results of the meta-model in the problem set LA.

Cases	$n \times m$	$\bar{x}$	$\sigma(x)$	R^2	Sig.	Cases	$n \times m$	$\bar{x}$	$\sigma(x)$	R^2	Sig.
La01	10×5	0.035	0.027	0.74	<0.01	La21	15×10	0.026	0.019	0.77	<0.01
La02	10×5	0.040	0.029	0.59	<0.01	La22	15×10	0.028	0.021	0.74	<0.01
La03	10×5	0.041	0.031	0.53	<0.01	La23	15×10	0.026	0.020	0.78	<0.01
La04	10×5	0.038	0.028	0.71	<0.01	La24	15×10	0.027	0.021	0.76	<0.01
La05	10×5	0.034	0.026	0.78	<0.01	La25	15×10	0.028	0.021	0.75	<0.01
La06	15×5	0.029	0.022	0.80	<0.01	La26	20×10	0.023	0.018	0.76	<0.01
La07	15×5	0.033	0.024	0.71	<0.01	La27	20×10	0.024	0.018	0.74	<0.01
La08	15×5	0.032	0.024	0.72	<0.01	La28	20×10	0.024	0.019	0.73	<0.01
La09	15×5	0.033	0.026	0.68	<0.01	La29	20×10	0.024	0.018	0.75	<0.01
La10	15×5	0.033	0.024	0.76	<0.01	La30	20×10	0.025	0.019	0.74	<0.01
La11	20×5	0.026	0.020	0.76	<0.01	La31	30×10	0.020	0.016	0.75	<0.01
La12	20×5	0.029	0.023	0.76	<0.01	La32	30×10	0.020	0.015	0.75	<0.01
La13	20×5	0.029	0.023	0.70	<0.01	La33	20×10	0.020	0.015	0.76	<0.01
La14	20×5	0.029	0.023	0.76	<0.01	La34	30×10	0.021	0.016	0.76	<0.01
La15	20×5	0.029	0.023	0.71	<0.01	La35	30×10	0.022	0.017	0.82	<0.01
La16	10×10	0.031	0.024	0.74	<0.01	La36	15×15	0.023	0.018	0.80	<0.01
La17	10×10	0.031	0.024	0.74	<0.01	La37	15×15	0.023	0.018	0.75	<0.01
La18	10×10	0.032	0.025	0.72	<0.01	La38	15×15	0.025	0.019	0.74	<0.01
La19	10×10	0.030	0.023	0.72	<0.01	La39	15×15	0.025	0.018	0.75	<0.01
La20	10×10	0.035	0.026	0.65	<0.01	La40	15×15	0.025	0.019	0.71	<0.01
Aver.	/	**0.032**	**0.025**	**0.71**	**<0.01**	**Aver.**	/	**0.024**	**0.018**	**0.76**	**<0.01**

The results can also be clearly presented by the quartile graphs of the absolute relative deviation $\chi(\Delta_c^a, \Delta_c^{sim})$, as shown in Figures 4 and 5. In Figure 4, the maximum value of the absolute relative deviations $\chi(\Delta_c^a, \Delta_c^{sim})$ for all problems in LA is about 0.19, but more than 75% of the values are less than 0.06 for all the problems in the problem set LA. Especially, when the problem scale is larger, such as the problems LA21-LA40, more than 75% of the values of $\chi(\Delta_c^a, \Delta_c^{sim})$ are less than 0.04. As for the problem set TA in Figure 5, the maximum value of the absolute relative deviation $\chi(\Delta_c^a, \Delta_c^{sim})$ for all problems is only about 0.12, and more than 75% of the values are less than 0.04 for all the test problems. Therefore, it can be concluded that the proposed meta-model has a very small estimation error for the EMD.

On the other hand, the results of the linear model ANOVA have also been provided in Tables 1 and 2. For the results in Table 1, except for the problems La02, La03, La09, and La20, we can find that all the values of R^2 are larger than 0.70. Especially for the problems La21-La40 with larger problem scales, the average of R^2 even reaches to 0.76. All the values of R^2 are larger than 0.70 for the problems in TA and the average value is about 0.76 as shown in Table 2. In addition, for all the problems in LA and TA, the significance level Sig. is less than 0.01. All these results show that the proposed meta-model have a significant linear correlation with the expected makespan.

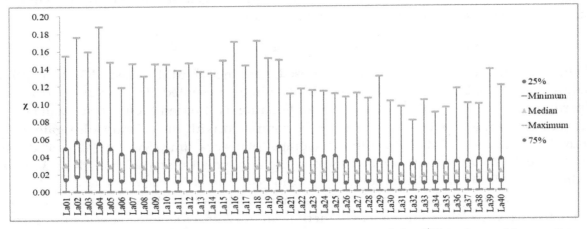

Figure 4. The quartile graph of the absolute relative deviation $\chi(\Delta_c^a, \Delta_c^{sim})$ in the problem set LA.

Table 2. The experimental results of the meta-model in the problem set TA.

Cases	$n \times m$	$\bar{\chi}$	$\sigma(\chi)$	R^2	Sig.	Cases	$n \times m$	$\bar{\chi}$	$\sigma(\chi)$	R^2	Sig.
Ta01	15×15	0.026	0.019	0.73	<0.01	Ta21	20×20	0.019	0.015	0.78	<0.01
Ta02	15×15	0.023	0.018	0.76	<0.01	Ta22	20×20	0.018	0.014	0.79	<0.01
Ta03	15×15	0.025	0.019	0.74	<0.01	Ta23	20×20	0.018	0.014	0.76	<0.01
Ta04	15×15	0.023	0.018	0.77	<0.01	Ta24	20×20	0.019	0.014	0.77	<0.01
Ta05	15×15	0.023	0.018	0.78	<0.01	Ta25	20×20	0.018	0.014	0.79	<0.01
Ta06	15×15	0.023	0.017	0.76	<0.01	Ta26	20×20	0.018	0.014	0.78	<0.01
Ta07	15×15	0.026	0.020	0.73	<0.01	Ta27	20×20	0.019	0.015	0.75	<0.01
Ta08	15×15	0.024	0.018	0.76	<0.01	Ta28	20×20	0.019	0.014	0.77	<0.01
Ta09	15×15	0.025	0.018	0.74	<0.01	Ta29	20×20	0.019	0.015	0.76	<0.01
Ta10	15×15	0.023	0.018	0.77	<0.01	Ta30	20×20	0.018	0.014	0.79	<0.01
Ta11	20×15	0.022	0.016	0.76	<0.01	Ta31	30×15	0.018	0.014	0.77	<0.01
Ta12	20×15	0.020	0.016	0.78	<0.01	Ta32	30×15	0.019	0.015	0.77	<0.01
Ta13	20×15	0.021	0.016	0.78	<0.01	Ta33	30×15	0.018	0.014	0.74	<0.01
Ta14	20×15	0.020	0.016	0.77	<0.01	Ta34	30×15	0.017	0.014	0.78	<0.01
Ta15	20×15	0.021	0.016	0.73	<0.01	Ta35	30×15	0.018	0.014	0.80	<0.01
Ta16	20×15	0.021	0.015	0.78	<0.01	Ta36	30×15	0.018	0.014	0.76	<0.01
Ta17	20×15	0.023	0.017	0.74	<0.01	Ta37	30×15	0.018	0.014	0.76	<0.01
Ta18	20×15	0.021	0.016	0.75	<0.01	Ta38	30×15	0.018	0.014	0.79	<0.01
Ta19	20×15	0.021	0.017	0.76	<0.01	Ta39	30×15	0.019	0.013	0.81	<0.01
Ta20	20×15	0.021	0.016	0.79	<0.01	Ta40	30×15	0.017	0.013	0.78	<0.01
Aver.	/	**0.023**	**0.017**	**0.76**	**<0.01**	**Aver.**	/	**0.018**	**0.014**	**0.77**	**<0.01**

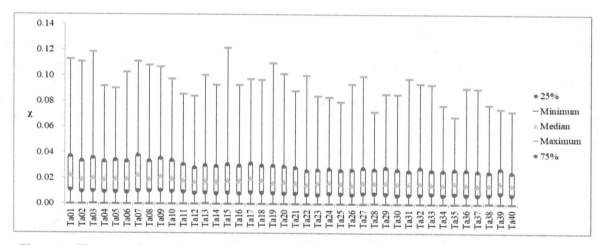

Figure 5. The quartile graph of the absolute relative deviation $\chi(\Delta_c^a, \Delta_c^{sim})$ in the problem set TA.

In summary, the proposed meta-model Δ_c^a have high evaluation accuracy and holds a strong linear correlation to the EMD. This means that the meta-model Δ_c^a is able to effectively distinguish the robustness of different schedules in the evolutionary algorithm.

4.3. Optimization Performance of The Proposed Algorithm

In this section, the performance of the proposed meta-model (MM)-based MOEA in optimizing the makespan and the EMD for the JSS under RMD will be presented. To show the performance of the algorithm, the Monte Carlo approximation in Equation (17)-based MOEA (MC) will be applied. In addition, the proposed meta-meta will also be compared with the existing surrogate measures, and thus the results on the MOEAs with the average total slack time (SM1) in [42] and the sum of free slack time (SM2) in [26] will also be provided. By implementing these algorithms with various approximations of EMD, four Pareto solution sets can be obtained for each problem.

To investigate the performance of MOEAs, many metrics have been developed and applied in the related research [44]. Since a single metric can only provide some specific but incomplete of performance, to comprehensively evaluate the performance of the proposed algorithm, both the average distance and the number of distinct choices will be used in our experiments to measure the convergence and diversity of the algorithm, respectively.

Average distance metric A_d in Equation (20) evaluates the closeness of the obtained Pareto solution set PF_{find} to the true Pareto solution set PF_{true}, where $d(z_i, a_j)$ denotes the Euclidean distance between z_i in PF_{find} and all points a_j in PF_{true}.

$$A_d = \frac{1}{|PF_{find}|} \sum_{i=1}^{|PF_{find}|} \min_{j=1}^{|PF_{true}|} d(z_i, a_j) \tag{20}$$

Number of distinct choices N_μ in Equation (21) focuses on the distribution of solutions, which defines the number of distinct choices for a pre-specified value of μ, $0 < \mu < 1$. In this metric, an m-dimensional objective space will be divided into $1/\mu^m$ number of small grids, where any solutions within the same grid are considered similar to one another. If there are individuals in the obtained Pareto set PF_{find} that fall into the region $T(l_m, \ldots, l_2, l_1)$, $NT(l_m, \ldots, l_2, l_1)$ is equal to one, otherwise zero. In our experiments, the value of μ for the metric N_μ is taken as 0.05.

$$N_\mu(PF_{find}) = \sum_{l_m=0}^{1/\mu-1} \cdots \sum_{l_2=0}^{1/\mu-1} \sum_{l_1=0}^{1/\mu-1} NT(l_m, \ldots, l_2, l_1) \tag{21}$$

Since the NP-hard nature of the JSS under RMD, the true Pareto set PF_{true} is not available for all test problems. In view of this, the approximate Pareto solution set which is provided by all comparison algorithms will be used to represent the true one. That is, under the obtained Pareto fronts $(PF_{find}^1, PF_{find}^2, \ldots, PF_{find}^{n_p})$ by different algorithms for a test problem, the true Pareto solution set can be approximated by Equation (22), where $a_j \prec b_i$ implies that a_j dominates b_i. Besides, in order to reduce the scale difference between different objectives, all Pareto fronts will be normalized by $PF_{find} = (PF_{find} - PF_{true}^{min})/(PF_{true}^{max} - PF_{true}^{min})$ based on the maximum and minimum of objectives of the true Pareto set PF_{true}.

$$PF_{true} \approx \left\{ b_i \big| \forall b_i, \neg \exists a_j \in (PF_{find}^1 \cup PF_{find}^2 \cup \ldots \cup PF_{find}^{n_p}) \prec b_i \right\} \tag{22}$$

The results on the metric A_d of the algorithms MC, MM, SM1, and SM2 have been provided in Tables 3 and 4 for the problem sets LA and TA, respectively. The results show that the algorithms SM1 and SM2 have the similar performance in the convergence, for the values of A_d of the algorithms SM1 and SM2 are always close to each other. For example, in Table 3, their average values of A_d in the problems La01–La20 are 1.27 and 1.26, and the average values of A_d in the problems La21–La40 are 0.21 and 0.21, respectively. The similar results can also be found in Table 4, the average values of A_d in the problems Ta01–Ta20 are 0.21 and 0.24, while they are 0.22 and 0.23 in the problems Ta21–Ta40.

By comparison, the proposed algorithm MM performs better in the convergence than the algorithms SM1 and SM2. This is because that, except for the problems La39, Ta14, and Ta39, all the values of A_d for the algorithm MM in the problem sets LA and TA are less than that of the algorithms SM1 and SM2. In average, the values of A_d for the algorithm MM in the problems La01–La20 and La21–La40 are 0.16 and 0.08, while the corresponding values of A_d for the algorithms SM1 and SM2 are about 1.26 and 0.21, respectively. And, in the problem set TA, the average values of A_d for the algorithm MM in the problems La01–La20 and La21–La40 are both 0.09, while the average values of A_d for the algorithms SM1 and SM2 are about 0.22.

On the other hand, the results also indicate that the convergence of the algorithm MM can even be very close to that of the algorithm MC. As shown in Table 3, the results show that the proposed algorithm MM can have the best convergence in the problems La04, La05, La07, La10, La12, La13, La14, La22, La24, La26, La27, and La31 from the problem set LA and Ta06, Ta09, Ta19, Ta23, Ta24, Ta37, and Ta37 from the problem set TA. In addition, the average of A_d for the algorithm MM in the problems La01–La21 with smaller problem scales is 0.16, which is 0.12 larger than that of the algorithm MC. But, in the problems with larger problem scales, such as the problems La21–La40 and Ta01–Ta40, the average of A_d for the algorithm MM is only 0.06 larger that of the algorithm MC. Therefore, we conclude that the proposed algorithm MM is better than the algorithms SM1 and SM2 and similar to the algorithm MC in convergence.

Table 3. The values of A_d for the algorithms Monte Carlo approximation-based MOEA (MC), meta-model (MM), total slack time (SM1), and free slack time (SM2) in the problem set LA.

Cases	$n \times m$	MC	MM	SM1	SM2	Cases	$n \times m$	MC	MM	SM1	SM2
La01	10×5	0.01	0.07	0.99	1.57	La21	15×10	0.00	0.10	0.31	0.34
La02	10×5	0.01	0.04	0.26	0.50	La22	15×10	0.03	0.01	0.19	0.13
La03	10×5	0.01	0.05	0.08	0.10	La23	15×10	0.00	0.14	0.19	0.31
La04	10×5	0.07	0.00	0.16	0.36	La24	15×10	0.04	0.03	0.20	0.12
La05	10×5	0.00	0.00	0.00	0.00	La25	15×10	0.00	0.07	0.19	0.30
La06	15×5	0.00	0.92	3.96	7.19	La26	20×10	0.02	0.02	0.23	0.17
La07	15×5	0.52	0.00	1.55	1.22	La27	20×10	0.06	0.02	0.26	0.06
La08	15×5	0.00	0.33	3.70	2.95	La28	20×10	0.00	0.11	0.18	0.15
La09	15×5	0.00	0.35	2.89	1.45	La29	20×10	0.01	0.07	0.17	0.08
La10	15×5	0.00	0.00	0.00	0.00	La30	20×10	0.02	0.04	0.26	0.24
La11	20×5	0.00	0.66	6.06	4.84	La31	30×10	0.15	0.00	0.21	0.25
La12	20×5	0.04	0.03	1.38	0.92	La32	30×10	0.00	0.18	0.24	0.24
La13	20×5	0.06	0.05	1.34	1.22	La33	20×10	0.00	0.17	0.24	0.09
La14	20×5	0.00	0.00	0.00	0.00	La34	30×10	0.00	0.10	0.27	0.08
La15	20×5	0.00	0.30	0.63	1.12	La35	30×10	0.01	0.16	0.18	0.26
La16	10×10	0.09	0.14	1.09	0.36	La36	15×15	0.00	0.12	0.19	0.38
La17	10×10	0.00	0.08	0.20	0.16	La37	15×15	0.00	0.12	0.22	0.25
La18	10×10	0.00	0.15	0.30	0.46	La38	15×15	0.00	0.04	0.18	0.27
La19	10×10	0.01	0.02	0.34	0.13	La39	15×15	0.00	0.13	0.04	0.20
La20	10×10	0.02	0.09	0.40	0.55	La40	15×15	0.00	0.05	0.24	0.31
Aver.	/	**0.04**	**0.16**	**1.27**	**1.26**	**Aver.**	/	**0.02**	**0.08**	**0.21**	**0.21**

Table 4. The values of A_d for the algorithms MC, MM, SM1 and SM2 in the problem set TA.

Cases	$n \times m$	MC	MM	SM1	SM2	Cases	$n \times m$	MC	MM	SM1	SM2
Ta01	15×15	0.00	0.08	0.19	0.20	Ta21	20×20	0.02	0.05	0.23	0.31
Ta02	15×15	0.00	0.08	0.22	0.33	Ta22	20×20	0.00	0.17	0.28	0.34
Ta03	15×15	0.00	0.04	0.17	0.09	Ta23	20×20	0.09	0.01	0.14	0.19
Ta04	15×15	0.01	0.12	0.21	0.17	Ta24	20×20	0.02	0.01	0.17	0.16
Ta05	15×15	0.00	0.15	0.15	0.24	Ta25	20×20	0.00	0.22	0.29	0.24
Ta06	15×15	0.04	0.01	0.23	0.22	Ta26	20×20	0.00	0.07	0.30	0.22
Ta07	15×15	0.00	0.14	0.24	0.26	Ta27	20×20	0.00	0.09	0.18	0.38
Ta08	15×15	0.01	0.02	0.08	0.11	Ta28	20×20	0.03	0.05	0.30	0.21
Ta09	15×15	0.06	0.03	0.27	0.30	Ta29	20×20	0.02	0.06	0.31	0.34
Ta10	15×15	0.06	0.10	0.29	0.22	Ta30	20×20	0.02	0.05	0.24	0.24
Ta11	20×15	0.00	0.22	0.29	0.30	Ta31	30×15	0.02	0.04	0.16	0.17
Ta12	20×15	0.01	0.04	0.24	0.19	Ta32	30×15	0.05	0.05	0.13	0.14
Ta13	20×15	0.00	0.08	0.14	0.29	Ta33	30×15	0.03	0.05	0.34	0.26
Ta14	20×15	0.01	0.12	0.10	0.17	Ta34	30×15	0.00	0.13	0.33	0.39
Ta15	20×15	0.00	0.21	0.26	0.37	Ta35	30×15	0.00	0.09	0.21	0.14
Ta16	20×15	0.00	0.06	0.23	0.21	Ta36	30×15	0.02	0.03	0.15	0.18
Ta17	20×15	0.03	0.06	0.14	0.33	Ta37	30×15	0.03	0.02	0.17	0.08
Ta18	20×15	0.00	0.07	0.24	0.30	Ta38	30×15	0.00	0.27	0.24	0.35
Ta19	20×15	0.09	0.00	0.30	0.34	Ta39	30×15	0.07	0.16	0.01	0.13
Ta20	20×15	0.00	0.14	0.17	0.19	Ta40	30×15	0.00	0.13	0.19	0.18
Aver.	/	**0.02**	**0.09**	**0.21**	**0.24**	**Aver.**	/	**0.02**	**0.09**	**0.22**	**0.23**

The results on the metric N_μ of the algorithms MC, MM, SM1 and SM2 are presented in Tables 5 and 6 for the problem sets LA and TA, respectively. The results show that the algorithms SM1 and SM2 also have the similar performance in the diversity. From the results in Table 5, we can found that the average values of N_μ for the algorithms SM1 and SM2 in the problems La01–La20 are 4.7 and 5.2, and the average values of A_d for the problems La21–La40 are 9.3 and 10.5, respectively. That is, the average difference of A_d between the algorithms SM1 and SM2 is only about 1.0 in average. The similar results can also be found in Table 6, the average values of N_μ for the problems Ta01–Ta20 are 10.2 and 9.7, while they are 8.9 and 8.4 in the problems Ta21–Ta40.

Table 5. The values of N_μ for the algorithms MC, MM, SM1, and SM2 in the problem set LA.

Cases	$n \times m$	MC	MM	SM1	SM2	Cases	$n \times m$	MC	MM	SM1	SM2
La01	10×5	11	12	2	4	La21	15×10	15	15	8	13
La02	10×5	12	9	5	4	La22	15×10	16	17	10	9
La03	10×5	11	8	2	6	La23	15×10	13	18	6	12
La04	10×5	9	8	4	4	La24	15×10	12	12	10	15
La05	10×5	1	1	2	3	La25	15×10	14	15	11	9
La06	15×5	3	3	3	6	La26	20×10	15	15	10	10
La07	15×5	11	6	4	8	La27	20×10	12	14	10	13
La08	15×5	5	7	3	9	La28	20×10	14	18	8	7
La09	15×5	7	9	9	7	La29	20×10	13	14	7	11
La10	15×5	1	2	4	2	La30	20×10	13	16	10	9
La11	20×5	4	5	6	5	La31	30×10	15	12	9	8
La12	20×5	11	8	5	7	La32	30×10	13	12	7	12
La13	20×5	12	7	7	6	La33	20×10	11	13	8	9
La14	20×5	1	1	3	1	La34	30×10	13	16	11	10
La15	20×5	12	16	7	6	La35	30×10	11	16	10	7
La16	10×10	9	8	2	2	La36	15×15	12	16	11	11
La17	10×10	10	11	7	7	La37	15×15	14	17	8	9
La18	10×10	12	14	8	4	La38	15×15	15	18	14	13
La19	10×10	12	12	6	6	La39	15×15	18	14	8	12
La20	10×10	12	14	4	7	La40	15×15	14	17	10	11
Aver.	/	**8.3**	**8.1**	**4.7**	**5.2**	**Aver.**	/	**13.7**	**15.3**	**9.3**	**10.5**

Table 6. The values of N_μ for the algorithms MC, MM, SM1, and SM2 in the problem set TA.

Cases	$n \times m$	MC	MM	SM1	SM2	Cases	$n \times m$	MC	MM	SM1	SM2
Ta01	15×15	16	18	9	9	Ta21	20×20	17	14	10	9
Ta02	15×15	14	10	10	12	Ta22	20×20	13	15	6	8
Ta03	15×15	15	19	12	10	Ta23	20×20	15	11	11	11
Ta04	15×15	14	19	11	11	Ta24	20×20	13	13	11	9
Ta05	15×15	17	15	9	11	Ta25	20×20	14	12	11	9
Ta06	15×15	16	14	9	10	Ta26	20×20	16	12	10	10
Ta07	15×15	15	17	12	10	Ta27	20×20	14	8	12	9
Ta08	15×15	17	11	13	9	Ta28	20×20	15	17	7	9
Ta09	15×15	15	14	10	8	Ta29	20×20	17	12	12	10
Ta10	15×15	15	14	11	12	Ta30	20×20	17	10	7	7
Ta11	20×15	13	15	10	10	Ta31	30×15	13	13	9	10
Ta12	20×15	12	14	8	7	Ta32	30×15	13	12	7	8
Ta13	20×15	16	13	8	10	Ta33	30×15	13	11	6	5
Ta14	20×15	13	14	9	10	Ta34	30×15	14	13	10	9
Ta15	20×15	17	18	12	11	Ta35	30×15	10	14	9	7
Ta16	20×15	19	13	8	8	Ta36	30×15	15	10	9	6
Ta17	20×15	15	11	10	9	Ta37	30×15	13	11	6	8
Ta18	20×15	16	15	10	9	Ta38	30×15	9	15	8	10
Ta19	20×15	10	13	12	8	Ta39	30×15	11	14	7	6
Ta20	20×15	16	17	11	10	Ta40	30×15	13	13	9	7
Aver.	/	**15.1**	**14.7**	**10.2**	**9.7**	**Aver.**	/	**13.8**	**12.5**	**8.9**	**8.4**

Compared with the algorithms SM1 and SM2, the proposed algorithm MM performs better in diversity. This is because that the values of A_d for the algorithm MM are larger than that of the algorithms SM1 and SM2 for most of the problems in the problem sets LA and TA as shown in Tables 5 and 6. In addition, the results have also shown the algorithm MM have the similar performance in diversity to that of the algorithm MC. For example, the average values of A_d for the algorithms MM and MC in the problems La01–La20 are about 8.1 and 8.3, while the average values of A_d are 15.3 and 13.7 in the problems La21–La40, respectively. Similar results can be found in Table 6 for the problem set TA. Therefore, we can conclude that the proposed algorithm MM is very close to the algorithm MC in diversity, but it is much better than the algorithms SM1 and SM2.

Taking the problems instances La06, La15, Ta15, and Ta36 as examples, the performance of the algorithms MC, MM, SM1, and SM2 can also be clearly illustrated by the Pareto fronts. As shown in Figure 6, the Pareto front of the algorithm MM is very close to that of the algorithm MC, while the Pareto fronts of the algorithms SM1 and SM2 are very far from that of the algorithm MC. On the other hand, the number of solutions in the Pareto front of the algorithm MM is approximately equal to that of the algorithm MC, while the number of solutions in the Pareto fronts of the algorithms SM1 and SM2 are much less in comparison.

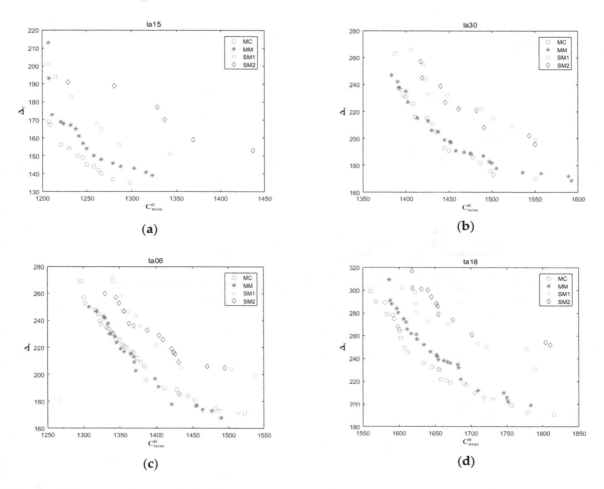

Figure 6. The Pareto fronts of algorithms MC, MM, SM1, and SM2. **(a)** For the problem La15; **(b)** for the problem La30; **(c)** for the problem Ta06; **(d)** for the problem Ta18.

However, as indicated earlier, the algorithm based on the Monte Carlo approximation will be very time-consuming. To investigate computational efforts for each algorithm, the average T_a and the relative value T_r of CPU time have been recorded, where T_r is the ratio of the average T_a of an algorithm (MC, MM, SM1, or SM2) to that of the algorithm MC. In this experiment, the simulation times for the Monte Carlo approximation are set as 30, which is generally the required minimum number of samples in statistical estimation [20]. As the results shown in Table 7, the algorithms SM1 and SM2 always consume the least time, while the algorithm MC consumes the most. By comparison, the time consumption of the proposed algorithm MM is almost equal to that of the algorithms SM1 and SM2, but it is much less than that of the algorithm MC. What is more, the time consumption of the algorithm MC increases significantly with the problem scale. For example, the average T_a of the algorithm MC in the problems La01-La05 is 66, which is close to that of the algorithm MM with the value 53. But, in the problems Ta31-Ta40, the time consumption of the algorithm MC is about 8 times of that of the algorithm MM. In more complex problems or uncertain scenarios, a larger sample size may be needed for the algorithm MC, which will result in a computational time that is unacceptable.

Table 7. Results on the CPU time (in seconds) of algorithms MC, MM, SM1, and SM2.

Cases	$n \times m$	MC		MM		SM1		SM2	
		T_a	T_r	T_a	T_r	T_a	T_r	T_a	T_r
La01–La05	10×5	66	1.00	53	0.80	50	0.76	50	0.76
La06–La10	15×5	83	1.00	54	0.65	52	0.63	50	0.60
La11–La15	20×5	113	1.00	55	0.49	55	0.49	52	0.46
La16–La20	10×10	102	1.00	54	0.53	54	0.53	51	0.50
La21–La25	15×10	153	1.00	56	0.37	55	0.36	54	0.35
La26–La30	20×10	220	1.00	60	0.27	59	0.27	57	0.26
La31–La35	30×10	398	1.00	73	0.18	70	0.18	68	0.17
La36–La40	15×15	238	1.00	65	0.27	62	0.26	60	0.25
Ta01–Ta10	15×15	231	1.00	63	0.27	61	0.26	59	0.26
Ta11–Ta20	20×15	351	1.00	75	0.21	70	0.20	68	0.19
Ta21–Ta30	20×20	543	1.00	85	0.16	82	0.15	83	0.15
Ta31–Ta40	30×15	733	1.00	95	0.13	92	0.13	89	0.12
Aver.	/	269.3	1.00	65.7	0.24	63.5	0.24	61.8	0.23

5. Conclusions

In this study, we have addressed the robust JSS with RMDs, in which the makespan and the EMD are considered simultaneously. To improve the efficiency of the MOEA, a meta-model has been constructed by using the data-driven response surface method. Then, with the individual-based evolution control, the meta-model-based MOEA has been proposed to solve this problem. The results have shown that regarding the convergence and diversity, the proposed algorithm yields better Pareto solution sets than the algorithms with the existing slack time-based surrogate measures. Moreover, the meta-model has high accuracy in evaluating the EMD similar to the Monte Carlo approximation. Overall, the proposed meta-model-based MOEA can effectively and efficiently solve the robust JSS with RMDs.

Author Contributions: Conceptualization, Z.W.; Formal analysis, S.Y.; Funding acquisition, T.L.; Investigation, S.Y.; Methodology, Z.W.; Supervision, T.L.; Writing—original draft, Z.W.; Writing—review and editing, T.L.

Notations:

JSS	Job shop scheduling problem	RMD	Random machine breakdowns
EMD	Expected makespan delay	MOEA	Multi-objective evolutionary algorithm
n	Number of jobs	m	Number of machines
J_j	Job j, $j = 1, 2, \ldots, n$	M_i	Machine i, $i = 1, 2, \ldots, m$
J	Set of jobs, $\{J_j | j = 1, 2, \ldots, n\}$	M	Set of machines $\{M_i | i = 1, 2, \ldots, m\}$
O_{ij}	Operation that job j is on machine i	O_j	Set of operations for job j
p_{ij}	Processing time of operation O_{ij}	st_{ij}	Starting time of operation O_{ij}
ct_{ij}	Completion time of operation O_{ij}	fs_{ij}	Free slack time of operation O_{ij}
ts_{ij}	Total slack time of operation O_{ij}	Pr_{ij}	Machine breakdown probability of O_{ij}
D_{ij}	Downtime when processing O_{ij}	C_{max}^0	Makespan of a schedule before execution
C_{max}^r	Actual makespan of a schedule	δ_c	Makespan delay of a schedule
Δ_c	Expression of expected makespan delay	Δ_c^a	Meta-model of Δ_c
Δ_c^{sim}	Monte Carlo approximation of Δ_c	O_n	Set of operations without slack time
O_y	Set of operations with slack time	p_s^n	Sum of processing time in the set O_n
p_s^y	Sum of processing time in the set O_y	fs_a	Average free slack time in the set O_y
ts_a	Average total slack time in the set O_y	λ_0	Machine failure rate of each machine

β_0 Expectation of the downtime P_0 Initial population

P_k Current population in generation k R_{k+1} Combined population in generation k

x Input vector $x = (\lambda_0, \beta_0, p_s^n, p_s^y, fs_a, ts_a)$ I_i A data instance $I_i = (x_i, \Delta_c^i)$

D_c Training data set s_i Schedule of ith individual in R_{k+1}

F_{k+1}^i Fitness of the ith individual in R_{k+1} F_{k+1} Fitness set of the population R_{k+1}

References

1. Sotskov, Y.N.; Egorova, N.G. The optimality region for a single-machine scheduling problem with bounded durations of the jobs and the total completion time objective. *Mathematics* **2019**, *7*, 382. [CrossRef]
2. Gafarov, E.; Werner, F. Two-machine job-shop scheduling with equal processing times on each machine. *Mathematics* **2019**, *7*, 301. [CrossRef]
3. Luan, F.; Cai, Z.; Wu, S.; Jiang, T.; Li, F.; Yang, J. Improved whale algorithm for solving the flexible job shop scheduling problem. *Mathematics* **2019**, *7*, 384. [CrossRef]
4. Turker, A.; Aktepe, A.; Inal, A.; Ersoz, O.; Das, G.; Birgoren, B. A decision support system for dynamic job-shop scheduling using real-time data with simulation. *Mathematics* **2019**, *7*, 278. [CrossRef]
5. Sun, L.; Lin, L.; Li, H.; Gen, M. Cooperative co-evolution algorithm with an MRF-based decomposition strategy for stochastic flexible job shop scheduling. *Mathematics* **2019**, *7*, 318. [CrossRef]
6. Zhang, J.; Ding, G.; Zou, Y.; Qin, S.; Fu, J. Review of job shop scheduling research and its new perspectives under Industry 4.0. *J Intell. Manuf.* **2019**, *30*, 1809–1830. [CrossRef]
7. Potts, C.N.; Strusevich, V.A. Fifty years of scheduling: A survey of milestones. *J. Oper. Res. Soc.* **2009**, *60*, S41–S68. [CrossRef]
8. García-León, A.A.; Dauzère-Pérèsb, S.; Mati, Y. An efficient Pareto approach for solving the multi-objective flexible job-shop scheduling problem with regular criterio. *Comput. Oper. Res.* **2019**, *108*, 187–200. [CrossRef]
9. Zhang, C.; Rao, Y.; Li, P. An effective hybrid genetic algorithm for the job shop scheduling problem. *Int. J. Adv. Manuf. Tech.* **2008**, *39*, 965–974. [CrossRef]
10. Li, L.; Jiao, L.; Stolkin, R.; Liu, F. Mixed second order partial derivatives decomposition method for large scale optimization. *Appl. Soft Comput.* **2017**, *61*, 1013–1021. [CrossRef]
11. Watanabe, M.; Ida, K.; Gen, M. A genetic algorithm with modified crossover operator and search area adaptation for the job-shop scheduling problem. *Comput. Ind. Eng.* **2005**, *48*, 743–752. [CrossRef]
12. Eswaramurthy, V.P.; Tamilarasi, A. Hybridizing tabu search with ant colony optimization for solving job shop scheduling problems. *Int. J. Adv. Manuf. Tech.* **2009**, *40*, 1004–1015. [CrossRef]
13. Mencía, C.; Mencía, R.; Sierra, M.R.; Varela, R. Memetic algorithms for the job shop scheduling problem with operators. *Appl. Soft. Comput.* **2015**, *34*, 94–105. [CrossRef]
14. Buddala, R.; Mahapatra, S.S. Two-stage teaching-learning-based optimization method for flexible job-shop scheduling under machine breakdown. *Int. J. Adv. Manuf. Tech.* **2019**, *100*, 1419–1432. [CrossRef]
15. Mehta, S.V.; Uzsoy, R.M. Predictable scheduling of a job shop subject to breakdowns. *IEEE Trans. Robotic. Autom.* **1998**, *14*, 365–378. [CrossRef]
16. Lei, D. Minimizing makespan for scheduling stochastic job shop with random breakdown. *Appl. Math. Comput.* **2012**, *218*, 11851–11858. [CrossRef]
17. Nouiri, M.; Bekrar, A.; Jemai, A.; Trentesaux, D.; Ammari, A.C.; Niar, S. Two stage particle swarm optimization to solve the flexible job shop predictive scheduling problem considering possible machine breakdowns. *Comput. Ind. Eng.* **2017**, *112*, 595–606. [CrossRef]
18. von Hoyningen-Huene, W.; Kiesmueller, G.P. Evaluation of the expected makespan of a set of non-resumable jobs on parallel machines with stochastic failures. *Eur. J. Oper. Res.* **2015**, *240*, 439–446. [CrossRef]
19. Jamili, A. Robust job shop scheduling problem: Mathematical models, exact and heuristic algorithms. *Expert Syst. Appl.* **2016**, *55*, 341–350. [CrossRef]
20. Xiong, J.; Xing, L.; Chen, Y. Robust scheduling for multi-objective flexible job-shop problems with random machine breakdowns. *Int. J. Prod. Econ.* **2013**, *141*, 112–126. [CrossRef]
21. Wu, Z.; Sun, S.; Xiao, S. Risk measure of job shop scheduling with random machine breakdowns. *Comput. Oper. Res.* **2018**, *99*, 1–12. [CrossRef]
22. Liu, N.; Abdelrahman, M.A.; Ramaswamy, S.R. A Complete Multiagent Framework for Robust and Adaptable Dynamic Job Shop Scheduling. *IEEE Trans. Syst. Man. Cybern. Part C* **2007**, *37*, 904–916. [CrossRef]

23. Xiao, S.; Sun, S.; Jin, J.J. Surrogate Measures for the Robust Scheduling of Stochastic Job Shop Scheduling Problems. *Energies* **2017**, *10*, 543. [CrossRef]

24. Zuo, X.; Mo, H.; Wu, J. A robust scheduling method based on a multi-objective immune algorithm. *Inform Sciences* **2009**, *179*, 3359–3369. [CrossRef]

25. Ahmadi, E.; Zandieh, M.; Farrokh, M.; Emami, S.M. A multi objective optimization approach for flexible job shop scheduling problem under random machine breakdown by evolutionary algorithms. *Comput. Oper. Res.* **2016**, *73*, 56–66. [CrossRef]

26. Al-Fawzan, M.A.; Haouari, M. A bi-objective model for robust resource-constrained project scheduling. *Int. J. Prod. Econ.* **2005**, *96*, 175–187. [CrossRef]

27. Goren, S.; Sabuncuoglu, I. Optimization of schedule robustness and stability under random machine breakdowns and processing time variability. *IIE Trans.* **2010**, *42*, 203–220. [CrossRef]

28. Deb, K.; Pratap, A.; Agarwal, S.; Meyarivan, T. A fast and elitist multiobjective genetic algorithm: NSGA-II. *IEEE Trans. Evol. Comput.* **2002**, *6*, 182–197. [CrossRef]

29. Li, L.; Yao, X.; Stolkin, R.; Gong, M.; He, S. An evolutionary multi-objective approach to sparse reconstruction. *IEEE Trans. Evol. Comput.* **2014**, *18*, 827–845.

30. Zhou, A.; Qu, B.; Li, H.; Zhao, S.; Suganthan, P.N.; Zhang, Q. Multiobjective evolutionary algorithms: A survey of the state of the art. *Swarm Evol. Comput.* **2011**, *1*, 32–49. [CrossRef]

31. Xiong, J.; Tan, X.; Yang, K.; Xing, L.; Chen, Y. A Hybrid Multiobjective Evolutionary Approach for Flexible Job-Shop Scheduling Problems. *Math. Probl. Eng.* **2012**, *2012*, 1–27. [CrossRef]

32. Hosseinabadi, A.A.R.; Siar, H.; Shamshirband, S.; Shojafar, M.; Nasir, M.H.N.M. Using the gravitational emulation local search algorithm to solve the multi-objective flexible dynamic job shop scheduling problem in Small and Medium Enterprises. *Ann. Oper. Res.* **2015**, *229*, 451–474. [CrossRef]

33. Hosseinabadi, A.A.R.; Kardgar, M.; Shojafar, M.; Shamshirband, S.; Abraham, A. GELS-GA: Hybrid metaheuristic algorithm for solving Multiple Travelling Salesman Problem. In Proceedings of the 2014 IEEE 14th International Conference on Intelligent Systems Design and Applications, Okinawa, Japan, 28–30 November 2014.

34. Jin, Y.; Branke, J. Evolutionary Optimization in Uncertain Environments: A Survey. *IEEE T. Evolut. Comput.* **2005**, *9*, 303–317. [CrossRef]

35. Al-Hinai, N.; Elmekkawy, T.Y. Robust and stable flexible job shop scheduling with random machine breakdowns using a hybrid genetic algorithm. *Int. J. Prod. Econ.* **2011**, *132*, 279–291. [CrossRef]

36. Chaari, T.; Chaabane, S.; Loukil, T.; Trentesaux, D. A genetic algorithm for robust hybrid flow shop scheduling. *Int. J. Comput. Integ. M.* **2011**, *24*, 821–833. [CrossRef]

37. Yang, F.; Zheng, L.; Luo, Y. A novel particle filter based on hybrid deterministic and random sampling. *IEEE Access* **2018**, *6*, 67536–67542. [CrossRef]

38. Yang, F.; Luo, Y.; Zheng, L. Double-Layer Cubature Kalman Filter for Nonlinear Estimation. *Sensors* **2019**, *19*, 986. [CrossRef] [PubMed]

39. Wang, X.; Li, T.; Sun, S.; Corchado, J.M. A survey of recent advances in particle filters and remaining challenges for multitarget tracking. *Sensors* **2017**, *17*, 2707. [CrossRef]

40. Mirabi, M.; Ghomi, S.M.T.F.; Jolai, F. A two-stage hybrid flowshop scheduling problem in machine breakdown condition. *J. Intell. Manuf.* **2013**, *24*, 193–199. [CrossRef]

41. Liu, L.; Gu, H.; Xi, Y. Robust and stable scheduling of a single machine with random machine breakdowns. *Int. J. Adv. Manuf. Technol.* **2006**, *31*, 645–654. [CrossRef]

42. Leon, J.; Wu, S.D.; Storer, R.H. Robustness measures and robust scheduling for job shops. *IIE Trans.* **1994**, *26*, 32–43. [CrossRef]

43. Jensen, M.T. Generating robust and flexible job shop schedules using genetic algorithms. *IEEE Trans. Evol. Comput.* **2003**, *7*, 275–288. [CrossRef]

44. Yen, G.G.; He, Z. Performance Metric Ensemble for Multiobjective Evolutionary Algorithms. *IEEE Trans. Evol. Comput.* **2014**, *18*, 131–144. [CrossRef]

8

Effect of Time-Varying Factors on Optimal Combination of Quality Inspectors for Offline Inspection Station

Muhammad Babar Ramzan [1], Shehreyar Mohsin Qureshi [2], Sonia Irshad Mari [3], Muhammad Saad Memon [3], Mandeep Mittal [4,*], Muhammad Imran [5] and Muhammad Waqas Iqbal [6]

[1] Department of Garment Manufacturing, National Textile University, Faisalabad 37610, Pakistan; babar_ramzan@yahoo.com

[2] Department of Industrial and Manufacturing Engineering, NED University of Engineering and Technology, Karachi 75270, Pakistan; sheheryar@neduet.edu.pk

[3] Department of Industrial Engineering and Management, Mehran University of Engineering and Technology, Jamshoro 76062, Pakistan; sonia.irshad@faculty.muet.edu.pk (S.I.M.); saad.memon@faculty.muet.edu.pk (M.S.M.)

[4] Department of Mathematics, Amity Institute of Applied Science, Amity University, Noida 201313, India

[5] Department of Industrial and Management Engineering, Hanyang University, Seoul 15588, Korea; Imran.ime13@gmail.com

[6] Department of Industrial Engineering, Hongik University, Seoul 04066, Korea; Waqastextilion@gmail.com

* Correspondence: mittal_mandeep@yahoo.com.

Abstract: With advanced manufacturing technology, organizations like to cut their operational cost and improve product quality, yet the importance of human labor is still alive in some manufacturing industries. The performance of human-based systems depends much on the skill of labor that varies person to person within available manpower. Much work has been done on human resource and management, however, allocation of manpower based on their skill yet not investigated. For this purpose, this study considered offline inspection system where inspection is performed by the human labor of varying skill levels. A multi-objective optimization model is proposed based on Time-Varying factors; inspection skill, operation time and learning behavior. Min-max goal programming technique was used to determine the efficient combination of inspectors of each skill level at different time intervals of a running order. The optimized results ensured the achievement of all objectives of inspection station: the cost associated with inspectors, outgoing quality and inspected quantity. The obtained results proved that inspection performance of inspectors improves significantly with learning and revision of allocation of inspectors with the proposed model ensure better utilization of available manpower, maintain good quality and reduce cost as well.

Keywords: human-based production system; offline inspection; optimization; inspection cost; outgoing quality; learning behavior

1. Introduction

Human labor and factors associated are one of the main engineering disciplines and play a vital role in maintaining good quality, manufacturing cost and productivity. Although researchers are working on automation and hybrid systems, however, the importance of human labor is not limited yet. One of the important advantage, of human labor over automation, is their decision-making ability. These type of abilities in human labor improves as skill level and experience increases. Organizations always want to utilize their manpower efficiently according to their capacity, yet there is a lack of studies that evaluate the human labor based on their skills. The present study has been conducted to fill this study gap by considering the skill level, operation time and learning behavior of human labor. For this purpose, a human-based quality control system is considered where most of the processes are carried out by human labor. Quality Control (QC) is an important part of quality management system that consists of monitoring activities along with quality planning, quality assurance and quality improvement [1]. The main objective of QC is to maintain the good level of quality by mitigating the root causes of defective products [2]. Inspection is the main activity of QC that is performed to decide the product's conformance and non-conformance at different stages of manufacturing [3]. The process of inspection is investigated here to highlight the importance of inspection skill and inspection time in a manufacturing environment where learning affects significantly. Inspection can either be online or offline where online inspect the product during the process and offline inspect the product after the completion of the process [4,5]. Although online inspection has been considered as an economical method, however sometimes it is not feasible. Thus inspection process has to be done offline on finished or semi-finished products [6]. This paper also considered offline station where 100% inspection is done by human labor.

In human based manufacturing setups, learning behavior imparts significant enhancements in the performance of labor and their skill improves with the passage of time. Researchers believed that any organization that learns faster will have a competitive advantage in the future. However, this learning varies person to person within an organization and help to classify the available manpower into their respective skill levels. Six types of learning have been identified and one of them is learning by doing like inspection process performed by human labor. While planning for the new order, allocation of manpower is done once, that is, before the start of order and same labor is used until the completion of the job. However, in the actual scenario, human labor learns from their experience and improve their performance with the passage of time. Thus, they will be able to do more work with better efficiency because of their improved skills. In this situation, the organization must revise the allocation of labor that may bring advantages like better utilization of available manpower, achievement of inspection targets, reduce cost and maintain good quality. Recently, the optimal number of quality inspectors have been determined to minimize cost [7,8]. However, the effect of Time-Varying factors, like learning behavior, on an efficient combination of inspectors is not considered yet. This study has kept this factor in contact and the process of inspection is investigated here to determine the optimal number of quality inspectors for inspection station over different time periods.

2. Literature Review

In past, plenty of work has been done on offline inspection to reduce the overall cost, increase company profit and improve product quality. These objectives have been achieved by giving due consideration to inspection policies, inspection systems and optimization of process target values. One of the pioneering work in developing inspection policy was done by Herer and Raz [9] to reduce the inspection cost using dynamic programming. The similar objective was also achieved by calculating optimal lot size and expected number of inspections [10]. After that plenty of work has been conducted to improve the effectiveness of inspection policy. Anily and Grosfeld-Nir [11] determined inspection policy and lot size for a single production run. Further investigation was done with two-time parameters and multiple productions run with rigid demand. Wang and Meng [12] developed a joint optimization model to determine the total cost function. Their model was compared with three policies like no inspection, full inspection and disregard the first s (DTF-s) items policies by a numerical example. Avinadav and Perlman [13] studied such process to minimize the cost by determining the optimal inspection interval. Sarkar and Saren [14] developed an inspection policy for an imperfect manufacturing system that has inspection error and warranty cost to reduce the inspection cost.

Other inspection strategies have also been developed that includes inspection disposition (ID) policy and inspection disposition and rework (IDR) policy. Raz, et al. [15] developed the first ID policy to minimize the cost function by solving the problem of economic optimization. After that their ID policy was extensively studied by other researchers with the consideration of different assumptions [16–21].

Continues sampling plan (CSP) is also a pioneering method of inspection in which 100% inspection and sampling inspection is alternatively conducted [22]. The basic sampling plan known as CSP-1 was developed by Dodge [23] to monitor the average outgoing quality level (AOQL). After that many modifications have been incorporated in the procedure of original CSP-1 by considering different assumptions [24–30].

The studies have also been conducted to optimize the process parameters by many investigators of quality control. After the pioneering work done by Springer [31], number of studies have been conducted to minimize the expected cost. Earlier a process target model (PTM) was proposed to optimize a single objective for three different types of screening problems [32]. Their aim was to cancel out the effect of error in inspection through the conception of cut off points that helped to divide the products into grade one, grade two and scrap. Duffuaa, et al. [33] proposed another PTM to increase the profit by assuming the independent characteristics of quality for a two-stage process. This PTM was also modified using acceptance sampling by Duffuaa, et al. [34] to achieve the same objectives. Recently, Multi-Objective Optimization (MOO) problem has been explored to find out the value of process parameters: income, profit and product uniformity [35–37]. The pioneer work on MOO was done considering 100% inspection policy to optimize the objective functions and Pareto optimal points were ranked by proposing an algorithm [36]. Their MOO model further reviewed by considering the sampling inspection however similar results were attained [37]. A further improvement was done considering two types of inspection errors because inspection system may be error-prone. After comparing the results of revised and previous models, it was concluded that inspection errors have a major effect on profit and uniformity. This study also worked on MOO and considered three important parameters to measure the performance of human labor while performing inspection process.

The philosophy of learning behavior is not only to improve the productivity but also look for other aspects that support the process of learning. That's why a number of studies have found a relationship with quality control techniques and learning which was summarized by Jaber [38]. This combination of learning and quality control was first suggested by Koulamas [39] to evaluate the effect of product design on quality and cost. Teng and Thompson [40] worked on the learning behavior of workers and assessed that how it affects the quality and cost of the product. Similarly, Franceschini and Galetto [41] reduced the non-confirming quantity in production plant by improving the skill of workers. Jaber and Guiffrida [42] worked on wright's learning curve [43] and proposed a quality learning curve (QLC) for a process that generates defects and required rework also. Further, this QLC was investigated by relaxing its different assumptions. Like Jaber and Guiffrida [44] assumed that an imperfect process can be interrupted to maintain quality and improved system's performance. Similarly, Jaber and Khan [45] further relaxed two assumptions and considered scrap after production along with a rework of a lot. They concluded that optimal performance improves with learning and deteriorates when learning in rework becomes faster. It is observed that quantity and cost of production have a direct link with quality and this subject will have particular interest when combined with learning behavior. A number of researchers have been investigating errors in screening, however, the relationship between quality and screening need to be studied further Jaber [38]. This study has considered learning behavior in the proposed model and its effect on inspection performance of inspectors.

Despite the above-mentioned literature, the researchers have investigated this research area with respect to the application of new trends, techniques and methodologies in the human labor selection and job assignment. It includes artificial intelligence, genetic algorithm, goal programming, fuzzy logic, data mining and data envelopment analysis [46–49]. In a human based production environment, assigning the job to workers according to their competence is an important step to keep overall cost in control and maintain production efficiency. A fuzzy logic interface method has been proposed to assign and verify production jobs to human labor. The proposed method has been applied to a discrete manufacturing system to reduce the cost due to human errors [46]. Similarly, a synchronized job assignment model has been proposed to overcome the problem of human performance due to deviation in skill level and fluctuation of cycle time. A multi-objective simulation integrated hybrid genetic algorithm was used as a job assignment model such that it promotes teamwork and overcome the effect of varying skill level [49]. However, there is a lack of studies in which such new trends have been applied in human-based inspection system. This study has also addressed this gap by applying multi-objective goal programming to the offline inspection station.

Table 1 has summarized the span of work done on offline inspection. It indicates that how different researchers have contributed to the field under study and compare them with the present study. Despite much work, human-based inspection system has not been studied yet considering the effect of learning on the performance of labor with different skill levels. The present study has focused this gap to contribute to the current literature and investigated that how learning behavior of different inspectors affect the inspection performance and total manpower required for inspection station. The MOO model has been presented here that can determine the group of inspectors having different skill levels such that all objectives of inspection station are achieved.

This study also incorporates the effect of learning behavior on inspection skill of human labor in terms of quality, cost and quantity. The proposed model is able to determine the optimal values of inspectors at different time periods and compares that how the requirement of manpower varies from time to time due to learning.

Table 1. Summary of contribution made by previous studies.

Authors	Inspection					Learning Behavior	Study Objective
	Strategy	Error	Cost	Time	Skill		
Jaber and Guiffrida [42]	Sampling	✓				✓	Proposed quality learning curve
Finkelshtein, Herer, Raz and Ben-Gal [16]	100%	✓	✓				Optimal ID policy
Duffuaa and Khan [50]	Both	✓	✓				Repeat inspection plan to measures the performance
Anily and Grosfeld-Nir [11]	100%		✓				Optimal inspection policy
Elshafei, et al. [51]	100%	✓	✓				Optimal inspection sequence for repeat inspection plan
Wang [17]	Sampling	✓	✓				Optimal ID policy
Duffuaa and Khan [52]	Both	✓	✓				Optimal inspection cycles
Wang and Hung [18]	Sampling	✓	✓				Optimal ID policy
Jaber and Guiffrida [44]						✓	Proposed QLC by relaxing assumptions
Wang and Meng [12]	Both	✓	✓				Optimal inspection policy
Colledani and Tolio [53]	Sampling	✓	✓				Analytical method of evaluation
Tzimerman and Herer [6]	Sampling	✓	✓				Optimal inspection policy
Bendavid and Herer [19]	Sampling	✓	✓				Optimal ID policy
Vaghefi and Sarhangian [54]	Sampling	✓	✓				Optimal inspection policy
Wang, Sheu, Chen and Horng [20]	Sampling	✓	✓				Optimal ID policy
Yu, Yu and Wu [28]	Both	✓	✓				Optimal inspection policy
Khan, et al. [55]	100%	✓				✓	Economic order quantity with learning in production
Jaber and Khan [45]	Both	✓	✓				Proposed QLC by relaxing assumptions
Yang [56]	Both	✓	✓				Optimization of K- stage inspection system
Khan, et al. [57]	100%	✓	✓				Economic order quantity
Tsai and Wang [21]	Sampling	✓	✓				Optimal IDR Policy
Yu and Yu [29]	Both	✓	✓				Optimal inspection policy
Khan, et al. [58]	Both	✓	✓				Effect on human factors on cost of supply chain
Avinadav and Sarne [59]	Sampling				✓		Selection of inspection systems
Avinadav and Perlman [13]	100%	✓	✓				Optimal inspection interval
Duffuaa and El-Ga'aly [36]	Sampling	✓	✓				Maximization of income, profit, product uniformity
Duffuaa and El-Ga'aly [37]	Sampling	✓	✓				Maximization of income, profit, product uniformity
Bouslah, et al. [60]	Sampling	✓	✓				Joint production control and economic sampling plan
Khan, et al [61]	100%	✓	✓			✓	Integrated supply chain model
Liu and Liu [62]	Sampling	✓					Resubmitted sampling scheme
Aslam, et al. [63]	Sampling	✓	✓				Mixed acceptance sampling plan
Yang and Cho [64]	100%	✓	✓				Optimal inspection cycles
Mohammadi, et al. [65]	Sampling	✓	✓				Effective robust inspection planning
Duffuaa and El-Ga'aly [35]	Sampling	✓	✓				Maximization of income, profit, product uniformity
Sarkar and Saren [14]	Sampling	✓	✓		✓		Product inspection policy
Ramzan and Kang [7]	Both	✓	✓		✓		MOO model to determine inspectors of different skills
Jaber [38]		✓	✓			✓	A review of studies linking quality with learning
Kang, Ramzan, Sarkar and Imran [8]	Both	✓	✓		✓		MOO model to determine inspectors for different products
This paper	Both	✓	✓	✓	✓	✓	MOO model to determine optimal quality inspectors

3. Model Formulation

3.1. Definition of Research Problem

Figure 1 indicates the movement of input material through production unit and inspection stations to complete the manufacturing process that is assumed to be an imperfect process. The output products transfer to an offline inspection station for two-step inspection processes: 100% inspection followed by sampling inspection. The first inspection station has J number of inspectors that perform the process of 100% inspection. They have varying skill levels which are defined based on their quantity inspected per day and errors in inspection per day. Each inspector classifies the output products either confirming or non-conforming. A batch of conforming products, having fixed quantity N, is then presented for sampling inspection. On the other hand, non-conforming products can either be reworked or rejected.

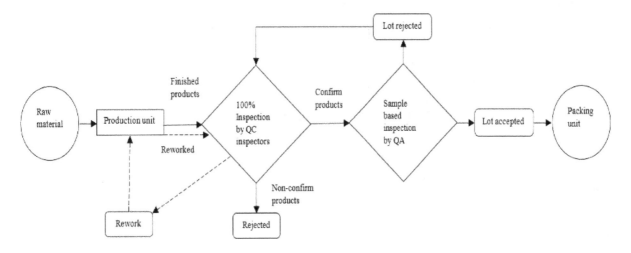

Figure 1. Flowchart of production unit and inspection stations of a manufacturing system.

A person with high inspection skill performs the Sampling inspection. The quantity n is randomly selected as a sample size from the presented batch/lot and the number of defective items d are separated. The value of d is compared with the threshold value c to make the final decision of lot acceptance or lot rejection. The decision will be to accept the lot if $d \leq c$ however lot will be rejected if $d > c$. The accepted lot is moved to the next process yet the rejected lot is returned to the same inspector for re-inspect. Defective items are separated from the rejected lot and exchanged with the conforming items to complete the batch for second sampling inspection. In order to calculate the quantity inspected per day and inspection cost per day of each inspector, number of accepted lots are used. Similarly, the value of outgoing quality is determined by the number of defectives items found. The value of Outgoing quality, accepted quantity and inspection cost depend on the number of inspectors and their skill levels that vary with the passage of time depending upon their learning behavior and experience.

3.2. Model Notations and Abbreviations

Model Notations

Sets

j	type of inspectors where, j = Low skill, Medium skill and High skill
l	low skill $l = 1, 2, 3, \ldots, L$
m	medium skill $m = 1, 2, 3, \ldots, M$
h	high skill $h = 1, 2, 3, \ldots, H$

Parameters

N	lot/batch size
n	sample size
IT_j	inspection time per unit taken by jth inspector
V	cost of inspection ($/min)
MI	maximum allowable quality inspector
ST	standard time of inspection of particular product
TVC_T	target of total cost for inspection station
AOQ_T	target of outgoing quality for inspection station
TIQ_T	target of accepted quantity for inspection station

Input variables

d_j	number of defective items present in sample size n inspected of jth inspector
b_j	learning rate of jth inspector
$d_1^{\pm}$	deviational variables for cost of inspectors
$d_2^{\pm}$	deviational variables for outgoing quality
$d_3^{\pm}$	deviational variables for accepted quantity
OQ_j	average outgoing quality of jth quality inspectors
IQ_j	inspected quantity by jth quality inspectors
VC_j	variable cost of jth quality inspectors

Decision variables

NI_j	number of jth type of skilled labor

3.3. Outgoing Quality

Maintaining an acceptable level of Outgoing Quality (OQ) is one of the main objectives and its dependents on the skill of quality inspectors. The value of OQ can be measured by sample-based inspection process by determining the number of defectives present in inspected quantity. Let quantity Q of finished products move from the manufacturing unit to the offline station where 100% inspection is done. If Q_j is the total quantity inspected by each inspector j and p_j is the probability of separating the non-conforming (NC) products from confirming (C) products than the value of NC and C can be calculated as:

$$NC_j = p_j \times Q_j$$

$$C_j = (1 - p_j) \times Q_j$$

The quantity NC_j can either be sent for rework or rejected. Rework quantity (RW_j) and rejected quantity (RE_j) can be calculated by the following equations:

$$RW_j = \alpha_j \times NC_j = \alpha_j \times (p_j \times Q_j)$$

$$RE_j = (1 - \alpha_j) \times NC_j = (1 - \alpha_j) \times (p_j \times Q_j)$$

where α_j is the probability of rework-able quantity. Similarly, the conforming quantity is moved for the process of sampling inspection as a lot/batch of size N. The following equation can be used to determine the value of OQ,

$$OQ = \frac{no\ of\ defective\ items}{Sample\ size}$$

$$OQ_j = \frac{d_j}{n_j} \ \forall j$$

where d shows number of defects present in sample size n. Since, this study has focused on learning behavior of quality inspectors along with their skill and inspection time. Thus, with the passage of time, quality inspectors will make less inspection error that will improve their individual OQ as well as of inspection station. A similar concept of reduction in defective percentage was also addressed by Jaber and Guiffrida [44], keeping in view the wright's learning curve. Their suggested formula is used here:

$$OQ(w) = OQ_s \times w^{-b}$$

where OQ_s is the initial value, b is the learning rate and $OQ(w)$ is the value of outgoing quality level at wth week. Similarly, the value of OQ for any inspector j can be calculated as:

$$OQ_j(w) = OQ_s \times w^{-b_j} \ \forall j$$

where b_j is the learning rate of inspector j. This study is investigating the human labor of J types of skill levels, thus Average Outgoing Quality (AOQ) can be calculated as:

$$AOQ(w) = \frac{\sum_{j=1}^{J} OQ_j(w)}{\sum_j NI_j} \ \forall j$$

$$AOQ(w) = \frac{OQ_l(w) + OQ_m(w) + OQ_h(w)}{\sum_j NI_j}$$

$$AOQ(w) = \frac{NI_L \left(OQ_{s,\,l} \times w^{-b_l}\right) + NI_M \left(OQ_{s,\,m} \times w^{-b_m}\right) + NI_H \left(OQ_{s,\,h} \times w^{-b_h}\right)}{\sum_j NI_j}$$

where b_l, b_m, b_h indicate the learning rate of inspector with low, medium and high inspection skill respectively. Finally, the value of AOQ for j type of quality inspectors is calculated by Equation.

$$AOQ = \frac{\sum_{j=1}^{J} NI_j \left(OQ_{s,\,j} \times w^{-b_j}\right)}{\sum_j NI_j} \ \forall j$$

3.4. Inspection Quantity

The second objective is to achieve the target of total inspection quantity to avoid any bottleneck and skill of quality inspector play a key role in this regard. Inspected quantity IQ is a quantity accepted by lot sampling process and is calculated for each inspector according to his inspection time. Quantity inspected by a jth inspector can be calculated as:

$$IQ = \frac{Time\ available}{Inspection\ time}$$

$$IQ_j = \frac{TA}{IT_j} \ \forall j$$

where IT_j is the inspection time taken by the jth quality inspector to inspect one item. With the passage of time, the efficiency of each quality inspector improves and inspected quantity increases because of reduction in inspection time due to learning. To calculate the improvement in inspection time, concept of wright's learning curve [43] is used that suggests the exponential relationship between man hour and cumulative production.

$$IT(w) = IT_s \times w^{-b}$$

where IT_s is the initial value of inspection time, b is the learning rate and $IT(w)$ is the inspection time at wth week. Similarly, the value of IT_j and IQ_j for a jth inspector can be calculated as:

$$IT_j(w) = IT_s \times w^{-b_j} \; \forall j$$

$$IQ_j(w) = \frac{TA}{IT_j(w)} = \frac{TA}{IT_{s,j} \times w^{-b_j}} \; \forall j$$

where b_j is the learning rate of the jth quality inspector. Total inspected quantity TIQ of the offline station will include all J types of inspectors.

$$TIQ(w) = \sum_{j=1}^{J} IQ_j(w) \; \forall j$$

$$TIQ(w) = IQ_l(w) + IQ_m(w) + IQ_h(w)$$

$$TIQ(w) = NI_l\left(\frac{TA}{IT_{s,l} \times w^{-b_l}}\right) + NI_m\left(\frac{TA}{IT_{s,m} \times w^{-b_m}}\right) + NI_h\left(\frac{TA}{IT_{s,h} \times w^{-b_h}}\right)$$

Total inspected quantity by J type of quality inspectors can be calculated by the following equation:

$$TIQ(w) = \sum_{j=1}^{J} NI_j\left(\frac{TA}{IT_{s,j} \times w^{-b_j}}\right)$$

3.5. Inspection Cost

Total inspection cost consists fixed cost (setup, inspection material, salaried workers etc.) and variable cost that is related to human labor. Since this study is investigating the skill of inspectors that vary with experience and learning of human labor, thus change in inspected quantity of inspector will also vary the related cost. This study is focusing more on the cost of quality inspectors that will be further used to optimize the total variable cost associated with all quality inspectors. By using inspected quantity IQ_j, the VC_j can be calculated on the basis of time earned TE_j for the jth quality inspector.

$$VC_j = TE_j \times V$$

$$TE_j = IQ_j \times ST$$

Thus

$$VC_j = (IQ_j \times ST) \times V \; \forall j$$

where ST is the standard time of inspection of a particular product and V is the cost of inspection ($\$$/min). As described earlier, a decrease in IT is observed based on the learning behavior of quality inspector that increase the IQ. Thus, the value of VC_j for jth inspector at any stage w will be calculated as:

$$VC_j(w) = \left(\frac{TA}{IT_j(w)}\right) \times ST \times V$$

$$VC_j(w) = \left(\frac{TA}{IT_{s,j} \times w^{-b_j}}\right) \times ST \times V$$

Total Variable Cost (TVC) of offline station that has J type of inspectors, will be calculated by as:

$$TVC(w) = \sum_{j=1}^{J} VC_j(w) \; \forall j$$

$$TVC(w) = \sum_{j=1}^{J} \left(\frac{TA}{IT_{s,j} \times w^{-b_j}} \right) \times ST \times V$$

$$TVC(w) = VC_l(w) + VC_m(w) + VC_h(w)$$

$$TVC(w) = \left\{ NI_l \left(\frac{TA}{IT_{s,1} \times w^{-b_l}} \right) \times ST \times V \right\} + \left\{ NI_m \left(\frac{TA}{IT_{s,m} \times w^{-b_m}} \right) \times ST \times V \right\}$$
$$+ \left\{ NI_h \left(\frac{TA}{IT_{s,h} \times w^{-b_h}} \right) \times ST \times V \right\}$$

$$TVC(w) = \left\{ NI_l \left(\frac{TA}{IT_{s,1} \times w^{-b_l}} \right) + NI_m \left(\frac{TA}{IT_{s,m} \times w^{-b_m}} \right) + NI_h \left(\frac{TA}{IT_{s,h} \times w^{-b_h}} \right) \right\} \times ST \times V$$

Finally, the total variable cost of all J type of inspectors can be calculated by:

$$TVC = \left\{ \sum_{j=1}^{J} NI_j \left(\frac{TA}{IT_{s,j} \times w^{-b_j}} \right) \right\} \times ST \times V$$

3.6. Objective Functions

The optimal values of decision variables are obtained using goal programming (GP) which is a type of multi-objective decision making and is widely used by many authors where more than one objective has to be achieved. The proposed model is also multi-objective that optimizes three objectives as mentioned below.

To keep the total cost per day TVC of all inspectors less than the target value of cost TVC_T.

$$Z_1 = \left\{ \sum_{j=1}^{J} NI_j \left(\frac{TA}{IT_{s,j} \times w^{-b_j}} \right) \right\} \times ST \times V$$

To keep the quality level of inspection.

$$Z_2 = \sum_{j=1}^{J} NI_j \left(\frac{TA}{IT_{s,j} \times w^{-b_j}} \right)$$

To meet the daily target of inspection quantity.

$$Z_3 = \frac{\sum_{j=1}^{J} NI_j \left(OQ_{s,j} \times w^{-b_j} \right)}{\sum_j NI_j}$$

In order to achieve these three objectives, the best combination of inspectors with respect to their skill levels need to be determined. GP variant, Min-max or Chebyshev GP, is used to determine the optimum decision variables by satisfying all the objective functions. In Chebyshev GP, the unwanted deviation for three goals was normalized. Percentage normalization was used in which each deviation is divided by target value of its respective objective. The objective function minimizes the worst or maximal deviation (λ) from amongst the set of three goals [66]. The GP formulation can be presented as follows:

$$Minimize\ Z = \lambda$$

Subject to

$$\frac{d_1^+}{TVC_T} \leq \lambda$$

$$\frac{d_2^+}{AOQ_T} \leq \lambda$$

$$\frac{d_3^-}{TIQ_T} \le \lambda$$

$$\left\{ \sum_{j=1}^{J} NI_j \left(\frac{TA}{IT_{s,j} \times w^{-b_j}} \right) \right\} \times ST \times V + d_1^- - d_1^+ = TVC_T$$

$$\frac{\sum_{j=1}^{J} NI_j \left(OQ_{s,j} w^{-b_j} \right)}{\sum_j NI_j} + d_2^- - d_2^+ = AOQ_T$$

$$\sum_{j=1}^{J} NI_j \left(\frac{TA}{IT_{s,j} \times w^{-b_j}} \right) + d_3^- - d_3^+ = TIQ_T$$

$$\sum_j NI_j \le MI \; NI_j \ge 0$$

$$d_t^-, d_t^+ \ge 0 \; \forall t \in \{1,2,3\}$$

4. Results and Discussion

The application of the proposed model is described here with the help of an example from garment manufacturing unit and an offline station is selected where the inspection of finished products is performed by human labor. The product selected for this study is a short sleeve polo shirt and the completion of the order will take 120 days. Since this study has incorporated the concept of learning and inspection skill of human labor will improve with the passage of time. This study has considered three skill levels, that is, low, medium and high, along with the three performance measures of inspection including cost, quality and quantity. Figure 2 indicates how these performance measures vary for three different skill levels.

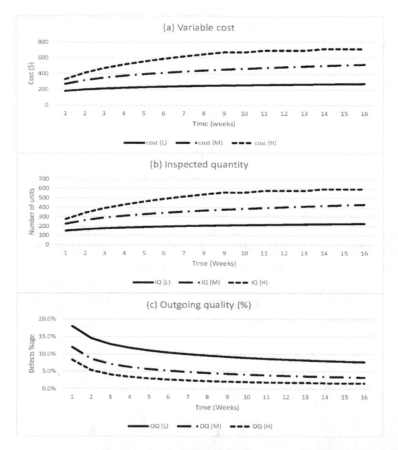

Figure 2. Influence of learning behavior on inspection performance of different inspectors.

At the start of order, the difference between three types of inspectors is not significant. However, the learning behavior varies person to person, that's why some inspectors learn quickly and improve their overall skill as compared to others. To achieve the objectives of the inspection station, an efficient combination of inspectors must be maintained that utilize the available manpower according to their skill levels. Thus, the requirement of manpower with respect to the skill levels will vary until we complete the order. That's why data were collected (Figure 2) for three different stages, that is, at the completion of 4th week (stage A), at the completion of 8th week (stage B) and at the completion of the 12th week (stage C). Keeping this scenario in view, data are collected for the selected product after the completion of each month and summarized in Table 2.

Table 2. Input data for short sleeve polo shirt.

Notation	At Stage A	At Stage B	At Stage C
ST (mins)	0.96	0.96	0.96
OQ_T	0.07	0.06	0.05
OQ	0.12	0.10	0.08
OQ_m	0.07	0.05	0.04
OQ_h	0.04	0.03	0.02
TC_T (\$)	3900	4690	5470
C_l (\$)	222	247	263
C_m (\$)	374	440	483
C_h (\$)	516	645	692
TIQ_T (Units)	3125	3750	4375
IQ_l (Units)	185	206	219
IQ_m (Units)	311	366	403
IQ_h (Units)	430	537	577
V (\$/min)	1.25	1.25	1.25
MI (Units)	12	12	12

In order to analyze the data in Table 2, an Optimization software, that is, Lingo 15.0, was applied by keeping the following system configuration: Intel® Core™ i7-7500U CPU @ 2.70 GHz Intel, 8.00 GB of RAM. Min-max GP method was used to calculate the optimal values of decision variables that also gave the optimized results of objective functions. The obtained results are summarized in Table 3 for all three stages and analysis can be divided into two parts: analysis of decision variable and analysis of objective function.

The decision variable analysis shows the optimum number of inspectors with their respective skill levels for each stage. These results ensure that all the objectives (cost, quantity and quality) have been achieved. Since the study incorporated learning behavior in this proposed model, thus the value of incoming quantity also vary along with the skill of inspectors as the order progress. At the early stage, when required targets of objective functions were low and the performance of inspectors of each skill level was also at the initial stage. The optimal combination that can achieve all targets of inspection station requires more inspectors with high inspection skill in comparison to low and medium. This is the confirmation of the fact that if an offline station consists of low skill inspectors mainly as compared to medium or high skill inspectors, the cost of inspection station may be low but the target of inspection quantity and quality level will be difficult to maintain for offline station. Therefore, the organization like to maintain an inspection station that consists of the best combination of inspectors to achieve all targets simultaneously.

As the order progress, the skill of each quality inspectors improved so as the incoming quantity which changed the targets of inspection station as well. Thus, at the second stage, the optimal results were obtained to satisfy the revised targets. However, this time, a combination of inspectors is changed and more medium skill inspectors are included. It is because of the fact that learning improves the performance of all inspectors and then the inspection station was able to achieve targets with less utilization of high skill labor. Similarly, at the last stage, the optimal combination consists of more low and medium skill quality inspectors to fulfill the revised targets. It is because of the fact that skill of both low and medium skill inspectors was improved enough meet the demands and less contribution was required from high skill inspectors.

Table 3. Optimized results of decision variables and objective functions for different stages.

Decision Variables	Values	Objectives	Target		Deviation Variables	
			Set	Achieved	d^+	d^-
Stage A						
Low skill	3	Inspection cost ($)	3900	3852	0	48
Medium skill	3	Outgoing quality	0.07	0.07	0	0
High skill	4	Inspected quantity (Units)	3125	3208	83	0
Stage B						
Low skill	3	Inspection cost ($)	4688	4671	0	17
Medium skill	6	Outgoing quality	0.06	0.06	0	0
High skill	2	Inspected quantity (Units)	3750	3888	138	0
Stage C						
Low skill	4	Inspection cost ($)	5469	5280	0	189
Medium skill	5	Outgoing quality	0.05	0.05	0	0
High skill	2	Inspected quantity (Units)	4375	4403	28	0

In a labor-intensive industrial setup like garment manufacturing, where the process of inspection is mainly performed by human labor, the presence of manpower with varying skill levels develops an environment that encourages the labor to compete with each other. Such a scenario provides them an opportunity to learn quickly that improve the level of their inspection skill at a faster rate. However, product type can significantly affect the rate of improvement in inspection skill. In case of a simple or basic garment, human labor can learn the things quickly because these products consist of fewer parts, a smaller number of operations or characteristics/features that a human inspector needs to inspect. On the other hand, this learning ability not only reduce but vary from person to person as the type of product moves to slightly complex, complicated or highly fashioned garments. This is because of the fact that these have more parts, increased number of operations and tough characteristics/features that an inspector need to inspect with concentration. Such products can affect the level of inspection skill of human labor that ultimately increases the inspection costs and decrease the outgoing quality. Similarly, the required manpower also changes with respect to product type to fulfill the requirements of the inspection station.

Analysis of the objective function, on the other hand, demonstrates the variance between the target values and the actual values of each goal at different stages, where underachieved values defined as d^- and overachieved value as d^+. Min-max GP method provided optimum results of decision variables such that the set target of each objective function is attained. Even though underachieved and overachieved values are also there for different objective functions but all these deviational values do not violate the given conditions. Like in Table 3, overachieved value of the inspection quantity (d^+) are 83, 138 and 28 for stage A, B and C respectively. However, it is still according to the constraints given in Section 3.6. Inspection quantity per day should not be less than the set target but presented results gave over achieved value, which is a positive side of the results. Similarly in Table 3, underachieved values of variable cost (d^-) are 48, 17 and 189 for stage A, B and C respectively. Since the constraint of the proposed model is to retain this variable cost low as much as possible so, these underachieved values also fulfill the already mentioned constraints.

In actual scenario, organization/managers allocate manpower only once, that is, at the start of the order and do not change till the completion of the order. This situation is not in favor of organizations as they are not using their labor according to their capacity. It may cause different problems like bottleneck and poor outgoing quality. Figure 3 demonstrates this fact, where the group of inspectors with their respective skill level is kept same for a full order. Variation in achieved values and targets values was evaluated. For this purpose optimal combination obtained at stage A (Table 3) is used here. It highlights not only the importance of skill of inspectors and learning but also explains that why it is important to revise the allocation of manpower at the periodical interval.

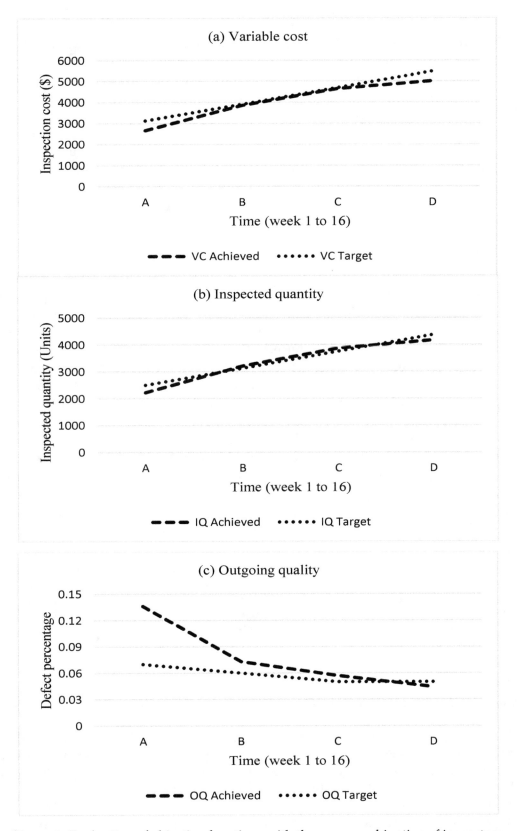

Figure 3. Evaluation of objective functions with the same combination of inspectors.

It is evident from the Figure 3 that the combination of inspectors of different skill levels could not achieve the targets throughout the order even though learning is also considered. Especially, outgoing quality is not kept under control due to the high percentage of inspection error. On the other hand, inspected quantity hit the targets on some stages but underachieved as well that creates a bottleneck. Such a situation will increase the workload on inspectors, increase the chance of overtime and affect the quality of product also due to work in progress. However, in the actual scenario, the performance of labor is not the same and they improve with time due to learning and experience. Thus, revision of optimal combination of inspectors at different intervals will not only save cost and improve quality but also avoid overtime and utilize the manpower of organization efficiently. In this way, the organization will be able to use their high skill labor for inspection of complex products where more skilled labor is required. This study also provides a way how to imply the available labor and get work from them according to their skill capacity. Also, such systems provide competitive environments that will help the employee to improve their skills. However, further work must be done to explore the ways that increase the learning process and also provide some bases to establish the pay/salary scale for employees based on their improvement with time.

5. Conclusions

In this study, multi-objective optimization model is developed to utilize the manpower efficiently and assign them job according to their capacity. For this purpose, offline inspection system is considered where inspection is performed by the manpower of varying skill levels. A multi-objective optimization model is proposed based on inspection skill, operation time, learning behavior. Min-max goal programming technique was used to determine the efficient combination of inspectors of each skill level at different time intervals of running order. The optimized results ensured that all the objectives of offline inspection station are attained that contains: the cost associated with inspectors, outgoing quality and inspected quantity. The results proved that the performance of inspectors improves significantly with learning and allocation of inspectors should be revised after regular interval keeping in view the improvement in their skill levels. For this purpose, the proposed model is helpful for organizations to ensure better utilization of available manpower, maintain good quality and reduce cost as well. Moreover, this study provides the basis to the researchers to further explore this research area for its practical application in the human-based manufacturing system. Such studies can be used to develop specific software for the assessment of human labor and job assignment. Also, this study has considered the offline inspection, while future work should also be done on online inspection.

Author Contributions: The contribution of the respective authors are as follows: M.B.R. conducted the complete study with main contribution in conceptualization and original draft preparation under the supervision of M.M. While S.I.M. and M.S.M. contributed in developing and defining the methodology, formal analysis, and validation. S.M.Q. conducted the process of revision and editing. Lastly, M.I. and M.W.I. jointly contributed in applying the optimization software and data collection from the relevant industry.

References

1. Purushothama, B. *A Practical Guide on Quality Management in Spinning*; Woodhead Publishing: Delhi, India, 2011.
2. Babu, V.R. *Industrial Engineering in Apparel Production*; Woodhead Publisher: Delhi, India, 2012.
3. Ullah, M.; Kang, C.; Qureshi, A.S.M. A Study of Inventory Models for Imperfect Manufacturing setup Considering Work-in-Process Inventory. *J. Soc. Korea Ind. Syst. Eng.* **2014**, *37*, 231–238. [CrossRef]
4. Tirkel, I.; Rabinowitz, G. Modeling cost benefit analysis of inspection in a production line. *Int. J. Prod. Econ.* **2014**, *147*, 38–45. [CrossRef]
5. Tirkel, I.; Rabinowitz, G. The relationship between yield and flow time in a production system under inspection. *Int. J. Prod. Res.* **2012**, *50*, 3686–3697. [CrossRef]

6.   Tzimerman, A.; Herer, Y.T. Off-line inspections under inspection errors. *IiE Trans.* **2009**, *41*, 626–641. [CrossRef]

7.   Ramzan, M.B.; Kang, C.W. Minimization of inspection cost by determining the optimal number of quality inspectors in the garment industry. *Indian J. Fibre Text. Res.* **2016**, *41*, 346–350.

8.   Kang, C.W.; Ramzan, M.B.; Sarkar, B.; Imran, M. Effect of inspection performance in smart manufacturing system based on human quality control system. *Int. J. Adv. Manuf. Technol.* **2018**, *94*, 4351–4364. [CrossRef]

9.   Herer, Y.T.; Raz, T. Optimal parallel inspection for finding the first nonconforming unit in a batch—An information theoretic approach. *Manag. Sci.* **2000**, *46*, 845–857. [CrossRef]

10. Grosfeld-Nir, A.; Gerchak, Y.; He, Q.-M. Manufacturing to order with random yield and costly inspection. *Oper. Res.* **2000**, *48*, 761–767. [CrossRef]

11. Anily, S.; Grosfeld-Nir, A. An optimal lot-sizing and offline inspection policy in the case of nonrigid demand. *Oper. Res.* **2006**, *54*, 311–323. [CrossRef]

12. Wang, C.-H.; Meng, F.-C. Optimal lot size and offline inspection policy. *Comput. Math. Appl.* **2009**, *58*, 1921–1929. [CrossRef]

13. Avinadav, T.; Perlman, Y. Economic design of offline inspections for a batch production process. *Int. J. Prod. Res.* **2013**, *51*, 3372–3384. [CrossRef]

14. Sarkar, B.; Saren, S. Product inspection policy for an imperfect production system with inspection errors and warranty cost. *Eur. J. Oper. Res.* **2016**, *248*, 263–271. [CrossRef]

15. Raz, T.; Herer, Y.T.; Grosfeld-Nir, A. Economic optimization of off-line inspection. *IiE Trans.* **2000**, *32*, 205–217. [CrossRef]

16. Finkelshtein, A.; Herer, Y.T.; Raz, T.; Ben-Gal, I. Economic optimization of off-line inspection in a process subject to failure and recovery. *IiE Trans.* **2005**, *37*, 995–1009. [CrossRef]

17. Wang, C.-H. Economic off-line quality control strategy with two types of inspection errors. *Eur. J. Oper. Res.* **2007**, *179*, 132–147. [CrossRef]

18. Wang, C.-H.; Hung, C.-C. An offline inspection and disposition model incorporating discrete Weibull distribution and manufacturing variation. *J. Oper. Res. Soc. Japan* **2008**, *51*, 155–165. [CrossRef]

19. Bendavid, I.; Herer, Y.T. Economic optimization of off-line inspection in a process that also produces non-conforming units when in control and conforming units when out of control. *Eur. J. Oper. Res.* **2009**, *195*, 139–155. [CrossRef]

20. Wang, W.-Y.; Sheu, S.-H.; Chen, Y.-C.; Horng, D.-J. Economic optimization of off-line inspection with rework consideration. *Eur. J. Oper. Res.* **2009**, *194*, 807–813. [CrossRef]

21. Tsai, W.; Wang, C.-H. Economic optimization for an off-line inspection, disposition and rework model. *Comput. Ind. Eng.* **2011**, *61*, 891–896. [CrossRef]

22. Montgomery, D.C. *Introduction to Statistical Process Control*, 6th ed.; John Wiley & Sons, Inc.: Hoboken, NJ, USA, 2009.

23. Dodge, H.F. A sampling inspection plan for continuous production. *Ann. Math. Stat.* **1943**, *14*, 264–279. [CrossRef]

24. Chen, C.-H.; Chou, C.-Y. Design of a CSP-1 plan based on regret-balanced criterion. *J. Appl. Stat.* **2000**, *27*, 697–701. [CrossRef]

25. Govindaraju, K.; Kandasamy, C. Design of generalized CSP-C continuous sampling plan. *J. Appl. Stat.* **2000**, *27*, 829–841. [CrossRef]

26. Richard Cassady, C.; Maillart, L.M.; Rehmert, I.J.; Nachlas, J.A. Demonstrating Deming's kp rule using an economic model of the CSP-1. *Qual. Eng.* **2000**, *12*, 327–334. [CrossRef]

27. Chen, C.-H.; Chou, C.-Y. Economic design of continuous sampling plan under linear inspection cost. *J. Appl. Stat.* **2002**, *29*, 1003–1009. [CrossRef]

28. Yu, H.-F.; Yu, W.-C.; Wu, W.P. A mixed inspection policy for CSP-1 and precise inspection under inspection errors and return cost. *Comput. Ind. Eng.* **2009**, *57*, 652–659. [CrossRef]

29. Yu, H.-F.; Yu, W.-C. A Joint Inspection Policy between CSP-1 and Precise Inspection for Non-repairable Products under Inspection Errors and Return Cost. *J. Qual.* **2011**, *18*, 61–73.

30. Galindo-Pacheco, G.M.; Paternina-Arboleda, C.D.; Barbosa-Correa, R.A.; Llinás-Solano, H. Non-linear programming model for cost minimisation in a supply chain, including non-quality and inspection costs. *Int. J. Oper. Res.* **2012**, *14*, 301–323. [CrossRef]

31. Springer, C. A method for determining the most economic position of a process mean. *Ind. Qual. Control* **1951**, *8*, 36–39.

32. Duffuaa, S.O.; Siddiqui, A.W. Process targeting with multi-class screening and measurement error. *Int. J. Prod. Res.* **2003**, *41*, 1373–1391. [CrossRef]

33. Duffuaa, S.O.; Al-Turki, U.M.; Kolus, A.A. A process targeting model for a product with two dependent quality characteristics using 100% inspection. *Int. J. Prod. Res.* **2009**, *47*, 1039–1053. [CrossRef]

34. Duffuaa, S.; Al-Turki, U.; Kolus, A. Process-targeting model for a product with two dependent quality characteristics using acceptance sampling plans. *Int. J. Prod. Res.* **2009**, *47*, 4031–4046. [CrossRef]

35. Duffuaa, S.O.; El-Ga'aly, A. Impact of inspection errors on the formulation of a multi-objective optimization process targeting model under inspection sampling plan. *Comput. Ind. Eng.* **2015**, *80*, 254–260. [CrossRef]

36. Duffuaa, S.O.; El-Ga'aly, A. A multi-objective mathematical optimization model for process targeting using 100% inspection policy. *Appl. Math. Model.* **2013**, *37*, 1545–1552. [CrossRef]

37. Duffuaa, S.O.; El-Ga'aly, A. A multi-objective optimization model for process targeting using sampling plans. *Comput. Ind. Eng.* **2013**, *64*, 309–317. [CrossRef]

38. Jaber, M.Y. *Learning Curves: Theory, Models, and Applications*; CRC Press: Boca Raton, FL, USA, 2016.

39. Koulamas, C. Quality improvement through product redesign and the learning curve. *Omega* **1992**, *20*, 161–168. [CrossRef]

40. Teng, J.-T.; Thompson, G.L. Optimal strategies for general price-quality decision models of new products with learning production costs. *Eur. J. Oper. Res.* **1996**, *93*, 476–489. [CrossRef]

41. Franceschini, F.; Galetto, M. Asymptotic defectiveness of manufacturing plants: An estimate based on process learning curves. *Int. J. Prod. Res.* **2002**, *40*, 537–545. [CrossRef]

42. Jaber, M.Y.; Guiffrida, A.L. Learning curves for processes generating defects requiring reworks. *Eur. J. Oper. Res.* **2004**, *159*, 663–672. [CrossRef]

43. Wright, T.P. Factors affecting the cost of airplanes. *J. Aeronaut. sci.* **1936**, *3*, 122–128. [CrossRef]

44. Jaber, M.Y.; Guiffrida, A.L. Learning curves for imperfect production processes with reworks and process restoration interruptions. *Eur. J. Oper. Res.* **2008**, *189*, 93–104. [CrossRef]

45. Jaber, M.Y.; Khan, M. Managing yield by lot splitting in a serial production line with learning, rework and scrap. *Int. J. Prod. Econ.* **2010**, *124*, 32–39. [CrossRef]

46. Kłosowski, G.; Gola, A.; Świć, A. Application of fuzzy logic in assigning workers to production tasks. In Proceedings of the 13th International Conference Distributed Computing and Artificial Intelligence, Sevilla, Spain, 1–3 June 2016; pp. 505–513.

47. Kuo, Y.-H.; Kusiak, A. From data to big data in production research: The past and future trends. *Int. J. Prod. Res.* **2018**, 1–26. [CrossRef]

48. Jasiulewicz-Kaczmarek, M.; Saniuk, A. Human factor in sustainable manufacturing. In *International Conference on Universal Access in Human-Computer Interaction*; Springer: Cham, Switzerland, 2015; pp. 444–455.

49. Muhammad Imran, C.W.K. A Synchronized Job Assignment Model for Manual Assembly Lines Using Multi-Objective Simulation Integrated Hybrid Genetic Algorithm (MO-SHGA). *J. Korean Soc. Ind. Syst. Eng.* **2017**, *40*, 211–220. [CrossRef]

50. Duffuaa, S.; Khan, M. Impact of inspection errors on the performance measures of a general repeat inspection plan. *Int. J. Prod. Res.* **2005**, *43*, 4945–4967. [CrossRef]

51. Elshafei, M.; Khan, M.; Duffuaa, S. Repeat inspection planning using dynamic programming. *Int. J. Prod. Res.* **2006**, *44*, 257–270. [CrossRef]

52. Duffuaa, S.O.; Khan, M. A general repeat inspection plan for dependent multicharacteristic critical components. *Eur. J. Oper. Res.* **2008**, *191*, 374–385. [CrossRef]

53. Colledani, M.; Tolio, T. Performance evaluation of production systems monitored by statistical process control and off-line inspections. *Int. J. Prod. Econ.* **2009**, *120*, 348–367. [CrossRef]

54. Vaghefi, A.; Sarhangian, V. Contribution of simulation to the optimization of inspection plans for multi-stage manufacturing systems. *Comput. Ind. Eng.* **2009**, *57*, 1226–1234. [CrossRef]

55. Khan, M.; Jaber, M.; Wahab, M. Economic order quantity model for items with imperfect quality with learning in inspection. *Int. J. Prod. Econ.* **2010**, *124*, 87–96. [CrossRef]

56. Yang, M. Minimization of Inspection Cost in an Inspection System Considering the Effect of Lot Formation on AOQ. *Int. J. Manag. Sci.* **2010**, *16*, 119–135.

57. Khan, M.; Jaber, M.Y.; Bonney, M. An economic order quantity (EOQ) for items with imperfect quality and inspection errors. *Int. J. Prod. Econ.* **2011**, *133*, 113–118. [CrossRef]

58. Khan, M.; Jaber, M.; Guiffrida, A. The effect of human factors on the performance of a two level supply chain. *Int. J. Prod. Res.* **2012**, *50*, 517–533. [CrossRef]

59. Avinadav, T.; Sarne, D. Sequencing counts: A combined approach for sequencing and selecting costly unreliable off-line inspections. *Comput. Oper. Res.* **2012**, *39*, 2488–2499. [CrossRef]

60. Bouslah, B.; Gharbi, A.; Pellerin, R. Joint production and quality control of unreliable batch manufacturing systems with rectifying inspection. *Int. J. Prod. Res.* **2014**, *52*, 4103–4117. [CrossRef]

61. Khan, M.; Jaber, M.Y.; Ahmad, A.-R. An integrated supply chain model with errors in quality inspection and learning in production. *Omega* **2014**, *42*, 16–24. [CrossRef]

62. Liu, N.-C.; Liu, W.-C. The effects of quality management practices on employees' well-being. *Total Qual. Manag. Bus. Excell.* **2014**. [CrossRef]

63. Aslam, M.; Wu, C.-W.; Azam, M.; Jun, C.-H. Mixed acceptance sampling plans for product inspection using process capability index. *Qual. Eng.* **2014**, *26*, 450–459. [CrossRef]

64. Yang, M.H.; Cho, J.H. Minimisation of inspection and rework cost in a BLU factory considering imperfect inspection. *Int. J. Prod. Res.* **2014**, *52*, 384–396. [CrossRef]

65. Mohammadi, M.; Siadat, A.; Dantan, J.-Y.; Tavakkoli-Moghaddam, R. Mathematical modelling of a robust inspection process plan: Taguchi and Monte Carlo methods. *Int. J. Prod. Res.* **2015**, *53*, 2202–2224. [CrossRef]

66. Jones, D.; Tamiz, M. *Practical Goal Programming*; Springer: Berlin, Germany, 2010; Volume 141.

9

Low Carbon Supply Chain Coordination for Imperfect Quality Deteriorating Items

Yosef Daryanto [1,2], Hui Ming Wee [1,*] and Gede Agus Widyadana [3]

[1] Department of Industrial and Systems Engineering, Chung Yuan Christian University, 200 Chung-Pei Rd., 32023 Chung-li, Taoyuan, Taiwan; yosef.daryanto@uajy.ac.id

[2] Department of Industrial Engineering, Universitas Atma Jaya Yogyakarta, Jl. Babarsari 43, 55281 Yogyakarta, Indonesia

[3] Department of Industrial Engineering, Petra Christian University, Surabaya, East Java 60236, Indonesia; gede@peter.petra.ac.id

* Correspondence: weehm@cycu.edu.tw

Abstract: Nowadays, many countries have implemented carbon pricing policies. Hence, the industry adapts to this policy while striving for its main goal of maximizing financial benefits. Here, we study a single manufacturer–retailer inventory decision considering carbon emission cost and item deterioration for an imperfect production system. This study examines two models considering two cases of quality inspection. The first is when the buyer performs the quality inspection, and the second is when the quality inspection becomes the vendor's responsibility so that no defective products are passed to the buyer. Carbon emission costs are incorporated under a carbon tax policy, and we consider the carbon footprint from transporting and warehousing the items. The objective is to jointly optimize the delivery quantity and number of deliveries per production cycle that minimize the total cost and reduce the total carbon emissions. This study provides solution procedures to solve the models, as well as two numerical examples.

Keywords: supply chain inventory; imperfect quality; inspection; carbon emission; deteriorating items

1. Introduction

Supply chain coordination has a favorable effect on inventory replenishment decisions. Supply chain coordination can be realized through information sharing and joint decision-making. Coordination brings many advantages such as lower inventory-related costs and quality improvement [1]. This study considers supply chain management coordination and examines its effect on both economic and environmental performance. This study proposes supply chain inventory models that consider carbon emission costs and the existence of defective items under different inspection coordination mechanisms. Further, the models also consider the effect of item deterioration. In real life, many inventory items deteriorate over time due to spoilage, physical depletion, or obsolescence.

Due to increasing pressure from legislation, customers, and other organizations, business and industry are striving for more eco-friendly operation. The production, distribution, consumption, and other post-consumption processes of a product are sources of carbon emission. Therefore, the concept of a low-carbon supply chain has gained massive interest among researchers and industry practitioners [2,3]. The objective is to control and reduce CO_2 emissions (the major part of greenhouse gas emission) from the supply chain. Recently, Kazemi et al. [4] considered the effect of carbon emissions on several economic order quantity (EOQ) models. Sarkar et al. [5] considered warehouse emissions in the EOQ model with a rework for the defective items. The model also considered partial backorder and multi-trade-credit-period. Taleizadeh et al. [6] proposed economic production quantity

(EPQ) models that considered carbon emissions. Recently, Sarkar et al. [7,8] and Daryanto and Wee [9] incorporated a carbon tax in a supply chain total cost model. Wahab et al. [10], Jauhari et al. [11], Sarkar et al. [12], Jauhari [13], Gautam and Khanna [14], and Tiwari et al. [15] incorporated both carbon emissions and imperfect quality in a low-carbon supply chain model. The quality inspection is performed by the buyer, and the defective products are sent back to the vendor or sold into the secondary market at a discounted price.

Table 1 illustrates the research gap by comparing this paper with the existing literature. This study focuses on supply chain inventory models for a system that contains imperfect quality items. The decisions of the supply chain dealing with the defective items in the imperfect production processes affect carbon emissions, because defective item processing also adds to the total emissions. Moreover, the loss due to imperfect quality and deterioration also forces the manufacturer to produce more products to satisfy customer demand per period, resulting in the increase in carbon emission from production, holding, and distribution. The objectives of these studies are to simultaneously minimize the total cost and reduce carbon emissions. This paper also contributes to low-carbon supply chain models by considering two cases of quality inspection. In the first case, the buyer performs the quality inspection, and in the second case, the quality inspection becomes the vendor's responsibility. The first model extends the studies of Wahab et al. [10], Jauhari et al. [11], Sarkar et al. [12], Jauhari [13], and Gautam and Khanna [14] to consider the effect of deterioration. In addition to the fixed and variable inspection costs, the model also extends Tiwari et al.'s [15] model by introducing weight and distance-dependent transportation cost and emission variables. The second model extends the first model by introducing an inspection option to prevent defective products from being shipped to the buyer. This model reduces the expected total costs and emission costs of the supply chain.

Table 1. Gap analysis with existing literature.

Authors	Imperfect Quality		Deteriorating Item	Variable Transportation Cost	Carbon Emission
	Vendor's Inspection	Buyer's Inspection			
Huang (2002)		✓			
Goyal et al. (2003)		✓			
Wee et al. (2006)		✓	✓		
Wahab et al. (2011)		✓			✓
Benjaafar et al. (2013)					✓
Lee and Kim (2014)		✓	✓		
Bazan et al. (2014)	✓				
Bozorgi et al. (2014)					✓
Jauhari et al. (2014)		✓			✓
Bozorgi (2016)					✓
Ghosh et al. (2016)					✓
Sarkar et al. (2016b)		✓		✓	✓
Yu and Hsu (2017)		✓			
Sarkar et al. (2017)	✓			✓	
Toptal and Çetinkaya (2017)					✓
Bouchery et al. (2017)					✓
Dwicahyani et al. (2017)					✓
Wangsa (2017)					✓
Li et al. (2017)					✓
Anvar et al. (2018)					✓
Hariga et al. (2018)					✓
Ji et al. (2018)					✓
Wang and Ye (2018)					✓
Gosh et al. (2018)					✓
Ma et al. (2018)					✓
Darom et al. (2018)					✓
Jauhari (2018)		✓			✓
Gautam and Khanna (2018)		✓			✓
Wangsa and Wee (2018)				✓	
Tiwari et al. (2018)		✓	✓		✓
Kundu and Chakrabarti (2019)			✓		✓
This paper	✓	✓	✓	✓	✓

This study incorporates carbon emissions, item deterioration, and defective percentage to guide the supply chain managers to make the inventory decisions on the delivery size and the number of deliveries per cycle. This introduction section is followed by reviews of previous related studies in

Section 2. Then, Section 3 defines the problem, assumptions, and notations in this study. Section 4 presents two mathematical models. Section 5 provides two numerical examples and the sensitivity analysis to find some insights from the proposed models. In the end, Section 6 summarizes the findings and discusses some opportunities for further research.

2. Literature Review

This study incorporates both economic and emission costs in a two-echelon supply chain production–inventory model assuming that defective products exist in each delivered lot. This section presents the existing literature that supports this study.

2.1. Imperfect Quality Inventory Model

In many industries, production systems are imperfect, producing a certain percentage of defective products. Rosenblatt and Lee [16] and Porteus [17] studied the relationship between the optimal lot size and quality performance. Rosenblatt and Lee [16] studied the optimal production cycle through considering the proportion of defective items, while Porteus [17] related the model to the opportunity for quality improvement and setup cost reduction through investment. Salameh and Jaber [18] incorporated defective items into the EPQ model and considered the screening time and cost. Many other researchers have continued the research on the EOQ and EPQ models with imperfect quality. Those researchers assume that at the end of the screening period, or the end of the cycle, the defective products will be sold at a lower price.

Other researchers bring the effect of imperfect quality items into the integrated vendor–buyer or multi-echelon inventory model. Huang [19] considered imperfect quality and assumed that the vendor provides a product warranty for the defective items. The buyer conducts a 100% inspection, and at the end, the vendor treats the faulty items. Goyal et al. [20] extended the previous model with a single production and multiple deliveries containing defective products. They assumed that the buyer sells the defective items at a discounted price. Figure 1 illustrates the scenario. Wee et al. [21] considered imperfect quality, shortage backorder, and item deterioration in an integrated production–inventory model. Lee and Kim [22] also developed an integrated production–inventory model of imperfect quality deteriorating items.

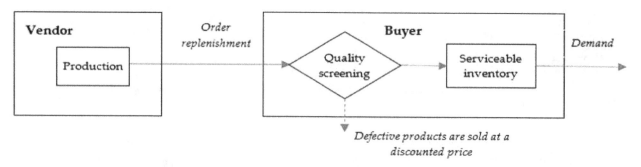

Figure 1. Illustration of an integrated inventory model for imperfect quality items where defective products are sold at a discounted price.

Bazan et al. [23] studied the effect of imperfect quality in different vendor–buyer inventory models. In their study, the vendor performs the inspection and considers one of three possible decisions regarding the defective items: (1) scrap off, (2) salvage at a discounted price, and (3) rework. Figure 2 illustrates the scenario when the vendor performs the inspection. Sarkar et al. [24] studied the integrated inventory model with two-stage inspection by the vendor considering the rework process and variable transportation cost. Yu and Hsu [25] developed a production–inventory model in which the defective items are returned to the vendor immediately for rework.

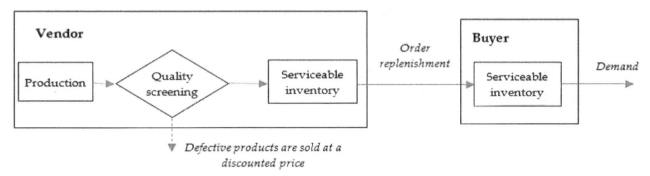

Figure 2. Illustration of an integrated inventory model for imperfect quality items with vendor's inspection.

2.2. Low-Carbon Supply Chain Management

Research on low-carbon supply chain management has increased rapidly in recent years and has been marked by a surge in the amount of literature in this area. Much of this research revealed that supply chain collaboration and the adjustment on operational decisions could reduce carbon emissions without significantly increasing their costs. Wahab et al. [10] studied the optimal shipment size and number of shipments for a two-echelon supply chain with carbon emission cost from transporting the inventory. The emissions are affected by the distance traveled, vehicle fuel efficiency, and the actual shipment weight. Benjaafar et al. [26] modified the traditional supply chain model by associating the carbon footprint from placing an order to the supplier, production setup, production process, and inventory holding. Fahimnia et al. [27] studied the impact of carbon pricing on a closed-loop supply chain through a case study.

Bozorgi et al. [28] considered carbon emissions from transporting and storing cold items that require temperature-controlled trucks and freezers. Bozorgi [29] extended the previous model considering multi-product cold items under limited capacity. Hariga et al. [30] incorporated carbon emissions from transporting and storing the cold items in a three-echelon supply chain. Ghosh et al. [31] considered carbon emissions from production, inventory holding, and transportation in a vendor–buyer supply chain under a single setup and multiple deliveries policy. Toptal and Çetinkaya [32] studied the effect of supply chain coordination and carbon emissions on vendor–buyer order quantity under lot-for-lot delivery. Bouchery et al. [33] examined different supply chain coordination configurations considering carbon emissions under limited vehicle capacity. Dwicahyani et al. [34] incorporated carbon emission costs, energy cost, and waste disposal for a two-echelon supply chain with remanufacturing. Li et al. [35] considered joint carbon tax and cap-and-trade policies for a two-echelon supply chain production–distribution model with transportation outsourcing. Wangsa [36] incorporated the government's penalties and incentive policies to reduce carbon emissions.

Anvar et al. [37] considered emissions from transportation and inventory-holding activities in a one-supplier multi-retailer supply chain. Hariga et al. [38] considered carbon tax and carbon cap policies for a two-echelon supply chain with vendor-managed consignment inventory partnership. The model incorporated emissions from the ordering process, production setup, and holding the inventory. Ji et al. [39] considered a carbon reduction investment from the supplier to get higher customer demand. Wang and Ye [40] compared the effect of considering carbon emissions on just-in-time and economic order quantity decisions for two-echelon supply chain inventory models. Ghosh et al. [41] considered a carbon tax regulation to minimize the total expected cost of a supply chain under stochastic demand and shortage backorder. Ma et al. [42] considered the effect of the carbon tax scheme between suppliers and buyer for production, procurement, and pricing decisions. Darom et al. [43] developed a manufacturer–retailer inventory model considering disruption risks and recovery with safety stock and the effect of carbon emission costs. The model considered carbon emissions from the transportation activities for a better recovery plan. Huang et al. [44] studied inventory and pricing decisions considering carbon emission, production disruption, and controllable deterioration using preservation technology. Recently, Daryanto et al. [45] proposed a low-carbon three-echelon supply chain inventory model considering item deterioration. Kundu and Chakrabarti [46] developed a low-carbon supply chain inventory model taking into account the effect of inflation and the time-value of money. Other researchers incorporated carbon emissions in supplier selection and order allocation [47–49].

3. Problem Definition, Assumption, and Notations

3.1. Problem Definition

This study considers a manufacturer–retailer supply chain that produces one type of item sold solely through one channel. The retailer orders n deliveries of equal lot size (Q) per cycle. The manufacturer implements single-setup multiple-deliveries (SSMD). Hence, it produces nQ units of item per production cycle. This study develops two models considering two cases of quality inspection. (1) In the first, the buyer performs a complete quality inspection process. (2) In the second, the vendor performs the quality inspection so that no defective products are passed to the buyer. The defective items are sold at a discounted price with no additional cost in both scenarios. Both the vendor and the buyer consider the carbon emission costs in their decision to comply with the carbon tax regulation. Model 1 is an extension of Tiwari et al.'s [15] model by introducing weight and distance-dependent transportation costs in addition to the fixed and variable inspection costs. Later, the second model extends the first model by studying another inspection option to reduce the expected total costs and emissions.

3.2. Assumption and Notation

This study explores real-life problems of cost minimization and carbon emission reduction under certain assumptions of a controlled situation. The assumptions are listed below, while the notations are presented in Table 2.

1.   The retailer's demand rate and the manufacturer's production rate are known and constant.
2.   The manufacturer implements a single-setup multiple-deliveries (SSMD) policy. Based on the retailer's order, the manufacturer produces nQ units of item per production cycle to reduce the setup time and cost. Then, it delivers the item in an equal lot sizes and constant time intervals [50].
3.   The replenishment is instantaneous.
4.   The items deteriorate in the manufacturer and retailer's inventory. The deterioration rate for both the manufacturer and retailer are equal and constant.
5.   The defective percentage, u, has a uniform distribution where $0 \leq \alpha < \beta < 1$.
6.   Good products are always available during the quality inspection as $x > D$.
7.   The retailer (in Model 1) and the manufacturer (in Model 2) perform a 100% quality inspection to ensure an excellent service.
8.   The fixed inspection cost per cycle is constant, whether performed by the buyer or the manufacturer.
9.   Carbon emissions come from the fuel and electricity consumption during transporting and holding the inventory.
10.   Shortage is not considered.
11.   The additional fuel consumption is a linear function of truckloads. Figure 3 illustrates the linear fuel consumption model, which is similar to that of Hariga et al. [30] with an example of the dataset from Volvo Corporation [51].

Table 2. List of notations.

Symbol	Definition
D	demand rate (unit/year);
P	production rate (unit/year);
R	production quantity; $R = PT_1$;
θ	deterioration rate; ($0 \leq \theta < 1$);
u	the probability of defective products per delivery lot size;
x	quality screening rate (unit/year);
i_c	fixed quality inspection cost (\$/cycle);
u_c	unit inspection cost (\$/unit);
c	retailer's ordering cost (\$/order);
h_d	retailer's holding cost (\$/unit/year);
d_d	retailer's deteriorating cost (\$/unit);
s	manufacturer's setup cost (\$/order);
h_p	manufacturer's holding cost (\$/unit/year);
d_p	manufacturer's deteriorating cost (\$/unit);
t_f	manufacturer's fixed transportation cost per delivery (\$/delivery);
t_v	fuel price for manufacturer's variable transportation cost (\$/liter);
d	distance traveled from vendor to buyer (km);
w	product weight (ton/unit);
c_1	average vehicle fuel consumption when empty (liter/km);
c_2	average additional fuel consumption per ton of load (liter/km/ton);
T_x	carbon emission tax (\$/tonCO$_2$);
F_e	average emissions from fuel combustion (tonCO$_2$/liter);
E_e	average emissions from electricity generation (tonCO$_2$/kWh);
e_1	transportation emission cost (\$/km); $e_1 = c_1 F_e T_x$;
e_2	average additional transportation emission cost per unit product (\$/unit/km); $e_2 = c_2 w F_e T_x$;
e_c	average warehouse energy consumption per unit product (kWh/unit/year);
w_e	warehouse emissions cost per unit product (\$/unit/year); $w_e = e_c E_e T_x$;
T	cycle length;
T_1	production period for the manufacturer in each cycle;
T_2	nonproduction period for the manufacturer in each cycle;
T_i	inspection time per delivery for the retailer;
T_b	inventory cycle length per delivery for the retailer; $T_b = T/n$;
$I_p(t)$	manufacturer's inventory level at time t;
$I_{pd}(t)$	manufacturer's inventory for defective products at time t;
$I_d(t)$	retailer's inventory level at time t;
ETC_d	retailer's expected total cost per year (\$/year);
ETC_p	manufacturer's expected total cost per year (\$/year);
ETC	joint expected total cost per year (\$/year);
ETE_d	retailer's expected total carbon emissions per year (tonCO$_2$/year);
ETE_p	manufacturer's expected total carbon emissions per year (tonCO$_2$/year);
ETE	joint expected total carbon emissions per year (tonCO$_2$/year);

Decision variables

Q	delivery lot size (unit);
n	number of deliveries per order (positive integer).
$*$	indicates optimal solution

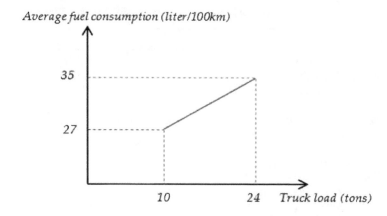

Figure 3. Linear function of average fuel consumption vs. total weight for regional traffic (Data source: Volvo Corporation, 2018).

4. Model Development

This section provides model development for two inspection cases.

4.1. Model Development with Retailer Inspection

This sub-section presents model development when quality inspection becomes the retailer's responsibility. The model is adapted from Tiwari et al. [15]. However, this study considers weight and distance-dependent transportation cost.

The inventory level of the manufacturer and the retailer is illustrated in Figure 4. In one production cycle, the manufacturer produces PT_1 units of the item, and delivers all the produced items to the retailer n times with a constant lot size Q. Right after receiving each lot, the retailer starts the quality inspection that ends at T_i. At T_i, uQ units of defective products will be removed from the inventory. During the period $[0, T/n]$, the retailer's inventory decreases due to demand.

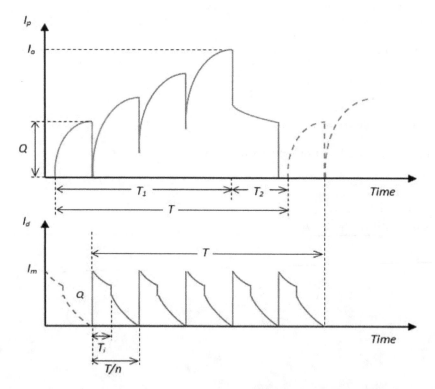

Figure 4. Manufacturer's and retailer's inventory model for constantly deteriorating items with retailer's inspection for $n = 5$.

4.1.1. Retailer Cost and Emission

As c is the retailer's ordering cost, the ordering cost per year is given by c/T (Lee and Kim [22], Yang and Wee [52]). After a lot arrived, the 100% quality inspection starts and then finishes at T_i. As there are fixed inspection costs per delivery, i_c, and unit inspection costs, u_c (Sarkar et al. [12]), the inspection cost per year is given by:

$$i_c \frac{n}{T} + u_c Q \frac{n}{T} = \frac{n}{T}(i_c + u_c Q) \tag{1}$$

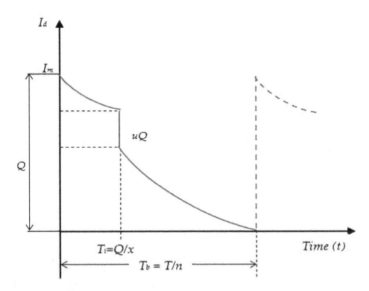

Figure 5. Retailer's inventory model with imperfect quality per delivery cycle.

Figure 5 illustrates the retailer's on-hand inventory per delivery cycle. The inventory level, considering deterioration and imperfect quality, has been studied by researchers such as Jaggi et al. [53] and results in the following equations:

$$I_d(t) = Qe^{-\theta t} + \frac{D}{\theta}\left(e^{-\theta t} - 1\right), \, 0 \le t \le Q/x \tag{2}$$

$$I_d(t) = Qe^{-\theta t} + \frac{D}{\theta}\left(e^{-\theta t} - 1\right) - uQ, Q/x \le t \le T/n \tag{3}$$

At $t = T/n$, $I_d(T/n) = 0$, therefore equation (3) becomes:

$$Qe^{-\theta T/n} + \frac{D}{\theta}\left(e^{-\theta T/n} - 1\right) - uQ = 0$$

Solving the equation for Q, one has:

$$Q = -\frac{D\left(e^{-\theta T/n} - 1\right)}{\theta\left(e^{-\theta T/n} - u\right)} = \frac{D\left(e^{-\theta T/n} - 1\right)}{\theta\left(u - e^{-\theta T/n}\right)} \text{ which is } = \frac{D\left(e^{\theta T/n} - 1\right)}{\theta\left(1 - ue^{\theta T/n}\right)} \text{ (Jaggi et al. [53])}$$

Hence:

$$Q = I_d(0) = \frac{D\left(e^{\theta T/n} - 1\right)}{\theta\left(1 - ue^{\theta T/n}\right)} \tag{4}$$

Further, the on-hand inventory per year for the retailer is:

$$\frac{n}{T}\left[\int_0^{Q/x} I_d(t)dt + \int_{Q/x}^{T/n} I_d(t)dt\right]$$

$$\frac{n}{T}\left[\frac{Q}{\theta}\left(1-e^{-\frac{\theta Q}{x}}\right) - \frac{D}{\theta^2}\left(\frac{Q\theta}{x}+e^{-\frac{\theta Q}{x}}-1\right) - \frac{1}{\theta}\left(e^{-\frac{\theta T}{n}}-e^{-\frac{\theta Q}{x}}\right)\left(Q+\frac{D}{\theta}\right)-\left(\frac{T}{n}-\frac{Q}{x}\right)\left(uQ+\frac{D}{\theta}\right)\right] \tag{5}$$

We assumed that storing the items requires electrical energy with a certain amount of carbon footprint. Therefore, substituting Equations (4) with (5) and considering the retailer's holding costs and emissions, the inventory holding and emission cost per year becomes:

$$(h_d+w_e)\frac{n}{T}\left[\frac{D}{\theta^2\left(ue^{\frac{\theta T}{n}}-1\right)^2}\left(\frac{uD}{x}\left(1+e^{\frac{2\theta T}{n}}-2e^{\frac{\theta T}{n}}\right)\right.\right.$$
$$\left.\left.+u\left(1-e^{\frac{2\theta T}{n}}+ue^{\frac{2\theta T}{n}}-ue^{\frac{\theta T}{n}}\right)+\frac{\theta T}{n}\left(u-1+ue^{\frac{\theta T}{n}}-u^2e^{\frac{\theta T}{n}}\right)+e^{\frac{\theta T}{n}}-1\right)\right] \tag{6}$$

Considering the expected probability value of the defective products ($E[u]$), the average warehouse energy consumption per unit product (e_c), and the average emission from electricity generation (Ee), from Equation (6), the retailer's expected carbon footprint (ETE_d) per year of holding the inventory is:

$$\begin{aligned}ETE_d &= (e_cE_e)\frac{n}{T}\left[\frac{D}{\theta^2\left(E[u]e^{\frac{\theta T}{n}}-1\right)^2}\left(\frac{E[u]D}{x}\left(1+e^{\frac{2\theta T}{n}}-2e^{\frac{\theta T}{n}}\right)\right.\right.\\ &\quad\left.+E[u]\left(1-e^{\frac{2\theta T}{n}}+E[u]e^{\frac{2\theta T}{n}}-E[u]e^{\frac{\theta T}{n}}\right)\right.\\ &\quad\left.\left.+\frac{\theta T}{n}\left(E[u]-1+E[u]e^{\frac{\theta T}{n}}-E[u]^2e^{\frac{\theta T}{n}}\right)+e^{\frac{\theta T}{n}}-1\right)\right]\end{aligned} \tag{7}$$

The retailer's deteriorating cost per year is:

$$\frac{d_dn}{T}\left(Q-uQ-\frac{DT}{n}\right) = d_d\left(\frac{(1-u)n}{T}\frac{D\left(e^{\theta T/n}-1\right)}{\theta\left(1-ue^{\theta T/n}\right)}-D\right) \tag{8}$$

The retailer's total cost is the sum of the ordering, inspection, deteriorating, inventory holding, and emission costs. Therefore, considering the probability of the defective products, the expected total cost per year is:

$$\begin{aligned}ETC_d &= \frac{c}{T}+\frac{n}{T}\left(i_c+u_c\frac{D\left(e^{\frac{\theta T}{n}}-1\right)}{\theta\left(1-E[u]e^{\frac{\theta T}{n}}\right)}\right)+d_d\left(\frac{(1-E[u])n}{T}\frac{D(e^{\theta T/n}-1)}{\theta(1-E[u]e^{\theta T/n})}-D\right)\\ &\quad+(h_d+w_e)\frac{nD}{T\theta^2\left(E[u]e^{\frac{\theta T}{n}}-1\right)^2}\left(\frac{E[u]D}{x}\left(1+e^{\frac{2\theta T}{n}}-2e^{\frac{\theta T}{n}}\right)\right.\\ &\quad+E[u]\left(1-e^{\frac{2\theta T}{n}}+E[u]e^{\frac{2\theta T}{n}}-E[u]e^{\frac{\theta T}{n}}\right)\\ &\quad\left.+\frac{\theta T}{n}\left(E[u]-1+E[u]e^{\frac{\theta T}{n}}-E[u]^2e^{\frac{\theta T}{n}}\right)+e^{\frac{\theta T}{n}}-1\right)\end{aligned} \tag{9}$$

4.1.2. Manufacturer Cost and Emission

After the arrival of the retailer's order, the manufacturer starts the production of nQ units of the item at a production rate P. Since s is the setup cost per production cycle, the manufacturer's setup cost per year is s/T.

The first delivery occurs as soon as the quantity is met. The following deliveries occur at T/n intervals. The transportation cost belongs to the manufacturer and consist of fixed and variable costs. Swenseth and Godfrey [54], Nie et al. [55], Rahman et al. [56], and Wangsa and Wee [57] incorporated the variable transportation cost, which is affected by the shipping distance and truckloads. The manufacturer's transportation cost per delivery is given by:

$$t_f+2dc_1t_v+dQwc_2t_v \tag{10}$$

The first element is the fixed transportation setup cost. The second element calculates the transportation cost of an empty truck. As the truck goes from the manufacturer to the retailer and then goes back, the distance is multiplied by two. Then, the transportation cost for the truckload is calculated, which depends on the delivery distance and quantity, product weight, additional fuel consumption per ton per km, and the fuel price. Substituting Equation (4) to (10), the manufacturer's transportation cost per year is given by:

$$\frac{n}{T}\left(t_f + 2dc_1 t_v + d\frac{D\left(e^{\theta T/n} - 1\right)}{\theta\left(1 - ue^{\theta T/n}\right)} wc_2 t_v\right) \tag{11}$$

Wahab et al. [10] identified that the emissions from transportation were affected by the delivery distance, actual shipment weight, fuel consumption per km, and CO_2 emissions per liter of fuel. Therefore, the amount of the manufacturer's carbon emission per year as the result of transportation activity can be derived as follows:

$$\frac{n}{T}(2dc_1 + dQwc_2)F_e = \frac{n}{T}\left(2dc_1 + d\frac{D\left(e^{\theta T/n} - 1\right)}{\theta\left(1 - ue^{\theta T/n}\right)} wc_2\right)F_e \tag{12}$$

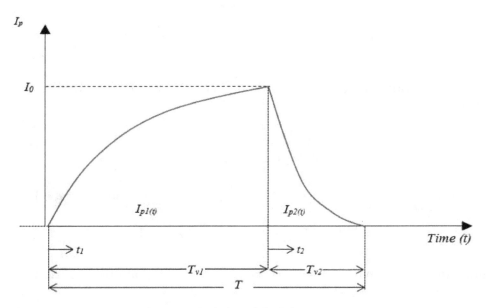

Figure 6. $I_{p1}(t_1)$ and $I_{p2}(t_2)$ vs. time.

As depicted in Figure 6, Lee and Kim [22] studied a similar inventory model for the manufacturer using Yang and Wee's [52] approach. Both production and consumption occur during T_1, while only consumption occurs during T_2. Hsu [58] suggested some revision considering the effect of defective products. Due to defective products and the retailer's quality inspection, the effective demand rate for the manufacturer becomes $D/(1-u)$. Therefore, the inventory functions are as follows:

$$I_{p1}(t_1) = \frac{P - (D/(1 - u))}{\theta}\left(1 - e^{-\theta\, t_1}\right), \; 0 \le\, t_1\, \le T_1 \tag{13}$$

$$I_{p2}(t_2) = \frac{(D/(1 - u))}{\theta}\left(e^{\theta\,(T_2 - t_2)} - 1\right), 0\; t_2\, \le T_2 \tag{14}$$

From the boundary condition $I_{p1}(T_1) = I_{p2}(0)$ and following Misra's [59] approximation:

$$\left(P - \frac{D}{1 - u}\right)T_1\left(1 - \frac{1}{2}\theta T_1\right) = \left(\frac{D}{1 - u}\right)T_2\left(1 + \frac{1}{2}\theta T_2\right)$$

Hence, one has:

$$T_1 \approx \frac{D}{(1-u)P - D} T_2 \left(1 + \frac{1}{2}\theta T_2\right) \tag{15}$$

$$T \approx \frac{T_2}{(1-u)P - D} \left((1-u)P + \frac{1}{2}D\theta T_2\right) \tag{16}$$

From Yang and Wee [52], the manufacturer's inventory per cycle is:

$$\int_0^{T_1} I_{p1}(t_1)dt_1 + \int_0^{T_2} I_{p2}(t_2)dt_2 - n\int_0^{T/n} I_d(t)dt \tag{17}$$

Hence, the manufacturer's holding cost per year is:

$$
\begin{aligned}
&\frac{h_p}{T}\left[\frac{P-(D/(1-u))}{\theta}T_1 + \frac{P-(D/(1-u))}{\theta^2}\left(e^{-\theta\,T_1} - 1\right)\right.\\
&\quad -\frac{(D/(1-u))T_2}{\theta} - \frac{(D/(1-u))}{\theta^2}\left(1 - e^{\theta\,T_2}\right)\\
&\quad -n\left(\frac{D}{\theta^2\left(ue^{\frac{\theta T}{n}}-1\right)^2}\left(\frac{uD}{x}\left(1 + e^{\frac{2\theta T}{n}} - 2e^{\frac{\theta T}{n}}\right) + u\left(1 - e^{\frac{2\theta T}{n}} + ue^{\frac{2\theta T}{n}} - ue^{\frac{\theta T}{n}}\right)\right.\right.\\
&\quad \left.\left.\left. + \frac{\theta T}{n}\left(u - 1 + ue^{\frac{\theta T}{n}} - u^2e^{\frac{\theta T}{n}}\right) + e^{\frac{\theta T}{n}} - 1\right)\right)\right]
\end{aligned}
\tag{18}
$$

The amount of a manufacturer's carbon emissions per year as the result of warehousing activity can be derived as follows:

$$
\begin{aligned}
&\frac{e_cE_e}{T}\left[\frac{P-(D/(1-u))}{\theta}T_1 + \frac{P-(D/(1-u))}{\theta^2}\left(e^{-\theta\,T_1} - 1\right)\right.\\
&\quad -\frac{(D/(1-u))T_2}{\theta} - \frac{(D/(1-u))}{\theta^2}\left(1 - e^{\theta\,T_2}\right)\\
&\quad -n\left(\frac{D}{\theta^2\left(ue^{\frac{\theta T}{n}}-1\right)^2}\left(\frac{uD}{x}\left(1 + e^{\frac{2\theta T}{n}} - 2e^{\frac{\theta T}{n}}\right) + u\left(1 - e^{\frac{2\theta T}{n}} + ue^{\frac{2\theta T}{n}} - ue^{\frac{\theta T}{n}}\right)\right.\right.\\
&\quad \left.\left.\left. + \frac{\theta T}{n}\left(u - 1 + ue^{\frac{\theta T}{n}} - u^2e^{\frac{\theta T}{n}}\right) + e^{\frac{\theta T}{n}} - 1\right)\right)\right]
\end{aligned}
\tag{19}
$$

The manufacturer's carbon emissions per year come from Equations (12) and (19). Therefore, the manufacturer's carbon emission cost is:

$$
\begin{aligned}
&\frac{n}{T}\left(2de_1 + d\frac{D\left(e^{\theta T/n}-1\right)}{\theta\left(1-ue^{\theta T/n}\right)}e_2\right)\\
&+\frac{w_e}{T}\left[\frac{P-(D/(1-u))}{\theta}T_1 + \frac{P-(D/(1-u))}{\theta^2}\left(e^{-\theta\,T_1} - 1\right) - \frac{(D/(1-u))T_2}{\theta} - \frac{(D/(1-u))}{\theta^2}\left(1 - e^{\theta\,T_2}\right)\right.\\
&\quad -n\left(\frac{D}{\theta^2\left(ue^{\frac{\theta T}{n}}-1\right)^2}\left(\frac{uD}{x}\left(1 + e^{\frac{2\theta T}{n}} - 2e^{\frac{\theta T}{n}}\right) + u\left(1 - e^{\frac{2\theta T}{n}} + ue^{\frac{2\theta T}{n}} - ue^{\frac{\theta T}{n}}\right)\right.\right.\\
&\quad \left.\left.\left. + \frac{\theta T}{n}\left(u - 1 + ue^{\frac{\theta T}{n}} - u^2e^{\frac{\theta T}{n}}\right) + e^{\frac{\theta T}{n}} - 1\right)\right)\right]
\end{aligned}
\tag{20}
$$

The loss due to deterioration in the manufacturer's inventory is the total production during the period T_1, minus the total delivered products to the retailer's inventory. Therefore, the manufacturer's deteriorating cost per year is:

$$\frac{d_p}{T}\left(PT_1 - n\left(\frac{D\left(e^{\theta T/n} - 1\right)}{\theta\left(1 - ue^{\theta T/n}\right)}\right)\right) \tag{21}$$

From Equations (11), (18), (20), and (21), as well as the setup cost, and considering the probability of the defective products, the manufacturer's expected total cost per year is:

$$
\begin{aligned}
ETC_p &= \frac{s}{T} + \frac{n}{T}\left(t_f + 2dc_1t_v + d\frac{D\left(e^{\theta T/n}-1\right)}{\theta\left(1-E[u]e^{\theta T/n}\right)}wc_2t_v\right) \\
&+ \frac{(h_p+w_e)}{T}\left[\frac{P-(D/(1-E[u]))}{\theta}T_1 + \frac{P-(D/(1-E[u]))}{\theta^2}\left(e^{-\theta\,T_1}-1\right)\right. \\
&\left. -\frac{(D/(1-E[u]))T_2}{\theta} - \frac{(D/(1-E[u]))}{\theta^2}\left(1-e^{\theta\,T_2}\right)\right. \\
&- n\left(\frac{D}{\theta^2\left(E[u]e^{\frac{\theta T}{n}}-1\right)^2}\left(e^{\frac{\theta T}{n}}-1+\frac{E[u]D}{x}\left(1+e^{\frac{2\theta T}{n}}-2e^{\frac{\theta T}{n}}\right)\right.\right. \\
&\left.+E[u]\left(1-e^{\frac{2\theta T}{n}}+E[u]e^{\frac{2\theta T}{n}}-E[u]e^{\frac{\theta T}{n}}\right)\right. \\
&\left.\left.+\frac{\theta T}{n}\left(E[u]-1+E[u]e^{\frac{\theta T}{n}}-E[u]^2e^{\frac{\theta T}{n}}\right)\right)\right] \\
&+ \frac{n}{T}\left(2de_1 + d\frac{D\left(e^{\theta T/n}-1\right)}{\theta\left(1-E[u]e^{\theta T/n}\right)}e_2\right) + \frac{d_p}{T}\left(PT_1 - n\left(\frac{D\left(e^{\theta T/n}-1\right)}{\theta\left(1-ue^{\theta T/n}\right)}\right)\right)
\end{aligned}
\tag{22}
$$

4.1.3. The Integrated Manufacturer and Retailer Cost Function

In an integrated decision, the manufacturer and the retailer jointly specify n, which minimizes the expected total cost (ETC). The ETC is the sum of ETC_d and ETC_p in Equations (9) and (22).

Using Taylor's series expansion for a small value of $\theta T/n$, θT_1, and θT_2, we can solve the cost function by assuming e^x as $1 + x + x^2/2 + x^3/6$. Furthermore, the expected total emissions (ETE) per year from the manufacturer and the retailer can be derived from Equations (7), (12), and (19).

4.1.4. Methodology and Solution Search

The objective is to determine the optimal number of deliveries (n^*) that minimize the expected total cost function (ETC). The value of n^* and the respective T, T_1, and T_2 will lead us to the optimal delivery quantity Q^* and production quantity R. The proposed procedure to derive the positive integer decision variable n is adapted from Tiwari et al. [15] and Yang and Wee [52] as follows:

Step 1. Substitute the T_1 and T functions in Equations (15) and (16) into ETC;

Step 2. Input all the known parameters;

Step 3. Set $n = 1$;

Step 4. Derive the partial derivative of ETC with respect to T_2 and set it to zero. Solve the equation to find the value of T_2;

Step 5. Use the known n and T_2 to find the value of T_1 and T using Equations (15) and (16).

Step 6. Derive the corresponding ETC;

Step 7. If $ETC(n) > ETC(n-1)$, then $n^* = n - 1$ and go to Step 8; otherwise, set $n = n + 1$ and go back to Step 4;

Step 8. Use n^* and the corresponding T^* to find Q^* from Equation (4) and calculate $R = PT_1{}^*$.

4.2. Model Development with Manufacturer Inspection

This sub-section presents the model development when quality inspection becomes the manufacturer's responsibility. The purpose of such a policy is to prevent transporting defective products. The manufacturer performs a quality inspection of all the produced products and keeps the defective products separately until the end of the production period T_1. The defective products will be sold at a discounted price to the secondary market. The inventory level for both the manufacturer (I_p) and the retailer (I_d), including the manufacturer's inventory of the defective products (I_{pd}), is illustrated in Figure 7. In this model, the I_{pd} is accumulated during the T_1 period. Besides, I_d decreases solely due to demand.

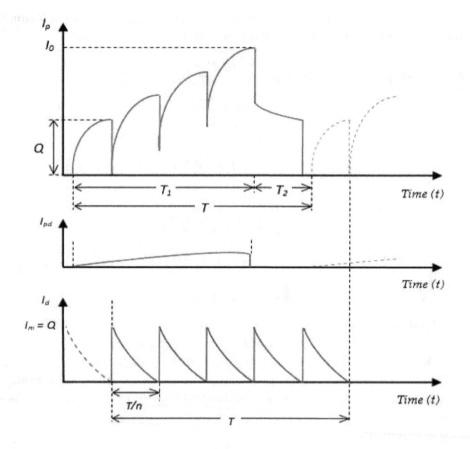

Figure 7. Manufacturer's and retailer's inventory model for constant deteriorating items with manufacturer's inspection for $n = 5$.

4.2.1. Retailer Cost and Emission

The retailer's total cost is the sum of the ordering, inventory holding, deteriorating, and emission costs. The ordering cost per year is given by c/T, which is similar to Model 1 (Section 4.1.1). During the T/n period, I_d decreases due to demand and deterioration. From Yang and Wee [52], the inventory function is as follows:

$$I_d(t) = \frac{D}{\theta}\left(e^{\theta(\frac{T}{n} - t)} - \right), 0 \ t \ \leq T/n \tag{23}$$

and

$$Q = I_d(0) = \frac{D}{\theta}\left(e^{\frac{\theta T}{n}} - 1\right) \tag{24}$$

and the holding cost per year is:

$$h_d\frac{n}{T}\left(\int_0^{T/n} I_d(t)dt\right) = h_d\frac{n}{T}\left(\frac{D}{\theta}\left(\frac{1}{\theta}\left(e^{\frac{\theta T}{n}} - 1\right) - \frac{T}{n}\right)\right) \tag{25}$$

Further, the deteriorating cost per year is:

$$d_d\frac{n}{T}\left(Q - D\frac{T}{n}\right) = d_d\frac{n}{T}\left(\frac{D}{\theta}\left(e^{\frac{\theta T}{n}} - 1\right) - \frac{DT}{n}\right) \tag{26}$$

$$ETE_d = e_c E_e\left(\frac{n}{T}\frac{D}{\theta}\left(\frac{1}{\theta}\left(e^{\frac{\theta T}{n}} - 1\right) - \frac{T}{n}\right)\right) \tag{27}$$

Equation (27) shows the retailer's carbon emission (ETE_d) from holding the inventory. Therefore, the retailer's carbon emission cost per year is:

$$w_e \left(\frac{n}{T} \frac{D}{\theta} \left(\frac{1}{\theta} \left(e^{\frac{\theta T}{n}} - 1 \right) - \frac{T}{n} \right) \right) \tag{28}$$

The retailer's expected total cost per year (ETC_d) becomes:

$$ETC_d = \frac{c}{T} + (h_d + w_e) \frac{n}{T} \left(\frac{D}{\theta} \left(\frac{1}{\theta} \left(e^{\frac{\theta T}{n}} - 1 \right) - \frac{T}{n} \right) \right) + d_a \frac{n}{T} \left(\frac{D}{\theta} \left(e^{\frac{\theta T}{n}} - 1 \right) - \frac{DT}{n} \right) \tag{29}$$

4.2.2. Manufacturer Cost and Emission

Due to some percentage of defective products, the production rate of the perfect product is $(1 - u)P$. The manufacturer's setup cost per year is s/T. In this model, the manufacturer will have an additional inspection cost. Since the total number of products being produced per production cycle is PT_1, considering a fixed inspection cost per cycle (i_c) and unit inspection cost (u_c), the manufacturer's inspection cost per year is:

$$\frac{i_c}{T} + \frac{u_c PT_1}{T} \tag{30}$$

The manufacturer's transportation function is similar to Equation (10); therefore, the transportation cost and emissions per year become:

$$\frac{n}{T} \left(t_f + 2dc_1 t_v + d\frac{D}{\theta} \left(e^{\frac{\theta T}{n}} - 1 \right) wc_2 t_v \right) \tag{31}$$

$$\frac{n}{T} \left(2dc_1 + d\frac{D}{\theta} \left(e^{\frac{\theta T}{n}} - 1 \right) wc_2 \right) F_e \tag{32}$$

From Figure 6, the inventory differential equations are:

$$dI_{p1}(t_1) = ((1 - u)P - D)dt_1 - \theta I_{p1}(t_1)dt_1, \ 0 \le t_1 \le T_1$$

$$dI_{p2}(t_2) = -Ddt_2 - \theta I_{p2}(t_2)dt_2, \ 0 \le t_2 \le T_2$$

For the boundary condition for $t_1 = 0$, $I_1(0) = 0$ and for $t_2 = 0$, $I_2(0) = I_o$ and for $t_2 = T_2$, $I_2(T_2) = 0$, the manufacturer's inventory functions for the good products are:

$$I_{p1}(t_1) = \frac{(1 - u)P - D}{\theta} \left(1 - e^{-\theta t_1} \right), \ 0 \le t_1 \le T_1 \tag{33}$$

$$I_{p2}(t_2) = \frac{D}{\theta} \left(e^{\theta (T_2 - t_2)} - 1 \right), 0 \ t_2 \le T_2 \tag{34}$$

From the boundary condition $I_{p1}(T_1) = I_{p2}(0)$, we have the following equation:

$$\frac{((1 - u)P - D)}{\theta} \left(1 - e^{-\theta T_1} \right) = \frac{D}{\theta} \left(e^{\theta T_2} - 1 \right) \tag{35}$$

From Taylor's series expansion and the assumption of $\theta T \ll 1$, following Misra's [59] approximation, one has:

$$((1 - u)P - D)T_1 \left(1 - \frac{1}{2}\theta T_1 \right) = DT_2 \left(1 + \frac{1}{2}\theta T_2 \right)$$

$$T_1 \approx \frac{D}{(1-u)P - D} T_2 \left(1 + \frac{1}{2}\theta T_2\right)$$
(36)

$$T \approx \frac{T_2}{(1-u)P - D} \left((1-u)P + \frac{1}{2}D\theta T_2\right)$$
(37)

Therefore, the manufacturer's inventory for good products becomes:

$$\int_0^{T_1} \frac{(1-u)P - D}{\theta} \left(1 - e^{-\theta\, t_1}\right) dt_1 + \int_0^{T_2} \frac{D}{\theta} \left(e^{\theta\,(T_2 - t_2)} - 1\right) dt_2 - n \left[\frac{D}{\theta}\left(\frac{1}{\theta}\left(e^{\frac{\theta T}{n}} - 1\right) - \frac{T}{n}\right)\right]$$
(38)

Besides, there is an inventory of defective products. From Figure 6, the inventory differential equation for the defective products is:

$$dI_{pd}(t_1) = uP dt_1 - \theta I_{pd}(t_1) dt_1,\ 0 \le t_1 \le T_1$$

For the boundary condition for $t_1 = 0$, $I_1(0) = 0$, the manufacturer's inventory function for the defective products is:

$$I_{pd}(t_1) = \frac{uP}{\theta}\left(1 - e^{-\theta\, t_1}\right),\ 0 \le t_1 \le T_1$$

Therefore, the manufacturer's inventory of the defective products becomes:

$$\int_0^{T_1} \frac{uP}{\theta}\left(1 - e^{-\theta\, t_1}\right) dt_1$$
(39)

Hence, the manufacturer's holding cost per year is:

$$\frac{h_p}{T}\left(\frac{(1-u)P - D}{\theta} T_1 + \frac{(1-u)P - D}{\theta^2}(e^{-\theta T_1} - 1) - \frac{DT_2}{\theta} - \frac{D}{\theta^2}(1 - e^{\theta T_2}) \right.$$
$$\left. - n\left(\frac{D}{\theta}\left(\frac{1}{\theta}\left(e^{\frac{\theta T}{n}} - 1\right) - \frac{T}{n}\right)\right) + \frac{uPT_1}{\theta} + \frac{uP}{\theta^2}(e^{-\theta T_1} - 1)\right)$$
(40)

Therefore, based on Equations (32) and (40), the manufacturer's carbon emission cost and the total expected carbon emissions per year can be calculated as follows:

$$\frac{n}{T}\left(2de_1 + d\frac{D}{\theta}\left(e^{\frac{\theta T}{n}} - 1\right)e_2\right)$$
$$+ \frac{w_e}{T}\left(\frac{(1-u)P - D}{\theta} T_1 + \frac{(1-u)P - D}{\theta^2}(e^{-\theta T_1} - 1) - \frac{DT_2}{\theta}\right.$$
$$- \frac{D}{\theta^2}(1 - e^{\theta T_2}) - n\left(\frac{D}{\theta}\left(\frac{1}{\theta}\left(e^{\frac{\theta T}{n}} - 1\right) - \frac{T}{n}\right)\right) + \frac{uPT_1}{\theta}$$
$$\left. + \frac{uP}{\theta^2}(e^{-\theta T_1} - 1)\right)$$
(41)

$$ETE_p = \frac{n}{T}\left(2dc_1 + d\frac{D}{\theta}\left(e^{\frac{\theta T}{n}} - 1\right)wc_2\right)F_e$$
$$+ \frac{e_c E_e}{T}\left(\frac{(1-u)P - D}{\theta} T_1 + \frac{(1-u)P - D}{\theta^2}(e^{-\theta T_1} - 1) - \frac{DT_2}{\theta}\right.$$
$$- \frac{D}{\theta^2}(1 - e^{\theta T_2}) - n\left(\frac{D}{\theta}\left(\frac{1}{\theta}\left(e^{\frac{\theta T}{n}} - 1\right) - \frac{T}{n}\right)\right) + \frac{uPT_1}{\theta}$$
$$\left. + \frac{uP}{\theta^2}(e^{-\theta T_1} - 1)\right)$$
(42)

The number of deteriorated items in the manufacturer's inventory is the total production during the period T_1, minus the total products delivered to the buyer and the inventory of the defective products. Therefore, the manufacturer's deteriorating cost per year is:

$$\frac{d_p}{T}\left((1-u)PT_1 - n\left(\frac{D}{\theta}\left(e^{\frac{\theta T}{n}} - 1\right)\right) + \left(uPT_1 - \frac{uP}{\theta}\left(1 - e^{-\theta\, T_1}\right)\right)\right)$$
(43)

Considering the additional inspection cost and the probability of the defective products, the manufacturer's expected total cost per year is:

$$
\begin{aligned}
ETC_p &= \tfrac{s}{T} + \tfrac{i_c}{T} + \tfrac{u_c PT_1}{T} + \tfrac{n}{T}\left(t_f + 2dc_1 t_v + d\tfrac{D}{\theta}\left(e^{\frac{\theta T}{n}} - 1\right)wc_2 t_v\right) \\
&\quad + \tfrac{n}{T}\left(2de_1 + d\tfrac{D}{\theta}\left(e^{\frac{\theta T}{n}} - 1\right)e_2\right) \\
&\quad + \tfrac{(h_p + w_e)}{T}\left(\tfrac{(1-E[u])P - D}{\theta}T_1 + \tfrac{(1-E[u])P - D}{\theta^2}\left(e^{-\theta T_1} - 1\right)\right. \\
&\quad - \tfrac{DT_2}{\theta} - \tfrac{D}{\theta^2}\left(1 - e^{\theta T_2}\right) - n\left(\tfrac{D}{\theta}\left(\tfrac{1}{\theta}\left(e^{\frac{\theta T}{n}} - 1\right) - \tfrac{T}{n}\right)\right) + \tfrac{E[u]PT_1}{\theta} \\
&\quad \left. + \tfrac{E[u]P}{\theta^2}\left(e^{-\theta T_1} - 1\right)\right) \\
&\quad + \tfrac{d_p}{T}\left(\left(1 - E[u]\right)PT_1 - n\left(\tfrac{D}{\theta}\left(e^{\frac{\theta T}{n}} - 1\right)\right)\right. \\
&\quad \left. + \left(E[u]PT_1 - \tfrac{E[u]P}{\theta}\left(1 - e^{-\theta T_1}\right)\right)\right)
\end{aligned}
\tag{44}
$$

4.2.3. The Integrated Manufacturer and Retailer Cost Function

The *ETC* of the integrated system is the sum of Equations (29) and (44). Using Taylor's series expansion for a small value of $\theta T/n$, θT_1, and θT_2, we can solve the cost function by assuming e^x as $1 + x + x^2/2 + x^3/6$. Furthermore, the *ETE* can be derived from Equation (27) and Equation (42).

4.2.4. Methodology and Solution Search

Similar to Model 1, the objective is to determine the optimal number of deliveries (n^*) that minimize the expected total cost function *ETC*. The proposed procedure to search for the optimum solution is as follows:

Step 1. Substitute the T_1 and T functions in Equations (36) and (37) into *ETC*;
Step 2. Input all the known parameters;
Step 3. Set $n = 1$;
Step 4. Derive the partial derivative of *ETC* with respect to T_2 and set it to zero. Solve the equation to find the value of T_2;
Step 5. Use the known n and T_2 to find the value of T_1 and T using Equations (36) and (37).
Step 6. Derive the corresponding *ETC*;
Step 7. If $ETC(n) > ETC(n-1)$ then $n^* = n - 1$ and go to step 8, otherwise set $n = n + 1$ and back to Step 4;
Step 8. Use n^* and the corresponding T^* to find Q^* from Equation (24) and calculate $R = PT_1{}^*$.

5. Numerical Example and Management Insights

5.1. Numerical Example 1

The values of the parameters are considered by adopting data from Yang and Wee [52], Hariga et al. [30], and Tiwari et al. [15] as $P = 2{,}000{,}000$ units/year, $D = 500{,}000$ units/year, $x = 1{,}725{,}000$ unit/year, $i_c = \$500$/delivery, $u_c = \$0.5$/unit, $c = \$2{,}000$/order, $s = \$100{,}000$/setup, $h_d = \$60$/unit/year, $h_p = \$40$/unit/year, $d_d = \$600$/unit, $d_p = \$400$/unit, $\theta = 0.1$, $d = 100$ km, $t_f = \$1000$/delivery, $t_v = \$0.75$/liter, $w = 0.01$ ton/unit, $c_1 = 27$ L/100 km, $c_2 = 0.57$ L/100 km/ton truckload, $e_c = 1.44$ kWh/unit/year, $T_x = \$75$/tonCO$_2$, $F_e = 2.6 \times 10^{-3}$ tonCO$_2$/L (US. EPA [60]), $E_e = 0.5 \times 10^{-3}$ tonCO$_2$/kWh (McCarthy [61]), and u is uniformly distributed in which $\alpha = 0$ and $\beta = 0.04$, with $E[u] = 0.02$.

The minimum value of joint expected total cost can be obtained at $n = 7$ with $T_2 = 0.0651856$, $T_1 = 0.0223966$, and $T = 0.0875822$, as shown in Table 3. The ETC is \$2,834,922/year, which is from Equation (4), the optimum Q is 6,387.7 units. The optimum R is 44,793.2 units, and the ETE is 30.598 tonCO$_2$/year. If the supply chain solely minimizes the total amount of carbon footprint, the decision is to perform a single-setup single-delivery (SSSD) as $n = 1$ with $ETE = 18.460$ tonCO$_2$/year (saving 39.7%). However, this situation increases the ETC into \$3,366,391 (18.7%). Figure 8 shows the convexity of ETC when $n = 7$.

Table 3. Expected total cost for different n in Model 1.

n	$T_2(10^{-5})$	$T_1(10^{-5})$	$T(10^{-5})$	ETC_d	ETC_p	ETC	ETE
1	4960	1703	6663	2,348,991	1,017,400	3,366,391	18.460
2	5641	1937	7578	1,463,323	1,568,493	3,031,816	21.333
3	5961	2048	8009	1,122,012	1,799,193	2,921,205	23.501
4	6161	2117	8278	941,509	1,930,509	2,872,018	25.422
5	6306	2167	8473	830,673	2,017,748	2,848,421	27.216
6	6422	2206	8628	756,370	2,081,526	2,837,896	28.935
7 *	6518	2240	8758	703,611	2,131,311	2,834,922	30.598
8	6603	2269	8872	664,620	2,172,067	2,836,687	32.218
9	6680	2295	8976	634,952	2,206,651	2,841,603	33.805
10	6751	2320	9071	611,889	2,236,823	2,848,712	35.360

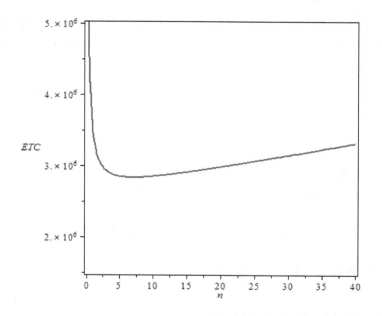

Figure 8. Graphical representation of expected total cost (ETC) for a fixed n in Model 1.

When the probability of defective products, unit inspection costs, carbon tax, and variable transport cost are equal to zero ($E[u] = u_c = T_x = t_v = 0$), the results are $n = 7$, $T = 0.08791$, and $ETC = $ \$2,559,246 which are similar to the results of Yang and Wee [52].

5.2. Numerical Example 2

We consider the parameters in numerical example one and solve it using the Model 2 results of the following values. The minimum value of joint expected total cost can be obtained at $n^* = 9$ and $T = 0.08869$, as shown in Table 4. The Q, R, and ETC are 4,929.6 units, 45,360.7 units, and \$2,782,396/year, respectively. The ETE is 33.52 tonCO$_2$/year.

Table 4. Expected total cost for different n in Model 2.

n	$T_2(10^{-5})$	$T_1(10^{-5})$	$T(10^{-5})$	ETC_d	ETC_p	ETC	ETE
1	4977	1709	6686	2,041,005	1,312,795	3,353,800	18.22
2	5653	1941	7595	1,167,506	1,844,193	3,011,699	21.07
3	5963	2048	8011	827,178	2,067,759	2,894,937	23.21
4	6151	2113	8264	644,684	2,195,273	2,839,957	25.12
5	6282	2158	8441	530,652	2,280,088	2,810,741	26.91
6	6384	2193	8577	425,568	2,342,142	2,794,711	28.63
7	6467	2222	8689	395,714	2,390,607	2,786,322	30.29
8	6538	2246	8784	352,240	2,430,297	2,782,747	31.92
9*	6601	2268	8869	318,411	2,463,985	2,782,396	33.52
10	6658	2288	8945	290,923	2,493,378	2,784,301	35.11

Table 5 provides the cost comparison between the two models for the result of examples one and two. The number of deliveries per cycle (n) is higher in Model 2 (when the manufacturer performs the quality inspection), while the delivery lot size (Q) is lower. All the retailer's cost components decrease, while all the manufacturer's cost components increase, except for the setup cost. In total, the ETC of Model 2 is 1.85% lower than the ETC in Model 1. However, the retailer's total costs were reduced by 54.7%, while the manufacturer's total costs increased by 15.6%. Considering this situation, cost-saving compensation from the retailer to the manufacturer is an alternative solution so that both parties take advantage of the implementation of the second inspection policy. Based on Goyal [62]:

$$z = \frac{ETC_{d-case1}}{ETC_{case1}}$$

z is the retailer's cost coefficient. Therefore, ETC_d and $ETCp$ after cost-saving compensation are

$$ETC_d{}^a = zETC_{case2}$$

$$ETC_p{}^a = (1-z)ETC_{case2}$$

Table 5. Comparison between Model 1 and Model 2.

Decision Variables and Cost Items	Model 1	Model 2	Saving (%)
Number of deliveries per cycle ($n*$)	7	9	
Cycle time (T)	0.08758	0.08869	
Delivery lot size (Q); units	6387.7	4929.6	
Ordering cost ($)	22,835.7	22,550.7	1.25
Inspection cost ($)	295,230.7	0	100
Inventory holding cost ($)	190,027.5	147,863.7	22.2
Deteriorating cost ($)	195,346.3	147,863.7	24.3
Emission cost ($)	171.0	133.1	22.2
Total retailer's cost per year ($)	703,611.2	318,909.1	54.7
Total retailer's cost per year after compensation ($)		690,574.4	*1.85*
Setup cost ($)	1,141,784.6	1,127,534.2	1.25
Inspection cost ($)	0	261,366.3	−100
Transportation cost ($)	85,289.5	107,690.0	−26.3
Inventory holding cost ($)	539,976.9	567,658.3	−5.13
Deteriorating cost ($)	362,122.2	397,345.0	−9.73
Emission cost ($)	2,138.0	2390.9	−11.8
Total manufacturer's cost per year ($)	2,131,311.2	2,463,984.8	−15.6
Total manufacturer's cost per year after compensation ($)		2,091,821.6	*1.85*
Expected total cost ($)	2,834,922.4	2,782,396.0	1.85
Expected total emission (tonCO$_2$/year)	30.598	33.523	−9.56

Hence, the retailer and manufacturer total cost per year become $690,574.4 and $2,091,821.6, respectively. Finally, by using this compensation policy, the cost decreases $13,036.7 for the retailer and $39,489.6 for the vendor, or 1.85% for both parties. Table 5 also shows that the ETE of Model 2 is 33.52 $tonCO_2$/year, which is 9.55% higher than the ETE in Model 1. We can obtain both the cost-saving and emissions-reducing objectives from Table 4, as there is a chance to reduce the ETE of Model 2. For $n = 7$, the ETE is 30.292, and the ETC is $2,781,779 in which now the ETE and the ETC are 1.0% and 1.87% lower than those of Model 1, respectively. Thus, the objectives of cost efficiency and carbon footprint level reduction can be obtained simultaneously. The new comparison between the two models is presented in Table 6. It is also observed that the total delivered products to the retailer in Model 2 after adjustment (Model 2 ^{adj}) is less than those in Model 1.

Table 6. Comparison between Model 1 and the adjusted Model 2.

Decision Variables and Cost Items	Model 1	Model 2 ^{adj}	Saving (%)
Number of deliveries per cycle (n^*)	7	7	
Cycle time (T)	0.08758	0.08704	
Delivery lot size (Q); units	6,387.7	6221.2	
Ordering cost ($)	22,835.7	22,977.4	−0.62
Inspection cost ($)	295,230.7	0	100
Inventory holding cost ($)	190,027.5	186,596.1	1.80
Deteriorating cost ($)	195,346.3	186,596.1	4.48
Emission cost ($)	171.0	167.9	1.81
Total retailer's cost per year ($)	703,611.2	396,337.5	43.7
Total retailer's cost per year after compensation ($)		690,428.8	1.87
Setup cost ($)	1,141,784.6	1,148,869.4	−0.62
Inspection cost ($)	0	261,461.4	−100
Transportation cost ($)	85,289.5	85,764.5	−0.55
Inventory holding cost ($)	539,976.9	529,446.7	1.95
Deteriorating cost ($)	362,122.2	357,812.1	1.20
Emission cost ($)	2,138.0	2117.7	0.95
Total manufacturer's cost per year ($)	2,131,311.2	2,385,471.8	−11.9
Total manufacturer's cost per year after compensation ($)		2,091,380.5	1.87
Expected total cost ($)	2,834,922.4	2,781,809.3	1.87
Expected total emission ($tonCO_2$/year)	30.598	30.292	1.00

Sensitivity analysis is performed by increasing or decreasing the value of the parameter by ±25% and ±50% from the original values, as shown in Table 7. The results confirm that the second model is superior to the first model in terms of total cost. The number of deliveries per cycle (n) is sensitive to changes in parameters P, D, s, h_d, h_p, d_d, d_p, and t_f. As the values of parameters P, h_p, d_p, and t_f increase, the smaller the value of n. Contradictory conditions occur for parameters D, s, h_d, and d_d. The expected total cost is highly sensitive to the changes in parameters P, D, θ, s, u_c, h_d, h_p, d_d, d_p, and t_f, and almost insensitive to the changes in other parameters.

It is observed that when the deterioration rate (θ) increases, the expected total cost and the number of deliveries increase, but the delivery quantity decreases. When the probability of defective products (u) increases, the expected total cost increases very slightly, especially when the inspection is performed by the vendor. When the carbon tax (T_x) increases, the number of deliveries remains stable. Otherwise, the delivery quantity and expected total cost increase are very small.

Table 7. Sensitivity analysis of the two models.

Parameter	Value Change	Model 1					Model 2				
		n^*	T	Q^a	ETC	%CTC	n^*	T	Q^b	ETC	%CTC
$P = 2,000,000$	+50%	7	0.0816	5949.3	3,024,249	6.68	8	0.0819	5120.3	2,966,117.1	6.60
	+25%	7	0.0839	6117.1	2,948,615	4.01	8	0.0842	5263.2	2,892,821.2	3.97
	0	7	0.0876	6387.7	2,834,922	0	9	0.0887	4929.6	2,782,396.0	0
	−25%	8	0.0959	6120.6	2,643,862	−6.74	9	0.0957	5322.0	2,596,679.1	−6.67
	−50%	8	0.1147	7321.0	2,253,495	−20.5	11	0.1153	5296.5	2,217,427.4	−20.3
$D = 500,000$	+50%	8	0.0816	7811.6	3,190,858	12.5	10	0.0822	6168.2	3,136,392.1	12.7
	+25%	8	0.0841	6705.8	3,044,190	7.38	9	0.0840	5833.6	2,989,178.5	7.43
	0	7	0.0876	6387.7	2,834,922	0	9	0.0887	4929.6	2,782,396.0	0
	−25%	7	0.0958	5242.7	2,548,150	−10.1	8	0.0962	4510.9	2,499,238.8	−10.2
	−50%	6	0.1100	4683.3	2,151,051	−24.1	8	0.1120	3501.7	2,108,977.7	−24.2
$c = 2000$	+50%	7	0.0880	6415.9	2,846,315	0.40	9	0.0891	4951.6	2,793,646.2	0.40
	+25%	7	0.0878	6401.8	2,840,625	0.20	9	0.0889	4940.6	2,788,027.5	0.20
	0	7	0.0876	6387.7	2,834,922	0	9	0.0887	4929.6	2,782,396.0	0
	−25%	7	0.0874	6373.5	2,829,207	−0.20	9	0.0885	4918.6	2,776,752.0	−0.20
	−50%	7	0.0872	6359.3	2,823,479	−0.40	9	0.0883	4907.5	2,771,095.4	−0.41
$s = 100,000$	+50%	9	0.1074	6090.8	3,348,784	18,1	11	0.1081	4917.3	3,292,159.7	18.3
	+25%	8	0.0979	6250.1	3,104,546	9.51	10	0.0988	4945.1	3,049,823.5	9.61
	0	7	0.0876	6387.7	2,834,922	0	9	0.0887	4929.6	2,782,396.0	0
	−25%	6	0.0760	6464.7	2,529,737	−10.8	8	0.0773	4834.4	2,480,006.3	−10.9
	−50%	5	0.0625	6383.9	2,169,316	−23.5	6	0.0631	5257.7	2,122,805.7	−23.7
$i_c = 500$	+50%	7	0.0883	6437.1	2,854,827	0.70	9	0.0888	4935.1	2,785,213.3	0.10
	+25%	7	0.0879	6412.4	2,844,894	0.35	9	0.0887	4932.4	2,783,805.1	0.05
	0	7	0.0876	6387.7	2,834,922	0	9	0.0887	4929.6	2,782,396.0	0
	−25%	7	0.0872	6362.9	2,824,912	−0.35	9	0.0886	4926.8	2,780,986.3	−0.05
	−50%	7	0.0869	6338.0	2,814,883	−0.71	9	0.0886	4924.1	2,779,575.6	−0.10
$u_c = 0.5$	+50%	7	0.0876	6387.5	2,962,557	4.50	9	0.0887	4929.0	2,910,260.4	4.60
	+25%	7	0.0876	6387.6	2,898,740	2.25	9	0.0887	4929.3	2,846,328.1	2.30
	0	7	0.0876	6387.7	2,834,922	0	9	0.0887	4929.6	2,782,396.0	0
	−25%	7	0.0876	6387.8	2,771,105	−2.25	9	0.0887	4929.9	2,718,463.9	−2.30
	−50%	7	0.0876	6387.9	2,707,289	−4.50	9	0.0887	4930.2	2,654,531.7	−4.60
$h_d = 60$	+50%	9	0.0872	4947.9	2,916,253	2,87	11	0.0880	4003.7	2,848,604.1	2.38
	+25%	8	0.0873	5571.5	2,878,457	1.54	10	0.0883	4014.8	2,817,636.9	1.27
	0	7	0.0876	6387.7	2,834,922	0	9	0.0887	4929.6	2,782,396.0	0
	−25%	6	0.0882	7502.8	2,782,702	−1.84	7	0.0885	6327.8	2,739,318.4	−1.55
	−50%	5	0.0893	9119.2	2,716,341	−4.18	5	0.0889	8901.6	2,680,745.8	−3.65
$h_p = 40$	+50%	5	0.0779	7955.9	3,075,129	8.47	5	0.0776	7768.5	3,033,547.3	9.03
	+25%	6	0.0823	7002.8	2,962,650	4.51	7	0.0827	5908.5	2,915,155.6	4.77
	0	7	0.0876	6387.7	2,834,922	0	9	0.0887	4929.6	2,782,396.0	0
	−25%	8	0.0940	5999.5	2,691,834	−5.05	10	0.0951	4758.0	2,634,200.0	−5.33
	−50%	9	0.1020	5786.3	2,531,836	−10.7	13	0.1051	4044.5	2,468,523.7	−11.3
$d_d = 600$	+50%	9	0.0872	49441	2,918,318	2,94	11	0.0880	4003.7	2,848,604.1	2.38
	+25%	8	0.0873	5569.0	2,879,619	1.58	10	0.0883	4416.4	2,817,636.9	1.27
	0	7	0.0876	6387.7	2,834,922	0	9	0.0887	4929.6	2,782,396.0	0
	−25%	6	0.0882	7507.4	2,781,144	−1.90	7	0.0885	6327.8	2,739,318.4	−1.55
	−50%	3	0.0872	14852.7	2,703,928	−4.62	5	0.0889	8901.6	2,680,745.8	−3.65
$d_p = 400$	+50%	7	0.0820	5981.9	3,010,061	6,18	6	0.0806	6721.3	2,957,798.8	6.30
	+25%	7	0.0847	6174.8	2,923,924	3.14	7	0.0839	5999.6	2,875,189.0	3.33
	0	7	0.0876	6387.7	2,834,922	0	9	0.0887	4929.6	2,782,396.0	0
	−25%	8	0.0922	5884.4	2,738,923	−3.39	10	0.0933	4668.1	2,679,457.1	−3.70
	−50%	9	0.0976	5538.2	2,632,492	−7.14	12	0.0997	4155.5	2,566,509.0	−7.76
$\theta = 0.1$	+50%	7	0.0794	5794.4	3,100,001	9.35	9	0.0804	4470.6	3,041,924.7	9.33
	+25%	7	0.0832	6069.2	2,970,737	4.79	9	0.0843	4683.2	2,915,364.1	4.78
	0	7	0.0876	6387.7	2,834,922	0	9	0.0887	4929.6	2,782,396.0	0
	−25%	7	0.0927	6762.9	2,691,447	−5.06	9	0.0939	5219.8	2,641,938.0	−5.05
	−50%	7	0.0989	7213.9	2,538,850	−10.4	8	0.0992	5516.8	2,492,404.9	−10.4
$t_f = 1000$	+50%	6	0.0874	7440.5	2,872,436	1.32	7	0.0883	6308.3	2,826,288.0	1.58
	+25%	7	0.0883	6437.1	2,854,827	0.70	8	0.0886	5542.6	2,805,413.7	0.83
	0	7	0.0876	6387.7	2,834,922	0	9	0.0887	4929.6	2,782,396.0	0
	−25%	8	0.0879	5612.0	2,814,046	−0.74	10	0.0885	4425.0	2,756,197.9	−0.94
	−50%	9	0.0880	4991.1	2,790,972	−1.55	12	0.0884	3685.7	2,725,660.0	−2.04
$t_v = 0.75$	+50%	7	0.0876	6391.8	2,837,605	0.09	9	0.0888	4933.7	2,785,501.1	0.11
	+25%	7	0.0876	6389.7	2,836,264	0.05	9	0.0887	4931.6	2,783,948.8	0.06
	0	7	0.0876	6387.7	2,834,922	0	9	0.0887	4929.6	2,782,396.0	0
	−25%	7	0.0876	6385.7	2,833,581	−0.05	9	0.0886	4927.6	2,780,842.7	−0.06
	−50%	7	0.0875	6383.6	2,832,239	−0.09	9	0.0886	4925.5	2,779,289.1	−0.11

Table 7. *Cont.*

Parameter	Value Change	Model 1					Model 2				
		n^*	T	Q^a	ETC	%CTC	n^*	T	Q^b	ETC	%CTC
$d = 100$	+50%	7	0.0877	6392.8	2,838,309	0.12	9	0.0888	4934.7	2,786,313.0	0.14
	+25%	7	0.0876	6390.3	2,836,616	0.06	9	0.0887	4932.2	2,784,355.0	0.07
	0	7	0.0876	6387.7	2,834,922	0	9	0.0887	4929.6	2,782,396.0	0
	−25%	7	0.0875	6385.1	2,833,229	−0.06	9	0.0886	4927.0	2,780,436.7	−0.07
	−50%	7	0.0875	6382.6	2,831,535	−0.12	9	0.0886	4924.5	2,778,476.4	−0.14
$E[u] = 0.02$	+50%	7	0.0874	6437.8	2,843,908	0.32	9	0.0887	4931.3	2,784,137.7	0.063
	+25%	7	0.0875	6412.6	2,839,414	0.16	9	0.0887	4930.5	2,783,248.6	0.031
	0	7	0.0876	6387.7	2,834,922	0	9	0.0887	4929.6	2,782,396.0	0
	−25%	7	0.0877	6363.1	2,830,435	−0.16	9	0.0887	4928.7	2,781,579.0	−0.029
	−50%	7	0.0878	6338.7	2,825,951	−0.32	9	0.0887	4927.7	2,780,796.5	−0.058
$w = 0.01$	+50%	7	0.0876	6387.7	2,835,956	0.04	9	0.0887	4929.6	2,783,408.9	0.036
	+25%	7	0.0876	6387.7	2,835.439	0.02	9	0.0887	4929.6	2,782,902.6	0.018
	0	7	0.0876	6387.7	2,834,922	0	9	0.0887	4929.6	2,782,396.0	0
	−25%	7	0.0876	6387.7	2,834,405	−0.02	9	0.0887	4929.6	2,781,889.5	−0.018
	−50%	7	0.0876	6.387.7	2,833,889	−0.04	9	0.0887	4929.6	2,781,383.0	−0.036
$c_1, c_2 = 0.27,$ 0.0057	+50%	7	0.0876	6388.7	2,835,627	0.02	9	0.0887	4930.5	2,783,244.8	0.031
	+25%	7	0.0876	6388.2	2,835,275	0.01	9	0.0887	4930.0	2,782,838.6	0.016
	0	7	0.0876	6387.7	2,834,922	0	9	0.0887	4929.6	2,782,396.0	0
	−25%	7	0.0876	6387.2	2,834,570	−0.01	9	0.0887	4928.9	2,782,026.3	−0.013
	−50%	7	0.0876	6386.7	2,834,218	−0.02	9	0.0887	4928.4	2,781,620.2	−0.028
$e_c = 1.44$	+50%	7	0.0876	6386.6	2,835,372	0.016	9	0.0887	4928.7	2,782,845.7	0.016
	+25%	7	0.0876	6387.1	2,835,148	0.008	9	0.0887	4929.2	2,782,620.8	0.008
	0	7	0.0876	6387.7	2,834,922	0	9	0.0887	4929.6	2,782,396.0	0
	−25%	7	0.0876	6388.3	2,834,698	−0.008	9	0.0887	4930.0	2,782,171.2	−0.008
	−50%	7	0.0876	6388.8	2,834,472	−0.016	9	0.0887	4930.5	2,781,946.2	−0.016
$T_x = 75$	+50%	7	0.0876	6387.7	2,836,077	0.04	9	0.0887	4929.8	2,783,658.0	0.045
	+25%	7	0.0876	6387.7	2,835,500	0.02	9	0.0887	4929.7	2,783,027.1	0.023
	0	7	0.0876	6387.7	2,834,922	0	9	0.0887	4929.6	2,782,396.0	0
	−25%	7	0.0876	6387.7	2,834,345	−0.02	9	0.0887	4929.5	2,781,764.9	−0.023
	−50%	7	0.0876	6387.6	2,833,768	−0.04	9	0.0887	4929.4	2,781,134.2	−0.045

6. Conclusions and Future Research

This study considers a two-echelon supply chain consisting of a manufacturer and a retailer where the production activities are resulting in a certain percentage of defective products. The supply chain entities are willing to reduce their environmental impact by coordinating the delivery quantity and number of deliveries per cycle. The effect of carbon emissions, item deterioration, and two choices of inspection are examined. The models are illustrated with two numerical examples, and the results give some insights. This study is an initial exploratory study that attempts to provide a mathematical solution for a controlled situation; it may be applied to handle larger problems of cost minimization and carbon emission reduction in the future.

From the research finding, it is observed that the numbers of delivered products from the manufacturer are less when the inspection is performed by the vendor. As a result, the total cost of the supply chain is less, because the total inventory-holding cost and the total deteriorating cost are decreasing. However, the vendor's total cost becomes higher when it performs the inspection. Therefore, the retailer needs to compensate a certain amount of cost-saving to the manufacturer so that both parties take advantage.

The research finding also revealed that although the total cost is less when the inspection is performed by the vendor, it does not guarantee a reduction in emissions. However, both the cost-saving and emission-reducing objectives can still be obtained simultaneously by reducing the level of cost savings. In this situation, there is a tradeoff between cost savings and reduction in carbon emissions.

Although this study addresses some practical aspects of a supply chain scenario to deal with lower carbon emissions, the scope has a wide opportunity to be extended. Applying the approach in a three-echelon supply chain or more is one opportunity. Future works can consider the possibility of reworking the defective products, the capacity of the vehicle and storage facility, and investment to reduce the carbon emissions. This study assumes a 100% inspection by the manufacturer. Future research may assume a sampling inspection by the manufacturer, as well as incorporate the issue of imperfect quality inspection.

Author Contributions: Conceptualization, Y.D.; Methodology, Y.D.; Software, Y.D.; Validation, G.A.W. and H.M.W.; Formal Analysis, Y.D.; Investigation, Y.D.; Resources, H.M.W.; Writing—Original Draft Preparation, Y.D.; Writing—Review & Editing, H.M.W. and G.A.W.; Visualization, Y.D.; Supervision, H.M.W.

Acknowledgments: The authors express their gratitude to the editor and the two anonymous reviewers for their comments and valuable suggestions to improve this paper. The first author also thanks to the United Board for Christian Higher Education in Asia for financing his study.

References

1. Glock, C.H. The joint economic lot size problem: A review. *Int. J. Prod. Econ.* **2012**, *135*, 671–686. [CrossRef]
2. Luo, Z.; Gunasekaran, A.; Dubey, R.; Childe, S.J.; Papadopoulos, T. Antecedents of low carbon emissions supply chains. *Int. J. Clim. Chang. Strateg. Manag.* **2017**, *9*, 707–727. [CrossRef]
3. Das, C.; Jharkharia, S. Low carbon supply chain: A state-of-the-art literature review. *J. Manuf. Technol. Manag.* **2018**, *29*, 398–428. [CrossRef]
4. Kazemi, N.; Abdul-Rashid, S.H.; Ghazilla, R.A.R.; Shekarian, E.; Zanoni, S. Economic order quantity models for items with imperfect quality and emission considerations. *Int. J. Syst. Sci. Oper. Logist.* **2018**, *5*, 99–115. [CrossRef]
5. Sarkar, B.; Ahmed, W.; Choi, S.B.; Tayyab, M. Sustainable inventory management for environmental impact through partial backordering and multi-trade-credit period. *Sustainability* **2018**, *10*, 4761. [CrossRef]
6. Taleizadeh, A.A.; Soleymanfar, V.R.; Govindan, K. Sustainable economic production quantity models for inventory system with shortage. *J. Clean. Prod.* **2018**, *174*, 1011–1020. [CrossRef]
7. Sarkar, B.; Ganguly, B.; Sarkar, M.; Pareek, S. Effect of variable transportation and carbon emission in a three-echelon supply chain model. *Transp. Res. Part E Logist. Transp. Rev.* **2016**, *91*, 112–128. [CrossRef]
8. Sarkar, B.; Ahmed, W.; Kim, N. Joint effects of variable carbon emission cost and multi-delay-in-payments under single-setup-multiple-delivery policy in a global sustainable supply chain. *J. Clean. Prod.* **2018**, *185*, 421–445. [CrossRef]
9. Daryanto, Y.; Wee, H.M. Single vendor-buyer integrated inventory model for deteriorating items considering carbon emission. In Proceedings of the 8th International Conference on Industrial Engineering and Operations Management (IEOM), Bandung, Indonesia, 6–8 March 2018; pp. 544–555.
10. Wahab, M.I.M.; Mamun, S.M.H.; Ongkunarak, P. EOQ models for a coordinated two-level international supply chain considering imperfect items and environmental impact. *Int. J. Prod. Econ.* **2011**, *134*, 151–158. [CrossRef]
11. Jauhari, W.A.; Pamuji, A.S.; Rosyidi, C.N. Cooperative inventory model for vendor-buyer system with unequal-sized shipment, defective items and carbon emission cost. *Int. J. Logist. Syst. Manag.* **2014**, *19*, 163–186. [CrossRef]
12. Sarkar, B.; Saren, S.; Sarkar, M.; Seo, Y.W. A Stackelberg game approach in an integrated inventory model with carbon-emission and setup cost reduction. *Sustainability* **2016**, *8*, 1244. [CrossRef]
13. Jauhari, W.A. A collaborative inventory model for vendor-buyer system with stochastic demand, defective items and carbon emission cost. *Int. J. Logist. Syst. Manag.* **2018**, *29*, 241–269. [CrossRef]
14. Gautam, P.; Khanna, A. An imperfect production inventory model with setup cost reduction and carbon emission for an integrated supply chain. *Uncertain Supply Chain Manag.* **2018**, *6*, 271–286. [CrossRef]
15. Tiwari, S.; Daryanto, Y.; Wee, H.M. Sustainable inventory management with deteriorating and imperfect quality items considering carbon emissions. *J. Clean. Prod.* **2018**, *192*, 281–292. [CrossRef]
16. Rosenblatt, M.J.; Lee, H.L. Economic production cycles with imperfect production processes. *IIE Trans.* **1986**, *18*, 48–55. [CrossRef]
17. Porteus, E.L. Optimal lot sizing, process quality improvement and setup cost reduction. *Oper. Res.* **1986**, *34*, 137–144. [CrossRef]

18. Salameh, M.K.; Jaber, M.Y. Economic production quantity model for items with imperfect quality. *Int. J. Prod. Econ.* **2000**, *64*, 59–64. [CrossRef]

19. Huang, C.K. An integrated vendor-buyer cooperative inventory model for items with imperfect quality. *Prod. Plan. Control* **2002**, *13*, 355–361. [CrossRef]

20. Goyal, S.K.; Huang, C.K.; Chen, K.C. A simple integrated production policy of an imperfect item for vendor and buyer. *Prod. Plan. Control* **2003**, *14*, 596–602. [CrossRef]

21. Wee, H.M.; Yu, J.C.P.; Wang, K.J. An integrated production-inventory model for deteriorating items with imperfect quality and shortage backordering considerations. In Proceedings of the International Conference on Computational Science and Its Applications (ICCSA), Glasgow, UK, 8–11 May 2006; Springer: Berlin/Heidelberg, Germany, 2006; pp. 885–897.

22. Lee, S.; Kim, D. An optimal policy for a single vendor single-buyer integrated production-distribution model with both deteriorating and defective items. *Int. J. Prod. Econ.* **2014**, *147*, 161–170. [CrossRef]

23. Bazan, E.; Jaber, M.Y.; Zanoni, S.; Zavanella, L.E. Vendor managed inventory (VMI) with consignment stock (CS) agreement for a two-level supply chain with an imperfect production process with/without restoration interruptions. *Int. J. Prod. Econ.* **2014**, *157*, 289–301. [CrossRef]

24. Sarkar, B.; Shaw, B.K.; Kim, T.; Sarkar, M.; Shin, D. An integrated inventory model with variable transportation cost, two-stage inspection, and defective items. *J. Ind. Manag. Optim.* **2017**, *13*, 1975–1990. [CrossRef]

25. Yu, H.F.; Hsu, W.K. An integrated inventory model with immediate return for defective items under unequal-sized shipments. *J. Ind. Prod. Eng.* **2017**, *34*, 70–77. [CrossRef]

26. Benjaafar, S.; Li, Y.; Daskin, M. Carbon footprint and the management of supply chains: Insights from simple models. *IEEE Trans. Autom. Sci. Eng.* **2013**, *10*, 99–116. [CrossRef]

27. Fahimnia, B.; Sarkis, J.; Dehghanian, F.; Banihashemi, N.; Rahman, S. The impact of carbon pricing on a closed-loop supply chain: An Australian case study. *J. Clean. Prod.* **2013**, *59*, 210–225. [CrossRef]

28. Bozorgi, A.; Pazour, J.; Nazzal, D. A new inventory model for cold items that considers costs and emissions. *Int. J. Prod. Econ.* **2014**, *155*, 114–125. [CrossRef]

29. Bozorgi, A. Multi-product inventory model for cold items with cost and emission consideration. *Int. J. Prod. Econ.* **2016**, *176*, 123–142. [CrossRef]

30. Hariga, M.; As'ad, R.; Shamayleh, A. Integrated economic and environmental models for a multi stage cold supply chain under carbon tax regulation. *J. Clean. Prod.* **2017**, *166*, 1357–1371. [CrossRef]

31. Ghosh, A.; Jha, J.K.; Sarmah, S.P. Optimizing a two echelon serial supply chain with different carbon policies. *Int. J. Sustain. Eng.* **2016**, *9*, 363–377. [CrossRef]

32. Toptal, A.; Çetinkaya, B. How supply chain coordination affects the environment: A carbon footprint perspective. *Ann. Oper. Res.* **2017**, *250*, 487–519. [CrossRef]

33. Bouchery, Y.; Ghaffari, A.; Jemai, Z.; Tan, T. Impact of coordination on cost and carbon emissions for a two-echelon serial economic order quantity problem. *Eur. J. Oper. Res.* **2017**, *260*, 520–533. [CrossRef]

34. Dwicahyani, A.R.; Jauhari, W.A.; Rosyidi, C.N.; Laksono, P.W. Inventory decisions in a two-echelon system with remanufacturing, carbon emission, and energy effects. *Cogent Eng.* **2017**, *4*, 1–17. [CrossRef]

35. Li, J.; Su, Q.; Ma, L. Production and transportation outsourcing decisions in the supply chain under single and multiple carbon policies. *J. Clean. Prod.* **2017**, *141*, 1109–1122. [CrossRef]

36. Wangsa, I.D. Greenhouse gas penalty and incentive policies for a joint economic lot size model with industrial and transport emissions. *Int. J. Ind. Eng. Comput.* **2017**, *8*, 453–480.

37. Anvar, S.H.; Sadegheih, A.; Zad, M.A.V. Carbon emission management for greening supply chains at the operational level. *Environ. Eng. Manag. J.* **2018**, *17*, 1337–1347.

38. Hariga, M.; Babekian, S.; Bahroun, Z. Operational and environmental decisions for a two-stage supply chain under vendor managed consignment inventory partnership. *Int. J. Prod. Res.* **2018**. [CrossRef]

39. Ji, S.; Zhao, D.; Peng, X. Joint decisions on emission reduction and inventory replenishment with overconfidence and low-carbon preference. *Sustainability* **2018**, *10*, 1119.

40. Wang, S.; Ye, B. A comparison between just-in-time and economic order quantity models with carbon emissions. *J. Clean. Prod.* **2018**, *187*, 662–671. [CrossRef]

41. Ghosh, A.; Sarmah, S.P.; Jha, J.K. Collaborative model for a two-echelon supply chain with uncertain demand under carbon tax policy. *Sādhanā* **2018**, *43*, 144. [CrossRef]

42. Ma, X.; Ho, W.; Ji, P.; Talluri, S. Coordinated pricing analysis with the carbon tax scheme in a supply chain. *Decis. Sci.* **2018**, *49*, 863–900. [CrossRef]

43. Darom, N.A.; Hishamuddin, H.; Ramli, R.; Nopiah, Z.M. An inventory model of supply chain disruption recovery with safety stock and carbon emission consideration. *J. Clean. Prod.* **2018**, *197*, 1011–1021. [CrossRef]

44. Huang, H.; He, Y.; Li, D. Pricing and inventory decisions in the food supply chain with production disruption and controllable deterioration. *J. Clean. Prod.* **2018**, *180*, 280–296. [CrossRef]

45. Daryanto, Y.; Wee, H.M.; Astanti, R.D. Three-echelon supply chain model considering carbon emission and item deterioration. *Transp. Res. Part E Logist. Transp. Rev.* **2019**, *122*, 368–383. [CrossRef]

46. Kundu, S.; Chakrabarti, T. A fuzzy rough integrated multi-stage supply chain inventory model with carbon emissions under inflation and time-value of money. *Int. J. Math. Oper. Res.* **2019**, *14*, 123–145. [CrossRef]

47. Shalke, P.N.; Paydar, M.M.; Hajiaghaei-Keshteli, M. Sustainable supplier selection and order allocation through quantity discounts. *Int. J. Manag. Sci. Eng. Manag.* **2018**, *13*, 20–32.

48. Moheb-Alizadeh, H.; Handfield, R. An integrated chance-constrained stochastic model for efficient and sustainable supplier selection and order allocation. *Int. J. Prod. Res.* **2018**, *56*, 6890–6916. [CrossRef]

49. Moheb-Alizadeh, H.; Handfield, R. Sustainable supplier selection and order allocation: A novel multi-objective programming model with a hybrid solution approach. *Comput. Ind. Eng.* **2019**, *129*, 192–209. [CrossRef]

50. Cao, W.; Hu, Y.; Li, C.; Wang, X. Single setup multiple delivery model of JIT system. *Int. J. Adv. Manuf. Technol.* **2007**, *33*, 1222–1228. [CrossRef]

51. Volvo Truck Corporation. Emissions from Volvo's Truck. Issue 3. 09 March 2018. Available online: http://www.volvotrucks.com/content/dam/volvo/volvo-trucks/markets/global/pdf/our-trucks/Emis_eng_10110_14001.pdf (accessed on 25 September 2018).

52. Yang, P.C.; Wee, H.M. Economic ordering policy of deteriorated item for vendor and buyer: An integrated approach. *Prod. Plan. Control* **2000**, *11*, 474–480. [CrossRef]

53. Jaggi, C.K.; Goel, S.K.; Mittal, M. Economic order quantity model for deteriorating items with imperfect quality and permissible delay in payment. *Int. J. Ind. Eng. Comput.* **2011**, *2*, 237–248. [CrossRef]

54. Swenseth, S.R.; Godfrey, M.R. Incorporating transportation costs into inventory replenishment decisions. *Int. J. Prod. Econo.* **2002**, *77*, 113–130. [CrossRef]

55. Nie, L.; Xu, X.; Zhan, D. Incorporating transportation costs into JIT lot splitting decisions for coordinated supply chains. *J. Adv. Manuf. Syst.* **2006**, *5*, 111–121. [CrossRef]

56. Rahman, M.N.A.; Leuveano, R.A.C.; bin Jafar, F.A.; Saleh, C.; Deros, B.M.; Mahmood, W.M.F.W.; Mahmood, W.H.W. Incorporating logistic costs into a single vendor-buyer JELS model. *Appl. Math. Model.* **2016**, *40*, 10809–10819. [CrossRef]

57. Wangsa, I.D.; Wee, H.M. An integrated vendor-buyer inventory model with transportation cost and stochastic demand. *Int. J. Syst. Sci. Oper. Logist.* **2018**, *5*, 295–309.

58. Hsu, L.F. Erratum to: An optimal policy for a single-vendor single-buyer integrated production-distribution model with both deteriorating and defective items. [Int. J. Prod. Econ. 147 (2014) 161–170]. *Int. J. Prod. Econ.* **2016**, *178*, 187–188. [CrossRef]

59. Misra, R.B. Optimum production lot size model for a system with deteriorating inventory. *Int. J. Prod. Res.* **1975**, *13*, 495–505. [CrossRef]

60. The United States Environmental Protection Agency (US. EPA). Emission Facts: Average Carbon Dioxide Emissions Resulting from Gasoline and Diesel Fuel. February 2005. Available online: https://nepis.epa.gov/ (accessed on 25 September 2018).

61. McCarthy, J.E. EPA Standards for Greenhouse Gas Emissions from Power Plants: Many Questions, Some Answers. CRS Report for Congress, 7–5700. 2013. Available online: http://nationalaglawcenter.org/wp-content/uploads/assets/crs/R43127.pdf (accessed on 25 September 2018).

62. Goyal, S.K. An integrated inventory model for a single supplier-single customer problem. *Int. J. Prod. Res.* **1977**, *15*, 107–111. [CrossRef]

10

Change Point Detection for Airborne Particulate Matter ($PM_{2.5}$, PM_{10}) by using the Bayesian Approach

Muhammad Rizwan Khan [1] and Biswajit Sarkar [2,*]

[1]   Department of Industrial Engineering, Hanyang University, 222 Wangsimni-Ro, Seoul 133-791, Korea;
    mrizwankhan162@gmail.com
[2]   Department of Industrial & Management Engineering, Hanyang University, Ansan,
    Gyeonggi-do 15588, Korea
*   Correspondence: bsbiswajitsarkar@gmail.com.

Abstract: Airborne particulate matter (PM) is a key air pollutant that affects human health adversely. Exposure to high concentrations of such particles may cause premature death, heart disease, respiratory problems, or reduced lung function. Previous work on particulate matter ($PM_{2.5}$ and PM_{10}) was limited to specific areas. Therefore, more studies are required to investigate airborne particulate matter patterns due to their complex and varying properties, and their associated (PM_{10} and $PM_{2.5}$) concentrations and compositions to assess the numerical productivity of pollution control programs for air quality. Consequently, to control particulate matter pollution and to make effective plans for counter measurement, it is important to measure the efficiency and efficacy of policies applied by the Ministry of Environment. The primary purpose of this research is to construct a simulation model for the identification of a change point in particulate matter ($PM_{2.5}$ and PM_{10}) concentration, and if it occurs in different areas of the world. The methodology is based on the Bayesian approach for the analysis of different data structures and a likelihood ratio test is used to a detect change point at unknown time (k). Real time data of particulate matter concentrations at different locations has been used for numerical verification. The model parameters before change point (θ) and parameters after change point (λ) have been critically analyzed so that the proficiency and success of environmental policies for particulate matter ($PM_{2.5}$ and PM_{10}) concentrations can be evaluated. The main reason for using different areas is their considerably different features, i.e., environment, population densities, and transportation vehicle densities. Consequently, this study also provides insights about how well this suggested model could perform in different areas.

Keywords: airborne particulate matter; Bayesian approach; change point detection; likelihood ratio test; time series analysis; air quality

1. Introduction

Airborne particulate matter is one of the most dangerous air pollutants and harmful to human health. For the last two decades, information about the negative impacts of PM_{10} (particles less than 10 μm in diameter) and $PM_{2.5}$ (particles less than 2.5 micrometers in diameter) has increased enormously. Exposure to high concentrations of such particles may cause premature death, heart disease, respiratory problems, or reduced lung function through different mechanisms, which include pulmonary and systemic inflammation, accelerated atherosclerosis, and altered cardiac autonomic function (Heroux et al. [1] and Pope et al. [2]). Therefore, to control particulate matter (PM) pollution, and to make effective plans for counter measurements, it is important to measure the efficiency and effectiveness of policies applied by the Ministry of Environment. Every region has developed different kinds of extensive bodies of legislation, which establish air quality standards for key air pollutants to improve the air quality and to satisfy these standards. The European Environment Agency, the United States Environmental Protection Agency, and the Ministry of Environment in South Korea have each set their own air quality standards for all air pollutants. Thus, It is essential to follow established air quality monitoring systems to measure the PM concentrations on an hourly as well as daily basis, because some areas deviate from the established PM standards. This may cause adverse environmental effects and serious health problems.

Until now, a number of statistical methods have been established to model the hazards of PM from air quality standards. A Bayesian multiple change point model was proposed to measure the quantitative efficiency of pollution control programs for air quality, which estimate the hazards of different air pollutants. In the model, it was assumed as a nonhomogeneous Poisson process with multiple change points. The change points were identified, and a rate function was estimated by using a reversible jump MCMC algorithm (Gyarmati-Szabo et al. [3]). In another study, the changes in health effects due to simultaneous exposure to physical and chemical properties of airborne particulate matter were gauged through Bayesian approach and inferences were drawn via the Markov Chain Monte Carlo method (Pirani et al. [4]). A Bayesian approach was introduced to estimate the distributed lag functions in time series models, which can be used to determine the short-term health effects of particulate air pollution on mortality (Welty et al. [5]). Hybrid models were proposed to forecast the PM concentrations for four major cities of China; Beijing, Shanghai, Guangzhou, and Lanzhou (Qin et al. [6]).

A change point detection method for detecting changes in the mean of the one dimensional Gaussian process was proposed on the basis of a generalized likelihood ratio test (GLRT). The important characteristic of this method is that it includes data dependence and covariance of the Gaussian process. However, in case of unidentified covariance, the plug-in GLRT method was suggested which remains asymptotically near optimal (Keshavarz et al. [7]). A new method for acute change point detection was proposed for fractional Brownian motion with a time dependent diffusion coefficient. The likelihood ratio method has been used for change point detection in Brownian motion. A statistical test was also suggested to identify the significance of a calculated critical point (Kucharczyk et al. [8]). The change point detection technique in machine monitoring was suggested, which was based on two stages. In the first stage, irregularities are measured in time series data through the automatic regression (AR) model, and then the martingale statistical test is applied to detect the change point in unsupervised time series data (Lu et al. [9]). An integrated inventory model was developed to determine the optimal lot size and production uptime while considering stochastic machine breakdown and multiple shipments for a single-buyer and single-vendor (Taleizadeh et al. [10]).

A statistical change point algorithm based on nonparametric deviation estimation between time series samples from two retrospective segments was proposed in which the direct density ratio estimation method was applied for deviation measurement through relative Pearson divergence (Liu et al. [11]). A novel statistical methodology for online change point detection was suggested in which data for an uncertain system was composed through an autoregressive model. On the basis of nonparametric estimation of unidentified elements, an innovative CUSUM-like scheme was recommended for change detection. This estimation method could also be updated online (Hilgert et al. [12]). A new methodology, the Karhunen-Loeve expansions of the limit Gaussian

processes, was suggested for change point test in the level of a series. Firstly, change point detection in the mean was explained, which later extended to linear and nonlinear regression (Górecki et al. [13]). A Cramer-von Mises type test was presented to test the sudden changes in random fields which was dependent on Hilbert space theory (Bucchia and Wendler [14]). The continuous-review inventory model was developed for Controllable lead time for comparing two models; one with normally distributed lead time demand and the second assumes that there is no specific distribution for lead time demand (Shin et al. [15]).

A new technique was developed to identify the structural changes in linear quantile regression models. When a structural change in the relationship between covariates and response at a specific point exists, it may not be at the centre of response distribution, but at the tail. The traditional mean regression method might not be applicable for change point detection of such structural changes at tails. Subsequently, the proposed technique could be appropriate for it (Zhou et al. [16]). For detection of simultaneous changes in mean and variance, a new methodology called the fuzzy classification maximum likelihood change point (FCML-CP) algorithm was suggested. Multiple change points in the mean and variance of a process can be estimated by this method. This technique is much better than the normal statistical mixture likelihood method because it saves a lot of time (Lu and Chang [17]). A model for Partial Trade-Credit Policy of Retailer was developed in which deterioration of products was assumed as exponentially distributed (Sarkar and Saren [18]).

The Bayesian change point algorithm for sequential data series was introduced which has some uncertain limitations regarding location and number of change points. This algorithm was precisely based on posterior distribution to deduce if a change point has occurred or not. It can also update itself linearly as new data points are observed. Posterior distribution monitoring is the finest way to identify the presence of a new change point in observed data points. Simulation studies illustrate that this algorithm is good for rapid detection of existing change points, and it is also known for a low rate of false detection (Ruggieri and Antonellis [19]). Due to the probabilistic concept of Bayesian change point detection (BCPD), this methodology can overcome threats in identifying the location and number of change points.

The performance of two different methods for change point detection of multivariate data with both single and multiple changes was compared. The results illustrated adequate performance for both Expectation Maximization (EM) and Bayesian methods. However, EM exhibits better performance in case of minor changes and unsuitable priors while the Bayesian method has less computational work to do (Keshavarz and Huang [20]). The Bayesian multiple change point model was suggested for the identification of Distributed Denial of Service (DDoS) flooding attacks in VoIP systems in which Session Initiation Protocol (SIP) is used as signalling mechanism (Kurt et al. [21]). One of the well-known change detection techniques is post classification with multi temporal remote sensing images. An innovative post classification technique with iterative slow feature analysis (ISFA) and Bayesian soft fusion was suggested to acquire accurate and reliable change detection maps. Three steps were suggested in this technique, first was to get the class probability of images through independent classification. After that, a continuous change probability map of multi temporal images was obtained by ISFA algorithm. Lastly, posterior probabilities for the class combinations of coupled pixels were determined through the Bayesian approach to assimilate the class probability with the change probability, which is called Bayesian soft fusion. This technique could be widely applicable in land cover monitoring and change detection at a large scale (Wu et al. [22]).

The Bayesian change point technique was designed to analyse biomarkers time series data in women for the diagnosis of ovarian cancer. The identification of such kind of change points could be used to diagnose the disease earlier (Mariño et al. [23]). The Generalized Extreme Value (GEV) fused lasso penalty function was applied to identify the change point of annual maximum precipitation (AMP) in South Korea. Numerical analysis and applied data analysis were conducted in order to compare performance from the GEV fused lasso and Bayesian change point analysis, which shows that when water resource structures are hydrologically designed the GEV fused lasso method should be used to identify the change points (Jeon et al. [24]). The Bayesian method was recommended to identify the change point occurrence in extreme precipitation data, and the model follows a generalized Pareto distribution. This Bayesian change point detection was inspected for four different situations, one with no change model, second with a shape change model, third with a scale change model, and fourth with both a scale and shape change model. It was determined that unexpected and sustained change points need to be considered in extreme precipitation while making hydraulic design (Chen et al. [25]).

Bayesian change point methodology was presented to identify changes in the temporal event rate for a non-homogeneous Poisson process. This methodology was used to determine if a change in the event rate has occurred or not, the time for change, and the event rate before or after the change. The methodology has been explained through an example of earthquake occurrence in Oklahoma. This spatiotemporal change point methodology can also be used for identifying changes in climate patterns and assessing the spread of diseases. It permits participants to make real time decisions about the influence of changes in event rates (Gupta and Baker [26]). A new Bayesian methodology was recommended to analyze multiple time series with the objective of identifying abnormal regions. A general model was developed and it was shown that Bayesian inference allows independent sampling from the posterior distribution. Copy number variations (CNVs) are identified by using data from multiple individuals. The Bayesian method was evaluated on both real and simulated CNV data to provide evidence that this method is more precise as compare to other suggested methods for analyzing such data (Bardwell and Fearnhead [27]).

All the above mentioned methods are either too complex and complicated for application on random hazards of PM or not applicable to randomness of PM hazards. Therefore, still more studies are required to investigate the PM hazards, due to its complex and varying properties and associated (PM_{10} and $PM_{2.5}$) concentrations and compositions, to investigate the numerical productivity of pollution control programs for air quality. The primary purpose of this research is to develop models for change point detection of particulate matter ($PM_{2.5}$ and PM_{10}) concentrations if it occurs in different areas. The pollutant concentrations before and after a change point has to be critically analyzed so that the proficiency and success of environmental policies for particulate matter ($PM_{2.5}$ and PM_{10}) concentrations can be evaluated. The Bayesian approach is used to analyze random hazards of PM concentrations with a change point at an unknown time (k).

To demonstrate the proposed approach, real time data of random hazards of PM concentrations at different sites has been used. The PM concentrations change point (k), parameters before change point (θ), and parameters after change point (λ) have been comprehensively analyzed by using the Bayesian technique. Thus, simulation models have been constructed for different data structures. The main reason for using different areas is their considerably different features i.e., environment, population densities, and transportation vehicle densities. Consequently, this study also provides insight about how well this suggested model could perform in different areas. The paper is structured as follows: Section 2 refers to problem definitions, explaining assumptions along with notation, and Section 3 shows the formulation of mathematical models. Sections 4 and 5 depict numerical examples and results, respectively, to validate the practical applications of the proposed models. Section 6 discusses the depicted results of previous section, it also explains the managerial insights of results. Finally, Section 7 presents conclusions of this study. Table 1 depicts the comparative study of different authors who have contributed in the direction of research, while the last row of the table portrays the contribution of this research paper. On the other hand, Tables 2 and 3 compares the difference in previous workings and this work.

Table 1. Author's contribution in the direction of research.

Authors	Airborne Particulate Matters ($PM_{2.5}$, PM_{10})	Change-Point Detection	BCPD (Bayesian Change Point Detection)	Time Series Analysis
Lim et al. (2012) [28]	Ambient particulate matter (PM)	-	-	-
Rao et al. (2018) [29]	Particulate matter air pollution	-	-	-
Wei and Meng (2018) [30]	Airborne fine particulate matter ($PM_{2.5}$)	-	-	-
Wang et al. (2017) [31]	Inhaled particulate matter	-	-	-
Heroux et al. (2015) [1]	Ambient air pollutants	-	-	-
Wellenius et al. (2012) [32]	Ambient Air Pollution	-	-	-
Pirani et al. (2015) [4]	Airborne particles	-	-	Bayesian inference within Time series
Li et al. (2013) [33]	Airborne particulate matter	-	-	Time series analysis
Kim et al. (2018a) [34]	Particulate matter	-	-	-
Kim et al. (2017) [35]	Air pollution	-	-	Time series model
Qin et al. (2017) [36]	Air pollution	-	-	Time series analysis
Lee et al. (2015) [37]	Fine and coarse particles	-	-	Time series analysis
Cabrieto et al. (2018) [38]		kernel change point detection, correlation changes	-	-
Keshavarz et al. (2018) [7]	-	Generalized likelihood ratio test, One-dimensional Gaussian process	-	-
Kucharczyk et al. (2018) [8]	-	likelihood ratio test, fractional Brownian motion	-	-
Lu et al. (2017) [9]		Change-point detection, machine monitoring, Anomaly measure (AR model), Martingale test	-	Time series data
Hilgert et al. (2016) [12]	-	On-line change detection, autoregressive dynamic models, CUSUM-like scheme	-	-
Górecki et al. (2017) [13]		Change point detection, heteroscedastic, Karhunen-Loeve expansions	-	Time series data
Bucchia and Wendler (2017) [14]	-	Change point detection, bootstrap, Hilbert space valued random fields, (Cramer–von Mises type test)	-	Time series data
Zhou et al. (2015) [16]	-	Sequential change point detection, linear quantile regression models	-	-
Lu and Chang (2016) [17]	-	Detecting change points, mean/variance shifts, FCML-CP algorithm	-	-

Table 1. *Cont.*

Authors	Airborne Particulate Matters ($PM_{2.5}$, PM_{10})	Change-Point Detection	BCPD (Bayesian Change Point Detection)	Time Series Analysis
Liu et al. (2013) [11]	-	Change point detection, relative density ratio estimation	-	Time series analysis
Ruggieri and Antonellis (2016) [19]	-	-	Bayesian sequential change point detection	-
Keshavarz and Huang (2014) [20]	-	-	Bayesian and Expectation Maximization methods, multivariate change point detection	-
Kurt et al. (2018) [21]	-	-	Bayesian change point model, SIP-based DDoS attacks detection	-
Wu et al. (2017) [22]	-	-	Post classification change detection, iterative slow feature analysis, Bayesian soft fusion	-
Gupta and Baker (2017) [26]	-	-	Spatial event rates, change point, Bayesian statistics, induced seismicity	-
Marino et al. (2017) [23]	-	-	Change point, multiple biomarkers, ovarian cancer	-
Jeon et al. (2016) [24]	-	-	Abrupt change point detection, annual maximum precipitation, fused lasso	-
Bardwell and Fearnhead (2017) [27]	-	-	Bayesian Detection, Abnormal Segments	Time series analysis
Chen et al. (2017) [25]	-	-	Bayesian change point analysis, extreme daily precipitation	-
This study	Airborne Particulate Matter	Change point detection	Bayesian approach and likelihood ratio test for change point detection	Time series data

Table 2. Change point detection.

Authors	Change-Point Detection
Cabrieto et al. (2018) [38]	Detection of correlation changes by applying kernel change point detection on the running correlations
Keshavarz et al. (2018) [7]	Detecting a change in the mean of one-dimensional Gaussian process data in the fixed domain regime based on the generalized likelihood ratio test (GLRT)
Kucharczyk et al. (2018) [8]	Variance change point detection for fractional Brownian motion based on the likelihood ratio test
Lu et al. (2017) [9]	Graph-based structural change detection for rotating machinery monitoring by martingale-test method
Hilgert et al. (2016) [12]	On-line change detection for uncertain autoregressive dynamic models through nonparametric estimation (CUSUM-like scheme)
Górecki et al. (2017) [13]	Change point detection in heteroscedastic time series through Karhunen-Loeve expansions
Bucchia and Wendler (2017) [14]	Change point detection and bootstrap for Hilbert space valued random fields (Cramer-von Mises type test)
Zhou et al. (2015) [16]	A method for sequential detection of structural changes in linear quantile regression models.
Lu and Chang (2016) [17]	Detecting change-points for shifts in mean and variance using fuzzy classification maximum likelihood change-point (FCML-CP) algorithm
Liu et al. (2013) [11]	Change point detection in time-series data by relative density-ratio estimation
This study	Change point detection for airborne particulate matter ($PM_{2.5}$, PM_{10}) through Bayesian approach and likelihood ratio test

Table 3. BCPD (Bayesian change point detection).

Authors	BCPD (Bayesian Change Point Detection)
Ruggieri and Antonellis (2016) [19]	A sequential Bayesian change point algorithm was proposed that provides uncertainty bounds on both the number and location of change points
Keshavarz and Huang (2014) [20]	Bayesian and Expectation Maximization (EM) methods for change point detection problem of multivariate data with both single and multiple changes
Kurt et al. (2018) [21]	A Bayesian change point model for detecting SIP-based DDoS attacks
Wu et al. (2017) [22]	A post-classification change detection method based on iterative slow feature analysis and Bayesian soft fusion
Gupta and Baker (2017) [26]	Estimating spatially varying event rates with a change point using Bayesian statistics: Application to induced seismicity
Marino et al. (2017) [23]	Change-point of multiple biomarkers in women with ovarian cancer
Jeon et al. (2016) [24]	Abrupt change point detection of annual maximum precipitation through fused lasso penalty function by using the Generalized Extreme Value (GEV) distribution
Bardwell and Fearnhead (2017) [27]	Bayesian Detection of Abnormal Segments in Multiple Time Series
Chen et al. (2017) [25]	Bayesian change point analysis for extreme daily precipitation
This study	Change point detection for airborne particulate matter ($PM_{2.5}$, PM_{10}) through Bayesian approach and likelihood ratio test

2. Problem Definition, Notation and Assumptions

2.1. Problem Definition

The major objective of this research is to develop a more precise, well defined and user friendly method for application on random hazards of PM to detect the change point of subjected air pollutant hazards at any unknown time (k) if it occurs at any area across the globe. The existing methods are either too complex and complicated for the application on random hazards of PM due to its complex and varying properties or not applicable to randomness of PM hazards. Therefore, still more studies are required to develop a such kind of methodology, which is easily understandable and appropriate to model the hazards of the PM concentrations from air quality standards that can also detect change points in these hazards. Secondly, this method could be applicable for any kind of time series and data distributions. Analysis of these changes need to be done, whether these change points are favorable or not for the environment. For this, a comparison of subjected pollutant hazards before and after a change point has to be done for the evaluation of pollution control programs adopted by environmental protection agencies. If hazards occurrences increase after the change point, then environmental policies have a negative impact which marks the failure of pollution control program, but if the hazards occurrences reduce after the change point, then it demonstrates the effectiveness of the pollution control program. Thirdly, an alteration in occurrences must be measured to define the new pollution control policies for further improvements in the current level of subjected air pollutant hazards.

For anticipated goals, the Bayesian approach will be used to determine posterior probabilities of pollutant occurrences and the likelihood ratio test will be used for identifying the change point in that Bayesian model. This suggested model would be numerically validated by using real-time data of particulate matters' concentrations in different areas of Seoul, South Korea, observed from January 2004 to December 2013. The change point (k) for for particulate matter ($PM_{2.5}$ and PM_{10}) hazards, the rate before the change point (θ), and the rate after the change point (λ) would be comprehensively analyzed. The central idea for using different regions is their considerably different features i.e., environment, population densities, and transportation vehicle densities. Hence, this study can also be a vision for the implementation of recommended model in different areas.Air quality standards for particular matter $PM_{2.5}$ and PM_{10} are given in Table 4. Results have been determined by following these standards.

Table 4. Region-wise air quality standards for particulate matters ($PM_{2.5}$ and PM_{10}).

Air Quality Standards for $PM_{2.5}$ ($\mu g/m^3$)		Air Quality Standards for PM_{10} ($\mu g/m^3$)	
European Standard ($PM_{2.5}$)	25	European Standard (PM_{10}) 24 h	50
American Standard ($PM_{2.5}$)	35	American Standard (PM_{10}) 24 h	150
Korean Standard ($PM_{2.5}$) 24 h	50	Korean Standard (PM_{10}) 24 h	100

Tables 5 and 6 illustrate some details regarding data collected for Guro, Nowon, Songpa, and Yongsan which exhibit standard-wise and location-wise percentage of polluted days. In case of $PM_{2.5}$, more than 44%, 21% and 8% days are polluted as per European, American and Korean standards respectively, which is alarming. Similarly, in case of PM_{10}, the polluted days concentrations as per European and Korean standards is more than 40% and 6% respectively and it could not be acceptable. Hence, there is a need to control hazards of PM.

Table 5. Particulate matter ($PM_{2.5}$) location-wise data.

Particle Pollution	Criteria ($\mu g/m^3$)	Total Number of Days	Effective Readings	Dangerous Concentration	%Age against Total Days	%Age against Effective Readings
\multicolumn{7}{c}{$PM_{2.5}$ Guro's data (Seoul, South Korea)}						
European Standard	25	2498	2486	1125	45.04%	45.25%
American Standard	35	2498	2486	532	21.30%	21.40%
Korean Standard	50	2498	2486	207	8.29%	8.33%
\multicolumn{7}{c}{$PM_{2.5}$ Nowon's data (Seoul, South Korea)}						
European Standard	25	3228	3031	1371	42.47%	45.23%
American Standard	35	3228	3031	718	22.24%	23.69%
Korean Standard	50	3228	3031	255	7.90%	8.41%
\multicolumn{7}{c}{$PM_{2.5}$ Songpa's data (Seoul, South Korea)}						
European Standard	25	3653	3388	1547	42.35%	45.66%
American Standard	35	3653	3388	795	21.76%	23.47%
Korean Standard	50	3653	3388	281	7.69%	8.29%
\multicolumn{7}{c}{$PM_{2.5}$ Yongsan's data (Seoul, South Korea)}						
European Standard	25	3653	3456	1537	42.08%	44.47%
American Standard	35	3653	3456	746	20.42%	21.59%
Korean Standard	50	3653	3456	280	7.66%	8.10%

Table 6. Particulate matter (PM_{10}) location-wise data.

Particle Pollution	Criteria ($\mu g/m^3$)	Total Number of Days	Effective Readings	Dangerous Concentration	%Age against Total Days	%Age against Effective Readings
		PM_{10} Guro's data (Seoul, South Korea)				
European Standard	50	3653	3540	1580	43.25%	44.63%
American Standard	150	3653	3540	60	1.64%	1.69%
Korean Standard	100	3653	3540	279	7.64%	7.88%
		PM_{10} Nowon's data (Seoul, South Korea)				
European Standard	50	3653	3531	1444	39.53%	40.89%
American Standard	150	3653	3531	41	1.12%	1.16%
Korean Standard	100	3653	3531	239	6.54%	6.77%
		PM_{10} Songpa's data (Seoul, South Korea)				
European Standard	50	3653	3467	1490	40.79%	42.98%
American Standard	150	3653	3467	50	1.37%	1.44%
Korean Standard	100	3653	3467	240	6.57%	6.92%
		PM_{10} Yongsan's data (Seoul, South Korea)				
European Standard	50	3653	3508	1566	42.87%	44.64%
American Standard	150	3653	3508	60	1.64%	1.71%
Korean Standard	100	3653	3508	282	7.72%	8.04%

2.2. Notation

The list of notation to represent the random variables and parameters is as follows:

Indices

i replication or sequence, $i = 1, 2, \ldots$
j position in the chain, $j = 1, 2, \ldots n$

Random variables

Y random process
y variable (Y) at any given point
y_i variable (Y) at point i where $i \in 0, 1, 2 \ldots$

Parameters

k change point in the random process
θ parameter before change point k associated with probability distribution function of random variable Y
λ parameter after change point k associated with probability distribution function of random variable Y

Variables

$Pr(\theta)$ prior distribution for parameter θ
$Pr(\theta|y_i)$ posterior distribution for parameter θ
$Pr(\lambda|y_i)$ posterior distribution for parameter λ
$Pr(y_i|\theta)$ likelihood or sampling model
V mean of the chain or replications (Average of daily pollutant concentrations)
V_{ij} jth observation from the ith replication

V_i	mean of ith replication
V	mean of m replications
B	between sequence variance represents the variance of replications with the mean of m replications
S_i^2	variance for all replications
W	within sequence variance is the mean variance for m replications
$Var(V)$	overall estimate of the variance of V in the target distribution
$\sqrt{R}$	estimated potential scale reduction for convergence

2.3. Assumptions

The following assumptions were used for the proposed model:

1. Y represents the number of times an event occurs in time t and Y is always positive real numbers $y \in 1, 2...$ that can be any random value.
2. $Y(0) = 0$ means that no event occurred at time $t = 0$.
3. Time series random data observed on equal interval of lengths.
4. The particulate matter daily concentrations or occurrence of events follow specific random probability distribution function.
5. The particulate matter daily concentrations in any interval of length (t) is a random variable and number of times event occurs is also positive random variable with parameter $(rate = \theta)$.

3. Mathematical Model

3.1. Formulation of Mathematical Model

The probability distribution function of a random variable Y at any given point y in the sample space is given as follows:
$$f(y; \theta) = Pr(Y = y|\theta) \ for \ y \in 1, 2...$$

There could be a single parameter or multiple parameters depending upon the probability distribution function of random variable Y.

The change point for random process Y is being detected by the likelihood ratio test and that is a statistical test used for comparing the goodness of fit for two statistical models; one is null model and other is alternative model. The test is based on the likelihood ratio, which states how many times more likely the data are under one model than the other. This likelihood ratio compared to a critical value used to decide whether to reject the null model.

$$f(\text{Change point}|Y, \text{Exepectation before change point}, \text{Expectation after change point})$$
$$= \frac{L(Y; \text{Change point}, \text{Expectation before change point}, \text{Expectation after change point})}{\sum_{j=1}^{n} L(Y; j, \text{Change point}, \text{Expectation before change point}, \text{Expectation after change point})} \quad (1)$$

and parameters' comparison before and after the change-point is also being done.

Let the change point in the random process be denoted by k and θ be the random variable parameter before change point k while λ be the random variable parameter after change point k. It can be represented as:
$$y_i \sim pdf(\theta) \ for \ i = 1, 2, ..., k$$
$$y_i \sim pdf(\lambda) \ for \ i = k+1, k+2, ..., n$$

Hence,

$$f(y; \theta) = Pr(Y = y_i|\theta) \, for \, i = 1, 2, ..., k$$

$$f(y; \lambda) = Pr(Y = y_i|\lambda) \, for \, i = k+1, k+2, ..., n$$

The joint pdf (probability density function) is the product of marginal pdf. If random variable $Y = y_i$ with parameter θ is modelled, then joint pdf of our sample data will be as below:

$$Pr(Y = y_i|\theta) = \prod_{i=1}^{n} Pr(y_i|\theta) \, for \, i \in 0, 1, 2, ..., n$$

A class of prior densities is conjugate for the likelihood/sampling model $Pr(y_i|\theta)$ if the posterior distribution is also in the same class. Therefore, prior distribution $Pr(\theta)$ and posterior distribution $Pr(\theta|y_i)$ will follow the same conjugate prior distribution to the likelihood/sampling model $Pr(y_i|\theta)$. However, the likelihood $Pr(y_i|\theta)$ follows the random distribution based on data. Therefore, the prior distribution $Pr(\theta)$ of parameters and posterior distribution $Pr(\theta|y_i)$ of the same parameters must be same and conjugate for Bayesian analysis. Bayes theorem for parameter's θ and λ is as follows:

$$Pr(\theta|y_i) \propto Pr(\theta)Pr(y_i|\theta)$$

$$Pr(\lambda|y_i) \propto Pr(\lambda)Pr(y_i|\lambda)$$

By applying Bayes theorem, the posterior distribution of model parameters θ and λ can be determined

$$Pr(\theta|y_i) = \frac{Pr(y_i|\theta)Pr(\theta)}{Pr(y_i)} \, for \, i \in 1, 2, ..., k$$

$$Pr(\lambda|y_i) = \frac{Pr(y_i|\lambda)Pr(\lambda)}{Pr(y_i)} \, for \, i \in k+1, k+2, ..., n$$

As,

$$L(\theta|Y) = f_\theta(Y) = f(Y|\theta)$$

Now, apply likelihood ratio test statistic for change point detection

$$f(k|Y, \theta, \lambda) = \frac{L(Y; k, \text{Expectation before change point, Expectation after change point})}{\sum_{j=1}^{n} L(Y; j, \text{Expectation before change point, Expectation after change point})}$$

And likelihood will be determined as given by:

$$L(Y; k, \theta, \lambda) = \left[exp\left(k((\text{Expectation after } k \text{ point} - \text{Expectation before } k \text{ point}) \right) \left(\frac{\text{Expectation before } k}{\text{Expectation after } k} \right)^{\sum_{i=1}^{k} y_i} \right]$$

The change point k is uniform over y_i. Please note that θ, λ and k are all independent of each other.

3.1.1. Convergence of the Parameters

A single simulation run of a somewhat arbitrary length cannot represent the actual characteristics of the resulting model. Therefore, to estimate the steady-state parameters, the Gelman-Rubin Convergence diagnostic has to be applied in which target parameters are estimated by running multiple sequences of the chain. m replications of the simulation ($m \geq 10$) are made, each of length $n = 1000$. If the target distribution is unimodal then Cowles and Carlin recommends that we must run at least ten chains, as this approach monitors the scalar numbers of interest in the analysis. Therefore, the mean rate of pollutant concentrations is a parameter of interest that is denoted by V.

Scalar summary V = Mean of the chain (Average of daily pollutant concentrations)

Let V_{ij} be the jth observation from the ith replication

$$V_{ij}, \ i = 1, 2, ..., m \ j = 1, 2, ..., n$$

Mean of ith replication

$$V_i = \frac{1}{n} \sum_{j=1}^{n} V_{ij}$$

Mean of m replications

$$V = \frac{1}{m} \sum_{i=1}^{m} V_i$$

The between sequence variance represents the variance of replications with the mean of m replications calculated as follows:

$$B = \frac{n}{m-1} \sum_{i=1}^{m} (V_i - V)^2$$

Variance for all replications is calculated to determine the within sequence variance

$$S_i^2 = \frac{1}{n-1} \sum_{j=1}^{n} (V_{ij} - V)^2$$

The within sequence variance is the mean variance for k replications determined as given below:

$$W = \frac{1}{m} \sum_{i=1}^{m} S_i^2$$

Finally, the within sequence variance and between sequence variance are combined to get an overall estimate of the variance of V in the target distribution

$$Var(V) = \frac{n-1}{n} W + \frac{1}{n} B$$

Convergence is diagnosed by calculating

$$\sqrt{R} = \sqrt{\frac{Var(V)}{W}}$$

This factor $\sqrt{R}$ (estimated potential scale reduction) is the ratio between the upper and lower bound on the space range of V which is used to estimate the factor by which $Var(V)$ could be reduced through more iterations. Further iterations of the chain must be run if the potential scale reduction is high. Run the replications until R is less than 1.1 or 1.2 for all scalar summaries.

3.1.2. Flowchart

The flowchart (Figure 1) for change point k detction, for any random process Y, is given as follows:

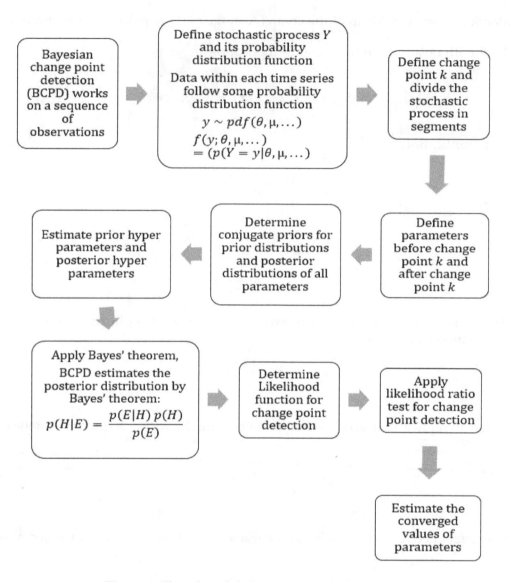

Figure 1. Flowchart for change point (k) detection.

3.2. Comparison Method for Change Point Detection

A change point analysis has been done by using a combination of CUSUM (cumulative sum control chart) and bootstrapping for comparative analysis.

3.2.1. The CUSUM (Cumulative Sum Control Chart) Technique

The CUSUM (cumulative sum control chart) is a sequential analysis technique typically used for monitoring change detection. CUSUM charts are constructed by calculating and plotting a cumulative sum based on the data. The cumulative sums are calculated as follows:

1. First calculate the average.

$$\bar{X} = \left(\frac{X_1 + X_2 + X_3 + ...,}{n} \right)$$

2. Start the cumulative sum at zero by setting $S_0 = 0$
3. Calculate the other cumulative sums by adding the difference between current value and the average to the previous sum, i.e.,

$$S_i = S_{i-1} + \left(X_i - \bar{X} \right)$$

Plot the series and the cumulative sum is not the cumulative sum of the values. Instead it is the cumulative sum of differences between the values and the average. Because the average is subtracted from each value, the cumulative sum also ends at zero.

Interpreting a CUSUM chart requires some practice. Suppose that during a period of time the values tend to be above the overall average. Most of the values added to the cumulative sum will be positive and the sum will steadily increase. A segment of the CUSUM chart with an upward slope indicates a period where the values tend to be above the overall average. Likewise a segment with a downward slope indicates a period of time where the values tend to be below the overall average. A sudden change in direction of the CUSUM indicates a sudden shift or change in the average. Periods where the CUSUM chart follows a relatively straight path indicate a period where the average did not change.

3.2.2. Bootstrap Analysis

A confidence level can be determined for the apparent change by performing a bootstrap analysis. Before performing the bootstrap analysis, an estimator of the magnitude of the change is required. One choice, which works well regardless of the distribution and despite multiple changes, is S_{diff} defined as:

$$S_{diff} = S_{max} - S_{min}$$

$$S_{max} = \max_{i=0,1,2,\ldots,} S_i$$

$$S_{min} = \min_{i=0,1,2,\ldots,} S_i$$

Once the estimator of the magnitude of the change has been selected, the bootstrap analysis can be performed. A single bootstrap is performed by:

1. Generate a bootstrap sample of n units, denoted $X^0_1, X^0_2, X^0_3, \ldots X^0_n$ by randomly reordering the original n values. This is called sampling without replacement.
2. Based on the bootstrap sample, calculate the bootstrap CUSUM, denoted $S^0_0, S^0_1, S^0_2, \ldots S^0_n$.
3. Calculate the maximum, minimum and difference of the bootstrap CUSUM, denoted S^0_{max}, S^0_{min} and S^0_{diff}.
4. Determine whether the bootstrap difference S^0_{diff} is less than the original difference S_{diff}.

The idea behind bootstrapping is that the bootstrap samples represent random reordering of the data that mimic the behavior of the CUSUM if no change has occurred. By performing a large number of bootstrap samples, it can be estimated that how much S_{diff} would vary if no change took place. It would be compared with the S_{diff} value calculated from the data in its original order to determine if this value is consistent with what has been expected if no change occurred. If bootstrap CUSUM charts tend to stay closer to zero than the CUSUM of the data in its original order, this leads one to suspect that a change must have occurred. A bootstrap analysis consists of performing a large number of bootstraps and counting the number of bootstraps for which S^0_{diff} is less than S_{diff}. Let N be the number of bootstrap samples performed and let X be the number of bootstraps for which $S^0_{diff} < S_{diff}$. Then the confidence level that a change occurred as a percentage is calculated as follows:

$$\text{Confidence Level} = 100 \frac{X}{N} \text{ percentage}$$

This is strong evidence that a change did in fact occur. Ideally, rather than bootstrapping, one would like to determine the distribution of S^0_{diff} based on all possible reordering of the data. However, this is generally not feasible. A better estimate can be obtained by increasing the number of bootstrap samples. Bootstrapping results in a distribution free approach with only a single assumption, that of an independent error structure. Both control charting and change-point analysis are based on the mean-shift model. Let $X_1, X-2, X_3, \ldots$ represent the data in time order. The mean-shift model can be written as

$$X_i = \mu_i + \epsilon_i$$

where μ_i is the average at time i. Generally $\mu_i = \mu_{i-1}$ except for a small number of values of i called the change-points. ϵ_i is the random error associated with the ith value. It is assumed that the ϵ_i are independent with means of zero. Once a change has been detected, an estimate of when the change occurred can be made. One such estimator is the CUSUM estimator. Let m be such that:

$$| \, S_m \, | = \max_{i=0,1,2,\ldots,} | \, S_i \, |$$

S_m is the point furthest from zero in the CUSUM chart. The point m estimates last point before the change occurred. The point $m+1$ estimates the first point after the change. Once a change has been detected, the data can be broken into two segments, one each side of the change-point, 1 to m and $m+1$ to 24, estimating the average of each segment, and then analyzing the two estimated averages.

4. Numerical Example

The formulated mathematical model has been used for the numerical verification and the validity of the model has also been checked. That is why real-time data of particulate matter hazards for four different sites of Seoul, South Korea has been utilized for this investigation.

4.1. Particulate Matter (PM$_{2.5}$) and (PM$_{10}$) Change Points for Four Different Sites

Two dissimilar cases need to be considered

4.1.1. Case 1—When There Is No Hazard

In this case, there is no hazard and concentrations of particulate matter does not exceed the threshold value of the standards. Therefore, there will be no polluted day and random variable Y would always be $y = 0$. Hence, due to zero hazard in the concentrations of particulate matter, this model has not been applied.

4.1.2. Case 2—When There Are Hazards

In this case, several polluted days for particulate matter ($PM_{2.5}$ and PM_{10}) concentrations are considered as a Poisson process. A counting process is a Poisson counting process with the rate $\theta > 0$. Here, we report the results obtained by applying the method described in Section 3 to the particulate matter ($PM_{2.5}$ and PM_{10}) concentrations for four different sites (Guro, Nowon, Songpa, and Yongsan) in Seoul, South Korea. We used the daily data observed from January 2004 to December 2013 to compute the change point of both pollutants.

$$f(y; \theta) = (Pr(Y = y|\theta)) = Poisson(y, \theta) = \frac{e^{-\theta}\theta^y}{y!} \; for \; y \in 1, 2, \ldots, n$$

Poisson distribution is the number of events occurring in a given time period. So in this case, occurrence of the number of polluted days in a month is taken as Poisson distribution. The rate of polluted days for both $PM_{2.5}$ and PM_{10} are given in Tables 7 and 8 respectively.

Table 7. $PM_{2.5}$ Poisson Process.

Area	Distribution	$PM_{2.5}$ Poisson Process (Rate) θ		
		European Standards	American Standards	Korean Standards
Guro	Poisson	13.720	6.488	2.524
Nowon	Poisson	12.934	6.774	2.406
Songpa	Poisson	12.892	6.625	2.342
Yongsan	Poisson	12.808	6.217	2.333

Table 8. PM_{10} Poisson Process.

Area	Distribution	PM_{10} Poisson Process (Rate) θ		
		European Standards	American Standards	Korean Standards
Guro	Poisson	13.167	0.500	2.325
Nowon	Poisson	12.033	0.342	1.992
Songpa	Poisson	12.417	0.417	2.000
Yongsan	Poisson	13.050	0.500	2.350

The change point for this Poisson process has to be detected to know whether a change has occurred, the most likely month in which change has occurred, and if the rate of polluted days has increased or decreased after the change point. It has been assumed that the number of polluted days for (particulate matter) $PM_{2.5}$ and PM_{10} concentrations follows a Poisson distribution with a mean rate θ until the month k. After the month k, the polluted days are distributed according to the Poisson distribution with a mean rate λ. It can be represented as:

$$y_i \sim Poisson(\theta) \; for \; i = 1, 2, ..., k$$

$$y_i \sim Poisson(\lambda) \; for \; i = k+1, k+2, ..., n$$

Hence,

$$f(y; \theta) = Pr(Y = y_i | \theta) \; for \; i = 1, 2, ..., k$$

$$f(y; \lambda) = Pr(Y = y_i | \lambda) \; for \; i = k+1, k+2, ..., n$$

If we model $Y = y_i$ as Poisson with mean rate θ then joint pdf of our sample data will be as below:

$$Pr(Y = y_i | \theta) = \prod_{i=1}^{n} pr(y_i | \theta) = \prod_{i=1}^{n} \frac{e^{-\theta} \theta^{y_i}}{y!} = c(y_1, y_2, ...y_n) e^{-n\theta} \theta^{\sum y_i} \; i \in 0, 1, 2, ..., n$$

This means that whatever our conjugate class of densities is, it will have to include terms like $e^{-C_2\theta} \theta^{C_1}$ for constants C_1 and C_2. The simplest class of such densities, which include these terms and corresponding probability distributions, are known as family of Gamma distributions. Therefore, prior distribution $Pr(\theta)$ and posterior distribution $Pr(Y = \theta | y_1, y_2, ...y_n)$ will follow a Gamma distribution, but likelihood or sampling model $Pr(y_1, y_2, ...y_n | \theta)$ follow a Poisson distribution.

Therefore, the prior distributions of θ and λ, uncertain positive quantities θ and λ has $Gamma(a_1, b_1)$ and $Gamma(a_2, b_2)$ distributions respectively, where a_1 is shape parameter and b_1 is rate parameter for θ while a_2 is shape parameter and b_2 is rate parameter for λ

$$Pr(\theta) = Gamma(\theta, a_1, b_1) = \frac{b_1^{a_1} e^{-b_1\theta} \theta^{a_1-1}}{\Gamma(a_1)}$$

$$Pr(\lambda) = Gamma(\lambda, a_2, b_2) = \frac{b_2^{a_2} e^{-b_2\lambda} \lambda^{a_2-1}}{\Gamma(a_2)}$$

Gamma distribution is also conjugate prior of the rate (inverse scale) parameter of the Gamma distribution itself. That is why the rate parameter b_1 and b_2 will also follow a Gamma distribution with different shape and rate parameters as given below:

$$b_1 \sim Gamma(c_1, d_1) \text{ where } c_1 = \text{shape parameter } d_1 = \text{rate parameter}$$

$$b_2 \sim Gamma(c_2, d_2) \text{ where } c_2 = \text{shape parameter } d_2 = \text{rate parameter}$$

By applying Bayes theorem, posterior distributions for rate parameters θ, λ, b_1 and b_2 will be determined in the following way. Likelihood and prior distributions of θ

$$Pr(y_1, y_2, y_3, ..., y_n | \theta) \sim Poisson(\theta)$$

$$Pr(\theta) = Gamma(\theta, a_1, b_1)$$

$$Pr(\theta | y_1, y_2, y_3, ..., y_n) = \frac{Pr(y_1, y_2, y_3, ..., y_n | \theta) Pr(\theta)}{Pr(y_1, y_2, y_3, ..., y_n)} = (e^{-b_1\theta}\theta^{a_1-1}) \times (e^{-n\theta}\theta^{\sum y_i}) \times c(y_1, y_2, y_3, ..., y_n)$$

$$= (e^{-(b_1+n)\theta}\theta^{a_1+\sum y_i-1}) \times c(y_1, y_2, y_3, ..., y_n, a_1, b_1)$$

$$(\theta | y_1, y_2, y_3, ..., y_n) \sim Gamma(a_1 + \sum_{i=1}^{n} y_i, b_1 + n)$$

This is evidently a Gamma distribution. Hence, the conjugacy of Gamma family for the Poisson sampling model or likelihood is confirmed. Hence, it is concluded from the above that if:

$$\theta \sim Gamma(a_1, b_1)$$

$$Pr(y_1, y_2, y_3, ..., y_n | \theta) \sim Poisson(\theta)$$

Then:

$$(\theta | y_1, y_2, y_3, ..., y_n) \sim Gamma(a_1 + \sum_{i=1}^{n} y_i, b_1 + n)$$

Similarly, the posterior distributions of all parameters θ, λ, b_1 and b_2 can be determined as given below:

$$(\theta | y, \lambda, b_1, b_2, k) \sim Gamma(a_1 + \sum_{i=1}^{k} y_i, k + b_1)$$

$$(\lambda | y, \theta, b_1, b_2, k) \sim Gamma(a_2 + \sum_{i=k+1}^{n} y_i, k + b_2)$$

$$(b_1 | y, \theta, \lambda, b_2, k) \sim Gamma(a_1 + c_1, \theta + d_1)$$

$$(b_2 | y, \theta, \lambda, b_1, k) \sim Gamma(a_2 + c_2, \lambda + d_2)$$

As Gamma is a two-parameter family of continuous probability distribution. As a result, the function:

$$L(\theta | Y) = f_\theta(Y) = f(Y|\theta)$$

The likelihood ratio test statistic is:

$$f(k | Y, \theta, \lambda) = \frac{L(Y; k, \theta, \lambda)}{\sum_{j=1}^{n} L(Y; j, \theta, \lambda)}$$

The likelihood is determined as given by:

$$L(Y; k, \theta, \lambda) = exp(k(\lambda - \theta)) \, (\theta/\lambda)^{\sum_{i=1}^{k} y_i}$$

For Bayesian approach, MATLAB has been used for change point detection of particulate matter ($PM_{2.5}$ and PM_{10}) data during the study period (2004–2013) for four different sites (Guro, Nowon, Songpa and Yongsan) in Seoul, South Korea. 10 replications of each simulation are made with 1100 observations in each replication. First 100 observations are discarded as a burn-in period. Replication Mean V_i of remaining 1000 observations has been taken for each replication as shown in Tables 9 and 10. Then mean (V) of replication mean has been taken to get the converged values of parameters.

Moreover, the CUSUM charts of polluted days as per European, American and Korean standards are shown in Figures 2–9 for four different sites Guro, Nowon, Songpa and Yongsan in Seoul, South Korea.

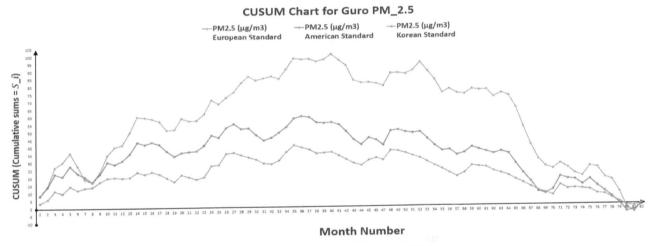

Figure 2. CUSUM chart for Guro $PM_{2.5}$.

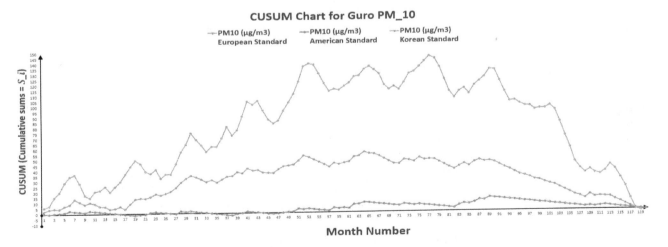

Figure 3. CUSUM chart for Guro PM_{10}.

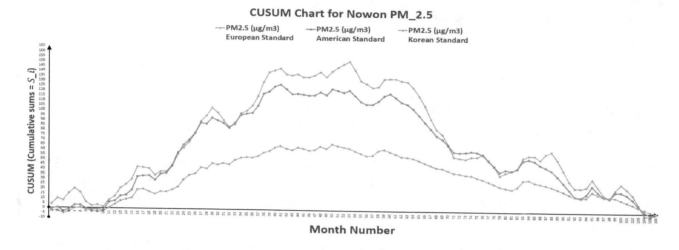

Figure 4. CUSUM chart for Nowon $PM_{2.5}$.

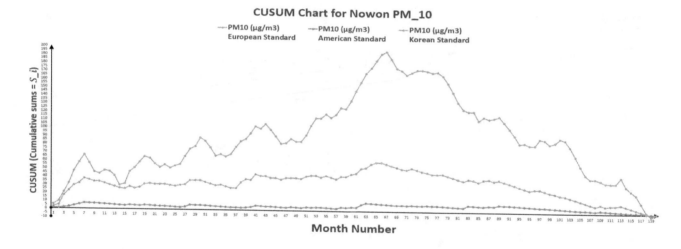

Figure 5. CUSUM chart for Nowon PM_{10}.

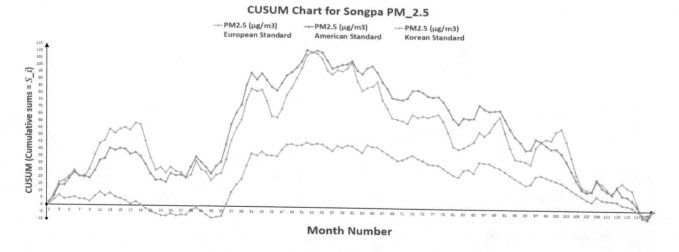

Figure 6. CUSUM chart for Songpa $PM_{2.5}$.

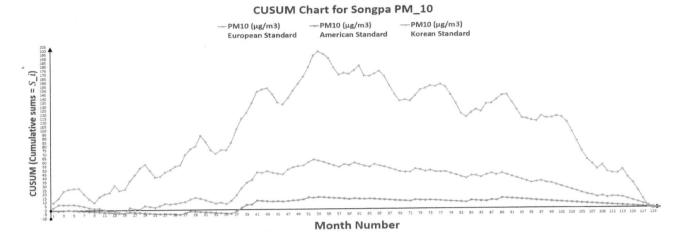

Figure 7. CUSUM chart for Songpa PM_{10}.

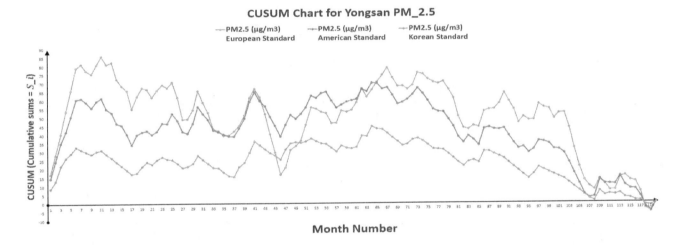

Figure 8. CUSUM chart for Yongsan $PM_{2.5}$.

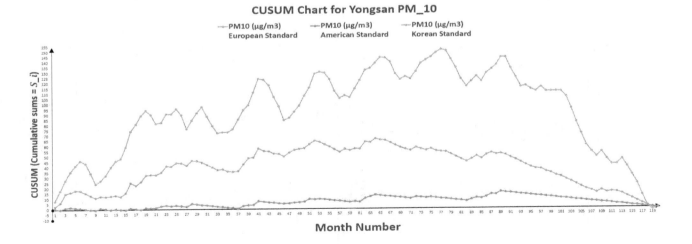

Figure 9. CUSUM chart for Yongsan PM_{10}.

Table 9. $PM_{2.5}$ Converged values of parameters (Bayesian approach).

$PM_{2.5}$ Converged Values of Parameters (Bayesian Approach)

Replication Mean	Guro			Nowon			Songpa			Yongsan		
	(θ) Replication Mean	(λ) Replication Mean	K Replication Mean	(θ) Replication Mean	(λ) Replication Mean	K Replication Mean	(θ) Replication Mean	(λ) Replication Mean	K Replication Mean	(θ) Replication Mean	(λ) Replication Mean	K Replication Mean
European standards												
V_1	15.96	11.17	43.29	15.88	10.30	49.98	14.93	11.24	53.69	24.80	12.13	6.92
V_2	16.03	11.25	42.53	15.89	10.34	49.83	14.90	11.28	53.81	24.46	12.15	8.07
V_3	16.00	11.18	43.12	15.90	10.32	49.76	14.91	11.25	53.92	24.81	12.07	7.49
V_4	16.01	11.17	43.19	15.90	10.30	49.96	14.91	11.24	54.05	24.77	12.14	7.75
V_5	15.98	11.12	43.52	15.88	10.26	50.13	14.93	11.23	53.59	24.56	12.09	7.48
V_6	15.96	11.14	43.61	15.87	10.28	50.12	14.89	11.24	53.98	24.07	12.08	9.48
V_7	15.95	11.17	43.41	15.84	10.30	50.12	14.88	11.26	53.91	24.61	12.03	8.20
V_8	16.04	11.21	42.76	15.94	10.34	49.65	14.93	11.26	53.73	24.69	12.13	7.87
V_9	16.01	11.19	42.75	15.88	10.30	49.78	14.90	11.24	53.71	24.50	12.10	7.83
V_{10}	15.96	11.15	43.59	15.85	10.30	50.23	14.88	11.25	54.07	24.23	12.12	8.30
(V) Mean of 10 replications	15.99	11.17	43.18	15.88	10.30	49.95	14.90	11.25	53.85	24.55	12.10	7.94
American standards												
V_1	8.35	5.32	33.46	9.82	4.77	42.11	8.73	4.95	53.32	16.12	5.69	6.17
V_2	8.24	5.33	33.67	9.84	4.80	41.76	8.72	4.96	53.31	16.04	5.71	6.17
V_3	8.22	5.30	34.31	9.82	4.78	42.12	8.72	4.95	53.35	16.00	5.69	6.21
V_4	8.29	5.30	34.10	9.84	4.79	41.75	8.72	4.95	53.32	16.08	5.68	6.18
V_5	8.31	5.30	33.49	9.86	4.77	41.67	8.72	4.93	53.32	16.05	5.67	6.17
V_6	8.27	5.31	33.70	9.80	4.77	42.11	8.71	4.94	53.39	15.96	5.68	6.20
V_7	8.24	5.30	34.01	9.88	4.79	41.66	8.70	4.95	53.33	15.92	5.69	6.19
V_8	8.25	5.32	33.70	9.86	4.80	41.61	8.74	4.96	53.25	16.16	5.69	6.16
V_9	8.47	5.33	32.46	9.83	4.78	41.66	8.72	4.94	53.21	15.99	5.68	6.16
V_{10}	8.38	5.33	33.28	9.82	4.79	41.89	8.71	4.95	53.42	15.96	5.69	6.21
(V) Mean of 10 replications	8.30	5.31	33.62	9.84	4.78	41.83	8.72	4.95	53.32	16.03	5.69	6.18

Table 9. *Cont.*

	\(PM_{2.5}\) Converged Values of Parameters (Bayesian Approach)											
	Guro			Nowon			Songpa			Yongsan		
Replication Mean	(θ) Replication Mean	(λ) Replication Mean	K Replication Mean	(θ) Replication Mean	(λ) Replication Mean	K Replication Mean	(θ) Replication Mean	(λ) Replication Mean	K Replication Mean	(θ) Replication Mean	(λ) Replication Mean	K Replication Mean
V_1	3.58	1.63	38.14	3.75	1.21	50.29	3.13	1.64	56.57	7.95	2.05	5.80
V_2	3.57	1.65	37.90	3.74	1.22	50.25	3.15	1.65	56.26	7.95	2.06	5.76
V_3	3.58	1.64	37.97	3.75	1.21	50.23	3.15	1.64	56.34	7.92	2.05	5.80
V_4	3.57	1.62	38.40	3.74	1.20	50.43	3.15	1.63	56.54	8.01	2.06	5.77
V_5	3.56	1.61	38.48	3.74	1.20	50.32	3.14	1.63	56.50	7.94	2.05	5.78
V_6	3.55	1.62	38.63	3.73	1.20	50.52	3.13	1.63	56.87	7.97	2.04	5.77
V_7	3.54	1.62	38.60	3.75	1.20	50.30	3.13	1.64	56.53	7.87	2.05	5.80
V_8	3.59	1.64	37.93	3.75	1.21	50.27	3.16	1.64	56.08	7.98	2.06	5.78
V_9	3.57	1.63	37.84	3.73	1.20	50.43	3.15	1.64	55.86	7.90	2.05	5.79
V_{10}	3.55	1.62	38.69	3.73	1.21	50.36	3.13	1.63	56.86	7.90	2.05	5.79
Mean of 10 replications (V)	3.56	1.63	38.26	3.74	1.21	50.34	3.14	1.64	56.44	7.94	2.05	5.78

Korean standards

Table 10. PM_{10} Converged values of parameters (Bayesian approach).

PM_{10} Converged Values of Parameters (Bayesian Approach)

Replication Mean	Guro (θ) Replication Mean	Guro (λ) Replication Mean	Guro K Replication Mean	Nowon (θ) Replication Mean	Nowon (λ) Replication Mean	Nowon K Replication Mean	Songpa (θ) Replication Mean	Songpa (λ) Replication Mean	Songpa K Replication Mean	Yongsan (θ) Replication Mean	Yongsan (λ) Replication Mean	Yongsan K Replication Mean
						European standards						
V_1	14.71	9.20	85.53	14.95	8.36	67.04	16.11	9.49	53.29	14.57	8.41	90.09
V_2	14.75	9.27	85.10	14.93	8.39	67.10	16.08	9.52	53.30	14.57	8.50	89.53
V_3	14.74	9.20	85.49	14.93	8.36	67.16	16.11	9.45	53.29	14.58	8.47	89.63
V_4	14.75	9.19	85.47	14.93	8.35	67.17	16.08	9.47	53.52	14.57	8.39	90.16
V_5	14.76	9.12	85.65	14.92	8.33	67.13	16.06	9.44	53.75	14.56	8.35	89.85
V_6	14.72	9.18	85.59	14.91	8.35	67.20	16.06	9.47	53.43	14.54	8.42	89.98
V_7	14.71	9.18	85.75	14.90	8.36	67.13	16.14	9.48	53.36	14.52	8.41	90.12
V_8	14.77	9.25	85.07	14.96	8.37	67.05	16.08	9.39	53.93	14.61	8.51	89.23
V_9	14.73	9.18	85.29	14.92	8.35	67.03	16.07	9.47	53.26	14.60	8.48	88.67
V_{10}	14.72	9.19	85.67	14.91	8.37	67.16	16.03	9.46	53.91	14.53	8.39	90.18
(V) Mean of 10 replications	14.73	9.20	85.46	14.93	8.36	67.12	16.08	9.46	53.50	14.56	8.43	89.74
						American standards						
V_1	0.63	0.12	90.65	0.69	0.13	66.56	0.56	0.07	87.63	0.66	0.04	91.61
V_2	0.63	0.12	90.76	0.63	0.11	72.52	0.55	0.07	89.08	0.66	0.04	91.33
V_3	0.63	0.12	90.67	0.52	0.08	81.79	0.56	0.07	87.86	0.66	0.04	91.46
V_4	0.63	0.12	90.34	0.53	0.09	81.32	0.57	0.07	86.80	0.66	0.04	91.41
V_5	0.63	0.12	90.23	0.76	0.14	60.70	0.56	0.06	88.35	0.67	0.04	91.03
V_6	0.63	0.12	90.48	0.52	0.08	81.91	0.56	0.07	87.98	0.66	0.04	91.50
V_7	0.63	0.12	90.53	0.45	0.06	89.85	0.56	0.06	88.72	0.66	0.05	91.18
V_8	0.63	0.12	90.63	0.82	0.15	56.42	0.56	0.09	88.73	0.66	0.04	91.11
V_9	0.63	0.13	89.33	0.64	0.11	71.37	0.56	0.07	88.19	0.66	0.04	91.69
V_{10}	0.64	0.12	89.79	0.59	0.11	75.61	0.56	0.07	88.26	0.66	0.04	91.29
(V) Mean of 10 replications	0.63	0.12	90.34	0.62	0.11	73.80	0.56	0.07	88.16	0.66	0.04	91.36

Table 10. *Cont.*

PM$_{10}$ Converged Values of Parameters (Bayesian Approach)

Replication Mean	Guro (θ) Replication Mean	Guro (λ) Replication Mean	Guro K Replication Mean	Nowon (θ) Replication Mean	Nowon (λ) Replication Mean	Nowon K Replication Mean	Songpa (θ) Replication Mean	Songpa (λ) Replication Mean	Songpa K Replication Mean	Yongsan (θ) Replication Mean	Yongsan (λ) Replication Mean	Yongsan K Replication Mean
						Korean standards						
V_1	2.89	0.91	85.25	2.92	0.89	65.68	3.16	1.09	52.78	3.32	1.11	67.44
V_2	2.90	0.92	85.17	2.91	0.89	65.67	3.17	1.10	52.65	3.33	1.13	66.93
V_3	2.89	0.90	85.96	2.92	0.89	65.69	3.17	1.09	52.79	3.32	1.12	67.52
V_4	2.88	0.88	86.67	2.91	0.88	65.69	3.17	1.09	52.83	3.30	1.08	68.72
V_5	2.90	0.91	84.97	2.91	0.88	65.67	3.16	1.08	52.79	3.30	1.09	68.37
V_6	2.88	0.89	86.13	2.91	0.88	65.72	3.16	1.09	52.75	3.27	1.06	69.89
V_7	2.87	0.87	87.12	2.90	0.89	65.70	3.16	1.09	52.64	3.28	1.08	68.93
V_8	2.89	0.89	86.14	2.92	0.88	65.67	3.18	1.09	52.59	3.33	1.12	67.09
V_9	2.88	0.89	86.27	2.90	0.88	65.63	3.16	1.09	52.56	3.31	1.10	67.66
V_{10}	2.88	0.90	86.17	2.90	0.89	65.74	3.15	1.09	53.15	3.30	1.10	68.08
(V) Mean of 10 replications	2.89	0.90	85.98	2.91	0.89	65.68	3.16	1.09	52.75	3.31	1.10	68.06

However, the bootstraps analysis of European standards has been shown in Figures 10–17 as given below.

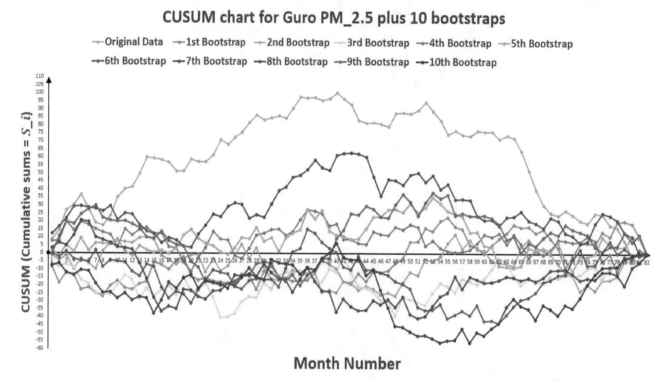

Figure 10. CUSUM chart for Guro $PM_{2.5}$ plus 10 bootstraps (European Standards).

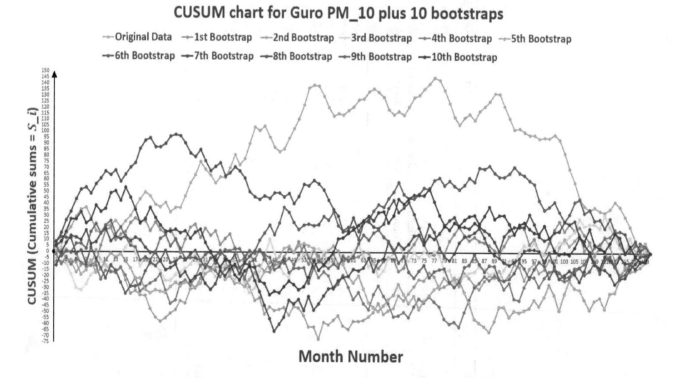

Figure 11. CUSUM chart for Guro PM_{10} plus 10 bootstraps (European Standards).

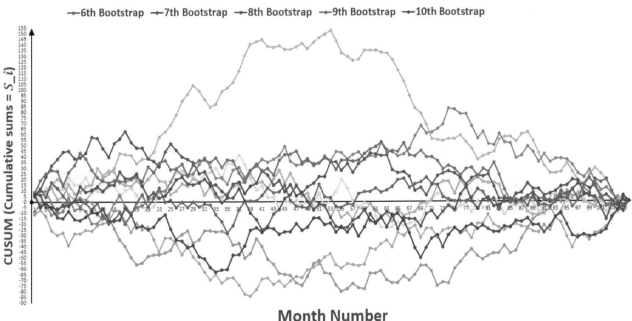

Figure 12. CUSUM chart for Nowon $PM_{2.5}$ plus 10 bootstraps (European Standards).

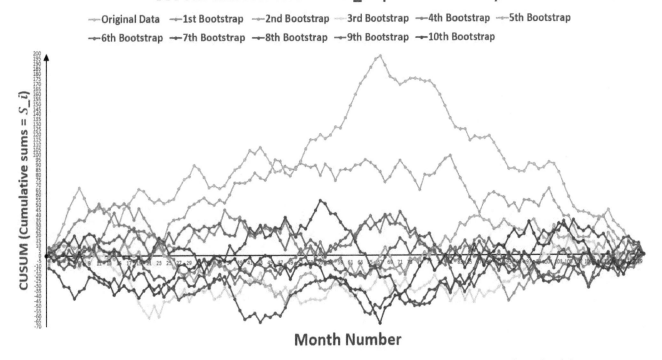

Figure 13. CUSUM chart for Nowon PM_{10} plus 10 bootstraps (European Standards).

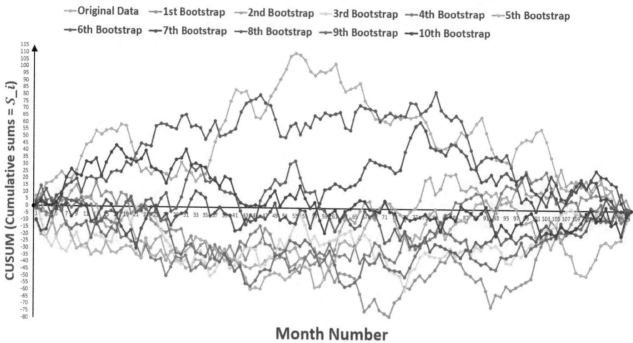

Figure 14. CUSUM chart for Songpa $PM_{2.5}$ plus 10 bootstraps (European Standards).

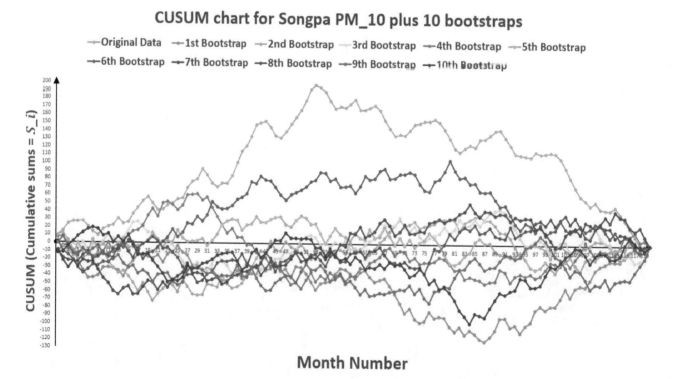

Figure 15. CUSUM chart for Songpa PM_{10} plus 10 bootstraps (European Standards).

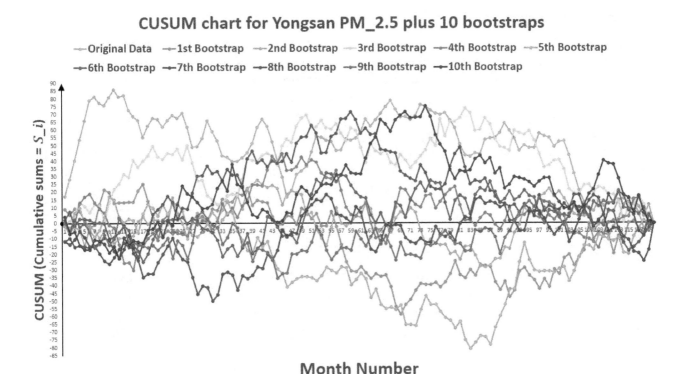

Figure 16. CUSUM chart for Yongsan $PM_{2.5}$ plus 10 bootstraps (European Standards).

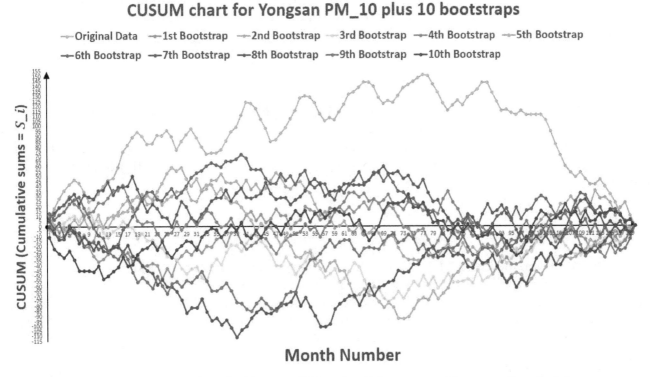

Figure 17. CUSUM chart for Yongsan PM_{10} plus 10 bootstraps (European Standards).

The change point k is discrete uniform over $(1, 2, 3 \ldots 120)$ as there are 120 months in 10 years. Please note that θ, λ and k are all independent of each other.

5. Numerical Results

Two dissimilar approaches have been used to attain the results. First one is Bayesian approach, which is based on probability distributions. It can be applicable to any kind of data distribution. For this, firstly data distributions are defined and then proposed method is applied to acquire the results. This approach is better to apply for random data structures and time series. While the second method is based on CUSUM charts, this technique is directly applicable on the raw data, which is good for deterministic data structures. Summarized forms of particulate matter ($PM_{2.5}$ and PM_{10}) change point (k), the rate before change point (θ) and the rate after change point (λ) during the study period (2004–2013) for four different sites (Guro, Nowon, Songpa and Yongsan) in Seoul, South Korea are given in Tables 11–14. The results have been computed by following the European, American, and Korean Standards as discussed in Table 4.

5.1. $PM_{2.5}$ Change Point (k) through Bayesian Approach

In Table 11, the results obtained through Bayesian approach have been described, where (k) is the predicted change point varies for different areas and different air quality standards. The results indicate the reduction of polluted days after change point (k) for $PM_{2.5}$. While (θ) represents the per month rate of polluted days before change point, (k) and (λ) be the rate of per month polluted days after change point (k).

5.2. $PM_{2.5}$ Last Point before Change (k) and First Point after Change (k + 1) through CUSUM Approach

Table 12 represents the results obtained for $PM_{2.5}$ through CUSUM approach, where (k) is the last point before change and ($k + 1$) be the first point after change point. So, the change point leis somewhere between (k) and ($k + 1$). This method also shows the reduction of polluted days after change point as (θ) represents the per month rate of polluted days before change point and (λ) be the rate of per month polluted days after change point.

5.3. PM_{10} Change Point (k) through Bayesian Approach

Table 13 explains the results obtained for PM_{10} through Bayesian approach. Hence, the expected change point is (k) that differs for different areas and various air quality standards. These results show the reduction of polluted days after change point (k) for PM_{10}. While (θ) is the per month rate of polluted days before change point (k) and (λ) represents the rate of per month polluted days after change point (k).

5.4. PM_{10} Last Point before Change (k) and First Point after Change (k + 1) through CUSUM Approach

The results obtained for PM_{10} through CUSUM approach have been described in Table 14, where the last point before change is (k) and the first point after change point is ($k + 1$). Therefore, the change point leis anywhere between (k) and ($k + 1$). This method also depicts the reduction of polluted days after change point. (θ) represents the per month rate of polluted days before change point and (λ) be the rate of per month polluted days after change point.

Table 11. $PM_{2.5}$ Change Point (k) for European, American and Korean Standards through Bayesian approach.

Area Seoul, South Korea	(θ) Rate before Change Point	(λ) Rate after Change Point	K Change Point	$\sqrt{R}\theta$ Convergence Parameter for (θ)	$Var(V)\theta$ Variance for (θ)	$\sqrt{R}\lambda$ Convergence Parameter for (λ)	$Var(V)\lambda$ Variance for (λ)	$\sqrt{R}K$ Convergence Parameter for K	$Var(V)K$ Variance for K
					European standards				
Guro	15.99	11.17	43.18	1.000408	0.583	1.000719	0.541	1.000747	59.219
Nowon	15.88	10.30	49.95	0.999943	0.783	1.000094	0.472	1.000036	34.238
Songpa	14.90	11.25	53.85	1.000199	0.302	1.000007	0.180	1.000870	9.719
Yongsan	24.55	12.10	7.94	1.000898	21.961	1.000943	0.477	1.002031	90.053
					American standards				
Guro	8.30	5.31	33.62	1.002540	1.064	1.000105	0.176	1.001256	75.773
Nowon	9.84	4.78	41.83	1.000595	0.296	1.000200	0.089	1.001159	13.007
Songpa	8.72	4.95	53.32	0.999857	0.172	0.999934	0.076	1.000255	2.395
Yongsan	16.03	5.69	6.18	0.99993	5.726	0.99956	0.101	1.000028	0.356
					Korean standards				
Guro	3.56	1.63	38.26	1.000475	0.132	1.000439	0.052	1.000865	41.605
Nowon	3.74	1.21	50.34	0.999959	0.083	1.000377	0.025	0.999978	9.024
Songpa	3.14	1.64	56.44	1.000200	0.068	1.000144	0.031	1.000588	45.887
Yongsan	7.94	2.05	5.78	1.000136	1.498	1.000237	0.018	0.999780	0.339

Bayesian Approach for Change Point Detection

Table 12. $PM_{2.5}$ Last point before change (k) and First point after change ($k+1$) for European, American and Korean Standards through CUSUM approach.

Area Seoul, South Korea	(θ) Average Rate before Change	(λ) Average Rate after Change	K Last Point before Change	$k+1$ First Point after Change	$\lvert S_m \rvert$ Most Extreme Point	S_{max} Highest Point in CUSUM	S_{min} Lowest Point in CUSUM	S_{diff} Magnitude of Change	Confidence Level %
					CUSUM Approach for Change Point Detection				
					European standards				
Guro	16.23	11.33	40	41	100.22	100.220	−5.280	105.500	100%
Nowon	15.81	10.06	53	54	152.50	152.500	−3.066	155.566	100%
Songpa	14.98	11.24	53	54	110.74	110.742	−6.108	116.850	100%
Yongsan	20.64	12.02	11	12	86.11	86.108	−5.192	91.300	70%
					American standards				
Guro	8.14	5.20	36	37	59.44	59.439	−5.024	64.463	100%
Nowon	9.90	4.80	41	42	128.28	128.283	−3.321	131.604	100%
Songpa	8.79	4.97	52	53	112.50	112.500	−5.375	117.875	100%
Yongsan	7.31	4.96	64	65	70.13	70.133	−4.783	74.917	100%
					Korean standards				
Guro	3.69	1.66	35	36	40.65	40.646	−1.476	42.122	100%
Nowon	3.76	1.20	50	51	67.72	67.717	−5.217	72.934	100%
Songpa	3.23	1.66	52	53	46.23	46.233	−8.275	54.508	100%
Yongsan	3.03	1.54	64	65	44.67	44.667	−1.667	46.333	100%

Change Point Detection for Airborne Particulate Matter (PM2.5, PM10) by using the Bayesian Approach

Table 13. PM_{10} Change Point (k) for European, American and Korean Standards.

Area Seoul, South Korea	(θ) Rate before Change Point	(λ) Rate after Change Point	K Change Point	Bayesian Approach for Change Point Detection					
				$\sqrt{R}\theta$ Convergence Parameter for (θ)	$Var(V)\theta$ Variance for (θ)	$\sqrt{R}\lambda$ Convergence Parameter for (λ)	$Var(V)\lambda$ Variance for (λ)	$\sqrt{R}K$ Convergence Parameter for K	$Var(V)K$ Variance for K
European standards									
Guro	14.73	9.20	85.46	1.000072	0.425	1.000427	0.925	0.999931	64.845
Nowon	14.93	8.36	67.12	0.999879	0.464	0.999925	0.327	1.000040	3.184
Songpa	16.08	9.46	53.50	1.000300	0.643	1.001282	0.310	1.003363	9.133
Yongsan	14.56	8.43	89.74	1.000123	0.597	1.000437	1.492	1.001094	75.750
American standards									
Guro	0.63	0.12	90.34	0.999840	0.009	1.000320	0.005	1.002821	31.264
Nowon	0.62	0.11	73.80	1.041187	0.173	1.036355	0.011	1.053574	1089.508
Songpa	0.56	0.07	88.16	1.000135	0.016	1.000253	0.037	1.000710	174.232
Yongsan	0.66	0.04	91.36	0.999851	0.016	1.000296	0.004	1.000219	32.243
Korean standards									
Guro	2.89	0.90	85.98	1.000820	0.046	1.001576	0.053	1.003429	59.252
Nowon	2.91	0.89	65.68	0.999881	0.045	1.000137	0.016	1.000338	0.567
Songpa	3.16	1.09	52.75	0.999935	0.066	1.000075	0.017	1.001445	7.194
Yongsan	3.31	1.10	68.06	1.002209	0.077	1.003709	0.050	1.004787	81.344

Table 14. PM_{10} Last point before change (k) and First point after change ($k+1$) for European, American and Korean Standards through CUSUM approach.

Area Seoul, South Korea	(θ) Average Rate before Change	(λ) Average Rate after Change	K Last point before Change	$k+1$ First Point after Change	$\lvert S_m \rvert$ Most Extreme Point	S_{max} Highest Point in CUSUM	S_{min} Lowest Point in CUSUM	S_{diff} Magnitude of Change	Confidence Level %
European standards									
Guro	15.05	9.79	77	78	145.17	145.167	−0.833	146.000	100%
Nowon	14.97	8.32	67	68	196.77	196.767	−2.967	199.733	100%
Songpa	16.15	9.46	53	54	197.92	197.917	−1.583	199.500	100%
Yongsan	15.01	9.53	77	78	151.15	151.150	−1.950	153.100	100%
American standards									
Guro	0.64	0.10	89	90	12.50	12.500	−2.000	14.500	100%
Nowon	0.51	0.16	63	64	10.48	10.475	0.000	10.475	80%
Songpa	0.70	0.19	53	54	14.92	14.917	−5.833	20.750	100%
Yongsan	0.67	0.00	89	90	15.50	15.500	−0.500	16.000	10%
Korean standards									
Guro	3.20	1.32	64	65	56.20	56.200	−0.675	56.875	100%
Nowon	2.91	0.87	66	67	60.55	60.550	−1.008	61.558	100%
Songpa	3.19	1.09	52	53	62.00	62.000	−4.000	66.000	100%
Yongsan	3.39	1.16	64	65	66.60	66.600	−0.650	67.250	100%

CUSUM Approach for Change Point Detection

6. Disussion

As the results of two different approaches have been described in the previous section.

1. Bayesian approach is based on probability distributions, which can be applicable on any kind of data distribution. In this case, firstly data distributions are defined and then proposed method is applied to acquire the results. This approach is better to apply for random data structures and time series.
2. CUSUM Approach is directly applied on the raw data, which is good for deterministic data structures.

6.1. Guro (Seoul, South Korea)

Guro is located in the southwestern part of Seoul, and has an important position as a transport link which includes railroads and land routes. The largest digital industrial complex in Korea is also positioned in Guro, centering on research and development activities as well as advanced information and knowledge industries. That is why, the policies of the Ministry of Environment in South Korea have influenced the concentrations of particulate matters ($PM_{2.5}$ and PM_{10}) in Guro and rate of polluted days has reduced in any of the cases.

6.1.1. Bayesian Approach

Bayesian method is better to apply for random time series data. If we look in case of Guro, Table 11 indicates that for $PM_{2.5}$ change-point (k) of polluted days were 43.18, 33.62, and 38.26 according to European, American, and Korean standards respectively. Therefore, a change occurred in the rate of polluted days, but it varied according to standards. At the minimum, the rate of polluted days ($\theta = 15.99$) was reduced 30.14% and the maximum reduction ($\theta = 3.56$) to ($\lambda = 1.63$) was 54.21% in the case of Korean standards. Similarly, Table 13 refers to the reduction of polluted days (θ) to (λ) for PM_{10} after change point (k) which were 85.46, 90.34, and 85.98 according to European, American, and Korean standards, respectively. Moreover, the decrease in the rate of polluted days ($\theta = 14.73$) to ($\lambda = 9.20$) was at least 37.54% for European standards, but it was 80.95% in the case of American standards. Figures 18 and 19 graphically represent the replications of monthly polluted days before and after the change point which are discussed in Tables 9 and 10.

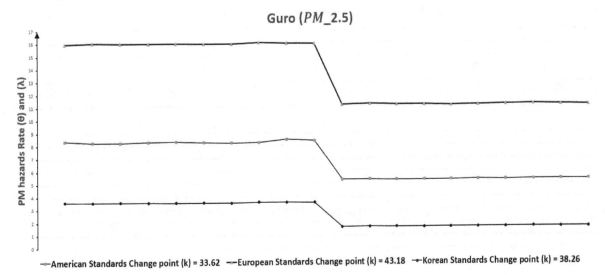

Figure 18. Guro (Seoul, South Korea) monthly polluted days before and after the change point due to $PM_{2.5}$.

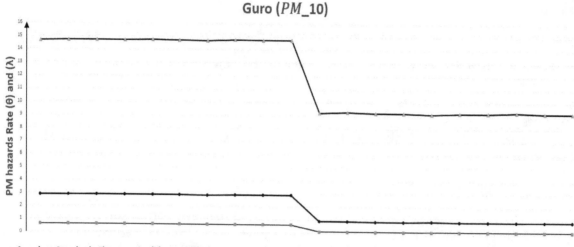

Figure 19. Guro (Seoul, South Korea) monthly polluted days before and after the change point due to PM_{10}.

6.1.2. CUSUM Approach

CUSUM Approach also indicates a reduction in hazards rate from (θ) to (λ) after change. As for Guro, Table 12 also represents the change of $PM_{2.5}$ polluted days through CUSUM approach, which shows that change point occurred between point 40 (k) and 41 ($k + 1$) for European standards, between point 36 (k) and 37 ($k + 1$) for American standards and it lies in-between point 35 (k) and 36 ($k + 1$) for Korean standards. While Table 14 indicates the change of PM_{10} polluted days through CUSUM approach with an indication of change point lies between point 77 (k) and 78 ($k + 1$) for European standards, point 89 (k) and 90 ($k + 1$) for American standards and point 64 (k) and 65 ($k + 1$) for Korean standards.

6.2. Nowon (Seoul, South Korea)

Nowon is located in the northeastern part of the city, and has the highest population density in Seoul with 619,509 persons living in 35.44 km², which is surrounded by mountains and forests on the northeast. The policies of the Ministry of Environment in Nowon have improved the rate of polluted days for $PM_{2.5}$ and PM_{10} hazards from θ to λ. Improvement in the reduction of polluted days varies case to case.

6.2.1. Bayesian Approach

Correspondingly, in case of Nowon, Table 11 depicts that change point (k) of polluted days for $PM_{2.5}$ were 49.95, 41.83, and 50.34 according to European, American, and Korean standards respectively. Particularly for this case, the change point was the same according to European and Korean standards, but varied for American standards. The rate of polluted days ($\theta = 15.88$) for European standards showed a minimum decrease of 35.14% after the change point and approached ($\lambda = 10.30$), but the maximum decrease was for Korean standards which was 67.65% with ($\theta = 3.74$) and ($\lambda = 1.21$). In the same manner, when we study Table 13, it elaborates that for PM_{10}, again there was a reduction in the rate of polluted days after change point (k) of 67.12, 73.80, and 65.68 to European, American, and Korean standards, respectively. That is comparable in cases of European and Korean standards, but a bit different for American standards. In addition, the reduction in the rate of polluted days for the European standard was at least 44.01% from ($\theta = 14.93$) to ($\lambda = 8.36$), while the maximum reduction was ($\theta = 0.62$) to ($\lambda = 0.11$) 82.25% for American standards. Figures 20 and 21 graphically represent the replications of monthly polluted days before and after the change point which are given in Tables 9 and 10.

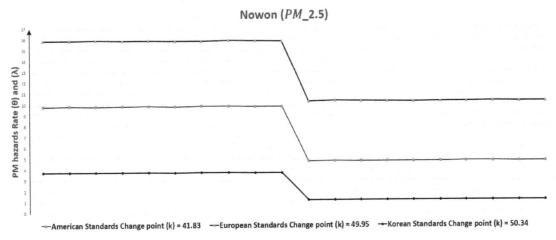

Figure 20. Nowon (Seoul, South Korea) monthly polluted days before and after the change point due to $PM_{2.5}$.

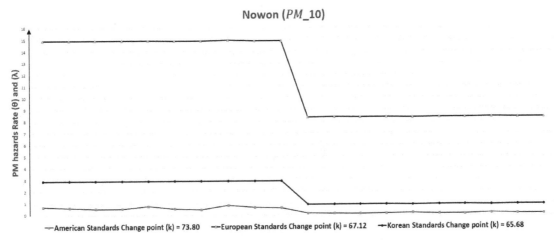

Figure 21. Nowon (Seoul, South Korea) monthly polluted days before and after the change point due to PM_{10}.

6.2.2. CUSUM Approach

Moreover, CUSUM Approach also validates the reduction of PM hazards. In case of Nowon, Table 12 represents the change of $PM_{2.5}$ polluted days through CUSUM approach, which shows that change point occurred between point 53 (k) and 54 ($k+1$) for European standards, between point 41 (k) and 42 ($k+1$) for American standards and it lies in-between point 50 (k) and 51 ($k+1$) for Korean standards. While Table 14 indicates the change of PM_{10} polluted days through CUSUM approach with an indication of change point lies between point 67 (k) and 68 ($k+1$) for European standards, point 63 (k) and 64 ($k+1$) for American standards and point 66 (k) and 67 ($k+1$) for Korean standards.

6.3. Songpa (Seoul, South Korea)

Songpa is located at the southeastern part of Seoul, and has largest population, with 647,000 residents. As per Ministry of Environment policies in Songpa, there is a smaller reduction for the rate of polluted days (θ) to (λ) as compared to Guro and Nowon, but still there is a significant reduction in PM hazards.

6.3.1. Bayesian Approach

Now for Songpa, we can check from Table 11 that change point (k) of polluted days for $PM_{2.5}$ were 53.85, 53.32, and 56.44 for European, American, and Korean standards respectively, which were all similar. The reduction in rate of polluted days was at least 24.50% for European Standards ($\theta = 14.90$)

to ($\lambda = 11.25$) while it was highest for Korean standards at 47.77% with ($\theta = 3.14$) and ($\lambda = 1.64$). Correspondingly, we can also inspect the improvement in the rate of polluted days from (θ) to (λ) for PM_{10} after change point (k) in Table 13. Change point (k) for the rate of polluted days due to PM_{10} concentration were 53.50, 88.16, and 52.75 according to European, American and Korean standards respectively, which was the same for European and Korean standards. The slightest improvement 41.17% has been in the case of European standards and ($\theta = 16.08$) is converted to ($\lambda = 9.46$). On the other hand, if we look at American standards, the rate of polluted days ($\theta = 0.56$) was already low which further decreased 87.5% to ($\lambda = 0.07$). Hence, this area is almost a meeting of the PM_{10} concentration requirements for American standards but not for other standards. Figures 22 and 23 graphically represent the replications of monthly polluted days before and after the change point which are given in Tables 9 and 10.

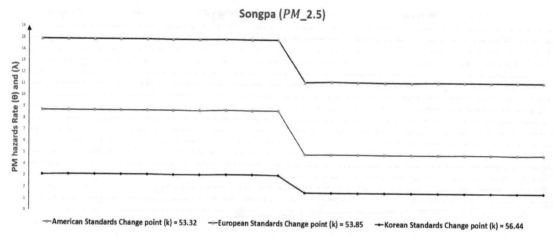

Figure 22. Songpa (Seoul, South Korea) monthly polluted days before and after the change point due to $PM_{2.5}$.

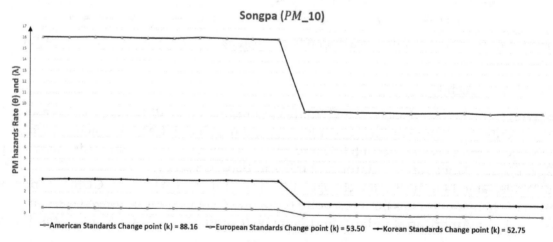

Figure 23. Songpa (Seoul, South Korea) monthly polluted days before and after the change point due to PM_{10}.

6.3.2. CUSUM Approach

As per CUSUM Approach, there is a decrease in PM hazards. Table 12 also represents the change of $PM_{2.5}$ polluted days through CUSUM approach, which shows that change point occurred between point 53 (k) and 54 ($k+1$) for European standards, between point 52 (k) and 53 ($k+1$) for American standards and it lies in-between point 52 (k) and 53 ($k+1$) for Korean standards. While Table 14 indicates the change of PM_{10} polluted days through CUSUM approach with an indication of change point lies between point 53 (k) and 54 ($k+1$) for European standards, point 53 (k) and 54 ($k+1$) for American standards and point 52 (k) and 53 ($k+1$) for Korean standards.

6.4. Yongsan (Seoul, South Korea)

Yongsan is a place in the center of Seoul in which almost 250,000 people reside. Prominent locations in Yongsan includes Yongsan station, electronic market and Itaewon commercial area with heavy traffic and transportation. Consequently, the policies of the Ministry of Environment in Yongsan has affected the particulate matter ($PM_{2.5}$ and PM_{10}) concentrations more than all the previous three locations (Guro, Nowon and Songpa). There is a remarkable decrease in rate of polluted days from (θ) to (λ).

6.4.1. Bayesian Approach

Similarly, in the case of Yongsan, Tables 11 and 13 tell us that the rate of polluted days (θ) for particulate matters ($PM_{2.5}$ and PM_{10}) was the highest in Seoul. The change occurred for $PM_{2.5}$ with the change point (k) 7.94, 6.18, and 5.78 with respect to European, American and Korean standards respectively, which was comparable for all the three standards. There was minimally a 50.71% fall in the rate of polluted days (θ = 24.55) to (λ = 12.10) for European standards, but the reduction in rate of polluted days was a maximum of 74.18% in the case of Korean standards. On the same note, Table 13 indicates that the change in the rate of polluted days has also occurred for PM_{10} concentrations. The change point (k) for it were 89.74, 91.36, and 68.06 for European, American and Korean standards, respectively. Furthermore, at least 42.10% rate of polluted days (θ = 14.56) was reduced to (λ = 8.43) for European standards but its maximum decrease was 93.93% for American standards (θ = 0.66) to (λ = 0.04), although, it is already approaching the requirements of this standard. Figures 24 and 25 graphically represent the replications of monthly polluted days before and after the change point which are given in Tables 9 and 10.

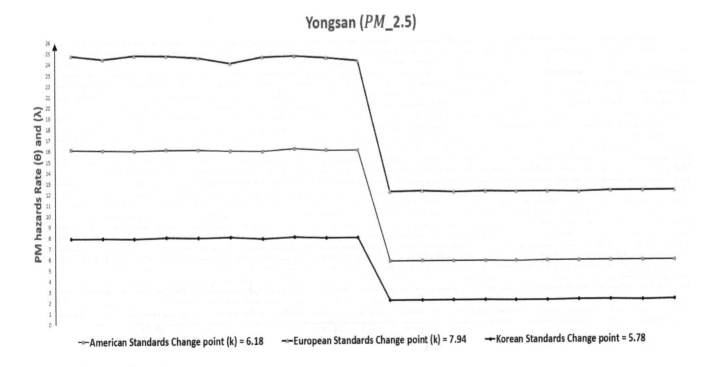

Figure 24. Yongsan (Seoul, South Korea) monthly polluted days before and after the change point due to $PM_{2.5}$.

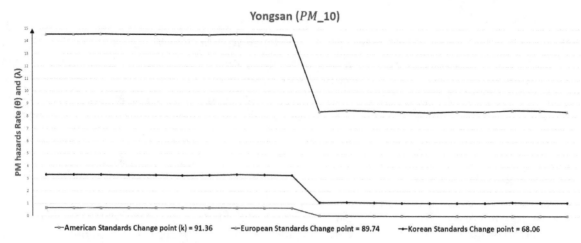

Figure 25. Yongsan (Seoul, South Korea) monthly polluted days before and after the change point due to PM_{10}.

6.4.2. CUSUM Approach

CUSUM Approach is directly applied on the raw data, which should be better for deterministic data structures. It also shows a reduction in PM hazards. In case of Yongsan, Table 12 also represents the change of $PM_{2.5}$ polluted days through CUSUM approach, which shows that change point occurred between point 11 (k) and 12 ($k+1$) for European standards, between point 64 (k) and 65 ($k+1$) for American standards and it lies in-between point 64 (k) and 65 ($k+1$) for Korean standards. While Table 14 indicates the change of PM_{10} polluted days through CUSUM approach with an indication of change point lies between point 77 (k) and 78 ($k+1$) for European standards, point 89 (k) and 90 ($k+1$) for American standards and point 64 (k) and 65 ($k+1$) for Korean standards.

6.5. Strengths

1. This approach is very precise, well defined, user friendly and easily understandable for applications on probability distributions, time series and random data.
2. The above mentioned model is an appropriate approach for detection of change points in random data structures.
3. Good technique for evaluation of process control programs by comparing the parameters before and after change point.

6.6. Limitations

1. Detection of only single change point is given in this model.
2. Further extension is required by making a model for a multiple number of change points for locating changed segments.

6.7. Managerial Insights

1. This model presents a suitable technique to analyze the air quality and pollutant hazards in the air.
2. By detecting change points in particulate matter ($PM_{2.5}$ and PM_{10}) concentrations and analyzing the occurrences of polluted days before and after a change point, environmental protection agencies can understand the role of their legislation efforts, and whether these change points are favorable or not for the environment.
3. A comparison of particulate matter hazards before and after a change point evaluates a pollution control program adopted by environmental protection agencies to make a decision. If these policies need further revision or not for the reduction of death rates and burden of diseases due airborne particulate matter concentrations in the air.

4. This study of pollutant hazards also defines the current levels of subjected air pollutant in the air which is helpful to make new pollution control policies for further improvements.

5. This research also brings an intuition to define new goals if previously defined goals have been achieved and also provides a vision if the environmental standards need to be revised, or not to overcome environmental challenges.

7. Conclusions

The main focus of this research work was to elucidate an appropriate change point detection model for occurrences of pollutant hazards due to higher concentrations of particulate matter ($PM_{2.5}$ and PM_{10}) in different locations. The rate of pollutant hazards before and after a change point was also estimated comprehensively to investigate the effectiveness of policies applied by the Ministry of Environment. To verify the model, four major locations (Guro, Nowon, Songpa, and Yongsan) in Seoul, South Korea were selected as study areas due to their different characteristics, such as climate zones, environment, populations and population densities. Three different environmental standards (European, American and Korean) were chosen as threshold values. Then, the model was applied to real time data sets in all cases and conclusions were drawn. The rate before and after the change point of particulate matter concentrations indicated a reduction in polluted days over a 10-year period. The overall results of our study confirm the effective role of legislation efforts used consistently to improve the air quality through the years but pollutant hazards still exist. Hence, further improvements are required to meet set standards to nullify hazards. This study can be further extended by making a multi-parameter change point model for a multiple number of change points considering the fact that different data structures follow different probability distributions.

Author Contributions: Conceptualization, Muhammad Rizwan Khan (M.R.K.) and Biswajit Sarkar (B.S.); methodology, M.R.K.; software, M.R.K.; validation, M.R.K. and B.S.; formal analysis, M.R.K.; investigation, M.R.K.; resources, M.R.K. and B.S.; data curation, M.R.K. and B.S.; writing—original draft preparation, M.R.K.; writing—review and editing, B.S.; visualization, M.R.K. and B.S.; supervision, B.S.; project administration, M.R.K. and B.S.; funding acquisition, B.S.

References

1. Héroux, M.E.; Anderson, H.R.; Atkinson, R.; Brunekreef, B.; Cohen, A.; Forastiere, F.; Hurley, F.; Katsouyanni, K.; Krewski, D.; Krzyzanowski, M.; et al. Quantifying the health impacts of ambient air pollutants: recommendations of a WHO/Europe project. *Int. J. Public Health* **2015**, *60*, 619–627. [CrossRef] [PubMed]

2. Pope, C.A.; Burnett, R.T.; Thurston, G.D.; Thun, M.J.; Calle, E.E.; Krewski, D.; Godleski, J.J. Cardiovascular mortality and long-term exposure to particulate air pollution: Epidemiological evidence of general pathophysiological pathways of disease. *Circulation* **2004**, *109*, 71–77. [CrossRef] [PubMed]

3. Gyarmati-Szabó, J.; Bogachev, L.V.; Chen, H. Modelling threshold exceedances of air pollution concentrations via non-homogeneous Poisson process with multiple change-points. *Atmos. Environ.* **2011**, *45*, 5493–5503. [CrossRef]

4. Pirani, M.; Best, N.; Blangiardo, M.; Liverani, S.; Atkinson, R.W.; Fuller, G.W. Analysing the health effects of simultaneous exposure to physical and chemical properties of airborne particles. *Environ. Int.* **2015**, *79*, 56–64. [CrossRef] [PubMed]

5. Welty, L.J.; Peng, R.; Zeger, S.; Dominici, F. Bayesian distributed lag models: Estimating effects of particulate matter air pollution on daily mortality. *Biometrics* **2009**, *65*, 282–291. [CrossRef]

6. Qin, S.; Liu, F.; Wang, J.; Sun, B. Analysis and forecasting of the particulate matter (PM) concentration levels over four major cities of China using hybrid models. *Atmos. Environ.* **2014**, *98*, 665–675. [CrossRef]

7. Keshavarz, H.; Scott, C.; Nguyen, X. Optimal change point detection in Gaussian processes. *J. Stat. Plan. Inference* **2018**, *193*, 151–178. [CrossRef]

8. Kucharczyk, D.; Wyłomańska, A.; Sikora, G. Variance change point detection for fractional Brownian motion based on the likelihood ratio test. *Phys. Stat. Mech. Its Appl.* **2018**, *490*, 439–450. [CrossRef]

9. Lu, G.; Zhou, Y.; Lu, C.; Li, X. A novel framework of change-point detection for machine monitoring. *Mech. Syst. Signal Process.* **2017**, *83*, 533–548. [CrossRef]

10. Taleizadeh, A.A.; Samimi, H.; Sarkar, B.; Mohammadi, B. Stochastic machine breakdown and discrete delivery in an imperfect inventory-production system. *J. Ind. Manag. Optim.* **2017**, *13*, 1511–1535. [CrossRef]

11. Liu, S.; Yamada, M.; Collier, N.; Sugiyama, M. Change-point detection in time-series data by relative density-ratio estimation. *Neural Netw.* **2013**, *43*, 72–83. [CrossRef]

12. Hilgert, N.; Verdier, G.; Vila, J.P. Change detection for uncertain autoregressive dynamic models through nonparametric estimation. *Stat. Methodol.* **2016**, *33*, 96–113. [CrossRef]

13. Górecki, T.; Horváth, L.; Kokoszka, P. Change point detection in heteroscedastic time series. *Econom. Stat.* **2018**, *7*, 63–88. [CrossRef]

14. Bucchia, B.; Wendler, M. Change-point detection and bootstrap for Hilbert space valued random fields. *J. Multivar. Anal.* **2017**, *155*, 344–368. [CrossRef]

15. Shin, D.; Guchhait, R.; Sarkar, B.; Mittal, M. Controllable lead time, service level constraint, and transportation discounts in a continuous review inventory model. *RAIRO-Oper. Res.* **2016**, *50*, 921–934. [CrossRef]

16. Zhou, M.; Wang, H.J.; Tang, Y. Sequential change point detection in linear quantile regression models. *Stat. Probab. Lett.* **2015**, *100*, 98–103. [CrossRef]

17. Lu, K.P.; Chang, S.T. Detecting change-points for shifts in mean and variance using fuzzy classification maximum likelihood change-point algorithms. *J. Comput. Appl. Math.* **2016**, *308*, 447–463. [CrossRef]

18. Sarkar, B.; Saren, S. Partial trade-credit policy of retailer with exponentially deteriorating items. *Int. J. Appl. Comput. Math.* **2015**, *1*, 343–368. [CrossRef]

19. Ruggieri, E.; Antonellis, M. An exact approach to Bayesian sequential change point detection. *Comput. Stat. Data Anal.* **2016**, *97*, 71–86. [CrossRef]

20. Keshavarz, M.; Huang, B. Bayesian and Expectation Maximization methods for multivariate change point detection. *Comput. Chem. Eng.* **2014**, *60*, 339–353. [CrossRef]

21. Kurt, B.; Yıldız, Ç.; Ceritli, T.Y.; Sankur, B.; Cemgil, A.T. A Bayesian change point model for detecting SIP-based DDoS attacks. *Digit. Signal Process.* **2018**, *77*, 48–62. [CrossRef]

22. Wu, C.; Du, B.; Cui, X.; Zhang, L. A post-classification change detection method based on iterative slow feature analysis and Bayesian soft fusion. *Remote. Sens. Environ.* **2017**, *199*, 241–255. [CrossRef]

23. Mariño, I.P.; Blyuss, O.; Ryan, A.; Gentry-Maharaj, A.; Timms, J.F.; Dawnay, A.; Kalsi, J.; Jacobs, I.; Menon, U.; Zaikin, A. Change-point of multiple biomarkers in women with ovarian cancer. *Biomed. Signal Process. Control.* **2017**, *33*, 169–177. [CrossRef]

24. Jeon, J.J.; Sung, J.H.; Chung, E.S. Abrupt change point detection of annual maximum precipitation using fused lasso. *J. Hydrol.* **2016**, *538*, 831–841. [CrossRef]

25. Chen, S.; Li, Y.; Kim, J.; Kim, S.W. Bayesian change point analysis for extreme daily precipitation. *Int. J. Climatol.* **2017**, *37*, 3123–3137. [CrossRef]

26. Gupta, A.; Baker, J.W. Estimating spatially varying event rates with a change point using Bayesian statistics: Application to induced seismicity. *Struct. Saf.* **2017**, *65*, 1–11. [CrossRef]

27. Bardwell, L.; Fearnhead, P. Bayesian detection of abnormal segments in multiple time series. *Bayesian Anal.* **2017**, *12*, 193–218. [CrossRef]

28. Lim, S.S.; Vos, T.; Flaxman, A.D.; Danaei, G.; Shibuya, K.; Adair-Rohani, H.; AlMazroa, M.A.; Amann, M.; Anderson, H.R.; Andrews, K.G.; et al. A comparative risk assessment of burden of disease and injury attributable to 67 risk factors and risk factor clusters in 21 regions, 1990–2010: A systematic analysis for the Global Burden of Disease Study 2010. *Lancet* **2012**, *380*, 2224–2260. [CrossRef]

29. Rao, X.; Zhong, J.; Brook, R.D.; Rajagopalan, S. Effect of particulate matter air pollution on cardiovascular oxidative stress pathways. *Antioxid. Redox Signal.* **2018**, *28*, 797–818. [CrossRef]

30. Wei, T.; Meng, T. Biological Effects of Airborne Fine Particulate Matter (PM2.5) Exposure on Pulmonary Immune System. *Environ. Toxicol. Pharmacol.* **2018**, *60*, 195–201. [CrossRef]

31. Wang, Y.; Xiong, L.; Tang, M. Toxicity of inhaled particulate matter on the central nervous system: neuroinflammation, neuropsychological effects and neurodegenerative disease. *J. Appl. Toxicol.* **2017**, *37*, 644–667. [CrossRef]

32. Wellenius, G.A.; Burger, M.R.; Coull, B.A.; Schwartz, J.; Suh, H.H.; Koutrakis, P.; Schlaug, G.; Gold, D.R.; Mittleman, M.A. Ambient air pollution and the risk of acute ischemic stroke. *Arch. Intern. Med.* **2012**, *172*, 229–234. [CrossRef]

33. Li, P.; Xin, J.; Wang, Y.; Wang, S.; Shang, K.; Liu, Z.; Li, G.; Pan, X.; Wei, L.; Wang, M. Time-series analysis of mortality effects from airborne particulate matter size fractions in Beijing. *Atmos. Environ.* **2013**, *81*, 253–262. [CrossRef]

34. Kim, S.E.; Bell, M.L.; Hashizume, M.; Honda, Y.; Kan, H.; Kim, H. Associations between mortality and prolonged exposure to elevated particulate matter concentrations in East Asia. *Environ. Int.* **2018**, *110*, 88–94. [CrossRef]

35. Kim, S.E.; Honda, Y.; Hashizume, M.; Kan, H.; Lim, Y.H.; Lee, H.; Kim, C.T.; Yi, S.M.; Kim, H. Seasonal analysis of the short-term effects of air pollution on daily mortality in Northeast Asia. *Sci. Total Environ.* **2017**, *576*, 850–857. [CrossRef]

36. Qin, R.X.; Xiao, C.; Zhu, Y.; Li, J.; Yang, J.; Gu, S.; Xia, J.; Su, B.; Liu, Q.; Woodward, A. The interactive effects between high temperature and air pollution on mortality: A time-series analysis in Hefei, China. *Sci. Total Environ.* **2017**, *575*, 1530–1537. [CrossRef]

37. Lee, H.; Honda, Y.; Hashizume, M.; Guo, Y.L.; Wu, C.F.; Kan, H.; Jung, K.; Lim, Y.H.; Yi, S.; Kim, H. Short-term exposure to fine and coarse particles and mortality: A multicity time-series study in East Asia. *Environ. Pollut.* **2015**, *207*, 43–51. [CrossRef]

38. Cabrieto, J.; Tuerlinckx, F.; Kuppens, P.; Wilhelm, F.H.; Liedlgruber, M.; Ceulemans, E. Capturing correlation changes by applying kernel change point detection on the running correlations. *Inf. Sci.* **2018**, *447*, 117–139. [CrossRef]

11

Dynamic Pricing in a Multi-Period Newsvendor under Stochastic Price-Dependent Demand

Mehran Ullah, Irfanullah Khan and Biswajit Sarkar *

Department of Industrial & Management Engineering, Hanyang University, Ansan, Gyeonggi-do 155 88, Korea;
mehrandirvi@gmail.com (M.U.); irfanullah13@outlook.com (I.K.)
* Correspondence: bsbiswajitsarkar@gmail.com.

Abstract: The faster growth of technology stipulates the rapid development of new products; with the spread of new technologies old ones are outdated and their market demand declines sharply. The combined impact of demand uncertainty and short life-cycles complicate ordering and pricing decision of retailers that leads to a decrease in the profit. This study deals with the joint inventory and dynamic pricing policy for such products considering stochastic price-dependent demand. The aim is to develop a discount policy that enables the retailer to order more at the start of the selling season thus increase the profit and market share of the retailer. A multi-period newsvendor model is developed under the distribution-free approach and the optimal stocking quantities, unit selling price, and the discount percentage are obtained. The results show that the proposed discount policy increases the expected profit of the system. Additionally, the stocking quantity and the unit selling price also increases in the proposed discount policy. The robustness of the proposed model is illustrated with numerical examples and sensitivity analysis. Managerial insights are given to extract significant insights for the newsvendor model with discount policy.

Keywords: price discounts; stochastic-price dependent demand; newsvendor; pricing policy

1. Introduction

In today's competitive economic environment, fluctuation in market demand is causing problems for businesses, especially those who are dealing with products having short life cycles. The example includes apparel products, fashion goods, seasonal clothing, personal computers, and other electronic goods. Demand uncertainty either leads to stock outs or overstocking; the short life cycles, further, aggravates the severity of the problem. In such situations, an important question arises: How to deal with these uncertain items? The newsvendor model offers a solution to such problems, in which the decision maker faces stochastic and exogenous demand. The newsvendor has to decide the order quantity ahead of the selling season by using the available information. The aim is to find the trade-off between overstocking and under-stocking conditions. In the classical newsvendor problem, the common practice is to dispose of the product at a salvage price considering no discount during the selling season. However, the past 30 years has reshaped the landscape of the retail industry; retailers prefer to avoid the stock outs by ordering larger lot sizes, and a discount is offered on the remaining stock at the end of the selling season. This increases the market share of the retailer because a strategic consumer waits patiently and buys the product when the price drops. This paper deals with such a business problem, in which the consumer can switch to alternative options with discounted prices; the retailer decides the lot size, finished products price, and the discount percentage on the price of the finished product at the end of the selling season.

As demand is selling price dependent, reducing the price, at the end of the selling season, increases the net demand. Moreover, in these strategic situations, the firms make decisions considering pricing and stocking. The retailer who deals in short-life-cycle/seasonal items faces stochastic demand and information on demand distribution is limited; however, the newsvendor has only an educated guess of the mean and variance of the demand. To find the optimal inventory level normal distribution of demand is employed; although, this does not provide the best performance compared to other distributions with the same mean and variance. Scarf [1] first addressed the distribution-free newsboy problem where mean and variance of demand were given, whereas the demand distribution assumption was not available. Considering the distribution-free approach, Scarf [1] developed a model for the optimal ordering quantity to get the maximum expected profit with the worst possible distribution of the demand. The min–max distribution-free approach developed by Scarf is good but is complex and difficult to understand. This problem was solved by Gallego and Moon [2], where they simplified Scarf's ordering rule for the newsboy problem.

This paper extends the classical newsvendor distribution-free model; the seller offers a progressive discount to generate more revenue. This model considers a retailer who is selling seasonal items and facing a stochastic demand. The retailer has only one opportunity to place the order before the start of the selling season. Reorders are not possible during the season; because the lead time is longer than the selling season. The newsboy takes the ordering decision based on historical data, which may possess high variance to the demand. In the classical newsvendor model, the selling price is assumed constant throughout the selling season, which prevents the retailer from generating revenue by price adjustment. This model is more realistic because it provides a price adjustment policy, which helps in generating extra revenue. This model specifically answers the following questions. What selling price should the retailer choose? How much to order considering the discounted policy later? And how much discount percent must the retailer offer at the end of the season?

The remainder of this paper is assembled as follows. In Section 2, this paper reviews the relevant literature. Section 3 provides notation and develops the mathematical model. Section 4 tests the developed model with numerical examples and provides a sensitivity analysis. In Section 5, the paper is concluded.

2. Literature Review

In this section we provide a summary of the relevant literature. This paper directly contributes to three streams of research, namely newsvendor models, price dependent stochastic demand, and price discounts in newsvendor. Therefore, relevant papers were reviewed in this section.

The classical newsboy problem is designed to find the optimal quantity of the items in a single period, probabilistic framework. The aim of calculating order quantity is to minimize the expected cost of overestimating and underestimating the probabilistic demand in the selling season. The newsboy problem has gained considerable attention since the pioneering paper of Arrow et al. [2]. Scarf [1] developed the min–max distribution-free procedure to calculate the optimal order quantity with only the mean and variance. Scarf proved the worst distribution of demand would be positive at two points. Gallego and Moon [3] simplified the proof of Scarf [1], the Scarf rule consists of a lengthy mathematical argument and is difficult to understand for researchers and managers. Anvari [4] maximizes the market value of the firm using the capital asset pricing model. An extensive literature review on the newsvendor problem can be found in the literature, for example in Khouja [5]. Bitran and Mondschein [6] dealt with seasonal items, they also developed a pricing policy based on time and inventory. As most of the newsvendor models deal with profit maximization, however, a few models deal with the probability of exceeding a specified minimum profit, as in Lau [7] and Parlar and Kevin Weng [8]. Sarkar [9] considered a service level constraint and variable lead time with the min–max distribution free approach, Sarkar [10] considered distribution-free approach with buyback contracts.

There exists an enormous amount of literature concerning the extension of the classical newsvendor model [11,12]. The comparison of applying the normal distribution and the scenario of the distribution-free approach (only mean and variance of the demand is available) with discounts is given by Moon et al. [13]; however, they did not consider price dependent demand, furthermore, their model is of a single period while this paper considered a multi period newsvendor problem. The consignment policy is considered in Sarkar et al. [14] in a single-period newsvendor problem with the distribution-free approach and retailer cost is reduced by the sustainable consignment contract. The classical inventory problem is extended by Kogan and Lou [15] to the multi-stage newsboy problem; further, they divided product flow into sequential stages for the reduction in underage or overage costs at the end-of-season. Matsuyama [16] considers a multi-period inventory problem; in their model, the ordering quantity is divided into many cycles, and if the inventory of the present cycle did not match that will affect the next cycle. The effect of coordination on stocking and pricing for two consecutive periods was studied by Lee [17], he analyzed a normal sales period and a leftover markdown sales period. Chen et al. [18] considers a multi-period supply chain model where the supplier is selling products to a multi-period newsvendor and calculated the optimal pricing for the supplier.

Petruzzi and Dada [19] argue that demand is price dependent in the newsvendor model, Khouja [20] developed the price-dependent demand policy and proved the concavity of the newsvendor problem. Arcelus et al. [21] considered the ordering policies in a newsvendor framework with a stochastic price-dependent demand. The classical single-period newsvendor model is extended in Chung et al. [22] with a price adjustment for the retailer in-season after receiving the demand; however, they assumed demand follows a normal distribution while this paper did not assume any distribution for the demand. Banerjee and Meitei [23] studied the effect of the selling price reduction and analyzed the optimal ordering policy for a single period inventory model. The demand is a stochastic function of the selling price in Abad [24] and he used the service level constraint to avoid the economic consequences of a stock-out situation. The relationships of the purchasing cost, price-dependent stochastic demand, and salvage value are shown by Ma et al. [25], they studied impacts of discounted schemes on the expected profit in a single-period newsvendor framework. Arcelus et al. [26] considered risk tolerance in the newsvendor problem with a price-dependent demand, and Hu and Su [27] optimized newsvendor expected profit with joint procurement planning and a pricing procedure.

The additive and multiplicative demand cases under the behavior of the strategic consumer are studied in Ye and Sun [28] in the newsvendor problem. Arcelus et al. [29] evaluated the pricing and ordering policies of a newsvendor facing risk-averse, risk-neutral, and risk-seeking situations with price-dependent stochastic demand. In their paper, they offer three types of sales policy: Pricing, rebates, and advertising for additive and multiplicative demand structure. He et al. [30] investigated the channel coordination issue in the newsvendor framework with the stochastic price and sales effort dependent demand. A coordination contract is studied by Chen et al. [31] in a stochastic demand case for fashionable products concerning the supplier–retailer channel. In their model, the supplier allows a fixed capacity of production, and retailers are not allowed to change the demand after the demand is realized. A decentralized supply chain is investigated in Chen and Bell [32], in this study the retailer determines the price and order quantity while facing the stochastic price-dependent demand and returns from the customer. Jadidi et al. [33] considered a single period model with quantity discounts, a transportation capacity problem, and price-dependent stochastic demand. Modak and Kelle [34] examined the dual-channel supply chain considering a stochastic demand dependent on retailer price and delivery-time.

The uncertain demand in the newsboy problem creates the need for price setting, which can lead to revenue maximization that is accomplished by increasing total sales. The newsboy deals with the overstocking situation by introducing discounts at the end of the season, he must clear the maximum leftover inventory by offering discounts on sales. Khouja [20] introduces the concept of multiple discounts in the newsvendor model, he further elaborated that discounts are applicable on the products until these items remain on the shelf. Khouja [35] extended Khouja [20] by offering quantity discounts with multiple discounts in the single period inventory problem. Cachon and Kök [36] develop the newsvendor model with a clearance price, they also showed how much discount should be offered if the inventory is remaining at the end of the season. The clearance sales theory is expressed by Nocke and Peitz [37], in their model the selling price was originally high; however, at the end-of selling period, they reduced the price to clear the remaining inventory. The effect of discounts on gift cards is analyzed by Khouja et al. [38] in the newsvendor framework. A discrete-time model is developed by Gupta et al. [39] for deciding clearance prices in the single period inventory problem by setting a bound on prices and the expected revenue. Cachon and Kök [36] considered a newsvendor problem with clearance pricing: Before the start of the selling season demand is stochastic and exogenous, during the season demand is endogenous and deterministic in their model. The optimal values for order quantity are calculated in Ullah and Sarkar [40]. Jammernegg and Kischka [41] developed a procedure to calculate the optimal values of the order quantity, expected profit, and selling price in the newsvendor framework. Mandal et al. [42] elaborates on the consumers switch to the alternative option as soon as they realize the lower price; likewise, firms make their pricing and stocking decisions. Hu and Su [27] eliminated the assumption on salvage and considered a clearance price as a decision variable. The revision of the interval environment is considered in Ruidas et al. [43].

3. Mathematical Model

The newsboy deals in short lifecycle items, which become obsolete after some time, the demand reduces after the selling season and other products with better performance replace them. This paper develops a joint pricing and inventory model for a multi-period newsboy with price-dependent stochastic demand. The newsboy also offers a discount at the end of the period to increase its revenue and market share. No assumption on demand is considered except that demand belongs to a class φ of the probability distribution functions with a known mean and variance; where a distribution-free approach is applied to solve the model.

3.1. Proposed Model

A multi-period newsvendor model was developed based on joint stocking and pricing decisions under demand uncertainty. The decision maker decides the order quantity at the start of the selling season. The newsvendor offers a discount on leftover inventory at the end of the season to enhance the sales; inventory still left after the discounted sales will be salvage in the next selling season. The combine multi-period and discount policy provide multiple selling opportunities, which reduce the risk considering the overstocking and understocking situations in the newsvendor model. The newsvendor is facing a price-dependent stochastic demand of the form $d_i(p, X) = a(p) + X_i$. The demand comprises of two components; the price dependent deterministic demand $(a(p))$ and random error (X_i), which is independent of the price; such type of demand considerations are common in the literature, for example see [19,41,44,45]. The deterministic price dependent demand is $a(p) = y - z * p$ that is linearly decreasing the function of the price p and it follows increasing the price elasticity (see [12,45,46]). Here y represents the market share and the z is the price sensitivity. The price dependent deterministic demand $a(p)$ is assumed to be positive. The stochastic price independent demand factor X_i, a random variable, is additive in nature because of the additive modeling framework. Further, the assumptions are considered that X_i follows a probability distribution function $f(X_i)$ and a cumulative probability distribution function $F(X_i)$ with mean μ_i and standard deviation σ_i.

The objective was to determine the stocking quantity (Q_i), selling price (p), and discount percentage (β) to maximize the expected profit of the newsvendor. The profit of the proposed system can be determined by calculating the revenue minus the total cost. In the proposed system, the revenue is obtained from three sources; selling finished products with price p, selling with discounted price $p(1 - \beta)$, and selling the leftover inventory from the previous period $((1 - \alpha(\beta))E(Q_{i-1} - d_{i-1})^+)$ with salvage value s. If the demand in the selling period does not exceed Q_i units, then the revenue is $pd_i(p, X)$, and the remaining units will be sold with a discount percentage β of the selling price (p). Otherwise the revenue is pQ_i, therefore, the total expected revenue, from selling with price p can be expressed as $pE(\min(Q_i, d_i))$. The cost consists of a purchasing cost cQ_i for Q_i units. The leftover after the discounted sales are held at a cost h per unit after the selling season that are salvaged in the next period with a salvage value s. Similarly, if the demand exceeds Q_i units, and the revenue is pQ_i, the shortage may arise and a penalty cost (b per unit) will be considered for the observed shortage. The profit for the multi-period newsvendor is the difference between the revenue generated $pE(\min(Q_i, d_i))$ and the cost incurred per item. The multi-period newsvendor expected profit function can be expressed as:

$$\pi = pE(\min(Q_i, d_i)) - cQ_i - bE(d_i - Q_i)^+ + \alpha(\beta)p(1 - \beta)E(Q_i - d_i)^+ - (1 - \alpha(\beta))hE(Q_i - d_i)^+ + s(1 - \alpha(\beta))E(Q_{i-1} - d_{i-1})^+. \tag{1}$$

In Equation (1) the first term $pE(\min(Q_i, d_i))$ is the expected profit generated from selling products with the full price. The second term is the purchase cost, the third term is the shortage cost, when the demand exceeds the order quantity, and the fourth term shows the expected revenue from discounted sales. As $E(Q_i - d_i)^+$ is the expected leftover after the end of season when the full price sales are completed, $\alpha(\beta)$ is the percentage of expected sales when the discount is offered. Where, $\alpha(\beta)$ is an increasing function of the discount percentage (β). $p(1 - \beta)$ shows the discounted price, thus, the total revenue from the discounted sales can be formulated as $(\alpha(\beta)p(1 - \beta)E(Q_i - d_i)^+)$. From the initial leftover $(E(Q_i - d_i)^+)$, $\alpha(\beta)$ percent is sold with a discount then $(1 - \alpha(\beta))$ percent remains after the discounted sales, for which the expected holding cost is $(1 - \alpha(\beta))hE(Q_i - d_i)^+$, and revenue from salvaging the expected leftover from the previous period is $s(1 - \alpha(\beta))E(Q_{i-1} - d_{i-1})^+$.

Where the discounted sales percentage $\alpha(\beta)$ is an increasing function of the discount percentage β (price), such that $\alpha(\beta) = \left(1 - e^{-\frac{\zeta*\beta}{\varrho}}\right)$. Where ζ and ϱ are the parameters; furthermore, $\alpha(\beta)$ shows a declining increment to increase in β and its behaviour is illustrated in Figure 1, when $\zeta = 0.2$ and $\varrho = 0.05$. Where, $\alpha(\beta)$ is a monotonically increasing function over β, as $\frac{\partial \alpha(\beta)}{\partial \beta} > 0$ and $\frac{\partial^2 \alpha(\beta)}{\partial \beta^2} < 0, \forall \beta$.

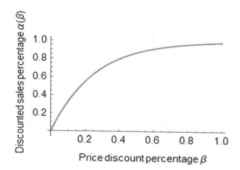

Figure 1. Discounted sales percentage plotted against the price discount percentage.

Observing that $\min(Q_i, d_i) = d_i - (d_i - Q_i)^+$, the expected profit can be written as,

$$\pi = pE(d_i) - cQ_i - (b + p)E(d_i - Q_i)^+ + (\alpha(\beta)p(1 - \beta) - (1 - \alpha(\beta))h)E(Q_i - d_i)^+ + (1 - \alpha(\beta))sE(Q_{i-1} - d_{i-1})^+. \tag{2}$$

As the newsvendor has partial (no distribution knowledge) information on demand, considering this situation, the expected leftover stock is $(Q_i - d_i)^+$ can be formulated as:

$$(Q_i - d_i)^+ = \frac{E|Q_i - d_i| + E(Q_i - d_i)}{2}. \tag{3}$$

By Cauchy Schwartz inequality:

$$E|Q_i - d_i| \leq \sqrt{E(Q_i - d_i)^2} = \sqrt{E(Q_i^2 - 2Q_i d_i + d_i^2)};$$

$$E|Q_i - d_i| \leq \sqrt{E(Q_i^2) - E(2Q_i d_i) + E(d_i^2)}. \tag{4}$$

The price dependent stochastic demand for period i is:

$$d_i = d_i(p, X).$$

The expected value of the price dependent stochastic price-dependent demand is equal to the expected value of random error plus the deterministic price dependent demand, which is greater than zero as:

$$E(d_i) = \mu_i + (a(p))^+.$$

The price dependent deterministic demand during the season is the maximum perceived cumulative deterministic (riskless) demand, i.e., market share plus the price sensitivity for the cumulative deterministic demand multiplied by price, such that:

$$a(p) = y - z * p.$$

Notice that:

$$E\left(Q_i^2\right) = (Q_i)^2,$$

and

$$E\left(d_i^2\right) = (\mu_i + a)^2 + \sigma_i^2.$$

Putting the values in inequality (4):

$$E|Q_i - d_i| \leq \sqrt{(Q_i)^2 - 2(Q_i)(\mu_i + a) + (\mu_i)^2 + \sigma_i^2}$$

$$= \sqrt{\sigma_i^2 + (Q_i)^2 - 2(Q_i)(\mu_i + a) + (\mu_i + a)^2}.$$

After simplification it can be written as:

$$E|Q_i - d_i| \leq \sqrt{\sigma_i^2 + \sigma_r^2 + (Q_i - \mu_i - a)^2}.$$

Putting the $E|Q_i - d_i|$ in Equation (3),

$$E(Q_i - d_i)^+ \leq \frac{1}{2}\left(\sqrt{\sigma_i^2 + (Q_i - \mu_i - a)^2} + (Q_i - \mu_i - a) \right).$$

Similarly, one can easily prove that,

$$E(d_i - Q_i)^+ \leq \frac{1}{2}\left(\sqrt{\sigma_i^2 + (\mu_i + a - Q_i)^2} - (Q_i - \mu_i - a) \right),$$

and

$$E(Q_{i-1} - d_{i-1})^+ \leq \frac{1}{2}\left(\sqrt{\sigma_{i-1}^2 + (Q_{i-1} - \mu_{i-1} - a)^2} + (Q_{i-1} - \mu_{i-1} - a) \right).$$

Utilizing these inequalities, the expected profit can be written as:

$$\pi = \sum_{i=1}^{n} \left(\begin{array}{l} p(\mu_i + a) - cQ_i - \frac{(b+p)}{2}\left(\sqrt{\sigma_i^2 + (\mu_i + a - Q_i)^2} - (Q_i - \mu_i - a) \right) \\ +\left(\left(1 - e^{-\frac{\zeta\beta}{\varrho}}\right)p(1 - \beta) - h\left(e^{-\frac{\zeta\beta}{\varrho}}\right)\right)\frac{1}{2}\left(\sqrt{\sigma_i^2 + (Q_i - \mu_i - a)^2} + (Q_i - \mu_i - a) \right) \\ +\left(e^{-\frac{\zeta\beta}{\varrho}}\right)\frac{s}{2}\left(\sqrt{\sigma_{i-1}^2 + (Q_{i-1} - \mu_{i-1} - a)^2} + (Q_{i-1} - \mu_{i-1} - a) \right) \end{array} \right). \tag{5}$$

3.2. Optimal Policies

Taking the first derivative of (5) with respect to Q_i, p, and β, and equating to zero the optimal values of Q_i^*, p^*, and β^* can be obtained, such that,

$$\frac{\partial \pi}{\partial Q_i} = \sum_{i=1}^{n}\left(-c + \frac{1}{2}\left(-e^{-\frac{\beta\zeta}{\varrho}}h + \left(1 - e^{-\frac{\beta\zeta}{\varrho}}\right)p(1-\beta)\right)\left(1 + \frac{-y+pz+Q_i-\mu_i}{\sqrt{(-y+pz+Q_i-\mu_i)^2+\sigma_i^2}}\right) - \right.$$
$$\left. \frac{1}{2}(b+p)\left(-1 - \frac{y-pz-Q_i+\mu_i}{\sqrt{(y-pz-Q_i+\mu_i)^2+\sigma_i^2}}\right)\right) = 0;$$

$$\frac{\partial \pi}{\partial p} = \sum_{i=1}^{n}\left(y - 2pz + \mu_i + \frac{1}{2}e^{-\frac{\beta\zeta}{\varrho}}s(z + \frac{z(-y+pz+Q_{-1+i}-\mu_{-1+i})}{\sqrt{(-y+pz+Q_{-1+i}-\mu_{-1+i})^2+\sigma_{-1+i}^2}}) + \frac{1}{2}(-e^{-\frac{\beta\zeta}{\varrho}}h +\right.$$
$$(1 - e^{-\frac{\beta\zeta}{\varrho}})p(1-\beta))(z + \frac{z(-y+pz+Q_i-\mu_i)}{\sqrt{(-y+pz+Q_i-\mu_i)^2+\sigma_i^2}}) + \frac{1}{2}(1 - e^{-\frac{\beta\zeta}{\varrho}})(1-\beta)(-y+pz+Q_i-$$
$$\mu_i + \sqrt{(-y+pz+Q_i-\mu_i)^2+\sigma_i^2}) - \frac{1}{2}(b+p)(-z - \frac{z(y-pz-Q_i+\mu_i)}{\sqrt{(y-pz-Q_i+\mu_i)^2+\sigma_i^2}}) + \frac{1}{2}(-y+$$
$$\left. pz + Q_i - \mu_i - \sqrt{(y-pz-Q_i+\mu_i)^2+\sigma_i^2})\right) = 0;$$

$$\frac{\partial \pi}{\partial \beta} = \sum_{i=1}^{n}\left(-\frac{e^{-\frac{\beta\zeta}{\varrho}}s\zeta\left(-y+pz+Q_{-1+i}-\mu_{-1+i}+ \sqrt{(-y+pz+Q_{-1+i}-\mu_{-1+i})^2+\sigma_{-1+i}^2}\right)}{2\varrho} + \frac{1}{2}(-(1-\right.$$
$$\left. e^{-\frac{\beta\zeta}{\varrho}})p + \frac{e^{-\frac{\beta\zeta}{\varrho}}h\zeta}{\varrho} + \frac{e^{-\frac{\beta\zeta}{\varrho}}p(1-\beta)\zeta}{\varrho})(-y+pz+Q_i-\mu_i+\sqrt{(-y+pz+Q_i-\mu_i)^2+\sigma_i^2})\right) = 0.$$

Q_i^*, p^*, and β^* obtained from the above first order conditions are the global optimal if the hessian matrix of π is negative semidefinite.

See Appendix A for proof.

4. Numerical Example

The developed model is tested with a numerical experiment and sensitivity analysis of the input parameters. The numerical experiment considers a newsvendor problem with two periods. The data for the given example was taken from Alfares and Elmorra [47]. Here $c = 35.1$ $/unit, $b = 14$ $/unit, $h = 14$ $/unit/period, $s = 10$ $/unit, $\mu_1 = 100$, $\sigma_1 = 15$, $\mu_2 = 100$, $\sigma_2 = 15$, $y = 500$ units/period, $z = 5$, $\zeta = 0.05$, and $\rho = 0.08$.

Case 1. Case 1 is the proposed model with the discount policy. The newsvendor decides on the stocking quantity and price based on the available information. Initially, the product is offered to the consumer with the full price, and at the end of the season, the newsvendor offers a discount on the leftover inventory. The inventory left after the discounted sales are salvaged in the next season.

Case 2. This case is considered to study the impacts of a discount on the expected profit and optimal policies of the newsvendor. This case examines the traditional newsvendor that does not offer a discount. In this case, the newsvendor decides on the stocking quantity and price based on the available information. No discount is offered and, thus, the discount percentage is zero. All the leftover inventory after the selling season is salvaged. Results of both cases are summarised in Table 1.

Table 1. Optimal results of Case 1 and Case 2.

Decision Variables	Case 1	Case 2
Q_1 (Units)	219.77	218.25
Q_2 (Units)	217.95	216.54
P ($/product)	77.12	76.88
β (%)	51	0
Expected Profit π ($)	16,763.5	16,530

From the results, it is clear that the expected profit of the discount policy was higher compared to the non-discount policy. Furthermore, both the stocking quantities and the optimal price were higher in the discount policy compared to the non-discount policy. The higher stocking quantity decreases the risk of stock outs, and the overstocking risk was neutralized by the discount policy. Thus, the discount policy was more flexible compared to the traditional non-discount policy.

4.1. Sensitivity Analysis

The sensitivity analysis was performed for all the key parameters and results were compiled in Tables 2–4. The percentage of variation for all parameters is in the range of −50% to +50%. The sensitivity analysis results from Table 2 revealed the following insights on model parameters:

- Considering the profit of the system, the most effective parameter was purchasing cost; decreasing it by 50% increases the expected profit by 50.99%. However, on the positive side, the effect was a little lesser compared to the negative side. Increasing purchasing cost by 50% decreases the profit by 40.85%. Increasing purchasing cost decreases order quantity, increases the optimal price, and the discount percentage is almost unaffected. This shows that the discount percentage applies to both expensive and inexpensive products.

- The impacts of shortage cost, on the profit of the system, were almost symmetrical towards both negative and positive changes. Order quantity increased with an increase in the shortage cost, whereas, the effect on other variables was negligible.

- The holding cost directly influenced the discount percentage, increasing the holding cost increases the discount percentage. This provides interesting results for newsvendors with higher holding costs. They can increase their profits by discounted sales policy. We can see that the profit was more sensitive towards negative changes compared to the positive changes in the holding cost. The order quantity decreased whereas the price was unaffected.

Compared to the holding cost that had a direct relation with the discount percentage; the salvage value had an indirect relation with the discount percentage. Increasing the salvage value decreases the discount percentage; the expected profit behaves in an almost symmetric way, with little high changes on the positive side. The sensitivity of the holding cost and salvage value provides instructing results for the decision maker. For retailers where holding was higher, a high discount policy was better; and for retailers with high salvage value, a low discount policy was the optimal one.

Table 2. Sensitivity analysis for the key operational parameter.

Parameter	Percent Change in Value	Decision Variables				Percent Change in Expected Profit
		Q_1	Q_2	p	β	
c	−50	271.7	266.8	68.6	0.51	50.99
	−25	244.6	241.9	72.8	0.51	24.18
	+25	195.7	194.3	81.3	0.50	−21.66
	+50	172.1	170.9	85.6	0.50	−40.85
b	−50	218.9	217.1	77.0	0.51	0.483
	−25	219.3	217.5	77.1	0.51	0.237
	+25	220.1	218.3	77.1	0.51	−0.230
	+50	220.5	218.6	77.1	0.51	−0. 453
h	−50	221.1	218.8	77.1	0.47	0.647
	−25	220.4	218.3	77.1	0.49	0.314
	+25	219.2	217.5	77.0	0.53	−0.297
	+50	218.2	217.2	77.0	0.54	−0.581
s	−50	218.9	218.0	77.1	0.52	−0.222
	−25	219.3	218.0	77.1	0.51	−0.113
	+25	220.2	217.8	77.1	0.50	0.117
	+50	220.8	217.8	77.1	0.49	0.240

This paper assumed a stochastic price-dependent demand that composed of a deterministic price dependent part and a random error. Table 3 provides a sensitivity analysis of the demand parameters; the following insights are obtained from the results:

- Although changing the mean of the random errors in the demand affects the profit, the results were symmetric in both the direction. Increasing μ_1 or μ_2 by 50% increased the profit by 12.36%, because, the expected value of demand $d_i(p, X_i)$ increased with increasing μ_1 and μ_2. Price of the finished product increased with increases in demand; however, the discount percentage remained the same. This means the discount policy applied to both low and higher demands newsvendors.

- Compared to the random error μ_1 and μ_2 the standard deviations had much less impact on the profit of the system. However, the changes, in profit, were symmetric to both positive and negative changes in standard deviations of the demand. The stocking quantity increased with an increase in standard deviation. The result was clear because increasing standard deviation increased the uncertainty; therefore, the stocking quantity was increased. Furthermore, the price remained unaffected; however, the discount percentage decreased with increasing σ_1. This means, for a less uncertain demand, the newsvendor should increase the discount percentage to increase its profit and market share. However, as the uncertainty increased the discount rate was reduced to avoid extra loses from high-expected salvage quantity.

- The deterministic price-dependent demand had two parameters, which were y and z. Where y is the potential market size for the deterministic demand and z is the price sensitivity of the consumer. Increasing or decreasing y directly increased or decreased the expected demand; therefore, the profit of the system was affected accordingly. However, the results were asymmetric and the effect grew as y increased.

- On the other hand, increasing z reduced the profit; however, the impacts were asymmetric and the decrease in profit declined as z increased. For a higher value of z, the consumer was more sensitive to price; therefore, the optimal price decreased with increasing z. The discount percentage, on the other hand, continuously increased with an increase in z. This means a higher discount percentage applied to a consumer having high price sensitivity and vice versa. Stocking quantity decreased with an increase in z because the realized deterministic demand decreased with increasing z.

Table 3. Sensitivity analysis for the demand parameter.

Parameter	Percent Change in Value	Decision Variables				Percent Change Expected Profit
		Q_1	Q_2	p	β	
μ_1	−50	181.9	230.1	74.6	0.51	−12.15
	−25	200.8	224.0	75.86	0.51	−6.17
	+25	238.9	211.8	78.3	0.51	6.361
	+50	527.6	205.7	79.6	0.50	12.91
μ_2	−50	231.9	180.1	74.6	0.51	−12.15
	−25	225.8	199.0	75.86	0.51	−6.17
	+25	213.6	236.8	78.3	0.51	6.361
	+50	207.6	255.7	79.64	0.50	12.91
σ_1	−50	216.5	217.4	77.2	0.52	1.763
	−25	218.1	217.7	77.1	0.51	0.881
	+25	221.3	218.1	77.0	0.50	−0.880
	+50	222.9	218.41	77.0	0.50	−1.761
σ_2	−50	219.2	215.5	77.2	0.50	1.98
	−25	219.4	216.7	77.1	0.50	0.99
	+25	220.0	219.1	77.0	0.51	−0.989
	+50	220.3	220.2	77.0	0.51	−1.979
z	−50	217.8	268.6	137.3	0.48	203.7
	−25	244.4	242.2	97.15	0.50	66.14
	+25	196.0	194.3	65.1	0.51	−37.67
	+50	172.7	171.1	57.1	0.52	−61.17
y	−50	81.4	79.8	53.7	0.52	−87.0
	−25	155.3	153.7	64.5	0.52	−53.2
	+25	284.0	281.9	89.7	0.50	72.0
	+50	348.1	345.9	102.2	0.49	162.8

The discounted portion of sales ($\alpha(\beta)$) is a function of the discount percentage with parameters ζ and ϱ. Increasing the discount percentage reduces the price and discounted sales increases. A sensitivity analysis of the parameters of the discounted portion is given in Table 4; the results showed that:

- With the increase in the parameter (ζ) value, the expected profit of the system showed an asymmetric increase. For a 25% decrease, the expected profit decreased by −0.32%; however, with further decreases the profit remains unaffected. On the positive side, the profit increase by 0.31% for a 25% increase, and 0.628% for a 50% increase in the value of ζ. The discount percent decreased with an increase in ζ, price remains unaffected, and the stocking quantity increased with increasing ζ.

- By increasing the value of the parameter (ϱ), the asymmetric negative change occurred in the profit, the order quantity decreased, the price almost remained the same, and the discount percentage increased.

Table 4. Sensitivity analysis for the key discounted sales parameter.

Parameter	Percent Change in Value	Decision Variables				Percent Change in Expected Profit
		Q_1	Q_2	p	β	
ζ	−50	218.2	217.2	77.0	0.53	−0.329
	−25	219.3	217.0	77.0	0.52	−0.329
	+25	220.1	218.3	77.1	0.50	0.318
	+50	220.6	218.7	77.2	0.49	0.628
ϱ	−50	221.6	219.5	77.3	0.47	1.226
	−25	220.3	218.4	77.2	0.49	0.423
	+25	219.4	217.6	77.0	0.51	−0.262
	+50	219.2	217.4	77.0	0.52	−0.441

4.2. Managerial Insights

Based on the obtained results, the following recommendations were suggested to managers:

- The proposed discount policy increases both the price and order quantities, thus, managers can order high quantity compared to non-discount policy. Higher ordering quantities decrease the risk of shortage cost, whereas, the discount percentage decreases the risk of overstocking and leftovers. Therefore, in the proposed policy, both the risks are minimized.
- Another important insight is that the discount percentage increases with a decrease in market uncertainty, this means, a retailer having low variable demand can order more with a higher discount percentage. However, retailers with a highly variable demand, orders low quantity with a low discount percentage.
- The optimal discount percentage increases as the consumer price sensitivity increases, therefore, managers that are dealing with markets having higher consumer sensitivity are advised to offer higher discount percentage. This increases the discounted percentage and higher profit and market shares can be achieved.
- For the single period problem, the optimal ordering quantity and price decreases, where the discount percentage increases; the discounts on the successive periods leads to an increase in order quantity compared to the single period newsvendor problem. The increase in the ordered quantity and price is the result of discount percentage that reduces salvage quantity for the subsequent period; however, the selling price of the items is still more than the salvaged value of the product.
- The associated risk with salvaging leftover and shortage is high in the stochastic environment and it can be reduced by implying the distribution free approach with discount offering—discounts are helpful for mangers in increasing the profit generation. The major objective of the manager is to maximize the expected profit, which can be achieved by the proposed discounted policy for leftover items in successive periods.

5. Conclusions

This paper studied joint pricing and inventory policies for the newsvendor model with discounted sales. The classical multi-period distribution-free newsvendor model was extended with a discount policy to increase the sales and profit of the retailer. Stochastic-price dependent demand was considered, and a distribution-free approach was applied to solve the model. No specific assumptions on the distribution of the random error in the demand were considered, except that it had a known mean and variance. Two numerical examples were considered, and the results showed that the proposed discount policy increased the sales and profit of the system. Furthermore, the discount policy provided more flexibility to the newsvendor in deciding the optimal price. With this policy, the newsvendor, initially, decided a higher price compared to the one without the discount policy, and later on, the leftover is discounted with a lower price. Thus, the newsvendor can catch both the strategic and non-strategic consumer at the same time. The sensitivity results showed that the discount policy was applicable to both expensive and inexpensive products; retailers with a higher holding cost can use this policy to increase their profit. This study considered the inventory and pricing policy for only one player, however, in practice, every business directly deals with upstream and downstream linkages. Therefore, this study can be extended by considering more than one player, such as the models developed by Sarkar [9,10]; in this case, two different discount policies can be considered, discount for the final consumer and discount for the newsvendor. Another limitation of this study was that we considered only the single discount per period, considering multiple discounts in one period is a more practical extension of this study. A third possible extension is to consider deteriorating products, such as the study done by Ullah et al. [48]; in this case, the salvage value of the deteriorated product must be zero.

Author Contributions: Conceptualization, M.U.; Methodology, B.S. and M.U.; Software, M.U.; Validation, B.S.; Formal analysis, M.U. and I.K.; Investigation, B.S. and M.U.; Resources, M.U., B.S., and I.K.; Data curation, B.S. and M.U.; Writing—original draft preparation, I.K. and M.U.; Writing—review and editing, I.K. and M.U.; Visualization, M.U.; Supervision, B.S.

Notation

The following notation are used to establish the mathematical model:

Decision variables

p	Price of finished product per unit ($/unit)
β	Discount percentage (percent of finished product price)
Q_i	Ordering quantity ith period (units)

Parameters

i	Index for selling period, where $i = 1\ldots\ldots n$
b	Shortage cost per unit ($/unit)
c	Purchasing cost per unit ($/unit)
h	Holding cost ($/unit/period)
s	Salvage value ($/unit)
$d_i(p, X_i)$	Price dependent stochastic demand of period i
X_i	Random error in demand
μ_i	The expected value of random error
σ_i	The standard deviation of demand
$a(p) = y - z * p$	Deterministic price dependent demand in-season
y	Maximum perceived cumulative deterministic (riskless) demand i.e., market share (units/unit time)
z	Price sensitivity for cumulative deterministic demand
$E(d_i) = \mu_i + a(p)$	The expected value of price dependent stochastic demand
X^+	Max [X,0]
π	Expected profit ($)

Appendix A

If,

$$a_{1,1} = \frac{\partial}{\partial Q_1}\frac{\partial \pi}{\partial Q_1}; a_{1,2} = \frac{\partial}{\partial p}\frac{\partial \pi}{\partial Q_1}; a_{1,3} = \frac{\partial}{\partial \beta}\frac{\partial \pi}{\partial Q_1}; a_{1,4} = \frac{\partial}{\partial Q_2}\frac{\partial \pi}{\partial Q_1}; a_{2,1} = \frac{\partial}{\partial Q_1}\frac{\partial \pi}{\partial p}; a_{2,2} =$$

$$\frac{\partial}{\partial p}\frac{\partial \pi}{\partial p}; a_{2,3} = \frac{\partial}{\partial \beta}\frac{\partial \pi}{\partial p}; a_{2,4} = \frac{\partial}{\partial Q_2}\frac{\partial \pi}{\partial p} a_{3,1} = \frac{\partial}{\partial Q_1}\frac{\partial \pi}{\partial \beta}; a_{3,2} = \frac{\partial}{\partial p}\frac{\partial \pi}{\partial \beta}; a_{3,3} = \frac{\partial}{\partial \beta}\frac{\partial \pi}{\partial \beta}; a_{3,4} = \frac{\partial}{\partial Q_2}\frac{\partial \pi}{\partial \beta};$$

$$a_{4,1} = \frac{\partial}{\partial Q_1}\frac{\partial \pi}{\partial Q_2}; a_{4,2} = \frac{\partial}{\partial p}\frac{\partial \pi}{\partial Q_2}; a_{4,3} = \frac{\partial}{\partial \beta}\frac{\partial \pi}{\partial Q_2}; a_{4,4} = \frac{\partial}{\partial Q_2}\frac{\partial \pi}{\partial Q_2},$$

then the Hessian matrix of (4) can be expressed as:

$$H = \begin{pmatrix} a_{1,1} & a_{1,2} & a_{1,3} & a_{1,4} \\ a_{2,1} & a_{2,2} & a_{2,3} & a_{2,4} \\ a_{3,1} & a_{3,2} & a_{3,3} & a_{3,4} \\ a_{4,1} & a_{4,2} & a_{4,3} & a_{4,4} \end{pmatrix}.$$

At the optimal solutions $Q_1^* = 219.76$, $Q_2^* = 217.94$, $p^* = 77.12$, and $\beta^* = 0.51$ the Hessian matrix can be written as,

$$H = \begin{pmatrix} -2.32 & -11.20 & -1.43 & 0.00 \\ -11.20 & -139.07 & -0.79 & 0.00 \\ -1.43 & -0.79 & -1677.99 & 0.00 \\ 0.00 & -13.49 & 1.47 & -2.79 \end{pmatrix}.$$

The first four principle minors are -2.32, $+197.81$, $-331,668.04$, and $+926,141.46$. Hence total profit is strictly concave at $Q_1^* = 219.76$, $Q_2^* = 217.94$, $p^* = 77.12$, and $\beta^* = 0.51$.

References

1. Scarf, H. A min-max solution of an inventory problem. In *Studies in the Mathematical Theory of Inventory and Production*; Stanford University Press: Palo Alto, CA, USA, 1958.
2. Arrow, K.J.; Harris, T.; Marschak, J. Optimal inventory policy. *Econometrica* **1951**, 250–272. [CrossRef]
3. Gallego, G.; Moon, I. The distribution free newsboy problem: Review and extensions. *J. Oper. Res. Soc.* **1993**, 44, 825–834. [CrossRef]
4. Anvari, M. Optimality criteria and risk in inventory models: The case of the newsboy problem. *J. Oper. Res. Soc.* **1987**, 38, 625–632. [CrossRef]
5. Khouja, M. The single-period (news-vendor) problem: Literature review and suggestions for future research. *Omega* **1999**, 27, 537–553. [CrossRef]
6. Bitran, G.R.; Mondschein, S.V. Periodic pricing of seasonal products in retailing. *Manag. Sci.* **1997**, 43, 64–79. [CrossRef]
7. Lau, H.-S. The newsboy problem under alternative optimization objectives. *J. Oper. Res. Soc.* **1980**, 31, 525–535. [CrossRef]
8. Parlar, M.; Kevin Weng, Z. Balancing desirable but conflicting objectives in the newsvendor problem. *IIE Trans.* **2003**, 35, 131–142. [CrossRef]
9. Sarkar, B.; Majumder, A.; Sarkar, M.; Kim, N.; Ullah, M. Effects of variable production rate on quality of products in a single-vendor multi-buyer supply chain management. *Int. J. Adv. Manuf. Technol.* **2018**, 99, 567–581. [CrossRef]
10. Sarkar, B.; Ullah, M.; Kim, N. Environmental and economic assessment of closed-loop supply chain with remanufacturing and returnable transport items. *Comput. Ind. Eng.* **2017**, 111, 148–163. [CrossRef]
11. Qin, Y.; Wang, R.; Vakharia, A.J.; Chen, Y.; Seref, M.M. The newsvendor problem: Review and directions for future research. *Eur. J. Oper. Res.* **2011**, 213, 361–374. [CrossRef]
12. Porteus, E.L. Stochastic inventory theory. *Hdbk. Oper. Res. Manag. Sci.* **1990**, 2, 605–652.
13. Moon, I.; Yoo, D.K.; Saha, S. The distribution-free newsboy problem with multiple discounts and upgrades. *Math. Probl. Eng.* **2016**, 2016, 2017253. [CrossRef]
14. Sarkar, B.; Zhang, C.; Majumder, A.; Sarkar, M.; Seo, Y.W. A distribution free newsvendor model with consignment policy and retailer's royalty reduction. *Int. J. Prod. Res.* **2018**, 56, 5025–5044. [CrossRef]
15. Kogan, K.; Lou, S. Multi-stage newsboy problem: A dynamic model. *Eur. J. Oper. Res.* **2003**, 149, 448–458. [CrossRef]
16. Matsuyama, K. The multi-period newsboy problem. *Eur. J. Oper. Res.* **2006**, 171, 170–188. [CrossRef]
17. Lee, C.H. Coordination on stocking and progressive pricing policies for a supply chain. *Int. J. Prod. Econ.* **2007**, 106, 307–319. [CrossRef]
18. Chen, X.A.; Wang, Z.; Yuan, H. Optimal pricing for selling to a static multi-period newsvendor. *Oper. Res. Lett.* **2017**, 45, 415–420. [CrossRef]
19. Petruzzi, N.C.; Dada, M. Pricing and the newsvendor problem: A review with extensions. *Oper. Res.* **1999**, 47, 183–194. [CrossRef]
20. Khouja, M. The newsboy problem under progressive multiple discounts. *Eur. J. Oper. Res.* **1995**, 84, 458–466. [CrossRef]
21. Arcelus, F.J.; Kumar, S.; Srinivasan, G. Retailer's response to alternate manufacturer's incentives under a single-period, price-dependent, stochastic-demand framework. *Decis. Sci.* **2005**, 36, 599–626. [CrossRef]

22. Chung, C.-S.; Flynn, J.; Zhu, J. The newsvendor problem with an in-season price adjustment. *Eur. J. Oper. Res.* **2009**, *198*, 148–156. [CrossRef]

23. Banerjee, S.; Meitei, N.S. Effect of declining selling price: Profit analysis for a single period inventory model with stochastic demand and lead time. *J. Oper. Res. Soc.* **2010**, *61*, 696–704. [CrossRef]

24. Abad, P. Determining optimal price and order size for a price setting newsvendor under cycle service level. *Int. J. Prod. Econ.* **2014**, *158*, 106–113. [CrossRef]

25. Ma, S.; Jemai, Z.; Sahin, E.; Dallery, Y. Analysis of the Newsboy problem subject to price dependent demand and multiple discounts. *Am. Inst. Math. Sci.* **2018**, *14*, 931–951. [CrossRef]

26. Arcelus, F.J.; Kumar, S.; Srinivasan, G. Risk tolerance and a retailer's pricing and ordering policies within a newsvendor framework. *Omega* **2012**, *40*, 188–198. [CrossRef]

27. Hu, X.; Su, P. The newsvendor's joint procurement and pricing problem under price-sensitive stochastic demand and purchase price uncertainty. *Omega* **2018**, *79*, 81–90. [CrossRef]

28. Ye, T.; Sun, H. Price-setting newsvendor with strategic consumers. *Omega* **2016**, *63*, 103–110. [CrossRef]

29. Arcelus, F.J.; Kumar, S.; Srinivasan, G. Pricing, rebate, advertising and ordering policies of a retailer facing price-dependent stochastic demand in newsvendor framework under different risk preferences. *Int. Trans. Oper. Res.* **2006**, *13*, 209–227. [CrossRef]

30. He, Y.; Zhao, X.; Zhao, L.; He, J. Coordinating a supply chain with effort and price dependent stochastic demand. *Appl. Math. Model.* **2009**, *33*, 2777–2790. [CrossRef]

31. Chen, H.; Chen, Y.F.; Chiu, C.-H.; Choi, T.-M.; Sethi, S. Coordination mechanism for the supply chain with leadtime consideration and price-dependent demand. *Eur. J. Oper. Res.* **2010**, *203*, 70–80. [CrossRef]

32. Chen, J.; Bell, P.C. Coordinating a decentralized supply chain with customer returns and price-dependent stochastic demand using a buyback policy. *Eur. J. Oper. Res.* **2011**, *212*, 293–300. [CrossRef]

33. Jadidi, O.; Jaber, M.Y.; Zolfaghari, S. Joint pricing and inventory problem with price dependent stochastic demand and price discounts. *Comput. Ind. Eng.* **2017**, *114*, 45–53. [CrossRef]

34. Modak, N.M.; Kelle, P. Managing a dual-channel supply chain under price and delivery-time dependent stochastic demand. *Eur. J. Oper. Res.* **2019**, *272*, 147–161. [CrossRef]

35. Khouja, M. The newsboy problem with multiple discounts offered by suppliers and retailers. *Decis. Sci.* **1996**, *27*, 589–599. [CrossRef]

36. Cachon, G.P.; Kök, A.G. Implementation of the newsvendor model with clearance pricing: How to (and how not to) estimate a salvage value. *Manuf. Serv. Oper. Manag.* **2007**, *9*, 276–290. [CrossRef]

37. Nocke, V.; Peitz, M. A theory of clearance sales. *Econ. J.* **2007**, *117*, 964–990. [CrossRef]

38. Khouja, M.; Pan, J.; Zhou, J. Effects of gift cards on optimal order and discount of seasonal products. *Eur. J. Oper. Res.* **2016**, *248*, 159–173. [CrossRef]

39. Gupta, D.; Hill, A.V.; Bouzdine-Chameeva, T. A pricing model for clearing end-of-season retail inventory. *Eur. J. Oper. Res.* **2006**, *170*, 518–540. [CrossRef]

40. Ullah, M.; Sarkar, B. Smart and sustainable supply chain management: A proposal to use rfid to improve electronic waste management. In Proceedings of the International Conference on Computers and Industrial Engineering, Auckland, New Zealand, 2–5 December 2018.

41. Jammernegg, W.; Kischka, P. The price-setting newsvendor with service and loss constraints. *Omega* **2013**, *41*, 326–335. [CrossRef]

42. Mandal, P.; Kaul, R.; Jain, T. Stocking and pricing decisions under endogenous demand and reference point effects. *Eur. J. Oper. Res.* **2018**, *264*, 181–199. [CrossRef]

43. Ruidas, S.; Seikh, M.R.; Nayak, P.K.; Sarkar, B. A single period production inventory model in interval environment with price revision. *Int. J. Appl. Comput. Math.* **2018**, *5*, 7. [CrossRef]

44. Yao, L.; Chen, Y.F.; Yan, H. The newsvendor problem with pricing: Extensions. *Int. J. Manag. Sci. Eng. Manag.* **2006**, *1*, 3–16. [CrossRef]

45. Raza, S.A. Supply chain coordination under a revenue-sharing contract with corporate social responsibility and partial demand information. *Int. J. Prod. Econ.* **2018**, *205*, 1–14. [CrossRef]

46. Hsueh, C.-F. A bilevel programming model for corporate social responsibility collaboration in sustainable supply chain management. *Trans. Res. E Log.* **2015**, *73*, 84–95. [CrossRef]

47. Alfares, H.K.; Elmorra, H.H. The distribution-free newsboy problem: Extensions to the shortage penalty case. *Int. J. Prod. Econ.* **2005**, *93*, 465–477. [CrossRef]

48. Ullah, M.; Sarkar, B.; Asghar, I. Effects of preservation technology investment on waste generation in a two-echelon supply chain model. *Mathematics* **2019**, *7*, 189. [CrossRef]

Permissions

All chapters in this book were first published in MDPI; hereby published with permission under the Creative Commons Attribution License or equivalent. Every chapter published in this book has been scrutinized by our experts. Their significance has been extensively debated. The topics covered herein carry significant findings which will fuel the growth of the discipline. They may even be implemented as practical applications or may be referred to as a beginning point for another development.

The contributors of this book come from diverse backgrounds, making this book a truly international effort. This book will bring forth new frontiers with its revolutionizing research information and detailed analysis of the nascent developments around the world.

We would like to thank all the contributing authors for lending their expertise to make the book truly unique. They have played a crucial role in the development of this book. Without their invaluable contributions this book wouldn't have been possible. They have made vital efforts to compile up to date information on the varied aspects of this subject to make this book a valuable addition to the collection of many professionals and students.

This book was conceptualized with the vision of imparting up-to-date information and advanced data in this field. To ensure the same, a matchless editorial board was set up. Every individual on the board went through rigorous rounds of assessment to prove their worth. After which they invested a large part of their time researching and compiling the most relevant data for our readers.

The editorial board has been involved in producing this book since its inception. They have spent rigorous hours researching and exploring the diverse topics which have resulted in the successful publishing of this book. They have passed on their knowledge of decades through this book. To expedite this challenging task, the publisher supported the team at every step. A small team of assistant editors was also appointed to further simplify the editing procedure and attain best results for the readers.

Apart from the editorial board, the designing team has also invested a significant amount of their time in understanding the subject and creating the most relevant covers. They scrutinized every image to scout for the most suitable representation of the subject and create an appropriate cover for the book.

The publishing team has been an ardent support to the editorial, designing and production team. Their endless efforts to recruit the best for this project, has resulted in the accomplishment of this book. They are a veteran in the field of academics and their pool of knowledge is as vast as their experience in printing. Their expertise and guidance has proved useful at every step. Their uncompromising quality standards have made this book an exceptional effort. Their encouragement from time to time has been an inspiration for everyone.

The publisher and the editorial board hope that this book will prove to be a valuable piece of knowledge for researchers, students, practitioners and scholars across the globe.

List of Contributors

Giulio Di Gravio and Riccardo Patriarca
Department of Mechanical and Aerospace Engineering, Sapienza University of Rome, Via Eudossiana, 18-00184 Rome, Italy

Raffaele Cantelmi
Department of Mechanical and Aerospace Engineering, Sapienza University of Rome, Via Eudossiana, 18-00184 Rome, Italy
Land Armaments Directorate, Ministry of Defence, Via di Centocelle, 301-00187 Rome, Italy

Ahmed Shaban
Mechanical Engineering Department, Faculty of Engineering, Fayoum University, Fayoum 63514, Egypt

Mohamed A. Shalaby
Department of Mechanical Design and Production, Faculty of Engineering, Cairo University, Giza 12613, Egypt

Shaktipada Bhuniya and Sarla Pareek
Department of Mathematics and Statistics, Banasthali Vidyapith, Banasthali, Rajasthan 304 022, India

Muhammad Omair
Department of Industrial Engineering, Jalozai Campus, University of Engineering and Technology, Peshawar 25000, Pakistan

Misbah Ullah, Sahar Noor and Shahid Maqsood
Department of Industrial Engineering, University of Engineering and Technology, Peshawar 25000, Pakistan

Baishakhi Ganguly
Department of Mathematics & Statistics, Banasthali University, Rajasthan 304022, India

Rekha Guchhait
Department of Mathematics & Statistics, Banasthali Vidyapith, Rajasthan 304022, India
Department of Industrial & Management Engineering, Hanyang University, Ansan, Gyeonggi-do 15588, Korea

Jong Soo Kim, Eunhee Jeon and Jiseong Noh
Department of Industrial and Management Engineering, Hanyang University, Erica Campus, Ansan 15588, Korea

Jun Hyeong Park
KPMG Samjong Accounting Corp., Gangnam Finance Center, 152 Teheran-ro, Gangnam-gu, Seoul 06236, Korea

Zigao Wu
Department of Industrial Engineering, Northwestern Polytechnical University, Xi'an 710072, China

Shaohua Yu
Laboratoire Genie Industriel, CentraleSupélec, Université Paris-Saclay, 91190 Saint-Aubin, France

Tiancheng Li
Key Laboratory of Information Fusion Technology (Ministry of Education), School of Automation, Northwestern Polytechnical University, Xi'an 710072, China

Muhammad Babar Ramzan
Department of Garment Manufacturing, National Textile University, Faisalabad 37610, Pakistan

Shehreyar Mohsin Qureshi
Department of Industrial and Manufacturing Engineering, NED University of Engineering and Technology, Karachi 75270, Pakistan

Sonia Irshad Mari and Muhammad Saad Memon
Department of Industrial Engineering and Management, Mehran University of Engineering and Technology, Jamshoro 76062, Pakistan

Mandeep Mittal
Department of Mathematics, Amity Institute of Applied Science, Amity University, Noida 201313, India

Muhammad Imran
Department of Industrial and Management Engineering, Hanyang University, Seoul 15588, Korea

Muhammad Waqas Iqbal
Department of Industrial Engineering, Hongik University, Seoul 04066, Korea

Yosef Daryanto
Department of Industrial and Systems Engineering, Chung Yuan Christian University, 200 Chung-Pei Rd., 32023 Chung-li, Taoyuan, Taiwan
Department of Industrial Engineering, Universitas Atma Jaya Yogyakarta, Jl. Babarsari 43, 55281 Yogyakarta, Indonesia

Hui Ming Wee
Department of Industrial and Systems Engineering, Chung Yuan Christian University, 200 Chung-Pei Rd., 32023 Chung-li, Taoyuan, Taiwan

Gede Agus Widyadana
Department of Industrial Engineering, Petra Christian University, Surabaya, East Java 60236, Indonesia

Muhammad Rizwan Khan
Department of Industrial Engineering, Hanyang University, 222 Wangsimni-Ro, Seoul 133-791, Korea

Mehran Ullah, Irfanullah Khan and Biswajit Sarkar
Department of Industrial & Management Engineering, Hanyang University, Ansan, Gyeonggi-do 15588, Korea

Index